The Inventive Spirit of
African Americans

The Inventive Spirit of African Americans

Patented Ingenuity

Patricia Carter Sluby

 PRAEGER

Westport, Connecticut
London

Library of Congress Cataloging-in-Publication Data

Sluby, Patricia Carter.
    The inventive spirit of African Americans : patented ingenuity / Patricia
Carter Sluby.
       p. cm.
    Includes bibliographical references and index.
    ISBN 0–275–96674–7 (alk. paper)
    1. African American inventors.   I. Title.
  T39.S57   2004
  604.8996'073—dc22   2003064767

British Library Cataloguing in Publication Data is available.

Library of Congress Catalog Card Number: 2003064767
ISBN: 0–275–96674–7

First published in 2004

Praeger Publishers, 88 Post Road West, Westport, CT 06881
An imprint of Greenwood Publishing Group, Inc.
www.praeger.com

Printed in the United States of America

∞™

The paper used in this book complies with the
Permanent Paper Standard issued by the National
Information Standards Organization (Z39.48–1984).

10 9 8 7 6 5 4 3 2

R0403200742

Congress shall have power ... [t]o promote the progress of science and useful arts, by securing for limited times to authors and inventors the exclusive right to their respective writings and discoveries.

THE U.S. CONSTITUTION
Article 1, section 8

The issue of patents for new discoveries has given a spring to invention beyond my conception.

THOMAS JEFFERSON
President of the United States, 1801–1809

CONTENTS

PREFACE

Changes have come, dynasties have risen and faded away, kingdoms have stood and crumbled to dust under the weight of years; man has evolved from the lowest barbarism to the highest culture and refinement; the printing press has come and flooded the world with knowledge; the pine torch, the tallow drop, the candle and the oil lamp have given way before the brilliancy of the electric light; the steam car, the stage coach are retiring before the electric cars and automobiles. The wheel of progress, intelligence and invention is steadily rolling in the land of darkness and ignorance, and in this twentieth century, the woman or man who has brains and uses them is the woman or man who succeeds.

Maggie Lena Walker, 1925

A historical picture of life on planet Earth exposes four major periods. First, there was single-cell life that developed into multicellular life. Millions of years later, vertebrates appeared, then mammals, and thereafter modern man, *Homo sapiens*. Man hunted and gathered for survival and eventually began to till the land, starting the age of agriculture. A few thousand years ago, man founded towns and cities, and a few hundred years ago the Industrial Revolution dawned. The last quarter of the twentieth century to the present, described as the age of information, embodies rapid technological advances, which explosion of information now moves into the new millennium, spawning new problems to solve.

The stone or wooden wheel of millenniums past evolved into the automobile's modern steel-belted tire, while ancient hooks or other unprotected metal shafts used to fasten clothing, boots, and shoes gave

Model of Cotton Chopper, Scraper, and Cultivator, invention of L. D. Moore.
From the Patricia Carter Ives Sluby Collection.

way to the safety pin, the zipper, and then Velcro fastenings. Ideas for such items emanate from individuals known as inventors, whether female or male. Discoveries and improvements thereon have taken place for millions of years. Therefore, an account of inventiveness gives insight into society's ever-changing needs.

In an imaginary letter from the "pen of the Apostle Paul," Martin Luther King, Jr. writes:

> I have heard so much about you and of what you are doing. News has come to me regarding the fascinating and astounding advances that you have made in the scientific realm. I have learned of your dashing subways and flashing airplanes. Through your scientific genius you have dwarfed distance and placed time in chains. You have made it possible to eat breakfast in Paris, France, and lunch in New York City. I have also heard of your skyscraper buildings with their prodigious towers rising heavenward. I am told of your great medical advances and the curing of many dread plagues and diseases, thereby prolonging your lives and offering greater security and physical wellbeing. All of that is marvelous. You can do so many things in your day that I could not do in the Greco-Roman world of my day. You travel distances in a single day that in my generation required three months. That

is wonderful. What tremendous strides in the areas of scientific and technological development you have made!

But in spite of all the achievements King cites in "Paul's letter," he cautions that American Christians "have failed to employ . . . moral and spiritual genius to make of it a brotherhood."[1]

In past centuries, American people of color were acknowledged by whites for their talents for music and dance, but any mention of the "Negro's" innate ability in the realm of inventive genius was considered fantasy. Thought of as having little originality, if any, the darker race was presumed to possess mental deficiency in the mechanical and industrial arts and to be incapable of original thought. Even people of color themselves, coming from the previous condition of bondage and having very little opportunity for gaining knowledge in science, fine art, or literature, were unaware of members of their race who had a faculty for discovery. Indoctrinated with the debilitating thought of inferiority and general indifference, members of the black race doubted their usefulness as instruments of creativity. The generally held principle that the black man was inferior to his white brethren made it futile for him to perform like any person of the majority race.

Of unusual note disproving inferiority is the story of Stephen L. Bishop, a Kentucky slave who spoke the ancient languages, Latin and Greek, and was renowned for his adroitness and extraordinary skill in the exploration of Mammoth Cave. During the War of 1812, slaves in the cave mined saltpeter for gunpowder and detected Indian artifacts in the process. Bishop was the first human to discover uncommon sightless creatures and the earliest to traverse the frightening Bottomless Pit. He then became the first tour guide for visitors. As a maze of monstrous size, the cave was home to Bishop, the site's original mapmaker. Owned by Franklin Gorin, an attorney who bought the cave as a tourist attraction, Bishop entered it when he was seventeen years old in 1838, learning the routes and cave jargon from two white guides.

From his years of association with men and women of power and wealth from around the world who came to tour the cave, Bishop was exposed to the fineries of life and talk of politics, science, and the humanities. He learned to read, write, and converse among the white visitors with a confident bearing, and these skills made him a "social novelty." He had the power to command whites to follow his lead lest they encounter harm. Bishop's reputation was founded on his findings and recorded feats. He died mysteriously in 1857, a year after being freed. He and his wife Charlotte had planned to settle in Liberia through the help of the Kentucky Colonization Society.[2]

Added to the story of Bishop's extraordinary feat and amazing skill are the those of two renowned musicians. Scott Joplin, the ragtime impresario, was born to a father who left slavery behind in North Carolina and to a freeborn mother. Growing up in a musical family in Texarkana, where their father performed on the violin and their mother played banjo and sang, the five Joplin children were musically trained. Scott's sensational musical aptitude surfaced at a young age, inspiring his parents to allow him to study under a white teacher. His musical genius is historic.[3]

The natural skill of eminent author, composer, and arranger Justin Holland propelled him to the realm of a classical pioneer and the most pivotal American guitarist of the late 1800s. Born in 1819 in a rural area of Norfolk County, Virginia, Holland improvised music from words found in old songbooks that had no musical notes. He heard worshipers singing tunes to the words at a log meeting house. In Boston, Holland received initial guitar training, then furthered his studies at Oberlin College in Ohio. Holland, performer extraordinaire on the guitar, flute, and piano, triumphed over all barriers and ascended as an encouraging example to those who followed in his footsteps.[4]

In 1886, Professor R. R. Wright presented proof of black scholarship and inventiveness in an *A.M.E. Church Review* article on the Negro inventor. He stated, "[A]mple evidence of the Negro's capability, susceptibility and homogeneity can be found on the shelves of their libraries and in the very books of their daily reading. . . . [O]ur white friends, having eyes to see do not see." Expounding further on the skillfulness of the Negro, Wright quoted a section of Edward H. Everett's address before the Massachusetts Colonization Society in 1833:

"Go back to an earlier period in the history of the black race. See what they were and what they did three thousand years ago, in the period of their glory, when they occupied the forefront in the march of civilization; when they constituted, in fact, the whole civilized world of their time. . . . We received it from our European ancestors; they had it from the Greeks and Roman and Jews. But," said he, "where did the Greeks and Romans and Jews get it? They derived it from Ethiopia and Egypt—in a word, from Africa."[5]

For nearly four hundred years after reaching the shores of America, people of color conceived remarkable, clever inventions. Then exploited as slaves, legally cast as chattel, blacks displayed abundant ingenuity during the developing years of America. To know the history of America is to be aware of the cultural and social changes brought about by the result of African Americans' inspirations. Their mental prowess is legendary.

Lift up your eyes on high, and behold
who hath created these things,
that bringeth out their host by number:
he calleth them all by names
by the greatness of his might,
for that he is strong in power;
not one faileth.

                                                                        Isaiah 40:26

Early Africans in America, like their forebears, were expert artisans, making pottery, weaving textiles, carving wood, and sculpting ivory and metal, the mainlining crafts practiced by free and enslaved souls. As masters in a myriad of trades, Africans moreover excelled in mining, metal tooling, and construction, but the majority labored on plantations as skilled agrarian workers. The skill of the newly enslaved African was used swiftly for the construction of plantation buildings, stately manor homes and their outbuildings. Slaves alongside freemen made, and designed as well, much of the fine furniture commonly viewed in these households. The enslaved humans were forced to construct their own one-room living cabins, made with clay and tabby walls, dirt floors, and thatched roofs, styled after West African building customs. Around 1800, Louis Metoyer, the son of a free black woman in Louisiana, designed a house on the Melrose Plantation established by his mother, Marie Therese, fashioned also like a common West African structure. Those who escaped bondage by fleeing west triumphed over stone cutting, seafaring, or trailblazing. The slaves who ran away to various points north and to the far northeast escaped to freedom through an organized system known as the Underground Railroad and eked out livelihoods there as machinists, shoemakers, seamstresses, or house servants and even as distillers, butlers, or barbers. Along the extensive eastern seaboard and in some inland states, a meager number of free or manumitted people of color were educators, pastors, and orators, while an occasional professional practiced medicine, law, or journalism.

In the slave state of Maryland, though, during John Brown's disastrous attempt to liberate those in bondage in 1859, a large neighborhood of free blacks coexisted with bondsmen in the valleys along rail lines, working as skilled ironworkers on the B&O Railroad. These skills were passed down from their predecessors, who founded churches to meet spiritual needs in black enclaves.

During military conflicts of the Revolutionary War and the War of 1812 along with the Mexican and the Civil Wars, African Americans served honorably as soldiers and sailors. Throughout their service, they fashioned intricate weaponry and crafted mariners' tools and ornaments. While idle, mariners were extraordinary at the art of scrimshaw, carving beautiful art on whalebone or ivory.

The rise of African Americans in business, in the professions, and in inventive thought was promising. Showing unexpected progress, the freed bondsmen and the freeborn utilized their skill and overcame toil and pain by developing labor-saving tools and contraptions.

In the nineteenth and twentieth centuries, technical, professional, and trade organizations coexisted alongside the commonplace benefit societies, all formed to articulate the concerns of the enslaved and of the free blacks. Established as forums, these worthy groups set forth strategies and programs for the disadvantaged. Mutual aid societies initiated training for Americans of African descent, giving them a support structure vitally needed during a hostile, racist period.

MUTUAL AID AND BURIAL

Wisely, early African Americans saw the need to group together to protect themselves. To assist fugitive slaves and free blacks, mutual aid groups, secret fraternal orders, and burial societies were founded. Benevolent organizations were important factors in the life of these individuals, who often feared that they might die without mourners, regardless of any lifetime successes and friendships. Many associations were forerunners of African American insurance companies that were outgrowths of burying-ground societies. Major cities had dozens of benefit groups, whose members paid monies to the survivors of deceased members and cared for the sick. Nearly all Americans of African descent at that time joined one society or another regardless of their livelihood. Societies sprang up everywhere. The lawyer and the doctor belonged, as did the preacher, printer, blacksmith, clerk, carpenter, inventor, and railway worker.

Numerous societies were exemplary groups. In 1787, Richard Allen and Absalom Jones organized the Free African Society in Philadelphia, Pennsylvania. As the earliest organized African American group in the nation and forerunner of the African Church, the Free African Society was a political entity and a church as well that offered mutual aid. The church body applied dues, paid by its members, to expenses of burial, relief of the sick, and care of widows and orphans. Allen later founded the Bethel African Methodist Episcopal Church, and Jones became the first black priest of the Protestant Episcopal Church.[6]

The Columbian Harmony Society, established on November 25, 1825, in the District of Columbia, offered mutual assistance to its black population. Free Negroes who achieved despite repressive laws and social practices organized the society, formed only thirty-seven years after the ratification of the Constitution of the United States. Members promised "to aid each other in infirmity, sickness, disease, or accident, and to provide burial after death."

Slaves and freedmen in the District of Columbia endured many hardships. Statutes and custom limited employment openings, and numerous regulations governed their conduct in public. Burying a black family member was expensive because the free black was responsible for making and paying for all burial arrangements, but slave owners buried their own enslaved humans, usually at the owners' expense. Due to the absence of a suitable location for interment, burial sites posed a problem for freedmen. The Columbian Harmony Society (vital to this day) provided a partial solution through the purchase of land so that members could inter their loved ones in a dignified place. The society founded and operated a cemetery known as Harmony Memorial Park, a site favored by many inventors.[7]

William Washington Browne (1849–1897), a black Baptist minister, founded the benevolent Grand United Order of True Reformers in Alabama as the true way to "reform" adverse conditions of black people. The order was an outgrowth of the Independent Order of Good Templars of the World. Branches of the True Reformers spread quickly throughout southern states. When Browne relocated to Richmond, he reorganized the Virginia True Reformers branch and renamed it the Grand Fountain of the United Order of True Reformers, which established a mutual benefit fund in 1883 that subsequently became a large insurance company. Providing significant employment for tradesmen and various craftsmen, the Grand Fountain at Richmond built, separately, a hall, hotel, and home for "old folks" using the talent of black architects and building contractors. The organization established a real estate agency, a building and loan association, and cooperative grocery stores, all in a certain political ward called Jackson Ward inhabited by blacks and configured by one of its prominent residents. The Washington, D.C., unit built a large brick structure in 1903 at a cost of $100,000, designed by black architect John A. Lankford. During this growth the benefit began a weekly newspaper as well.[8] The Reformers benefited from the thriving enterprises that generated millions of dollars, and it profited immensely from the skills and business acumen of its members.

Former slave Mary Prout organized the Independent Order of St. Luke exclusively for women in Baltimore, Maryland, in 1867. Maggie Lena Walker (1867–1934), a product of Richmond's Jackson Ward, later took over leadership. She joined this benevolent society, established for the sick and bereaved, when she was a young girl. Advancing through the ranks, Walker rose to the position of executive secretary in 1899 and reorganized the society. She produced amazing results in ten years. Utilizing black skilled workers, Walker began a general department store and founded a weekly newspaper, which enterprises produced hundreds of thousands of dollars in assets. She established the St. Luke Penny Savings Bank in 1903, and by 1910 she was the bank's president, the first woman president of a bank anywhere in the world. The institution, later known as the Consolidated Bank and Trust Company (resulting from the merger of the Penny Savings Bank, the Second Street Savings Bank and Trust Company, and the Commercial Bank and Trust Company), then was the model for other mutual benefit societies that flourished.[9] The consolidation saved the smaller, younger banks and formed one strong bank with the greatest longevity of any African American bank in the nation. Incorporating smaller banks into one large bank provided the African American community with a confident source for loans and other financial services denied them at white institutions. Due to its conservative practices, the Consolidated Bank and Trust Company did not close during the infamous 1929 stock market crash in the United States. This was extremely unusual and rare. Although the Independent Order of St. Luke went out of existence in the latter part of the twentieth century, its bank and branches today thrive on assets in the millions of dollars, attesting to the astute business practices of people of color.

Religious sisterhoods and brotherhoods were founded in the 1800s to provide health aid, practical and religious training, and welfare for people of color, which helped them physically, mentally, and spiritually. Inclusive of several minority groups, the Congregation of the Sisters of the Blessed Sacrament for Indians and Colored People was established in 1889. Due to the dire needs of the American Indian and freed African Americans, the Right Reverend James O'Connor, bishop of Omaha, provided for their intellectual, moral, and physical regeneration. With financial assistance coming from his generous compatriot, Miss Katherine M. Drexel of Philadelphia, the bishop began boarding schools, day schools, orphanages, nursing care, the visitation of the sick, and the instruction of adults in Christianity.[10] The groups helped improve the conditions of the destitute newly freed people by giving them needed assistance and guidance lacking in the local and state governments.

BUSINESS AND TRADE

Gradually, in the nineteenth century, various business, mercantile, and professional groups established independent associations. Specific organizations, such as the Colored Farmer's National Alliance and Cooperative Union, the Agricultural and Mechanic Association, and the Colored American Institute for the Promotion of the Mechanic Arts and Sciences, appeared in the mid-1800s. African Americans, including inventors, found membership vital to their welfare.

Black Americans in the publishing business offered a few freeborn and manumitted blacks an opportunity in the early 1800s to express deep concern about their existence in a country struggling with and haggling over the thorny slave problem while in transition from an agrarian society to an industrial commonwealth. Black newspapers and journals flourished for years, having a wide minority readership. Their writers attempted to reach thousands of free people in the heavily populated northern cities and the great masses in the South. The news columnists praised the achievement of skilled tradesmen and craft experts, including the occasional inventor, whom they willingly promoted and proudly exalted. Although whites burned out some brave publishers and destroyed their presses, the pen's power prevailed. Upon relocating west or north, these journalists simply reorganized and began another publication.

Except in a few cases, the possession of currency was mostly foreign to the freed people living in the southern states at the end of the Civil War. However, they slowly and steadily plodded on to make ends meet using their skill, wit, and ingenuity, even competing with the influx of European immigrants who were skilled mechanics and craftsmen.

In 1900 in Boston, Massachusetts, Dr. Booker T. Washington founded the National Negro Business League (now the National Business League). The association consisted of diverse individuals who had succeeded in some business and could tell how they worked to achieve success and how each learned new mechanical and technological skills to help control his or her economic destiny. The object was to stimulate and to increase African American enterprises and capital. Washington, a graduate of Hampton Institute, was the founder of the Alabama-based Tuskegee Normal and Industrial Institute. The under-educated freedmen needed training to help secure employment and to sustain a meaningful livelihood. Institutions were founded, mostly in the South, to provide this opportunity through industrial education consisting of formalized courses. In reasoning why he started the alliance, Washington recounted:

> As I have travelled through the country from time to time I have been constantly surprised to note the number of colored men and women, often in small towns and remote districts, who are engaged in various lines of business. Sometimes in many cases the business is very humble, but nevertheless it was sufficiently advanced to indicate the opportunities of the race in this direction. My observation in this regard led me to believe that the time had come for the bringing together of the leading and most successful colored men and women throughout the country who are engaged in business.[11]

Officers of the National Negro Business League, including Booker T. Washington, president.
From *Proceedings of the National Negro Business League, Boston, 1900* (Boston: J. R. Hamm, 1901). From the Patricia Carter Ives Sluby Collection.

Washington's innovative group united African Americans from varied fields, including tradesmen, artisans, businesspeople, professionals, and others, who readily joined the new organization. The overall thrust was "In union there is strength," the recognized bulwark of all nations. Many inventors who had established businesses were staunch members. Inventor Andrew Hilyer delivered a passionate speech on the immense sum of money blacks now saved and invested in the country in enterprises managed by them when considering the poverty and training of freed blacks some thirty-five-odd years before.

At the beginning of an educational drive at African American normal, mechanical, and agricultural schools, a new breed of builders and craftsmen were trained to assist with rebuilding the South. A new generation of professionally taught architects of color surfaced, some of whom formulated mechanical and building trade programs at several black college campuses. By the new twentieth century, these builders and architects founded businesses and designed black communities, hotels, commercial buildings, insurance companies, and banks for black fraternal organizations. Expanding rapidly, chapters of the league sprang up in virtually every major jurisdiction in the country. Delegates were determined and serious at annual conventions that were held in major cities having sufficient accommodations for African Americans.

The most successful and enduring black businesses in the country around the early 1900s were in Jackson Ward in Richmond, Virginia. In a huge black enclave, shaped by Colonel Giles B. Jackson, black banks and insurance companies flourished, some of which were the first African American–owned financial institutions in the country. The most important bank between 1887 and 1910 was the True Reformers' Bank, organized in 1887. Its articles of incorporation were written by Jackson, who was the first African American in Virginia to pass the bar. Although the Freedman's Bank in Washington, D.C., antedated the Reformers' Bank, it was neither black owned nor chartered, and it collapsed in 1873.[12]

Charles M. Christian chronicled in *Black Saga: The African American Experience* the decline of black-owned banks, found mostly in the South. For the year 1934, he observed that "there were only twelve banks owned by Blacks in this country—despite the fact that more than one hundred thirty-four had been created since 1888. . . . Black banks had spread to every state in the South by 1930. Although they expanded and proliferated rapidly, they were also short-lived. Most of these banks failed in the same year they were established."[13] These Americans, unfortunately, had lost confidence in their own enterprises.

A few resulting insurance and savings and loan enterprises survived, providing financial backing for blacks and quality jobs that sharpened their financial skills when nearly all of the parent beneficial societies disappeared. A few visionary African Americans in 1899 organized the North Carolina Mutual and Provident Association, subsequently changing its name to the North Carolina Mutual Life Insurance Company, which survived the great crash and the depression due to the brilliant leadership of its president, C. C. Spaulding. Following the depression, it became the largest African American business in the United States. With an initial investment of $350, North Carolina Mutual flourishes today with assets greater than $40 million.[14]

MEDICINE AND OTHER HEALTH SCIENCES

White institutions trained the early African American physicians, or white doctors apprenticed them, before the founding of the nation's African American medical schools. The earliest known free black associated with the art of healing in America was Lucas Santomee, who studied in Holland in the 1600s. James Derham is accorded the distinction of being the first African American physician in this country. Born a slave in Philadelphia in 1762, he was taught to read and write and became an assistant to physicians, who were also his masters, during and after the Revolutionary War. Well trained in medical healing techniques, Derham moved to New Orleans after purchasing his freedom and built up a profitable medical business there. The acclaimed physician Dr. Benjamin Rush signaled Derham as a skilled medical professional.[15]

James McCune Smith (1811–1865) was the first free black awarded a medical doctor degree, but having been denied entry at medical schools in the United States, he secured it at the foreign University of Glasgow in 1837. He skillfully practiced the healing art in the city of New York and diligently maintained two pharmacy establishments, the earliest of their kind.[16] Later in the 1800s, blacks very slowly were admitted to American colleges of medicine such as Harvard University or Rush Medical Center, which graduated David J. Peck, the earliest of his race to obtain a medical degree from an American institution.

In 1867, the first African American female physicians began their practice, being trained at white facilities. Rebecca Lee Crumpler graduated from New England Female Medical College, and Rebecca Cole received her degree at the Women Medical College of Pennsylvania in 1867. After practicing in Philadelphia until 1881, Cole relocated to Washington, D.C., and became the superintendent of the Home for Destitute Colored Women and Children.[17]

Washington, D.C., as the nation's capital, was a magnet to Americans of African origin. In 1862, the city abolished slavery, and in the succeeding year, the freed attended schools at no cost. New citizens were deprived though, and created serious health problems for the town. Freedman's Hospital, founded in 1862, emerged out of the Civil War to relieve these conditions. In the postwar era, thousands of people needed education, employment, and welfare services. After its founding in 1866, the federally funded and subsidized Howard University provided the necessary education and gave welfare services through its medical department that opened two years later with seven African American students and one white student. Freedman's Hospital (now known as Howard University Hospital) then became the teaching facility for medical students at the university. The skills they acquired aided the newly formed federal agencies that were established to offer relief of ignorance and personal suffering. The black population soon tripled. Thoughtfully, the institution held evening classes to allow those who had to work a chance to earn a living. In 1866, at Nashville, Tennessee, another medical school for African Americans was established and named Meharry Medical College. As part of Walden University, the college started with less than a dozen students.

In the decades that followed, numerous other medical schools were founded, but only Howard and Meharry survived. Black institutions, nearly all in the East, between 1880 and 1920, engaged in training doctors or toyed with the notion of forming medical schools, but, due to unsurmountable difficulties, administrators closed the institutions or abandoned the idea.[18] Nonetheless, the two schools that endured graduated more than 50 percent of African American physicians in the United States, many of whom developed novel procedures and techniques to improve general welfare such as sanitation, vaccinations, clinics, and diagnostic procedures.

Medicine was the most prestigious profession among African Americans, compared with other disciplines. It was expected that the advancement of physicians in the health professions was easy. This was not true. In the 1920s, when hostile medical discrimination policies were well entrenched at the white medical schools in the North and West, only one or two African Americans successfully gained admission in a class. Interestingly, the Howard University Medical Department in 1868 erected no barriers against white students or women, and the Medico-Chirurgical Society of the District of Columbia, the oldest African American medical association, likewise was nondiscriminatory at its inception in 1884.

Black doctors suffered badly under white prejudice and found racial polarization ever widening; nonetheless, the system did not crush their motivation to excel. Medical societies, like the medical schools and hospitals in the seventeen southern states and in the District of Columbia, maintained a segregated framework. It was not until 1952 that the American Medical Association (AMA) affirmed its resolution to urge constituent societies having racially restrictive membership provisions to remove the offensive restriction, and in the same year the District Medical Society complied (however, the Baltimore County Medical Society, an AMA affiliate, had discontinued its racial barriers in 1948). Health specialists knew the importance of community involvement in health care and the need to keep abreast of developments in their specialized science, so they organized health associations for these purposes.

People of color fashioned health organizations after the older white ones but, more important, formed them as a result of the exclusionary practices of their white counterparts. For more than a century in the United States, these health institutions served as the focal point of community health, training, and welfare, and they spearheaded the drive for equality and economic opportunity. Many groups emerged from others, and some were born of new issues and new goals. Early meetings were in homes, churches, and meeting halls, but, however humble the beginnings, many have risen to national prominence and influence.

The well-established National Medical Association (NMA) was founded in October 1895 during the convening of the Cotton States and International Exposition at Atlanta, Georgia. Its enormous membership serves as a network for African American physicians and as an advocate for an equitable health-care system in the United States. One founder, Dr. Daniel Hale Williams, performed the first open-heart surgery in 1893 known in the medical field, an astounding accomplishment given the limitations in equipment and other medical assistance then. The NMA's goals are to promote high standards in medical practice and education, to eliminate racial discrimination from all American medical institutions, and to educate the public on health issues. In 1892, Dr. Miles Vanderhurst Lynk, another founder, published the *Medical and Surgical Observer*, the first journal of its kind for African American practitioners. The NMA's interests cover legislation and active work for greater representation within the developing health-care systems and state health-planning agencies. Also, the NMA strives to increase the number of African Americans in health careers.

In 1908, graduate nurses sought professional recognition, so they established a forum to help their situation and to increase the pool and training of nurses. The result was the then National Association of Colored Graduate Nurses. Women completed the requisite courses at "colored" schools of nursing, for example, at Hampton, Virginia's Dixie Hospital, Washington, D.C.'s, Freedman's Hospital, and Chicago's Provident Hospital, along with the Lincoln Hospital of New York City, St. Philip's Hospital of Richmond, Virginia, and the Nurse Training School of Charleston, South Carolina.

Dr. Daniel Hale
Williams.
Courtesy of the Moorland-
Spingarn Research Center,
Howard University.

Dr. John Kenney of Tuskegee, who became the personal physician to Dr. Booker T. Washington, issued a proclamation in 1915 to establish National Negro Health Week, celebrated for a week in April of each year. This special observance served as an awareness program for the black community through which many young people were inspired to take up a medical career as a practitioner or researcher. The concept originated in Virginia in 1913 with the Negro Organization Society through the guidance of Robert Russa Moton (1867–1940), who inherited the principalship of Tuskegee, succeeding Washington. Kenney continued this program after Washington's death in 1915, but abolished it in the 1950s.

The best tool for African Americans in the early 1900s to disseminate scientific principles was the *Journal of the National Medical Associa-*

tion, the premier journal for medical expression. The eminent William E. B. Du Bois published a brilliant survey on the health of the American Negro in 1906. Had this medical publication taken advantage of its position by encouraging developments along the path delineated by Du Bois, the NMA would have performed a magnificent service for the United States and been a tremendous asset for minority practitioners.

Other well-established companion groups are the National Dental Association (founded in 1913), the National Pharmaceutical Association, the Association of Black Psychologists, and the National Black Nurses Association, as well as the Black Psychiatrists of America. These organizations serve the same basic needs as the larger health science organization and serve as forums to promote scientific principles, to encourage medical research, and to voice concerns about common problems.

A few decades ago, medical education in the African American community took a giant step when Morehouse College in Atlanta, Georgia, initiated a two-year medical program with twenty-five entrants in 1977. Dr. Louis C. Brown conceived the idea and succeeded in encouraging the president of Morehouse College, Dr. Hugh M. Gloster, to gamble on initiating another African American medical school. The class of 1981 was Morehouse's first full-fledged four-year class to receive medical degrees. Another later-established institution is the Charles Drew School of Medicine at Los Angeles, California. The facility helps to serve the needs of those on the west coast.

Medical and technical organizations, like others, function to distribute information on career and educational opportunities and to monitor federal legislation affecting African American groups in health and law. The associations reflect achievement and serve the needs of African American talent.

TECHNOLOGY

In 1925, a group of technically oriented individuals established the National Technical Association (NTA) at Chicago, Illinois. It is the oldest African American technical association in the world. Charles S. Duke, its first president, guided the group through six terms. The association is dedicated to assuring that science and technology attend to the needs of the minority community. This group publishes the quarterly *NTA Journal* and annually holds conferences. Its large membership includes architects, engineers, scientists, teachers, and other interested persons and organizations. The NTA aspires to provide information for members and to afford an opportunity for them to expand personal and professional horizons. Additionally, the association encourages the interchange of information between minorities in technology and aids and encourages African American youth in preparation for technical careers through its numerous professional and student chapters across the nation. It maintains information on skills and conducts national and regional meetings in conjunction with national scientific and technical career-awareness programs.

Formed in the latter decades of the twentieth century, the National Organization of Black Chemists and Chemical Engineers, the Black Physicists Association, the National Tooling and Machining Association, and the National Society of Black Engineers are alliances that have platforms expressing the importance of minority participation in the mainstream of society. Their emphasis on programs and strategies is essential to the survival of these trades.

ACKNOWLEDGMENTS

After my initial interest in inventions and inventors was aroused, I was compelled to find more about my sable folk. This pursuit, covering many years, was a journey into the unexpected realm of writing. First I was encouraged by colleagues and friends to write small articles, then pushed to write a book. Gathering names of patent holders of color was an immensely gratifying task, albeit painstaking in determining ethnic origin and sex.

In the course of my patent career, information came from colleagues and neighbors, from associates and inventors, and from friends and family. Other data emanated from institutions and organizations. Many people helped me more than can easily be imagined, so I hesitate to cite anyone for fear that I overlook others. While numerous names are expressed, I hope that the few who might be omitted will attach forgiveness to their other rectitudes.

I am deeply grateful for the enormous information and support given me by my former colleagues and coworkers along with intellectual property agents and attorneys: John R. Moses, Samuel R. Williamson, William L. Muckelroy, John H. Newsome, Herman O. Jones, Jerome D. Jackson, Henry Jiles, Vivian Garner, Willie Bowman, A. Hugo Word, Booker T. Hogan, Werten F. W. Bellamy, Sr., Edward G. Favors, J. Richard Everett, Doris Funderburk Penn, Wendell K. Fredericks, Edith R. Buffalow, Howard Flournoy, John Rollins, Ethel R. Cross, Harold Burks, Sr., Wallace Burk, Fred Samuels, Sandra Nolan, Anthony D. Miller, Lawrence Harbin, Howard S. Williams, Michael Williamson, Kenneth Dobyns, Daniel M. Pritchett III, Avalyn Pitts, Roscoe V. Parker, Jerome J. Norris, Theodore Morris, Kenneth Hairston, Paula Hairston, Bernice Moore Butler, Louis Rimrodt, Marshall Gaddis, James Otis Thomas, Lorenzo Hayes, Brenda Hines, George Walton,

Lawrence J. Goffney, Jr., Edith Jackmon Hunter, Harold Broome, Richard Johnson, James Davie, Sidney B. Williams, Jr., Fannie Evans, Eli Liebermann, Vincent D. Turner, John Wynn, Donald R. Valentine, Fred Denson, Dale Ore, Vera Clarke, Carl Brundidge, Alan Kennedy, Vivian Redd, Hosea Taylor, Philip G. Hampton II, Winston A. Douglas, Michael Drew, Harry Moatz, Lynne Anderson, Johnnie R. Brown, Christopher Henderson, George Lesmes, Isaac Fleischman, Robert Edmonds, Charlotte Douglas, James Turnipseed, Charles Edison Smith, Eugene Young, Leonard Williamson, Mose Montgomery, Raymond Benton Johnson, and Clyde E. Bailey, Jr.

Freely sharing information were researchers Barbara Wyche, Arlene Hambrick, Grace Nance, who worked on the life of Granville Woods, and Ernestine G. Lucas, whose genealogical work on her family uncovered inventive family members and others. Writers and journalists Simeon Booker, Jerry Malloy, Joseph O. Evans, Stacy Jones, Ira Rogers, Keith Holmes, Susanne Otteman, James G. Spady, Anne L. Macdonald, Dalton Narine, Art Cookfair, and Benjamin Verdery are most graciously thanked for all their hospitable assistance.

I especially thank recorders of sable history Kathleen Joyce Prestwidge, Carroll R. Gibbs, A'Lelia Bundles, Leroy Graham, Glennette Tilley Turner, Portia James, Lady Sala, Winifred Latimer Norman, Lawrence D. Hogan, Sylvia Lyons Render, Louise Hutchinson, Lester A. Lee, G. Theodore Catherine, John R. Kinard, Hattie Carwell, and Richard Mattis for their wonderful support and encouragement through the years. Without their constant urging, I might not have reached my goal.

Librarians Jean Blackwell Hutson, Ernest Kaiser, and Gail Redmann have been a treasure. They hold a special spot in my soul for doing research beyond the call of duty. Worthy of distinctive mention are Reese Taylor, Lloyd McAulay, Lucy T. Edwards, Joyce Colbert, Ernest Denny, Melody Noel Brown, Howard S. Jones, Jr., Sylvia Cook Martin, Joletha Robinson Brown, Paula Quick Hall, Eugene DeLoatch, Gabrielle Knecht, Zora Felton, Pat Haynes, Michael F. Dwyer, Valerie Thomas, Tim Rives, Hester Monk Adams, Patricia Powell Braxton, Gerry Jackson, Gary Harris, Norman Poe, James Cox, Kojo Nnamdi, and Bruce K. Smith. Their generosity at sharing information was more than one could expect.

With endless gratefulness I richly thank the innumerable inventors who assisted me. The number of these extraordinary, giving talents is so great that I dare not list them for fear of an omission. For the enormous support, energy, time, information, and love they have given this project, I express my deep gratitude. Driven and highly motivated, they believe in a system that can reward them.

Many institutions, organizations, and societies allowed me use of their research facilities or sent me material: the U.S. Patent and Trademark Office; the Moorland-Spingarn Research Center of Howard University, Washington, D.C.; the New York State Education Department in Albany, New York; the Library of Congress; the National Intellectual Property Law Association; the Chicago Historical Society; the Schomburg Center for Research in Black Culture of the New York Public Library; the Patent and Trademark Office Society; the Newberry Library in Chicago; the National Archives and Records Administration; the Historical Society of Washington, D.C.; the Anacostia Museum of the Smithsonian Institution; Queens Borough Public Library of New York City; and the St. Louis Public Library. To all I am sincerely grateful.

Individuals who have been especially helpful are my editor Heather Ruland Staines, Charles Eberline for his superb copy editing of the manuscript, and the production staff at Praeger Publishers. Heather has been a patient guiding light who has offered suggestions and assistance at every turn. I am indebted to Patricia C. Dunn, Maceo C. Dailey, and Fred M. B. Amram for their worthy and instructive critique of the manuscript, and to Robert Hall, Norman G. Torchin, Art Molella, and Claudine Klose I give my warmest thanks. To many friends and others whom I have not mentioned by name, I voice my heartiest thanks.

Most of all, I owe deep, deep gratitude to my husband, Paul E. Sluby, Sr., for his patience, unending assistance, and sage advice. To my daughters, Julia and Felicia, I give special, loving thanks for their belief in me and for their interest in this project.

Patricia Carter Sluby
Temple Hills, Maryland

INTRODUCTION

> Whoever invents or discovers any new and useful process, machine manufacture, or composition of matter, or any new and useful improvement thereof, may obtain a patent therefor, subject to the conditions and requirements of this title.
>
> Title 35, *U.S. Code* §101

When I was a novice patent examiner at the U.S. Patent and Trademark Office, I discovered that my neighbor's brother held several U.S. patents in chemistry, my career field. Excited at finding this African American inventor, I felt compelled to quiz him on the circumstances involved in receiving his patents. I did not realize that my early pursuit of collecting data on minority inventors would blossom. My search deepened my awareness of their omnipresence. This crusade consumed me for decades during my lengthy experience as a member of the examining corps. Now, after crossing over from being an examiner to being a registered patent agent, I bring my long quest to fruition.

A federally protected grant, resulting from the product of an inventor's brainchild, is called "intellectual property." Patents (along with trademarks, trade secrets, and copyrights) are representative of this property and are of great value to anyone who wants protection for his or her idea. Possession of this property is extremely valuable because the rights can be sold, transferred, inherited, mortgaged, and taxed. Rights and protection for those who own such property are founded on laws specific to the particular property.

Before 1790, American colonists petitioned the colonial or state legislature for patent rights, issued only by special acts. Because there were no general laws to provide for the granting of patents, it was necessary for an inventor to make a specific appeal to the governing body. Some colonial patents were recorded in Great Britain and were recognized in the colonies. Presently, it is unknown if any African American took advantage of these patent rights prior to the adoption of the Constitution of the United States and the beginning of our patent system since no known research has been done in this area.

The Constitution enabled Congress to enact the first patent law establishing U.S. patent rights on April 10, 1790, from which the modern patent system has gradually evolved. George Washington signed the first patent bill on that date. Its first administrator was Thomas Jefferson, then secretary of state.

The Patent Act of 1790 granted a patent for a fourteen-year period if the invention or discovery was deemed "sufficiently useful and important." A Patent Board was established at the State Department, but later was found burdensome to its administrators, who held other duties. Having absolute power, the board consisted of Thomas Jefferson, secretary of state; Henry Knox, secretary of war; and Edmund Randolph, attorney general. In the final outcome, Jefferson was the first administrator and as well the first patent "examiner." The first governing laws were changed substantially three years later bringing about the Patent Law of 1793, which abolished the board that gave rigid examination of applications in favor of a patent registration process and a validity review by the courts. It was not until 1836 that the examination system was reestablished when the Act of July 4 made it necessary to determine the novelty and the usefulness of an invention. The patent section at the State Department was reorganized and established as a separate bureau there called the Patent Office. A commissioner of patents was appointed by the president, and in addition to filing the application with drawings, the applicant had to submit a patent model; however, after 1880, models were no longer required.[1]

In order to process and examine the increasing volume of applications, the Patent Office hired scientists to examine the claimed merit of the invention. Allen Bland (1833?–1929?) was the earliest known African American appointed an examiner at the U.S. Patent Office, according to his daughter, Irene Bland Jurix, and Howard University professor Kelly Miller in the *Etude*.[2] Described in the 1870 federal census enumeration as "mulatto," thirty-seven years of age, Bland was born in South Carolina and attended school at Charleston. He attended preparatory school at Oberlin College and was graduated from Wilberforce University in 1849. He married Lydia Ann Cromwell of Wilmington, Delaware, in 1850, and moved his family to Flushing, New York, where his son James and two other sons were born. Then Bland resettled in Troy, New York, and also in Philadelphia, Pennsylvania, before relocating to Washington, D.C., in 1865 immediately after the

Civil War. By this time, he and his wife had several children, and they lived in various locations in the northwest sector, including a house in a row of houses built by General Oliver Otis Howard near Howard University. From 1870 through 1874, Bland is listed in Washington, D.C., city directories as an employee at the Patent Office. In 1870, he enrolled in law school at Howard University, continuing his training while working at the Patent Office. He remained in law school through 1872. Bland did tailoring work a few years earlier before his federal employment, and his famous son, James A. Bland, minstrel and songwriter of "Carry Me Back to Old Virginny," attended Howard at the same time; however, James dropped law in favor of music.[3]

Henry Edwin Baker (1857–1928) is the second known African American patent examiner. In 1877, Baker was hired as a "copyist" at the U.S. Patent Office. He worked at the building that was located then on Seventh Street in the northwest section of the capital city, and attained the position of second assistant examiner in "old Division 4" under Examiner Merritt, his chief.[4] After achieving this rare status, Henry Baker retired in the early 1920s. Almost twenty years passed before other African Americans reentered the field as examiners.

Born in Columbus, Mississippi, on September 18, 1857, and educated there, Baker was appointed by Mississippi representative H. W. Barry to the U.S. Naval Academy, where he was admitted in 1875 as the third African American cadet midshipman. Two years later, he left Annapolis because of severe harassment and prejudicial treatment by whites. In 1877, he began studies at the Ben-Hyde Benton School of Technology, which he completed in 1879. That year, he enrolled in law school at Howard University, graduating in 1881. Baker then began postgraduate work at Howard, which was completed in 1883. He married Violetta K. Clark of Detroit, Michigan, in May 1893 and was a member and treasurer of the Berean Baptist Church in Washington, D.C.[5]

Henry Baker, a pioneer, risk taker, and stalwart, succumbed to death on April 27, 1928, at Providence Hospital in the nation's capital. He had no children but was survived by a niece, Irene Warfield, and other relatives. His interment was held at Harmony Cemetery, then in Washington, D.C., now Harmony Memorial Park located in Maryland.[6]

Countless applicants have succeeded in receiving the desired federal patent protection, but the names of only a few patentees have become household words. Such inventors as Alexander Graham Bell, Thomas Alva Edison, Henry Ford, or Charles Goodyear are quickly recognized; however, patentees like George Washington Carver, Granville T. Woods, Jan Matzeliger, Percy Lavon Julian, Lewis Howard Latimer, or Elijah McCoy are not as well known to the general public. Historically, the names of African Americans have generally been excluded from publication lists that highlight inventors. Nonetheless, at a time when African Americans were classified as chattel and deprived of their human rights, the patent system provided the opportunity for free blacks to be known for their genius. Yet, for the most part, their ingenuity and creativity went unobserved since persons of color were ignored or ridiculed. In fact, the earliest African American granted a patent received it in 1821.

The ever-increasing number of African American inventors is a vital and productive force in our economy. Although people of color did not gain patents in great abundance in the 1800s, they secured a host of patents in the 1900s. Evidence of their presence in the new millennium guarantees more revelations. From their emergence African Americans have received several thousand U.S. patents out of the more than six million grants of record. The number will grow as sable inventors continue to apply for proprietary rights. Weekly issuance of these grants holds promise.

Under the Act of March 2, 1861, the inventor held a monopoly for seventeen years after the issuance date of the patent, but under new legislation arising from the General Agreement on Tariffs and Trade (GATT) that took effect on June 7, 1995, the patent holder's grant now expires twenty years from the date of filing the application. The inventor, however, has no patent rights from the time of filing to the date the patent issues. This is the "pendency period" during which the applicant files as a large or small entity with appropriate fees. Since the U.S. Patent and Trademark Office is a fee-funded government agency, the applicant must be financially prepared to traverse the system, including the payment of fees to keep the patent in force for its full number of years.

With the patent process being an ever-evolving system, periodically new laws are passed to help improve patent practice. One such law, signed by President George W. Bush on November 2, 2002, helps the U.S. Patent and Trademark Office keep up with modern technology. H.R. 2215 includes the Patent and Trademark Office Authorization Act of 2002, which provides electronic user-friendly patent filing for applicants. The Intellectual Property and High Technology Technical Amendments Act of 2002 is also a part of the new law.

As an examiner, I had the opportunity to witness the total picture of Yankee and foreign ingenuity. Firsthand knowledge of developments in all phases of endeavor is at the fingertips of an examiner— literally at a touch on the computer terminal keyboard. Additionally, an examiner is exposed to all types of inventions and can personally speak with inventors concerning their ingenuity. Such circumstances place the examiner in the unique position of viewing the breadth and depth of creative genius. I became aware of numerous African American inventors, many of whom were successful in obtaining patent grants. However, there were others who became frustrated with the system's failure to issue the coveted grant. Indeed, it is a difficult process to traverse.

The inventor's patent application must pass the rigid examination system and other technical requirements before the grant is issued, offically known as a U.S. letters patent. For approval of a patent application, the inventor must surrender documents containing statements and claims worded specifically about the invention. After an inventor submits the application to the Patent Office, it is assigned to an examiner who, knowledgeable in the subject matter, will determine the patentability of the claimed subject matter. To grasp the notion, the examiner begins with a careful study of the inventor's request. To understand what the applicant declares as the parameters of the invention or discovery, the examiner then analyzes the invention claims— the crucial part of the application. After searching the files of U.S. and foreign patents and various publications including journals, books, or even newspapers, the patent professional applies the three tests of patentability—novelty, usefulness, and unobviousness. If these tests are satisfactory and other technicalities are met, the examiner grants the patent to the inventor.

Most inventors want monetary gain besides personal satisfaction from their inventiveness. This is quite understandable since the path from creation to production can present substantial financial demands. Those inventors who choose to protect their product with a patent before going to market find that it is very expensive to have their application travel through the complexities of patent examination. Subsequently, additional time, energy, and money are spent to manufacture the product for its general or specialized purpose, whether patented or not protected. At this point, all must dig deep into their pockets since obtaining a patent does not ensure pecuniary rewards. This must come from individual effort. Apparently, inventors sustain themselves on ingredients including determination, fortitude, and courage, but many attribute their success to lots of good, solid luck. By chance, some talents gain power, fame, or glory, but very few become rich.

While a copyright is a form of protection given by law to authors of literary, dramatic, musical, artistic, and other intellectual works, and a trade secret is given protection by a state for a secret that is substantial and valuable, a patent is granted by the government to an inventor to bar others from making, using, or selling the invention throughout the United States. There are three basic types of patents for which an inventor can specifically apply: utility patents, design patents, and plant

Nº 3970955

THE UNITED STATES OF AMERICA

TO ALL TO WHOM THESE PRESENTS SHALL COME:

WHEREAS THERE HAS BEEN PRESENTED TO THE

COMMISSIONER OF PATENTS AND TRADEMARKS

A PETITION PRAYING FOR THE GRANT OF LETTERS PATENT FOR AN ALLEGED NEW AND USEFUL INVENTION THE TITLE AND DESCRIPTION OF WHICH ARE CONTAINED IN THE SPECIFICATIONS OF WHICH A COPY IS HEREUNTO ANNEXED AND MADE A PART HEREOF, AND THE VARIOUS REQUIREMENTS OF LAW IN SUCH CASES MADE AND PROVIDED HAVE BEEN COMPLIED WITH, AND THE TITLE THERE-TO IS, FROM THE RECORDS OF THE PATENT AND TRADEMARK OFFICE IN THE CLAIMANT(S) INDICATED IN THE SAID COPY, AND WHEREAS, UPON DUE EXAMI-NATION MADE, THE SAID CLAIMANT(S) IS (ARE) ADJUDGED TO BE ENTITLED TO A PATENT UNDER THE LAW.

NOW, THEREFORE, THESE LETTERS PATENT ARE TO GRANT UNTO THE SAID CLAIMANT(S) AND THE SUCCESSORS, HEIRS OR ASSIGNS OF THE SAID CLAIMANT(S) FOR THE TERM OF SEVENTEEN YEARS FROM THE DATE OF THIS GRANT, SUBJECT TO THE PAYMENT OF ISSUE FEES AS PROVIDED BY LAW, THE RIGHT TO EXCLUDE OTHERS FROM MAKING, USING OR SELLING THE SAID INVENTION THROUGHOUT THE UNITED STATES.

IN TESTIMONY WHEREOF *I have hereunto set my hand and caused the seal of the* PATENT AND TRADEMARK OFFICE *to be affixed at the City of Washington this* twentieth *day of* July *in the year of our Lord one thousand nine hundred and seventy-six, and of the Independence of the United States of America the two hundredth and first.*

Attest:

Ruth C. Mason
Attesting Officer

C. Marshall Dann
Commissioner of Patents and Trademarks

Cover of a patent grant, issued in 1976, celebrating the American Revolution Bicentennial.

patents. The utility patent is issued to anyone who invents or discovers a new and useful process, machine, manufacture, or composition of matter, or a new and useful improvement, subject to certain conditions. The design patent is granted to any person who has invented a new, original, and ornamental design for an article of manufacture. The plant patent may be issued to anyone who invents or discovers and asexually reproduces a distinct and new variety of plant. The trademark or service mark is a word, phrase, sound, or symbol used on or in association with goods and in performance of a service.

Applications for patents and trademarks do not require ethnic or sex identification. Thus determining either distinction is an arduous and difficult task. The process of just verifying the identity of women inventors is an endless excursion. Names like Johnnie, Frankie, Dale, Beverly, Posey, Carroll, or Marion can be masculine or feminine; therefore, primary source information is essential.

Various publications address the subject of patent ownership by African Americans; nevertheless, these works primarily concern popular or famous personalities or inventions. This writing attempts a full study of their inventive spirit from earliest time to the present to fill the void. In completing a task of this size, though, errors inescapably may appear. Many hidden names come to the public's attention for the first time, appearing with the more recognized African American geniuses. Although a sizeable number of minorities have secured patents in the United States and abroad as well, only domestic patents are of concern here.

The central purpose of this work is to bring to the forefront names of past and present gifted thinkers and tinkerers of African descent often overlooked in the annals of human endeavor. This labor should be useful to students in secondary education and those in higher intellectual pursuits who are concentrating on the humanities, on African American history and achievement, or on the social and physical sciences. The abundant intellectual property of black inventors should interest scholars working in the field of patents and trademarks and in the inventive process itself.

From evidence uncovered in Africa in metallurgy, science, architecture, medicine, and other fields, surprising discoveries support proof of the reasoning ability of Africans, including the ebony souls brought to America. The first chapter discusses the early historical contribution of people of color oiling the wheel of progress, intelligence, and invention from the dark continent to America's shores. The chapters that follow spotlight the plight of inventive slaves up to the Civil War juxtaposed with the situation of free blacks at that period. The Civil War era reveals Confederate legislation that provided patent rights for the enslaved. The postwar chapter incorporates the Reconstruction of the South, craft societies, and agricultural and industrial inventions developed by African Americans, some of which significantly altered the economic climate of major industries. Early-twentieth-century innovations, elaborated in another chapter, inclusive of military inventions produced during the world wars, showcase the diverse intellect of minorities. Novel technological advances are discussed in the mid-century chapter that highlight the involvement of black Americans on engineering teams at institutions, corporations, and government facilities. The closing chapter concerning the modern period embodies current minority inventors and their participation in the forefront of technology at the close of the twentieth century and in the new millennium.

Women inventors are given special attention in a separate chapter because, at one time, women were not encouraged or expected to use their brain creatively or inventively. More significantly, African American females' success at the U.S. Patent and Trademark Office is minuscule compared to that of their white female counterparts. Consequently, emphasizing their effort is fair. Of significant mention in the chapter is the inventive trend found in family lines having inherent abilities, and, therefore, particular reference is given to this phenomenon. Though one or two inventors are mentioned earlier, their presence here is appropriate.

Appendix I contains discussion of minorities in the practice of intellectual property law. Appendix II is the "Roster of African American Patentees" that lists the inventor's name, patent title, its number, and date of issue. While a significant number of black inventors own scores of grants, not all their documents may be listed. Inclusive of Henry E. Baker's research, the "Roster" embraces inventors who have utility patents for inventions that have use in the general chemical (inclusive of biotechnical concepts), mechanical, and electrical areas (inclusive of computer science and business practices). For inventors who have secured design patents for inventions having an ornamental look, see the final chapter.

Finally, the bibliography provides sources for additional inquiry that might interest scholars and encourage further research.

1

ONCE UPON A TIME

For wisdom is better than rubies;
and all the things that may be desired
are not to be compared to it.
I, wisdom, dwell with prudence,
and find out knowledge of witty inventions.

Proverbs 8:11–12

AFRICA'S CONTRIBUTION

The oldest remains of humans have been found in Kenya, the heart of the African continent. Only two types of artifacts from this early period remain today—partial skeletons and the tools with which people worked. The human who first took up the stone ax, the arrowhead, and the flint knife lived in innermost Africa, home of the darker races. Obviously, then, prehistoric man's presence gave rise to certain items of necessity and convenience. Ali A. Mazrui in *The Africans* speculates "that if there was a Garden of Eden where the first man and woman lived, that garden was in Africa." Then he reveals, "but Africa is not merely the probable cradle of Man and his initial culture: the continent is also the genesis of civilisation. Eastern Africa provided the birth of humanity and culture: several regions of Africa made a major contribution to the development of agriculture; and northern Africa initiated grand civilisation."[1]

The denizens of Africa worked in metal by fashioning spears, knives, and death masks of copper and iron. They were creating art while the tribes of Europe and Asia were not yet born. They were so advanced, in the sub-Saharan region, that they skipped a phase of cultural development. Advancing directly from the Stone Age to the Iron Age, these people bypassed the Bronze Age entirely because natural iron supplies are more abundant in the southern Sahara than copper. The immensely utile element was extracted from its ore and refined with bellows and charcoal fires. Here the skills of the blacksmith were sharpened as the metal was worked into useful tools.

In those days, great armies conquered distant lands; great African kings conceived intricate forms of government and developed distinguished learning centers. These peoples had the intelligence to survive eons of disease, famine, invasions, and the elements. Most of all, they had the intellect to shape stone, wood, bone, skins, plants and their by-products, clay, and metal. Their tribal ties were strong, binding one to the other by culture, mores, language, and tradition.

A huge engineering feat was accomplished in Egypt when plans to divert the course of the Nile were executed. The Suez Canal was begun by Africans during 609–593 B.C. Scholars have credited the Egyptians with numerous developments and innovations such as the merhet, a device used as an aid to map stars; the bega, the earliest known measure of weight; and medical procedures that include contraceptive jelly, a pregnancy test, and antibiotics. Scholars attest that many of these Egyptians were dark skinned or black like those in Ethiopia of old who fought, traded, and intermarried with the Egyptians.[2]

Further, Ivan Van Sertima, author of *Blacks in Science: Ancient and Modern*, profoundly writes, in part:

> Anthropology has had a long love affair with the primitive and has preferred to set its tent down among the African bushmen exploring the simplicities of tiny tribal communities rather than the complexities to be found in the primary centers of large African nations. Very partial and limited visions of the African hovering on the fringes of his vast world have come to represent the totality of his capacity and potential. . . .
>
> Five centuries of these falsehoods have been exploded in just five years. These years have seen the discovery of African steel-melting in Tanzania 1,500–2,000 years ago, an astronomical observatory in Kenya 300 years before Christ, the cultivation of cereals and other crops by Africans in the Nile Valley 7,000 years before any other civilization, the domestication of cattle in Kenya 15,000 years ago, the domestic use of fire by Africans 1,400,000 years ago (one million years before its first known use in China), the use of tetracyclene by an ancient African population fourteen centuries ago, an African glider-plane 2,300 years old, a probe by microwave beams of an American radar satellite beneath the sands of the Sahara, revealing cultures 200,000 years old and the traces of ancient rivers running from this African center. Some of these buried stream valleys seem to be "ancient connections to the upper Nile tributaries," towards which blacks migrated, later peopling Nubia and Egypt.[3]

The well-known oral tradition for preserving African history, passed on credibly by griots, was often detailed and lasting. Though the fact is not widely published, Africans did originate writing methods. A number of African writings were developed and used before Alexandria and Timbuktu were ravished, and prior to the destruction of Moorish chronicles.

Influenced somewhat by the Egyptians, the Nubians invented the Meroitic script. Several decades ago, a unique Egyptian hieroglyphic system was unearthed when the black kingdom of Ta-Seti was newly found in the Sudan. It was announced as the origin of Egyptian writings.

Egyptian Ability to Diagnose and Treat Diseases

According to J. A. Rogers:

There is evidence that the Egyptians, and perhaps Imhotep also, diagnosed and treated more than two hundred diseases, among them fifteen diseases of the abdomen, eleven of the bladder, ten of the rectum, twenty-nine of the eyes, and eighteen of the skin.

They knew how to detect disease by the shape, color, or position of the visible parts of the body, as the skin, hair, nails, tongue. They treated spinal tuberculosis, gall-stones, appendicitis, gout, rheumatoid arthritis, mastoid diseases, and dental caries. They practiced surgery, knew of auscultation, and extracted medicine from plants.

Source: J. A. Rogers, *World's Great Men of Color, 3000 B.C. to 1946 A.D.* (New York: Helga M. Rogers, 1947), vol. 1, p. 2.

People of color have been practicing in the field of medicine since before the birth of Christ. The ancient Egyptian Imhotep is believed to be the real "father of medicine." Greeks and Romans received their knowledge from this great practitioner. People of African descent have been inextricably tied with healing and with medicine since the beginning of time.

The "Dark Ages" swept Europe, Asia, and parts of Africa when these lands were overrun by the Visigoths, Huns, and Vandals. However, Africa was to become the center of knowledge. The West African kingdom of Ghana rose as a powerful entity about A.D. 800. Ghana's wealth came from its abundance of gold and iron, which emerged from the trans-Saharan trade, but it later declined.[4]

In the thirteenth century, Mali became the power state, and its economy, like Ghana's, rested on the trading of gold, salt, cloth, rubber, ivory, slaves, and metals. Mansa Kankan Mussa, king of Mali from 1307 to 1377, led thousands of his people in caravan safely across the Sahara Desert from Timbuktu to Mecca in 1324. The buildings in Timbuktu and other cities of the Sudan were designed by an architect Mussa brought back to his kingdom.[5]

At Mali's decline in the fifteenth century arose the kingdom of Songhay in western Sudan. Its king Sonni Ali Ber (1464–1492) created the most powerful empire in West Africa. He captured Timbuktu, conquered trade routes, and expanded his domain to encompass as much land mass as Napoleon did four centuries later. The Songhay empire became a major center for commerce, culture, and the Moslem religion. The next king of Songhay was General Askia Mohammed Toure, who seized power in 1493, one year after Columbus sailed to America. Formerly the prime minister, he reigned for nineteen years, ruling and administering Songhay strictly according to Islamic law. He was known as Askia, "the Great," a remarkable administrator who established a government renowned for its efficiency and detail.[6]

Timbuktu was well established as a center of trade and learning. The cities of Gao, Walata, and Jenne were additional learning centers. The University of Sankore had well-stocked libraries where one could study history, medicine, and astronomy.

During the first half of the sixteenth century, Affonso I, the king of the Congo, was the first monarch to modernize Africa on a large basis. He encouraged Christian beliefs and brought about the practice of using modern skills in masonry, carpentry, and agriculture. He modernized Congo politics and resisted the lures of the slave trade.

Between 1580 and 1617, just before the first blacks stepped on shore at Jamestown in the colony of Virginia, Idris Alooma, the sultan of Bornu, reunited the kingdoms of Kanem and Bornu. Because he was a devout Moslem, he replaced tribal laws with Islamic law. He also made a pilgrimage to Mecca. On this journey, he acquired Turkish firearms, which he used to conquer other territory. He deployed trained swordsmen on horseback, muskets, and armor—unusual war implements for that time.[7]

The powerful king of the warlike Ashanti nation was Osei Tutu, from 1680 to 1717, when the American colonies were being established and the French were exploring the Mississippi. The Ashanti nation was a great West African kingdom where gold was the prime source of wealth. The Ashanti's geographical area tripled in size during the reign of Tutu.

Carter G. Woodson and Charles H. Wesley in their 1972 *The Negro in Our History* commend the old strategy Africans used to educate their young. Giving merit to the system, they declare:

There is no formal school training in native Africa except the discipline of two societies found in most communities. The one for the boys is under the direction of a fatherly old man, and that for the girls under a trustworthy matron. They are carefully instructed in physiology and hygiene with special reference to fatherhood and motherhood. . . . Early in life about the regular school age in modern countries, the African boy begins his education. He is required to look after the kids, the young goats, and to make observation in agriculture methods. The boy is required later to tend larger animals and finally to herd cattle. He also undergoes circumcision very much like that of the Hebrews. The girls at the same age begin the study of household and domestic duties. . . . They continue at this sort of training until they reach the age of becoming housewives. After having been under strict supervision of matrons who have instructed them in the rudimentary instructions of motherhood and have taught them the duty of wives to their husbands, the course terminates with a ceremony.[8]

The unfortunate souls taken from their homeland against their will, filled with studious direction from the elders, were prohibited by design from bringing artifacts of their native land to the new shores. Nonetheless, slavers could not obliterate their mental faculty, resourcefulness, and craft skill, subsequently passed on to those who followed.

ABILITIES ABOUND

Four centuries ago, with the arrival of the slave ships, these natives were deprived of human rights. The African who was routed from his homeland came from ancient societies having well-organized governments and military warfare skills, taught to him by his ancestors, which he passed on to those born in the new land. He had a rich cultural life, being skilled at carving in bronze, wood, and ivory. The African also was a sophisticated artisan adept in weaving and pottery making and proficient as a musician and dancer. These abilities remained with the captured native chained as cargo on slave ships bound for North America. Competent in war, various slaves were sons of African kings and princesses who never had their spirit broken, though cowed by bondage.

The conditions were so severe that millions perished; however, a few overcame the injustices heaped upon them to become free. The Africans comingled with the native inhabitants of the New World and with their European captors. Consequently, different cultures and technologies blended. Portia James in *The Real McCoy* writes, "African-American craftsmen integrated African technological skills with the European and Native American technology that they learned in America to create new and unique African-American traditions in technol-

A. L. CRALLE.
ICE CREAM MOLD AND DISHER.

No. 576,395.   Patented Feb. 2, 1897.

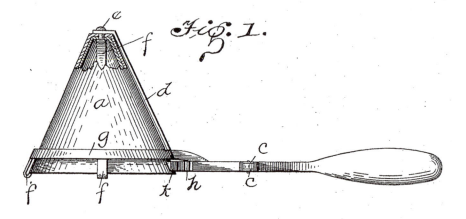

Fig. 1.

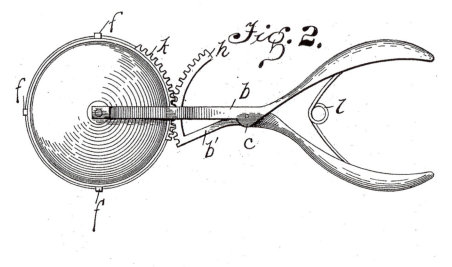

Fig. 2.

Witnesses:
A. R. Appleman
A. M. Wilson

Inventor:
Alfred L. Cralle.

BY Henry C. Earp Att'y.

Ice Cream Mold and Disher, patented invention of Alfred L. Cralle.

ogy."[9] New generations learned from the old; fathers taught sons; mothers instructed daughters. James further declares that a "closer examination of the period [seventeenth-century America] reveals that many aspects of the new technology can indeed be attributed to the innovations of early African-Americans."[10]

Beliefs about African People by Acclaimed Thinkers of History

I am apt to suspect the Negroes . . . to be naturally inferior to the White. There never was a civilized nation of any other complexion than white, nor even any individual eminent either in action or speculation, no ingenious manufacturers amongst them, no arts, or sciences.

Philosopher David Hume

The study of the Negro is the study of man's rudimentary mind. He would appear rather a degeneracy from the civilized man than a savage rising to the first step, were it not for his total incapacity for improvement.

Explorer and Writer Richard Burton

Why increase the sons of Africa, by planting them in America, where we have so fair an opportunity, by excluding all blacks and tawnys, or increasing the lovely white and red?

Scientist Benjamin Franklin

There is a physical difference between the white and the black races living together . . . while they do remain together there must be the position of superior and inferior, and I as much as any man am in favor of having the superior position assigned to the white race.

President Abraham Lincoln

Source: Anthony T. Browder, *Nile Valley Contributions to Civilization* (Washington, D.C.: Institute of Karmic Guidance, 1992), pp. 17–18.

Interestingly, the Confederate general Thomas J. "Stonewall" Jackson, when he was a professor at Virginia Military Institute, found time to teach at a Negro Sunday school for a number of years.

The paternalistic and denigrating attitudes of white supremacists permeated Western society, but in spite of their power and opinion, notable black ability and ingenuity prevailed. The white power structure overwhelmingly believed the Negro to be naturally inferior to the majority race; nevertheless, exceptional black talent repeatedly came to the forefront as ingenious in manufacturing and in the sciences and the arts. If blacks were inherently inferior, how is it that some achieved great distinction?

2

EARLY CREATIVE MINDS

The true measure of a nation's worth is its contribution to the
well-being of the world. This can be applied equally well to races,
and, judging by this standard, the Negro has nothing of which
to be ashamed.
   Giles B. Jackson and D. Webster Davis, *Industrial History*, 1908

INVENTIVE FREE PEOPLE OF COLOR

Despite the severe restrictions in slaveholding states to keep bondsmen
illiterate for fear that knowledge would foster organized rebellions,
many free African Americans, and some slaves, were learned. Ironically, the earliest public school for people of color and Native Americans was established in Virginia in 1620; however, by the 1700s, strong
opposition to the teaching of slaves surfaced throughout the slaveholding South. Those north of the Mason-Dixon line mostly found
educational opportunities that were a challenge to southern blacks. A
private school for slaves appeared early in New York City, and later in
the 1700s, a few schools for poor white, formerly enslaved, freeborn,
or Indian children appeared in communities in Ohio, Maryland, Pennsylvania, and Massachusetts, and even in North Carolina and South
Carolina. Overall, for the southern enslaved, a wellspring of alternative
mechanisms sprang forth to educate the disadvantaged bondsmen.
Clandestine schools popped up like mushrooms, to the dismay of the
white establishment. In a few Louisiana communities, the restrictive
rules and regulations luckily were ignored due to the protection of
powerful masters for various reasons. On occasion, a master or owner
sent his charge to Europe for an education, and, at times, the bonds-

man accompanied his master to an educational institution to serve his needs. In the process, the slave also received an education. Many brave slave parents also sought white instructors to teach their offspring. Numerous slaves were multilingual, speaking Spanish, French, "good English," or even Swedish, in addition to any African mother tongue.

The word *slave* originally came from "Slav," a term assigned to people of Indo-European background frequently enslaved in the ancient Middle Ages.

During slavery, a number of free African Americans conceived and developed industrial artifacts, mechanical tools, and other implements, and a few of them were even recognized for their ingenuity. The appellations mathematician, astronomer, surveyor, and gazetteer fully describe inventor Benjamin Banneker, born free on November 9, 1731. Banneker's mother, Mary, was a free mulatto, and his father was a slave. He was raised on a farm near Elk Ridge, Maryland. His grandmother was an English servant girl, Molly Welsh, and his grandfather was a slave African prince, anglicized as Robert.[1]

He began his education with a simple but private country training consisting of reading, writing, and basic arithmetic. Perhaps the equivalent of eighth-grade education, this training was supplemented with continued study and reading in the evenings after doing his chores on the farm.

With an eager mind and skilled hands, Banneker mastered certain mechanical concepts, enabling him to design and to effectively build a wooden clock. Completed in 1753, it kept accurate time and faultlessly struck the hours for twenty years. This was the first American-made clock.

Banneker was gifted in mathematics and astronomy. A neighbor loaned him books that he fervently read on the subjects, and instruments that he used. With this knowledge, he was able to predict the solar eclipse of 1789.

Two years later, when Banneker worked with the team that planned and laid out the nation's capital, he published a series of almanacs that contained data on astronomy, medicinal products, and tide tables for the Chesapeake Bay. His papers on the life of insects were widely read in the well-populated area of the United States and in Europe around the 1790s.

His surveying knowledge and prodigious memory brought him his greatest achievement. Earlier, he had assisted Andrew Ellicott and his three sons in building a mill near his home. At forty-one years of age, he assembled the machinery and apparatus for the mill. When the nation's capital was moved from Philadelphia to a new area to be known as Washington, Ellicott's son, Andrew, was appointed chief surveyor. Banneker was appointed as the third member of the team, with Major Pierre L'Enfant in charge. In a rage with officials over the plans for the city, L'Enfant resigned and quickly departed for France, taking the plans with him. Banneker volunteered to save the desperate situation by precisely reproducing the plans from memory. He was not honored in his native country for this outstanding accomplishment, but France accorded salutations to him, and Great Britain bestowed distinction upon him in its English Parliament records. Benjamin Banneker died on his farm on October 9, 1806, and is buried in the family plot.[2]

African Americans made significant contributions to the maritime industry as officers, common seamen, shipbuilders, tradesmen, and laborers. Two sterling maritime inventors developed distinct improvements in articles of manufacture for sailing and whaling. The seaport cities in the North drew large numbers of free black Americans seeking work after the Revolutionary War. Manufacturing and transportation in the early 1800s provided opportunities for black inhabitants. Consequently, substantial black settlements were founded in these maritime cities.

Absalom F. Boston, grandson of the slave Prince Boston, was a Nantucket captain who commanded the whaling ship *Loper*, where he employed black navigators and crews. As a free African American, John Mashow entered the maritime trade in South Dartmouth, Massachusetts, after seeking employment from the local shipbuilder, Laban Thatcher. Mashow founded a company in 1831 and became an outstanding shipbuilder himself.[3]

Robert Benjamin Lewis, born in 1802 at Gardiner, Maine, invented an oakum-picking machine useful in Maine's Shipbuilding interests, especially at the city of Bath.[4]

Inventor James Forten (1766–1842) of Philadelphia, Pennsylvania, was born of free American parents of color. At age fifteen, he became a powder boy on the colonial navy vessel *Royal Louis* during the Revolutionary War. Later he was an apprentice to a sailmaker at a loft and worked his way up to foreman in 1786. By 1798, Forten was the owner of the sail loft and subsequently invented a contraption to handle sails. Even though no record is found that he patented this invention, the apparatus helped him to amass a fortune of $100,000, which he used for his abolitionist activities. A prominent agent against slavery, Forten denied slave ships his sail-rigging and sail-handling tool. He is credited with influencing William Lloyd Garrison to stand against the evils of colonization.[5]

Inventor Lewis Temple (1800–1854), born in Richmond, Virginia, originated a whaling harpoon usually known as the toggle harpoon that revolutionized the whaling industry. Some writers refer to the device as Temple's toggle, the Temple iron, or Temple's iron. In any case, the skill and ingenuity of its originator are legendary. After its introduction to commercial whaling in 1848, the toggle harpoon virtually changed the way whalers caught their prey. Temple operated a craft shop at the New Bedford, Massachusetts, port whaling center. The Sag Harbor Whaling and Historical Museum at Long Island, New York, and the maritime museum in Bermuda exhibit prized original models of the Temple toggle harpoon. One original model is owned privately in Princeton, New Jersey.[6] As in Forten's case, no records indicate that Temple obtained a patent on his innovation.

Some black inventors, though, thought that indirect patent protection through the name of white business associates was best. Such was the thinking of successful cabinetmaker Henry Boyd (1802–1886), who formed a commercial venture with a white cabinet manufacturer. Born a Kentucky slave, Boyd purchased his freedom after apprenticing as a cabinetmaker and then went to Cincinnati to find work. Eventually, after a stint as an independent carpenter, he partnered with a white craftsman. By 1835, he accumulated $3,000 and also secured the freedom of his brother and sister. As a talented bed-frame designer and successful shop owner, Boyd wanted protection for his unusual sturdy frames, so he allowed his partner to get a patent in 1835 on the "Boyd Bedstead" design. Afterward, competitors saw immense benefit in the invention, and Boyd did the next best thing. In 1845, as Cincinnati's premier manufacturer of bedsteads, Boyd started identifying the profitable object by stamping his name on each product. As a result, several deliberate fires were started at his manufacturing facility, but he reconstructed the site each time. Finally, in 1863, he was compelled to retire.[7]

SLAVES AS ORIGINATORS

As is commonly known, in the South during the slave period, work in agriculture and in mechanics was performed mostly by slave labor. These unskilled laborers and skilled artisans faced various problems and often solved them through diligent, daily negotiation.

At the height of the slave trade, New England native Eli Whitney obtained a patent on March 14, 1794, for an invention dubbed the "cotton gin." This grant, issued a mere four years after the first U.S.

patent, gave Whitney full credit as the original, first, and sole inventor of the initial cotton engine. Was this true? Some doubt still lingers.

Whitney came south to study law and accepted a position as a tutor on a plantation called Mulberry Grove, a tract of land given by the state of Georgia to the Revolutionary War officer Major General Nathanael Greene, who died in 1786. Greene's widow, Catharine Littleton Greene, had previously met Whitney in 1792 and offered him a position at the plantation. Whitney eventually busied himself in the plantation shops.[8]

Horace King, born a slave, was one of the foremost bridge engineers in the South before and after the Civil War. Freed by his master, John Goodwin, who sent him north to be educated in engineering, he returned to build bridges in Georgia over the Chattahoochee River and others in Alabama, Mississippi, and South Carolina. Georgia and Alabama passed special laws giving him standing with white builders and contractors. King, in gratitude, erected a monument over the tomb of his former master.

Source: J. A. Rogers, *Africa's Gift to America* (St. Petersburg, Fla.: Helga M. Rogers, 1961), p. 228.

Mulberry Grove was in an area that produced upland cotton, a plant that had a greenish fuzzy seed that was difficult to manually separate from the lint. Nearby, off the coast of Georgia, was a different kind of cotton—the long, silky Sea Island cotton that easily was ginned. Though easy to process, it was not the favored cotton shipped offshore. By 1810, only one-tenth of Sea Island cotton, compared to upland cotton, was being exported.[9]

The enslaved labored intensely to loosen the seeds from the cotton lint. It took ten hours for the slave to pick a pound of lint from three pounds of mixed lint and seed. Some historians relate that Whitney saw people of color using a crude comblike instrument to perform this task. Being mechanically oriented from his earlier manufacturing days in his father's Westboro, Massachusetts, shop, Whitney improved upon and perfected the crude comb device. Contrarily, it was told that a bondsman called Sam bettered the device made by his father. Carter G. Woodson and Charles Wesley in *The Negro in Our History* recorded the opinion of patent examiner Henry E. Baker to be that "slaves made certain appliances, experimenting with the separation of the seed from cotton, which, when observed by Eli Whitney, were assembled by him as the cotton gin."[10]

In just ten days, allegedly, Whitney developed the famous cotton gin

E. Whitney,
Cotton Gin.

Patented Mar. 14, 1794.

NO·PRINTED COPY OF SPECIFICATION IN OFFICE.

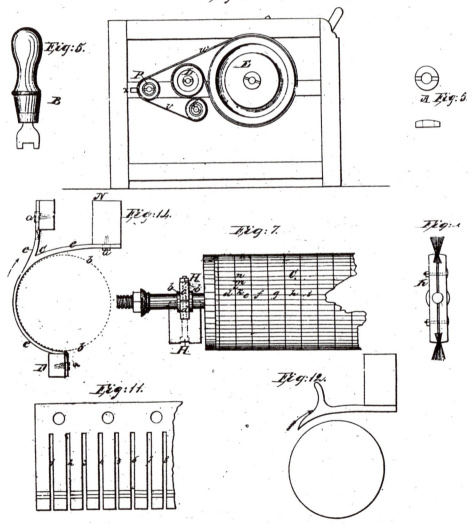

Cotton Gin, patented invention of Eli Whitney.

as an improvement over the crude apparatus to process cotton. The principal parts of his machine were the frame, the cylinder, the breast-work, the cleaner, and the hopper. The gin basically was a roller equipped with wire teeth that pulled the cotton fiber from the seed as spikes revolved between hopper slots. In a few years, cotton exported from the United States escalated from a mere 138,000 pounds per year to 6 million pounds per year.

However, Whitney's initial glory was short-lived. In 1796, another Georgia inventor also patented an improvement of the ginning method. This process employed circular saws rather than wire teeth. Infringement suits followed, with litigation lasting for years, but Whitney was triumphant. At settlement, he received payment for damages and used this money to further improve his invention. Eli Whitney died at age fifty-nine in New Haven, Connecticut, in January 1825.[11]

In contrast, a slave is recognized for an outstanding development in tobacco, another southern crop, when an unusual occurrence took place during its processing. S. N. Hawks, Jr., relates in *Principles of Flue-Cured Tobacco Production*:

> In the early part of the nineteenth century, fires on the floors of the open curing barns were being used to lower the humidity, thereby improving the natural curing conditions. In 1839, an eighteen-year-old Negro on the Slade farm in Caswell County, North Carolina, after allowing the fire to almost burn out, added charcoal to the fire. The renewed blast of heat cured the tobacco to a more yellow color than normal. This light colored tobacco sold for about four times the normal price. The use of heat to "yellow" tobacco and then dry the leaf on the Slade farm is often credited with being the start of "flue-cured" tobacco.[12]

The creation of flue-cured tobacco began from an accidental discovery made by the slave teenager Stephen, employed as a blacksmith and overseer on the Slade farm in North Carolina. The intelligent youth quickly discerned the leaf turning a bright yellow, creating a product that was an instant hit, selling for "forty cents a pound, as against the average ten cents," according to Nannie May Tilley.[13] The curiosity was a novel variety of fancy, fine gold leaf, which years later became the foundation of the cigarette business.

EARLIEST PATENTEE

Activist Thomas L. Jennings (1791–1859), a free person of color, developed an early dry-cleaning process, called scouring, to get rid of dirt and grease and renew clothing to its original appearance. He was successful at securing a utility patent for the method in 1821. Jennings's obituary, written by Frederick Douglass in the *Anglo-African Magazine* (1859), gave the first clue to his impressive accomplishment, and he thus is the earliest known African American to receive a U.S. letters patent. His letters patent, preserved in an antique gilded frame that hung above his bed at the time of his death, was signed by U.S. Secretary of State John Quincy Adams and by Attorney General William Wirt. Jennings was an apprentice to a famous New York tailor and later founded his own successful clothing establishment. As a New York City resident, he fought for the abolition of slavery in the early 1800s and backed his activities with earnings from his business. Jennings was a fervent fighter against peonage and often penned petitions against bondage. All his children were educated and each prospered in his or her enterprise. His son William was a progressive businessman, and another son, Thomas, built a large dental practice in New Orleans. His daughter Matilda became a dressmaker, and his other daughter, Elizabeth, taught school in New York City.[14] Of Jennings, noted historian J. A. Rogers writes:

> Thomas Jennings of New York, who owned one of the city's largest clothing stores, made a fortune from his patent for renovating clothes. His plucky daughter broke up the jim-crow car in New York. When she was ejected from the white car one Sunday morning, she employed Chester Arthur, later President of the United States, to take her case to the Supreme Court, and won.[15]

Chester Alan Arthur was the twenty-first president of the United States (1881–1885), coming into office on the death of James A. Garfield. Born in North Fairfield, Vermont, Arthur graduated from college in Schenectady, New York, in 1848. Six years later, he qualified to practice law and defended fugitive slaves in New York City. No doubt this inclination made him the ideal lawyer for minorities to engage as legal counsel. Arthur joined the Republican Party and became a rising star after aiding several politicians in various campaigns.

Jennings, the patentee, reaped direct benefit from the exclusive right to exclude others from making or selling his invention for a specified time, thereby demonstrating the value of a patent. In advancing science and the useful arts, the primary beneficiary is the consumer. Minus the consumer, the invention concept is without merit, doomed to failure. Jennings gave the public a better product and was rewarded by his customers' patronage. His patent provided a better level of living. Given Jennings's success, it can be reasoned that competitors surfaced with improvements, sparking more innovation.

RARE DISTINCTION

Between 1793 and 1836, federal patent practice shifted from an examination system to a registration system, in which time Jennings procured his patent. Coincidentally, at the juncture of return to the examination process in 1836, Henry Blair, a black inventor, received rare distinction in federal files by happenstance. Because of this, historians thought, erroneously, that Blair was the first person of color to receive a patent grant. Blair, a free illiterate of Glen Ross, Maryland, living in a rural agricultural area not far from the nation's capital, is the only inventor identified by race in official records, singularly noted as "colored man."[16] The notation made next to his name (in two instances) in a patent commissioner's report was inappropriate since patent laws exclude any reference to racial identification. Patent records are clear on differentiation of nationality, but are void of ethnic identity. However improper, the notations did provide the information that an African American took advantage of the patent system.

Patents awarded under the old system were unnumbered. The present system of numbering patents consecutively started with grants issued under the Patent Act of 1836. Thus patent number 1 was issued on July 13, 1836, for the making of potash and pearl ash, the invention of John Ruggles, a U.S. senator from Maine who launched congressional reform resulting in passage of the new patent act.

Later the government assigned numbers that ended with an "X" to patents issued before 1836. Blair's patents fell at the nexus of these systems. On December 15, 1836, a great fire completely destroyed 7,000 models, 9,000 drawings and 230 books, but the most serious loss was that of all the records of patent applications and grants. Congress appropriated revenue to replace the records and the valuable patent models ravaged. Fortunately, Blair's drawing of his first patent and the specification of his second patent were restored.

Source: The Story of the United States Patent Office (Washington, D.C.: published by the Pharmaceutical Manufacturers Association with the cooperation of the U.S. Department of Commerce on the occasion of the 175th anniversary of the First U.S. Patent Law, 1965), pp. 804–833. See also B. M. Frederico, "The Patent Office Fire of 1836," *Journal of the Patent Office Society*, 19 (November 1937): 804–833.

PATENTEES.	INVENTIONS OR DISCOVERIES.	PAGE.
Bigelow, Erastus B. -	Loom, weaving knotted counterpanes, -	110
Bill & Spalding, - -	Loom, webbing tape, &c. - - -	110
Biddis, John - -	Paper making, - - - -	113
Bird, George - -	Paper polishing, - - - -	114
Bissell, L., J. Hinman, L. C. Hinman, and B. Gains, -	Spinning cotton, - - - -	118
Bissell, L., L. C. Hinman and S. Wilson, - -	Spinning cotton, - - -	118
Billings, J. S. and B. J. -	Spinning machine, horizontal, -	122
Bird, Fitzgerald . -	Medicine, - - - -	150
Biddis, John -	Starch, potatoe, - -	159
Biddis & Bedwell, -	Tannin, extracting, - -	161
Bidwell, Henry L. -	Cooking stove or digestive furnace, - -	173
Bille, Keene A. -	Heat, produced by the, &c. - -	181
Bigelow, Louis -	Carriage, steam, - - -	198
Bigelow, Elisha -	Steam engine, - - - -	202
Bingham & Warner, -	Propelling boats, canal, - - -	221
Bishop, Naphtali -	Bridges, - - - -	241
Birkhead, Levin -	Springs, wooden, - - -	263
Bishop, Luna -	Bellows, - - - -	272
Bille, Keene A. -	Liquors, drawing and corking, - -	278
Billing, Seraphim -	Raising water, - - -	285
Bigelow, Jos. -	Press, cheese, &c. - - -	305
Bicknell, John -	Grist mill, - - - -	319
Bigelow, Elisha -	Grist mill, - - - -	321
Bisbee, Asa -	Power, extending, - - -	330
Bisbee, John -	Lathe, turning, - - -	342
Bissell, Luther -	Saw mills, - - - -	351
Bisbee, Ziba -	Staves and hoops, &c., splitting, - -	359
Bissell, Luther -	Marble, sawing, &c. - -	369
Bishop, Joseph S. -	Cutting leather, - - -	378
Bishop Garry -	Washing machine, - - -	401
Bishop, Garry -	Washing machine, and churn, - -	406
Binney, Archibald -	Types, mould for casting, - -	420
Binney, Archibald -	Types, mould, printer's, - -	420
Binney, Archibald -	Types, smoothing, &c. - -	420
Bigelow, Elijah -	Teeth, engrafting, - - -	432
Bishop, Nathaniel -	Combs, rolling the backs of, &c. -	438
Bishop, William C. -	Garments, draughting coats, &c. - -	439
Bille, Keene A. -	Bottles, washing, filling, &c. - -	444
Blake, Edward -	Bee hive, - - - -	2
Black, James A. -	Hoe, weeding, &c. - - -	16
Blake, Thatcher -	Hulling grass seed, - - -	19
Black, William -	Plough, - - - -	24
Blocher, John -	Seeding, corn planter, - -	31
Blair, Hy. (colored man,) -	Seeding, corn planter, - -	31
Blair, Hy. (colored man,) -	Seeding, cotton planter, - -	32
Blake, P., E. W. Blake, W. Blake, and J. A. Blake, -	Castors, for bedsteads, - -	55
Blake, P., E. W. Blake, and J. A. Blake, -	Lock, door, escutcheon, -	65
Blake, P. and E. W. -	Locks, mortise, - -	65
Blanvelt, Abraham -	Locks, spiral spring, &c. - -	59

Digest of Patents notating Henry Blair as "(colored man)."

18

19

On October 14, 1834, Blair received a utility patent on a seed planter and another on August 31, 1836, on a cotton planter. The seed planter, called a corn planter, was assigned number 8447x, and the cotton planter is number 15. The descriptive portion of the seed planter patent does not exist; however, the cotton apparatus specification describes an easy, useful device. As the horse pulls the machine, half-shovels on the left and right make a ridge by moving the dirt. The tongue plow makes the furrow. The cylinder revolves with two wheels and allows passage of the seeds, which drop into the furrow and are covered as the press cover closes the sides of the furrow. The adjustable apparatus conformed to different-sized furrows.

Blair probably was born about 1807 and died around 1860. To this date, nothing is known of his contacts or how he came to know of the patent process.

In identifying an inventor of color who lived at Hempstead Plains, Long Island, the 1839 *Farmer's Cabinet* news journal published information stating that the creator (unnamed) crafted a horse-drawn rake. Since the individual died in 1821, it can be safely assumed that the black inventor conceived the idea in the first decade of the nineteenth century. The invention was introduced first into Pennsylvania. Fearing an effect on their wages because it saved "at least one half of the expense of gathering hay," angry farmers destroyed the rake, which allowed farmhands to gather hay without manually raking. In spite of its destruction, the rake succeeded beyond expectations and spread worldwide, motivating subsequent improvements.[17] The inventor did not patent his idea and in all probability made no money from it either.

Apparently free, Joseph Hawkins of West Windsor, New Jersey, gained a patent in 1845 on a gridiron used to broil meat. He constructed and arranged bars to provide for saving all the liquid that falls from the meat during the cooking process. At one time, certain authors thought Hawkins unique in patent endeavors. An 1895 article about him titled "Genius of the Colored Man" highlights the belief that prior to 1867, "it appears that but one invention had been patented by a colored man." However, the authors obtained additional information by "a systematic and protracted investigation" and acknowledged that "many patents have been allowed in favor of the colored race, some of which have proven of much value, and have come into general use in some parts of the United States."[18]

Patent specification of the invention of Henry Blair, 1836, No. 15.

No. 15. 3571

Henry Blair, of Glen Ross, Md.

The Schedule referred to in these Letters Patent, and making part of the same, containing a description in the words of the said Henry Blair himself of his improvement in the Cotton planter,

To all etc ~~to whom these presents shall come~~ :

Be it Known that I, Henry Blair, of Glen Ross, in the County of Montgomery & State of Maryland, have invented a new and useful machine, called the "Cotton Planter," and that the following is a full and exact description thereof, viz; Two side pieces five feet six inches long, Six inches deep, and two and a half wide, A beam four feet long, rising in front six inches to the end of which is attached a clevis and screw wrench mortised into the front ends of the Side pieces, Three inches from the ends are two Crosspieces, the front of which is two feet six inches long, three inches broad and one and three fourth inches thick, The Second Six inches deep by two and a half width is Tenoned into the Side pieces, two feet six inches from the front of the front cross piece, into the Center of which is tenoned the beam, one foot three inches back is a similar Crosspiece, & twelve inches back another, into the Centers of which is tenoned a short beam through the Center of which beam is let a movable bar ten inches long, with a bolt and tap, attached to the lower end of which is a concave press cover Ten inches long, twelve wide in front, and nine back — Three feet seven inches from the front ends of the side pieces is a dropping slender, Two feet eight inches long, and six inches in diameter reduced to a square axle

Patent specification of the invention of Henry Blair, 1836, No. 15 (continued).

22

at each end, which is received into the hub of a wheel three feet high, and dished three inches. — The cylinder has holes on its periphery, which may be of any number, and of such size as to contain one or more See and grooved one inch from each end, and half inch deep to receive the head blocks, which are twelve inches long eight deep, and two, and a half wide, and the side pieces are cut into receive the cylinder behind the head blocks, and to the side pieces and framed in the usual way, the handles with the upper ends two feet above the frame. On the head blocks are two brace two inches deep by one and a half wide, transfixed to the head blocks, and side pieces by four bolts &a, between which, and touching upon one third the diameter, and two thirds of the length of the cylinder between the head blocks is a hopper, which is made to hold, one, two or more gallons, of seed, and made by two screw bolts passing through the sides of the hopper, and braces, Touching upon the upper unoccupied third of the cylinder is a draw door, which by means of a handle passing through the brace, is made to cover the holes on the cylinder within the hopper, so as to prevent the seed from dropping while turning or moving the machine, Attached to the outside, or inside of the front ends of the side pieces one at nine, and the other at fifteen inches from the ends by two bolts, and taps each are two plough bars, — eighteen inches long to the lower ends of each of which are attached by means of two scre

Patent specification of the invention of Henry Blair, 1836, No. 15 (continued).

23

bolts, two half shovels; twelve inches long, and ten wide at the wing; right and left, or two six inch bar-share ploughs; with six inch land side, right, and left to which are attached by bolts, and Taps in the usual way, a bar and share, and stayed by two rods, bolts and Taps, extending from the front cross piece to the bar – passing through the front beam, and attached by a bolt, and Tap, two feet two inches back, from the front cross piece is a plough bar nine inches long to the lower end of which is attached by two screw bolt a tongue plough six and a half inches long, and three inches wide at the Top.

Operation;

When the horses draw the machine, the right and left half shovels or bar shares (as the planter may choose) throws a ridge – The Tongue Plow makes the drill, the Cylinder is revolving with the wheels, catches the seed in the holes made on its periphery as they pass through the hopper, and lets them drop into the drill and the press cover closes the sides of the drill so as to cover the seed,

What I claim as new, and as my invention, and for which I shall claim Letters Patent, is the reversion of the disk of one, or both wheels, so as to command the different distances of the rows, and the shifting of the ploughs from the inside to the outside of the side place and vice versa, so as to throw a wide or narrow ridge

In Testimony that the above is a full and exact description of the construction, and operation

Patent specification of the invention of Henry Blair, 1836, No. 15 (continued).

Patent specification of the invention of Henry Blair, 1836, No. 15 (continued).

SUGAR, SUGAR

A few free African Americans in the 1800s had resources, and Louisianan Norbert Rillieux (1806–1894) was one of them, but he came from circumstances different from those of most free southern blacks. This was where rice, cotton, and sugar plantations were abundant with slave labor. Born on March 17, 1806, in New Orleans, Norbert was the son of the wealthy white engineer, inventor, and French planter Vincent Rillieux and quadroon Constance Vivant. He was baptized in St. Louis Cathedral, and because of his father's position he received the privileged education of the colored Creole. The elder Rillieux invented a steam-operated cotton-baling press from his engineering endeavors.

Norbert was a very intelligent son and was packed off for schooling to the finest engineering institution in France. At age twenty-four, he became an instructor in applied mechanics at L'Ecole Centrale in Paris, the youngest person to achieve this position. He was captivated by thermal dynamics and steam power and published a series of papers on "The Functions and Economic Implications of the Steam Engine."

Rillieux attempted to interest Parisian investors in his theory of multiple-effect evaporation, but without success. About 1834, he returned to his native home, where, as a youngster, he had been exposed to sugar processing on his father's plantation. Rillieux observed that the method for refining sugar from cane and beets was crude, back-

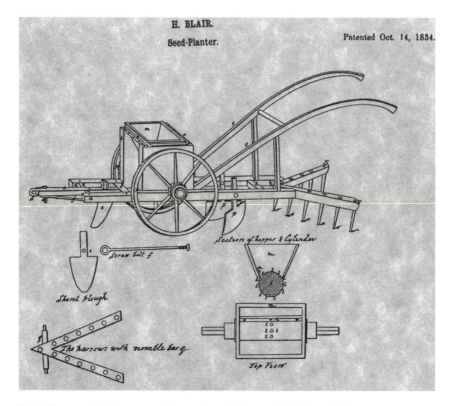

Seed Planter, 1834, patented invention of Henry Blair, No. 8447X.

breaking, and dangerous. This was the inefficient but popular "Jamaica train" process. Slaves hand-ladled boiling cane juice from one open vat to another to produce a dark, sticky sugar. Several scientists had previously designed vacuum pans and condensing coils, but without success. Accomplishing the goal to invent a new and useful improvement, the well-trained inventor designed an ingenious process that used an evaporating pan or boiler having an enclosed series of condensing coils in vacuum chambers. This clever design reduced labor and saved fuel since the saccharine juices and syrup boiled at a lower temperature, producing a better product. Rillieux filed for a patent and was issued his first grant, number 3,237, in 1843 for this improvement in sugar works. He had refined "the manner of connecting a steam engine with the evaporating pan or pans" at a required temperature and enhanced the process by combining the system with the "Howard Saccharine Evaporator" (the state-of-the-art equipment). Also, he adapted the "Champenoise column" and regulated the concentration of the syrup "by means of a differential thermometer." The

Patent model of Norbert Rillieux's invention the Sugar Works.
Courtesy of the Anacostia Museum and Center for African American History and Culture, Smithsonian Institution. Photographer Harold Dorwin.

saccharine juices and syrup, sensitive to heat, caramelized or turned brown at high temperature; at reduced pressure, the liquids boiled at lower temperatures.

On December 10, 1846, Norbert received patent number 4,879 for an improvement on his sugar-refining method. It was this second patent that captured the world's attention and revolutionized the sugar industry. The unique multiple-effect mechanism reduced the time, cost, and safety risk involved in producing a superior quality of sugarcane and beets product in the form of refined, granulated white sugar with the sweetness of the dark crude. White, refined sugar had been available, but at premium cost. With a finer-quality product at cheaper prices, the consumer knew a winner. The invention consisted of first "clarifying saccharine juices" before the evaporation process and then cooling "by a current of air" followed by a special arrangement of the "vacuum pans or evaporators." It was the special arrangement of the evaporators that led to the success of this innovation, which quickly spread in Louisiana and to the West Indies, setting the precedent for all improved evaporation systems.

Sugar manufacturer Theodore Packwood of Myrtle Grove Plantation

N. Rillieux,

Vacuum Pan,

Nº 3.237-

Patented Aug. 26, 1843.

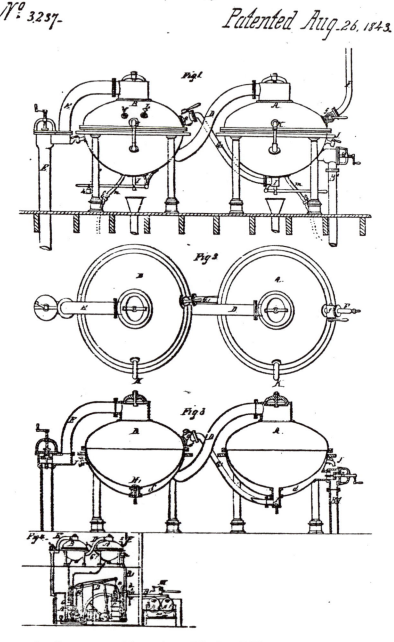

Evaporating Pan, patented invention of Norbert Rillieux.

gambled on Rillieux's invention, and his gamble paid off, making Rillieux's multiple-effect device the world's premier vacuum evaporator system. After previous years of misfortunes and several failures at attempts to refine his evaporator, Norbert Rillieux was finally triumphant.[19]

Following loud and rapid acclaim, Cuban and Mexican sugar refiners hastily adopted his process. This catapulted him to being the most celebrated engineer in Louisiana. On March 17, 1857, Rillieux received another patent, issued as reissue number 439, on his sugar-refining process. As with most successful operations, Rillieux's creative exploits were copied and pirated. Some of his designs were stolen and taken offshore to Europe. Although Rillieux had made a monumental contribution to the sugar industry and was recognized for it, he did not entirely enjoy his new position. As a free person of color, he suffered discrimination. After the influx of thousands of white southerners into his home state, their viewpoints and restrictive laws prevailed, and they excluded Rillieux from privileges he earlier had enjoyed before living in France. He returned to France in 1854, where he experienced practically no racial prejudice and became headmaster at his alma mater. There he engaged in engineering research, but received very little interest in his invention. Further, a German had pirated his designs, and European engineers misinterpreted their function, causing the process to operate poorly.

Rillieux abandoned sugar engineering, turned to archaeological pursuits, and became an Egyptologist. However, in France at age seventy-five, he returned to sugar refining, his passion, and obtained yet another patent in 1881 on a process of heating juices with vapors in a multiple-effect system. This economical process is still prevalent in cane and beet sugar factories worldwide. He filed for French patents on his sugar-refining processes, but lost the rights to one of them at age eighty-five because of a reluctance by experts to recognize the concept. Bitter over the European attitude, he died at age eighty-eight on October 8, 1894, survived by his wife, Emily Cuckow Rillieux. In spite of many obstacles, Norbert Rillieux accumulated enormous wealth from his inventions, and his widow was able to live a comfortable life until her death in 1912.[20]

Rillieux finally achieved recognition, though posthumously, for his outstanding accomplishment. A plaque honoring Rillieux's creative genius in the field of sugar refining is at the Louisiana State Museum in New Orleans, dedicated "by Corporations representing the Sugar Industry all over the world."

The movement to colonize American blacks in Africa had reached fervent heights and threatened the pool of black creative talent. Free Americans of color in the nation's North and the South as well were not keen on the idea of transplantation to Africa even though laws on the books in southern states controlled their movement about the area. In 1821, the colonizationists succeeded in establishing the colony of Liberia, which consisted of 43,000 square miles where free Negroes lived as citizens with full rights. There they were expected to help spread Christianity and to fight for the cessation of the slave trade. The scheme at first was benevolent, but conflict, doubt, and fear that the strong-willed would overcome the weak erupted. Several states had set up a process, outlined by the American Colonization Society, to return freed slaves and free people of color to Africa, ostensibly to benefit them. In actuality, the states initiated the process to rid the nation of ebony residents, but the scheme failed. Even though thousands of free blacks did leave for Liberia of their own accord and others were practically forced to leave, the majority saw through the strategy and denounced it. Ideas of colonizing elsewhere in the United States and in other places in the Americas or in Canada were also popular among some free persons; however, the outbreak of the Civil War effectively ended these notions.

PATENTS AND SLAVES

Black American inventors are no different from any other group of thinkers with ingenuity, ability, and an intense desire to solve problems, occasionally solving their dilemmas years before they attempt to patent or sell the concept. The exception is that minority inventors suffer and struggle to achieve their goal in the face of extraordinary hardship, thus demonstrating enormous self-confidence. They often are paranoid and very defensive about their "new" ideas, but show a sense of pride of ownership. The requirements necessary to obtain federal protection for a notion are the same for everyone, regardless of ethnic background, religion, gender, creed, or color. The presence and subsequent importance of minority inventors, however, are not well known. Historically, certain laws or customs have negatively influenced general public awareness of the quantity and quality of their input, and these laws or customs all but ignored the overall effect on the daily, business, and technical aspects of their worldly existence.

Enslaved thinkers and tinkerers in antebellum days were forced to assign their invention rights to their master because of a citizenship technicality in the patent application oath. Simply put, slaves could not hold patents because they, as noncitizens, could not own property. Classified as intellectual property, patents can be assigned, sold, or transferred like real estate, a function denied slaves but not the master who often secured patents for the inventions of his chattel (obviously attesting in an oath that *he* was the true inventor). The owner then reaped all manufacture and sale benefits.[21]

The matter of whether an enslaved soul had a right to hold U.S. patents apparently did not arise until four years before the beginning of the Civil War. In 1857, a letter to the U.S. secretary of the interior provoked the issue. On August 25, Oscar J. O. Stuart [spelled Stewart in the Attorney General's opinion], a lawyer and planter of Homesville, Mississippi, requested if the master of a slave could procure a patent for his slave's useful invention. Ned, a blacksmith owned by the estate of Stuart's late wife, had invented an improved cotton scraper for plowing cotton fields. The situation, being a new one to Secretary Jacob Thompson, was submitted to the attorney general.

Kenneth W. Dobyns in his work *The Patent Office Pony* reports, "Thompson presented the matter to United States Attorney General Jeremiah S. Black for an opinion, but he refused to give an advisory opinion, indicating that he would pass upon an actual pending patent application."[22] Stuart submitted all pertinent facts in an application, which included the slave's sworn affidavit that he was the original inventor of the machine, and forwarded it in Ned's own name. Upon his doing this, Black on June 10, 1858, rendered a final point of view that a new and useful machine invented by a slave could not be patented. With the endorsement of the commissioner of patents, Black resolved the issue in favor of the free human, a citizen who was the original inventor and who could make a contract and own property.[23] This action effectively ignored the enslaved originator, but, more important, disregarded the slave owner himself, who was not the original inventor. Thus neither the slave, Ned, nor Stuart received a favorable response to the request or petition.

Outraged by the official opinion of these public officials, Stuart attempted to get the laws changed to protect his double plow and double scraper, reasoning that "the master has the same rights to the fruits of the labor of the intilect [*sic*] of his slave."[24] Seeking support from fellow Mississippians, Stuart fired off letters to state politicians urging special legislation to protect his device. After failing in this pursuit, he sought endorsements that he used to promote the machine. A few years later, the Civil War began, and Stuart obtained the rank of colonel in the Confederate army.

On May 17, 1861, the Statutes at Large of the Confederate States of America carried a provision that gave slaves patent rights, reversing the national government's decision. After Jefferson Davis became president of the Confederate States of America, he endorsed the following legislation to provide for slave inventors:

INVENTION OF A SLAVE.

A new and useful machine invented by a slave cannot be patented.

ATTORNEY GENERAL'S OFFICE,
June 10, 1858.

SIR: I fully concur with the Commissioner of Patents in the opinion he has given on the application of Mr. O. T. E. Stewart, of Mississippi. For the reasons given by the Commissioner, I think as he does, that a machine invented by a slave, though it be new and useful, cannot, in the present state of the law, be patented. I may add

Invention of a Slave, published decision of U.S. Attorney General, 1858.

And be it further enacted, That in case the original inventor or discoverer of the art, machine or improvement for which a patent is solicited is a slave, the master of such slave may take oath that the said slave was the original; and on complying with the requisites of the law shall receive a patent for said discovery or invention, and have all the rights to which a patentee is entitled by law.[25]

Although the Confederacy gave aid to slave thinkers, a review of the Confederate Patent Office records shows no action by Stuart for his slave Ned.[26]

Interest in slave inventions arose when Jefferson Davis and his brother Joseph Emory Davis, just prior to the beginning of the Civil War, attempted to secure a patent for slave Benjamin T. Montgomery, who invented a propeller for a river steamboat, later adopted and used by the Confederate navy, which became aware of the invention due to favorable southern press reports. Joseph owned Montgomery, who worked on his plantation, Hurricane, and afterwards on Brierfield, the property of Jefferson Davis, repairing mechanical contraptions used on the farms. Montgomery, born in Virginia in 1819 and later sold at a slave market in Mississippi, was encouraged by his benevolent master to read and write, finally achieving great proficiency in mechanics, machining, and civil engineering. He even ran a small wares business on his own.

The U.S. Patent Office refused the petitions of each Davis brother based on the earlier decision of the nation's attorney general to deny patents for a slave's invention. The brothers wanted to be the patentee, and assignee as well, of the boat propeller invention. Benjamin Montgomery's biographer, Janet Sharp Hermann, writes in *The Pursuit of a Dream*:

> In the late 1850s he invented a boat propeller that promised to be an improvement on the paddle wheels used on river steamboats. Acting on "the canoe paddling principle," the blades cut into the water at an angle, causing less resistance and therefore less loss of power and jarring of the boat. With this propeller, which weighed a fraction of the conventional paddle wheel, there was no need for a wheelhouse. Ben made a prototype which he operated by hand on the Mississippi for a couple of years before the Civil War, but he dreamed of powering it with a steam engine so that its advantages could be truly tested. . . . he displayed a model of the invention at the Western Sanitary Fair in Cincinnati.[27]

Montgomery applied for a federal patent himself after moving to Ohio before the war's end, but was denied any rights. The *Cincinnati Daily Gazette* in its Christmas Day issue in 1863 described the advantages of his boat propeller, where, in particular, each crankshaft revolution carries two points of resistance to the water. This feature adjusts commendably to steam power. Also, the news article announced, "Ben D. [*sic*] Montgomery, a colored man, who has been in slavery for twenty-seven years . . . [and] came to Cincinnati last June, exhibits at the Sanitary Fair."[28] After a full and eventful life, Montgomery died in 1878.

Patent solicitor James H. Layman of Cincinnati in 1892 gave the following profound testament to the Honorable William Edgar Simonds, twenty-third commissioner of patents and former congressman who secured the passage of the first U.S. International Copyright Act:

> I have just received a copy of the official circular of March 8, in regard to collecting models for the Columbian Exposition, and would respectively call your attention to a very interesting display the Patent Office is capable of making. It is well known the office possesses a steamboat model made by Abraham Lincoln, but it is not so well known that it once contained a model constructed by Jefferson's Davis' body servant, a slave who indignantly repudiated the idea of having white blood in his veins. This slave was named Montgomery, and about the time Vicksburg was captured, he came to Cincinnati, and made an application for a patent on his invention, a substitute for paddle wheels.
>
> The application was placed in the hands of Knight Bros, of this city, and I prepared the drawings for them, and while I was at work on the case, the inventor told me that some of the rebel gun boats were to be provided with his propeller. He also showed me a number of Vicksburg papers that contained very flattering notices of the invention.
>
> I do not remember whether his application was allowed, or was forfeited

on account of nonpayment of the final fee, but for some reason the patent was not issued.

I was in Washington at the time Mr. Marble was Commissioner, called his attention to the matter, but he took no interest in it, and one of the attendants told me the model had been sent to some Eastern college.

As previously stated, the entire model, including the frame work and metallic portions, was made by this slave, and when it was submitted here to an expert model-maker, for the purpose of having it duplicated, he said there was not a man in his shop capable of doing such a finished piece of work.

Now, if the slave's propeller model could be procured and exhibited in the same case with the great emancipator's model of his boat, it would attract the attention of thousands.

It is my impression, however, that Lincoln's model would suffer by the comparison.

Respectfully yours,[29]
James H. Layman
Patent Solicitor

Apparently Layman was not aware of the decision by the U.S. attorney general refusing a patent for a slave's invention.

Isaiah Thornton Montgomery, founder of the prosperous all-black town of Mound Bayou, Mississippi, was one of several children born to Benjamin and Mary Montgomery on the Davis plantation. His father taught him to write, and a slave of Jefferson Davis taught him to read from a speller. He and his brother William served in the Union navy, and after discharge in 1864 both joined their father, who had moved to Ohio about the time of Vicksburg's capture. The father then returned south with his sons in 1865, eventually establishing the firm Montgomery and Sons that shipped merchandise. Having excellent business acumen, Isaiah subsequently founded a colony in Bolivar County in the Yazoo Delta and laid out the town of Mound Bayou. Isaiah spoke of his achievement at the initial proceedings of the National Negro Business League in 1900 at Boston. His followers had to prepare land for cultivation as a result of the railroad companies expanding their lines to southern cotton markets and "seeking to people its wild lands." He then held an elected office upon entering politics.

Sources: "He Tells His Own Life Story, His Early Life as a Slave and the Path to Its Success," *New York World*, September 27, 1890, pp. 1, 2; *The Proceedings of the National Negro Business League, Boston, 1900* (Boston: J. R. Hamm, 1901), p. 101.

Montgomery's son, Isaiah, communicated in a 1903 letter to patent examiner Henry Blair that his uncle, Peter I. Montgomery, also an

Isaiah Montgomery.
The Proceedings of the National Negro Business League, Boston, 1900 (Boston: J. R. Hamm, 1901) from the Patricia Carter Ives Sluby Collection.

inventor, had a "ditching plow" invention before the examiners at the patent office. He added that Peter's son, B.S.T. Montgomery, "had secured a patent for a device for holding books, papers etc., to be read or copied with a typewriter."[30]

Not surprisingly, the Patent Office of the Confederacy was fashioned after the U.S. patent system that had shifted from an early registry system to one that provided for an examination of the patent application. President Davis placed the position of commissioner of patents under the auspices of the attorney general and appointed Rufus R. Rhodes to fill it. The Confederate patent term lasted fourteen years, commensurate with the federal term. In addition to inventions relating to military devices, the granted patents embraced multiple agricultural implements.

Documents and massive ledgers of the Patent Office of the Confederacy at the Museum of the Confederacy at Richmond, Virginia, with hundreds of handwritten pages, record only 266 patents, granted between 1861 and 1864.[31] During these years, more than 16,000 patents were issued at the U.S. Patent Office.[32] In the records at the museum's library, it appears that no slave is identified as the original inventor, according to yearly lists maintained by the Confederate Patent Office. It is conceivable that a master may have applied on behalf of his slave but was not successful with the "requisites of the law." Interestingly, it appears that Davis himself never took advantage of his own provision.

3

UNDER HIS OWN PERSONAGE
Dutifully Logged

[A]nd I will get them praise and fame in every land where they
have been put to shame. At that time will I bring you again,
even in the time that I gather you: for I will make you a name
and a praise among all people of the earth, when I turn back
your captivity before your eyes, saith the Lord.

Zephaniah 3:19–20

The abundance of African American inventions is immeasurable. How
can one calculate a true number, given the potential of thinking human beings? If one yardstick is to check government records of those
who applied for patents but did not attain any, then one is out of luck
because federal laws prohibit access to these accounts. Another yardstick, the most practical because an individual can be sure of the actual
inventor, is the picture of the inventive talent that successfully sought
legal protection. His or her name is of permanent record in official
government files. Those recorders of history who identify ebony people
who are inventive and take out patents in their own names eliminate
any uncertainty about who these originators are because the designated patent number indicates that the description of the invention
can be tracked. The inventive skill of African Americans is quite broad,
in fact, as broad as that of any other ethnic group, and their range of
imaginativeness traverses the entire spectrum of patent documentation.

After April 1865, those previously held in bondage were free and
thus became citizens through the ratification of the Thirteenth
Amendment to the U.S. Constitution. Now they could enjoy the privileges whites and freedmen had earlier. A great number of people of

color, freeborn or freed, had been educated by others of their race, by their masters, by abolitionists, or by benevolent religious groups and could manage on their own. However, an overwhelming number of blacks had been severely deprived of basic freedoms.

At that time, the U.S. Congress established the Bureau of Refugees, Freedmen, and Abandoned Lands to assist the ex-slaves and to help them adjust to new independence, and revenue was allocated for employment, education, and medical services. Following the end of "great unpleasantness," the federal government chartered the Freedman's Savings and Trust Company—the Freedman's Bank—to inspire monetary thrift among the former slaves. The main office was set up in New York City, with branches opening shortly thereafter in Washington, D.C., Richmond, Nashville, New Orleans, and other sites, primarily in the South. Although more than thirty branches organized, the bank failed in 1874. Scandal and mismanagement were widespread.

State bureaus established processes to help with contractual alliances, schooling, and other associated skills for the distraught, displaced, and abandoned blacks. Headed by General O. O. Howard, the Freedmen's Bureau lasted five years, during which time money was spent to open hospitals and to start thousands of schools, including Howard University, named after the general. Other historically black colleges and universities established were Fisk University and Hampton Institute, among many.

During the Reconstruction of the South, state constitutions guaranteed political and civil rights to all, but Reconstruction was short-lived, lasting about seven years. Two African Americans from southern states were elected to national office, one to the U.S. House of Representatives and the other to the Senate. On March 30, 1870, the Fifteenth Amendment to the U.S. Constitution granted African Americans the right to vote. In 1870 also, the first African American was admitted to West Point but was forced to withdraw from the institution after a court-martial resulting from an infraction. James W. Smith of South Carolina was overwhelmed by a multitude of abuses and insults during his short tenure at the prestigious military school. Eventually, Henry O. Flipper made the grade in 1877, becoming the first black American graduate. Later, when he was in Nogales, Arizona Territory, he patented a tent in 1898.

Innovations by African Americans surfaced confidently. The former slave, like any other citizen, now lawfully could file for a patent grant under his or her own personage. By 1900, a few hundred people of color achieved the distinction of holding a U.S. letters patent.

But dreams of freedom were short-lived. The African American was driven from hope back to fear at the beginning of the twentieth century. Overwhelming odds of poverty, disease, ignorance, discrimination, and lack of employment and voting rights overshadowed the hope that blacks and whites could live side by side without segregation. The black minority then adapted to a new form of life, emulating much of the class and standards of whites while holding onto religious attitudes long prevalent in the South.

The period between 1880 and 1890 was perhaps the greatest inventive decade in history. Inventions such as the trolley car, the electric light, railroad innovations, the cash register, the dynamo, the pneumatic tire, smokeless gunpowder, transparent photographic film, electric welding, the steam turbine, and the electric furnace were patented. It was in this era of great intellect that the ubiquitous automatic shoe-lasting machine was devised.

SHOES EVERLASTING

Immigrants flooded to North America in the late 1800s with the same dream as that of the freed black men and women already planted on that soil. They wanted respect, economic power, and the ability to exercise their rights as citizens. But for the African American in the South, this aspiration was severely restricted after the Civil War through the enactment of black codes. Many blacks moved to the North looking for a better life; some of them migrated from various Caribbean islands and from nearby countries.

An immigrant to the United States from a colony of Holland known as Paramaribo, Surinam (Dutch Guiana), demonstrated remarkable creative genius when he labored to perfect a shoe-lasting machine. Patented in 1883, the lasting apparatus that could produce a complete shoe revolutionized the entire shoe industry worldwide.

Outstanding inventor Jan Earnst Matzeliger (1852–1889) was born on September 15, 1852, to a native Surinam woman and a Dutch engineer. Although immensely gifted, Jan Matzeliger apparently received limited schooling because later in life, when filing his patent applications, he signed them with his mark, an "X." At the young age of ten, he was apprenticed in machine shops and nine years later became a mariner. After two years at sea, Matzeliger came to Philadelphia, where he took an apprenticeship as a shoe cobbler. Shoes were made by hand in a slow, tedious fashion.

Around 1876, Matzeliger moved to Lynn, Massachusetts, and found work at a shoe factory, where he sat at a bench operating a sewing machine for the soles of shoes. He learned English and studied physics and other subjects to make up for his lack of formal education. He became puzzled at the hand labor necessary to connect the uppers to the soles of the shoe. This hard work accounted for only a few com-

Jan Earnst Matzeliger.
Courtesy of the Moorland-
Spingarn Research Center,
Howard University.

pleted boots or shoes in a single day. The drudgery inspired Matzeliger to seek a faster and easier way.

The answer came many years later as seven pages of complicated drawings and eight pages of printed material specifying how his invention worked. His inventive spirit, combined with familiarity with the lasting process, prompted Matzeliger to develop this complicated machinery. The machine attached the sole to the upper of the shoe in one minute's time. It held the shoe on the last, gripped and pulled the leather down around the heel, then guided and drove the nails in place, and finally discharged the completed shoe from the machine. It could automatically and speedily last shoes, enabling the production of up to seven hundred pairs of boots or shoes per day, cutting the cost of shoe production in half.

J. E. MATZELIGER.

LASTING MACHINE.

No. 274,207.

Patented Mar. 20, 1883.

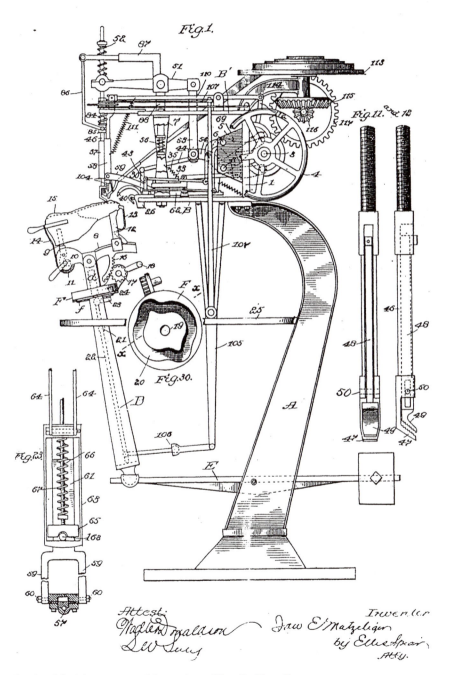

Fig.1.

Fig.11. and 12.

Fig.30.

Fig.33.

Attest:

Inventor

Jan E Matzeliger
by Ellis Spear
Atty.

Lasting Machine, patented invention of Jan E. Matzeliger.

From 1883 to 1891, Matzeliger received five patents on his innovation, all of which revolutionized the shoemaking industry. The first patent application, titled simply "Lasting Machine," perplexed the patent examiners at Washington, D.C., so the office dispatched an examiner to Lynn to see how the apparatus worked. Surprised and satisfied, the examiner, back at his office, issued the patent on the lasting machine on March 20, 1883. The application had been filed more than a year earlier.

Matzeliger needed investors to back his devices. Arduous searching finally paid off when businessmen C. H. Delnow and M. S. Nichols agreed to advance money, but at a premium for themselves. A two-thirds interest went to the backers, and the remaining third went to Matzeliger. The Union Lasting Machine Company coalesced from this agreement, founded to produce lasted shoes on a large scale. However, the partners needed more financial help, so the Consolidated Lasting Machine Company was established with financial assistance from George W. Brown and Sidney W. Winslow, a businessman who was to become the kingpin of machinery in New England. Winslow was quick to understand the significance of such inventions in the shoe industry. Thus the Consolidated Lasting Machine Company was born. The company bought the rights to Matzeliger's patents and paid him stock in the company, rather than money. Matzeliger, in the care of friends, was in poor health the last years of his life, suffering from tuberculosis. Never receiving any money for his inventions, he died poverty stricken on August 24, 1889, at age thirty-six.[1]

The final patents on Matzeliger's inventions were issued after his death; however, they were filed when he was ailing in late 1888. His second invention, titled "Mechanism for Distributing Tacks," merited a patent three months after his death in 1889. Two more improvements matured into patents in 1890, one on a nailing machine and another on a tack-separating and distributing mechanism; they listed George W. Moulton as administrator of Matzeliger's estate. The last patent on "certain improvements in lasting shoes" and "the mechanism therefor," titled like the first, was filed in 1885, but was granted six years later on September 22, 1891, two years posthumously. This patent was assigned to the Consolidated Hand Method Lasting Machine Company of Nashua, New Hampshire, with George W. Moulton stated now as executor of Matzeliger's estate.

The value of Matzeliger's stock was not realized until after his death. Entrepreneur and visionary Sidney W. Winslow later cleared a fortune from the ownership of the machine. Matzeliger's holdings in the two shoe companies, all he owned, were bequeathed to fifteen friends, his physician, Lynn's hospital, and North Congregational Church, the only religious institution that accepted him. The church gained enough profit from the sale of the stock to pay off the full mortgage. Perrie Lee, his foster son, received paintings and papers that eventually came into the hands of a neighbor, Ernest Rideout, whose family retained a few of them. Matzeliger is interred in Lynn at Pine Grove Cemetery.[2]

A merger of the Consolidated Lasting Machine Company with forty-one smaller shoe manufacturers in 1899 formed the New Jersey corporation called the United Shoe Machinery Corporation, which soon became a multimillion-dollar business. Although Matzeliger did not survive to witness the greatness of his ingenuity, he left an indelible monument in the good he did for people. Each time we consider the purchase of a new pair of shoes, we have cause to think about this inventive genius who made them more affordable for every man, woman, and child. The governor of Massachusetts signed legislation in 1984 to name a bridge in Lynn for Matzeliger, and in 1991, the U.S. Postal Service issued a twenty-nine-cent first-class postage stamp in his honor.

The African American inventor has shown diversity, and proficiency as well, in many branches of art or science. Indeed, he or she has endeavored in the many useful fields of industrial, mechanical, and electrical arts, along with the other art fields. The times dictate trends, and people of color have been no stranger to shifts in consumer desires or needs. Diversity of invention in industry or business is self-evident among the following talents.

LIGHT BULB BREAKTHROUGH

Lewis Howard Latimer (1848–1928) was lucky. He achieved the light bulb breakthrough that allowed the manufacture of carbon filaments for Thomas Alva Edison's incandescent bulb. Beginning a career as a patent illustrator, Latimer executed drawings for Alexander Graham Bell and for Edison; Latimer, a pioneer, became an early builder of the electric light industry, and he was famed as the developer of long-lasting carbon filaments.

Born in Chelsea, Massachusetts, on September 4, 1848, to fugitive slave parents, George and Rebecca Latimer, who had fled Norfolk, Virginia, on October 4, 1842, Lewis Howard Latimer was the youngest of four children. The police arrested his father in Boston four days after his arrival when his owner appeared before authorities demanding imprisonment for George until he was returned to slavery. News of the arrest spread, and abolitionists such as William Lloyd Garrison and Frederick Douglass supported the call for Latimer's release and raised $400 to purchase George's freedom. Louis Haber in *Black Pioneers of Science and Invention* remarked that Latimer's case was "the first of several famous Boston fugitive-slave cases," which resulted in the

Lewis Howard Latimer.
Courtesy of the Latimer-
Norman Collection.

Lewis Howard Latimer.
Courtesy of the Latimer-
Norman Collection.

passage of a Massachusetts law "forbidding state officers from participating in hunting for fugitive slaves."[3]

At age sixteen, Latimer enlisted in the Union navy in 1864 and
served as landsman aboard the side-wheel gunboat U.S.S. *Massasoit*,
which was part of the North Atlantic Blockading Squadron. Latimer
received an honorable discharge after the vessel returned to Boston in
1865. When he was looking for work, he happened upon a young black
woman who had been asked to suggest a "colored boy" as a helper in
the office of solicitors Crosby and Gould. They needed an office boy
with a "taste for drawing." The firm of Crosby and Gould was a noted
patent law establishment in Boston that hired a corps of drafters to
design patent drawings. Latimer taught himself drafting and requested
permission to do some drawings. His employers reluctantly acquiesced
and then discovered an outstanding talent. Eventually Latimer rose to
the position of chief draftsman. His work was well respected, and he
remained at the firm for eleven years. In later years, the firm was renamed Crosby and Gregory and was located near the school where Alexander Graham Bell was teaching and experimenting on his
telephone.[4] In January 1874, apparently influenced by his office spe-
ciality and showing his ingenuity, Latimer, with coinventor Charles W.
Brown of Salem, filed a patent application at the U.S. Patent Office in

(No.Model.)

L. H. LATIMER.

PROCESS OF MANUFACTURING CARBONS.

No. 252,386.   Patented Jan. 17, 1882.

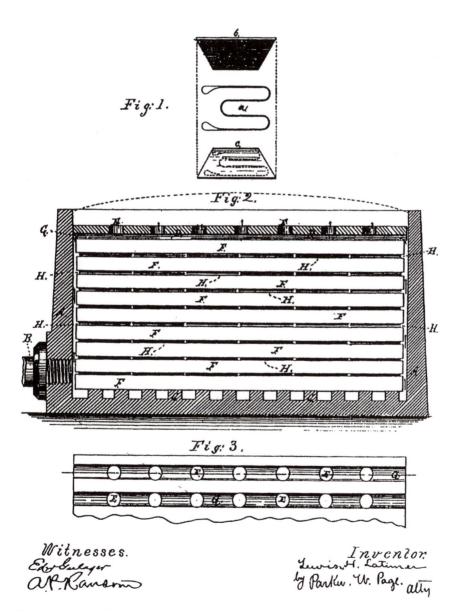

Witnesses.
Edw Guleyer
A. P. Ransom

Inventor.
Lewis H. Latimer
by Parker W. Page. atty

Process of Manufacturing Carbons, patented invention of Lewis Latimer.

Washington, D.C., for an improvement in water closets (toilets) for railroad cars, and received the patent the following month on February 10. They modified the standard water closet by providing a pivoted bottom to the hopper that was automatically opened and closed by closing and raising the seat cover, respectively. Crosby and Gould, as might be expected, were their patent attorneys.

Latimer met Bell and became good friends. "When Bell learned that Latimer was a draftsman, he asked Latimer to draw up the plans" for his telephone invention, writes Glennette Turner in *Lewis Howard Latimer*.[5] Bell began work on the telephone in September 1875. Latimer assisted Bell in preparing the patent application and also helped him with various drawings. Bell's patent was issued on March 7, 1876.

In 1880, Latimer, now living in Bridgeport, Connecticut, near a sister, began to work as a draftsman for the United States Electric Lighting Company under chief engineer and founder Hiram Maxim, who was impressed with Latimer's ability. Here Latimer was introduced to the emerging technology of electric light and learned of the genius of Thomas Edison, who had invented the incandescent carbon-filament electric lamp in 1879, which was patented on January 27, 1880. Maxim, Edison, and other upstart electric companies competed for solving the problem of providing a long-lasting filament. Latimer, who had moved to New York City, teamed with Joseph V. Nichols of Brooklyn and filed an application for an electric lamp in 1881. They received a patent for producing "incandescence of a continuous strip of carbon secured to metallic wires" attached to the electric lamp base on September 13 of the same year.

Six days before the 1881 patent was issued, Latimer, alone, filed an application for the breakthrough patent on a process of manufacturing carbon filaments. Latimer formulated a process of carbonizing material by enclosing it between cardboard, rather than the standard material, tissue paper or cloth. The cardboard expanded at high temperatures at the same time as the carbonizing material, thereby producing an exceptional filament that had an extended life. The patent was issued on January 17, 1882, and was assigned to the United States Electric Lighting Company. Interestingly, inventor Joseph Nichols was listed on the patent as one of his witnesses, and Parker W. Page was his new patent attorney. Latimer was still employed by Maxim, so the carbon filaments were initially used in Maxim's lamp. Several months later in 1882, Latimer and another inventor, John Tregoning of Philadelphia, patented a globe supporter for electric lamps, assigned also to Maxim's company.

After installing some new lamps in various facilities in New York and Philadelphia, Maxim sent Latimer to Canada and to London to teach and supervise the innovative method. After Latimer returned to America, he left Maxim and went to work for the Brooklyn company Olmstead Electric, then moved to Acme Electric Light Company of New York City, where he made the Latimer Lamp. The company folded, and Latimer then became a draftsman and general assistant with the Imperial Electric Light Company. However, by 1884, he was working for the Thomas Alva Edison Electric Light Company as an engineer, chief draftsman, and expert witness on the Board of Patent Control, a position critical to determine the outcome of patent lawsuits among competitors. Latimer was a distinguished member of the Edison Pioneers and wrote the definitive book on incandescent electric lighting in 1890.

Latimer was a Renaissance man—draftsman, engineer, expert technical witness, author, poet, and inventor of unusual creativity. In 1886, he turned his inventive ability away from electric lamps to patenting an apparatus for cooling, deodorizing, and disinfecting rooms and other areas. In 1896, he received a patent on a locking rack for hats, coats, umbrellas, canes, and the like, and in 1905, he patented a book supporter. Latimer died on December 11, 1928, after an esteemed, illustrious career. The Edison Pioneers, the scientific team that helped Edison in his pioneering work, mourned his passing and paid tribute to Latimer, the only African American in the organization.[6] A Brooklyn, New York, public school was named for him on May 10, 1968.[7]

Inventor Samuel R. Scottron, an ancestor of the renowned actress Lena Horne, through trial and tribulation well understood the essence of diversification between the late 1870s and 1893, when he worked on his inventions. He recounted in the *Colored American* in 1906 that a "patent which can be simplified by another is worth nothing. . . . knowledge of mechanics will show you how to use the simplest methods in obtaining certain desired results . . . [but contact] with the market will show you whether what you wish to accomplish will be worth anything . . . even if you succeed in making the thing." Scottron found that years "are spent by some in trying to do something by way of a patented article, that even if made, wouldn't be wanted by a sufficient number of persons to make it desirable." The invention business was risky, to put it mildly.[8]

Scottron's first idea was a profitable design of an adjustable mirror. It was arranged in an opposing fashion such that a view of every side could be seen all at once. His success at mirrors spurred other patentable concepts. However, the cornice business caught his attention so he abandoned the mirror business. The successful manufacturing and marketing of his patented extension cornices for curtains in the early 1880s was eventually cut short by a newfangled fad. Fashionable curtain poles had killed the cornice business. Accordingly, the capricious trade made him diversify by force rather than by choice. He then joined the ranks of the curtain-pole makers and subsequently patented curtain-rod combinations in 1892 and 1893. Ultimately, Scottron set off in still another direction, that of manufacturing "porcelain onyx" cylinders used by lamp and candlestick producers. Set up in Brooklyn, New York, this imitation onyx business proved quite stable and highly profitable.

Moses William Binga, born in 1841 at Anderdon, Ontario, Canada, a haven for a fugitive slave who had escaped through the Underground Railroad, secured a patent for an improvement in a street-sprinkling apparatus in 1879 when he resided in Cincinnati, Ohio.[9] Like many who sold a part of their patent rights, Binga assigned one-half to H. L. Morey of Hamilton, Ohio. His invention consisted "of a perforated pipe journaled in bearings attached to a curb stone, sidewalk, street, road or lawn." The device could direct the water jets to any side of the street and wash gutters. Most roads and streets at that time were dirt pathways.

At this period and beyond, the rise of African American entrepreneurship came to the attention of both blacks and whites through books, newspapers, journals, and associations' convenes. This progress, though, was hard fought, in part because of business shifts and an unpredictable market. But a few African Americans realized handsome profits.

EARLY CREATIVE GENIUS IN THE CAPITAL CITY

The attraction of the nation's capital drew African Americans, many of whom had creative ability. The District of Columbia, created from the Maryland and Virginia slaveholding countryside in 1790, included Washington City, the seat of the nation's government, established there in 1800. "Of the District's 14,093 inhabitants at that time," says Paul E. Sluby, Sr., in his November 2000 speech "History of the Columbian Harmony Society," "there were over 3,000 slaves and nearly 800 free blacks."[10] By the 1880s, well after emancipation, the black population escalated to more than 59,000. In the latter part of the nineteenth century, records reveal the steady growth of "colored" inventors with patents emerging in Washington City. Both genders appeared in evidence. There were no legal handicaps to restrain their access to federal protection. Many worked for the federal government, and this status gave them job security and a pension.

Landrow Bell was a diversified inventor who patented an improvement in a smokestack for locomotives in May 1871. Intended to prevent the dangerous effluence of sparks and cinders that harmed passengers and combustible property near the rail line, Bell's contrivance consisted of a division in the crescent-shaped flue that helped the cinders and sparks to be confined to the ash pan and engine fire-box. The following year he achieved federal protection for an improvement in dough kneaders. Bell, a waiter in the food-service industry, lived on Eighth Street in the southwest section of Washington.[11]

Originator William A. Lavalette, a printer, improved the construction and arrangement of a printing press. His two patent grants were obtained in 1878, when he resided in the northeast quadrant of Washington. Lavalette died on January 19, 1914, at age seventy-three.[12]

Another inventor of the city was Leonard C. Bailey, who patented a combined truss and bandage for supporting lower-body hernias in 1883. Adopted by the Army Medical Board, the invention netted him millions. Bent on exercising his creative thought, Bailey secured another patent for a folding bed in 1899. Becoming a prominent businessman, Bailey cofounded the Capitol Savings Bank and served as its president. He was a director of the Manassas Industrial School and a member of the first integrated jury impanelled in Washington, D.C. He survived his wife and passed away suddenly on September 1, 1918.[13] Bailey, a Columbia Harmony Society treasurer, is buried in a section of its cemetery (now National Harmony Memorial Park, located in Largo, Maryland, outside of the capital city) that is named for him.[14]

David A. Fisher, Jr., a furniture-board maker, received two grants. The earlier invention was an improved joiner's clamp patented in 1875, and the second was an improvement in furniture casters. The clamp readily adjusted the nut component, and the caster provided for a wheel to remain secure in its socket. Fisher, a prominent businessman in the city, was the second president of the Columbian Harmony Society.[15]

Inventor Andrew Franklin Hilyer patented two devices in 1890, one a water evaporator attachment for hot-air registers and the other an evaporator for hot-air registers. The devices, attached to a register, allowed the heater to provide greater humidity to a room for the occupant's health and comfort. Hilyer, born a slave in 1858 in Walton County, Georgia, migrated with his widowed mother to St. Louis, Missouri, then to Nebraska following her death. He moved to Minneapolis and became the first black graduate of the University of Minnesota in 1882. After relocating to the District of Columbia, he received a law degree from Howard University, graduating as the class valedictorian.[16]

James Wormley, renowned in Washington, D.C., was granted a patent on a lifesaving apparatus in 1881. Floats having a rope twisted and passed into sleeves or tubes in the outer side or bulwarks of a boat provided lifesaving support for occupants. Wormley was a wealthy caterer and the hotel proprietor of the famed Wormley Hotel (or Wormley House), which opened in 1871. Authors of the *Wormeley-Wormley* lineage Stanton Wormley, Sr. and Jr. (descendants), and Paul E. Sluby,

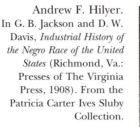

Sr., wrote that the Wormley Hotel "was also the site of the well-known and historically important 'Wormley Compromise of 1877,' which solved the crisis of whether Rutherford B. Hayes or Samuel J. Tilden had been elected President of the United States." A deal was made whereby Tilden's supporters gave Hayes the necessary electoral votes to win in exchange for ending Reconstruction in the South. Ironically, this deal, which signaled the retreat of federal support for civil rights and southern political gains for people of color, was sealed in a black-owned and operated hotel. Born of free parents on January 16, 1819, in Washington, D.C., Wormley died at Boston, Massachusetts, on October 18, 1884. He was interred in Harmony Cemetery at the capital city.[17]

Inventor Jonas Cooper, a janitor, obtained his patent on a shutter and fastening device in 1883. Lockrum Blue devised a hand corn-shelling implement intended for speedily and productively removing the grain from the ears of corn, patented in 1884. A small metallic blade attached to a bench accommodated a single tooth used in the initial step to detach two rows of grain, and the concave knife-edged section completed the removal. Blue was interred at Harmony Cemetery after his death in February 1894.[18]

Henry Brown was rewarded in 1886 for his invention of a receptacle for storing and preserving documents and especially "carbon paper."

(No Model.)

A. F. HILYER.
WATER EVAPORATOR ATTACHMENT FOR HOT AIR REGISTERS.

No. 435,095.   Patented Aug. 26, 1890.

Fig 1

Fig. 2.

Attest.

Victor J. Evans.

R. J. Campbell

Inventor

Andrew F. Hilyer.

By G. W. Balloch

Atty.

Water Evaporator Attachment for Hot Air Registers, patented invention of Andrew F. Hilyer.

James Wormley.
Courtesy of Mrs. Freida
H. Wormley.

Resident Joseph Sidney Coolidge secured a grant in 1888 on a harness attachment for horses that hooked onto any harness without affecting the device itself. It was uncomplicated and economical to construct and durable and easy to use. Coinventors John E. Purdy and Daniel E. Sadgwar acquired a grant in 1889 for a folding chair that was inexpensive, strong, and durable "so as to be easily portable."

Joint inventors William Snow and James A. Johns patented a liniment "consisting of tobacco, Jamestown seed, quill-wort, poke-root, salt, Cayenne pepper, resin, lard, and water in 1890." Interestingly, Johns signed the grant with "his mark," an "X."

Hugh M. Browne, a nephew of Wormley, was granted several patents. The first, acquired in 1890, was for a sewer trap that automatically provided against backwater or floodwater by hydrostatic power. The second patent was issued in 1908 on a damper regulator for a furnace. Browne graduated from Howard University in 1875 and from the theological department of Princeton University in 1878. He studied at universities in Germany and Scotland. Afterward he became an educator at Monrovia College in Monrovia, Africa; a teacher of physics at a Washington, D.C., high school and at Hampton Institute; and next the principal of schools in Baltimore and Philadelphia. Browne died in 1923 at age eighty-two. Browne Junior High School in Washington, D.C., commemorates his contributions to education.[19]

Cabinetmaker Henry A. Jackson was allowed a patent in 1896 on an improved kitchen table adapted "for use in small rooms." *Boyd's Directory of the District of Columbia, 1897,* places Jackson in the northwest sector of the nation's capital.

Diversified creative genius Charles V. Richey was a prolific inventor. When he was living in Atlanta, Georgia, he received a patent for a railroad switch and another for a car coupling. He was in Washington, D.C., when he received a patent for a fire-escape bracket and afterward patented a railroad switch. The following year, he obtained still another patent for a combined cot, hammock, and stretcher. Interestingly, four of Richey's patents were assigned, in part, to inventor Leonard C. Bailey. At one point they both employed the same patent attorney, H. B. Willson. By 1904, Richey was employed at the Bureau of Printing. Years afterward, he patented a meter device to register the number of originating telephone calls and a lockout system to prevent unauthorized use. Richey set up the Delaware-registered Richey Telephone Lock and Call Register Company to promote the concepts.[20]

Engineer Thomas Henry Edmonds invented a separating screen used with pipes of automatic valve regulators to filter foreign matter in 1897. Useful in any water supply pipe, the screen, made of two plates screwed together to hold the wire material rigidly in place, kept out lint, scales, shells, and other undesirable substances. That year he lived on Rock Creek Church Road.

RECORDERS OF HISTORY

Toward the close of the nineteenth century, certain recorders of history and black journals attempted to erase the insidiously prevailing impression that "colored" people, collectively, had not made any progress or had not improved their lot since emancipation. The supplement of the *Cleveland* (Ohio) *Gazette,* a Negro newspaper established in 1883 by Harry C. Smith, credited "Negroes of Brains" in its November 26, 1892, issue. Averring the "advancement of the Negro race during the past twenty-five years . . . most clearly evidenced in the careers of its leaders," the article illuminates those having brilliant and exceptional success.[21]

Inspired by the progress of an enslaved race set free, black authors wholeheartedly hailed evidence of their achievement. Major Richard R. Wright, Sr., educator, politician, editor, and banker, was annoyed at the myth of African Americans' inferiority in the field of inventions, so he penned an article "The Negro as an Inventor" that ran in the *A.M.E. Church Review.* William H. Quick in *Negro Stars in All Ages of the World,* 1898, devoted a chapter to colored inventors with patents and their business enterprises as outgrowths. Quick's work gives credit to George Morsel Williams of Newark, Delaware, for seven mechanical inventions, including a corn planter, a drill tube for seeding machines, mower knives that had a spiral shape, pawl and ratchet mechanisms, a lawn mower with grass gatherer and dropper, and a lawn mower with an adjustable bed knife. Quick also printed a patent list provided by researcher and chronicler Henry E. Baker.[22]

Anthony Bowen

Twenty years before the Civil War, Anthony Bowen, a Washington, D.C., resident, became the first African American clerk in the U.S. Patent Office. From 1841 to his death in 1871, Bowen advanced through a succession of promotions. Born into slavery in 1809 on the estate of William Bradley in Prince George's County, Maryland, Bowen moved to the capital city a free person. He eventually purchased his first wife's freedom. His son James served in the U.S. Coast Guard and was valedictorian among the first graduates of the medical school at Howard University in 1871. Bowen opened doors for free Negroes in the city, establishing Sunday school at Wesley Church and evening school for free black men. Further, he founded St. Paul AME Church and became an ordained minister. Most notably, he organized the first Young Men's Christian Association for Colored Men and Boys in 1853, becoming its first president. With the assistance of John F. Cook and other free men, Bowen helped many young men of his kind. A southwest Washington, D.C., public school is named for him.

Source: "Anthony Bowen, 1809–1871, Founder (A Biographical Sketch)," by Ella Payne Moran, great-granddaughter. From the Patricia Carter Ives Sluby Collection.

In *Evidences of Progress among Colored People,* author G. F. Richings, too, borrows from Baker's work and recognizes the steam-trap invention of prolific inventor Henry Creamer as "an automatic steam pump that seems to have made a good impression among those who have tested it, for it is very highly spoken of." Richings describes J. B. Randolph, a minister of Trenton, New Jersey, as having "taken out a patent on an apparatus for heating and cooking, claiming that at least one-half of the fuel now used in heating a house can be saved by the use of his patent." D. F. Black of Mechanicsburg, Pennsylvania, is recounted to possess several patents and was engaged "in manufacturing a coconut food" that "met with fair success."[23]

In the U.S. patent records, prolific inventor Turner Byrd, Jr., received patents for appliances for a horse and wagon or carriage in addition to car couplings. Other innovators granted patents before 1900 include Alexander P. Ashbourne of Oakland, California, who worked on food products and a kitchen utensil, and John P. Parker of Ripley, Ohio, who manufactured screws for tobacco presses.

In early years, the widely circulated journal *Crisis*, published by the National Association for the Advancement of Colored People (NAACP), and the *Negro Yearbook*, by Monroe Nathan Work of Tuskegee Institute, diligently recognized the achievement of various thinkers and tinkerers. Some innovators found fame and fortune; some just happened upon success.

During 1917–1918, Negroes made a large number of inventions. Many of these related to the war. Charles Stevenson of Amarillo, Texas, invented a glass war bomb. . . . L. A. Hayden invented an airship stabilizer which was adopted by the British Government. . . . Julius Hart of Columbus, Georgia, invented three war bombs . . . that for one the War Department gave him $15,000. . . . William D. Polite of Charlotte, North Carolina, has patented an anticraft gun. . . . James Davis of Alexandria, Louisiana, . . . invented a new kind of machine gun. Horace G. Anderson of Washington, District of Columbia, has patented a new type of explosive bullet that will illuminate the place struck. John Martin of Calexico, California, has patented a gun which an operator miles away is to fire by electricity. . . . Jacob W. F. Berry of Decatur, Alabama, invented an electrically driven submarine. . . . H. A. Cooper of Sabetha, Kansas, invented a submarine detector. . . . Henry Grady of Westbourne, Tennessee, has had patented a Torpedo-Catcher and a Mine Destroyer. George Bryan of Asbury Park, New Jersey invented a device for protecting ships at sea called an "apartment torpedo and mine shield." He also invented a war bomb. He claims that in 1914 he invented a street signal "Stop and Go" . . . says . . . it was put in operation in a different form and claimed by some else. . . . Charles V. Richey of Brooklyn, New York, has invented a device for preventing the destruction of ships at sea by submarines. He is also the inventor of an electric slot piano player and an automobile shifting speed controller. His piano player device permits a person from any part of a store, cafe or amusement place to drop a nickel in a box and play any one of the pieces in the piano he chooses.

Source: Monroe N. Work, ed., *Negro Year Book, 1918–1919* (Tuskegee Institute, Ala.: Negro Year Book Publishing Company, 1919), p. 5.

Honor for these achievements was paramount for the black psyche since a host of African Americans were skeptical and suspicious of their own people's accomplishments. They thought that any pronouncement would bring the race into disrepute. With the help of the unfriendly recorders of events, not even African Americans knew of the extent of their contributions, except in terms of sweat, blood, and tears.

The story of an unusual talent whose father was an African, is found in the *Maryland Historical Magazine.* Frank W. Porter III in his article entitled "John Widgeon: Naturalist, Curator, and Philosopher" writes about this African American who was a janitor and custodian of the Maryland Academy of Sciences for fifty-five years and "was an invaluable contributor to its early development." The academy is the oldest academy of science in the United States. A man born "into slavery and entirely self-educated," John Widgeon was noted as a naturalist, museum curator, collector, and philosopher. Porter writes that the Baltimore *Sun* labeled him "industrious,... self-respecting,... educated and intelligent."[24] Widgeon, during the latter decades of the nineteenth century, was authorized to collect, to classify, and to exhibit many significant collections of the academy.

Born in 1850 in Northampton County, Virginia, Widgeon was unschooled until age sixteen but displayed an early interest in collecting and observing insects and animals near his home. After only two years of formal training, Widgeon left Virginia to look for meaningful employment. He went from one menial job to another before he found significant work in Baltimore, Maryland, at the academy. For his diligence and resourcefulness in the science of collecting paleontological specimens, especially two tons of coral and a forty-foot finback female whale, during his career, Widgeon was awarded the degree of master of science. He passed away in 1937 at his home in Fairfield, Maryland.[25]

The United States had been winding down from the ten-month Spanish-American War only to see more global fighting action in less than a decade when Eugene Burkins was rewarded in 1900 for his breech-loading cannon that was a type of rapid-fire gun. The same year John F. Pickering became a patent holder for his airship invention. Philadelphian William B. Purvis received numerous patents on a paper-bag machine and he acquired patents on a fountain pen, hand stamp, an electric railway, and a magnetic car-balancing device as well. The diverse inventor sold a number of his patents on the paper-bag machine to the New York Union Paper Bag Company.

Ned E. Barnes enjoyed patent rights from 1905 through 1928. He conceived multiple inventions, most on rail and tie braces for the railway. During this period, patentee Brinay Smartt of Tennessee developed reversing valves, valve gears, and a wheel device, and Lewis Dorcas received his patent on a stove. Oscar Robert Cassell not only patented a flying machine, he patented further a bedstead extension and an angle indicator.

Richard B. Spikes of San Francisco, California, received his first pat-

Joseph H. Dickinson. In G. F. Richings, *Evidences of Progress among Colored People* (Philadelphia: George S. Ferguson Co., 1905). From the Patricia Carter Ives Sluby Collection.

ent on a billiard rack in 1910. Sixteen years later he obtained a grant for a combination milk-bottle opener and cover. Afterwards he received patents on transmission and gear-shift means and on a process for sampling tank liquids. Decades later Spikes patented an automatic safety brake system.

Renowned makers of musical instruments. Joseph Hunter Dickinson and his son, Samuel Dickinson, who received a patent on a reed organ and on a phonograph, are credited with more than a dozen ingenious concepts, some concerning mechanical means for player pianos and the reed organ. G. F. Richings mentions:

> Joseph H. Dickinson was born June 22, 1855. He attended school in Detroit, Mich. At the age of fifteen he enlisted in the United States Revenue Service. At age seventeen he entered the employ of the Clough and Warren Organ Co. . . . in whose service some of his best work has been accomplished. . . . [He] formed a partnership with his father-in-law, known as the Dickinson-Gould Organ Co., for the manufacture of parlor and chapel organs. This firm sent to the New Orleans exhibition a large chapel organ as an exhibit showing the progress of the colored people in manufacturing. Prior to this, for the Centennial Exposition in 1876, Mr. Dickinson helped to construct a large combination organ for the Clough & Warren Organ Co., which received a diploma and medal.[26]

James Doyle received his first patent in 1900 for inventing a serving apparatus for dining rooms. Twelve years later he patented an automatic serving system and subsequently patented a particular server for that system. David Baker held patent grants on a railway signal apparatus, on a signal device to indicate high water for bridges, and on interliners to prevent tire punctures. The patented automatic glass-gathering machine of Ross D. Brown inspired at least three glass companies to use it at their plants.

Joining the ranks of African American inventors at this new century's turn was Kentuckian Shelby Davidson (1868–1931), a lawyer and a tinkerer with adding machines. Curator Portia James in the Smithsonian catalog *The Real McCoy* gives insight into his creativity:

> Davidson came . . . to Washington, D.C., in 1887, where he began working in the auditing department of the U.S. Post Office Department. In 1906, Davidson began to study adding machines with an eye toward how they might be improved to handle government auditing functions more efficiently. He visited several factories to observe exactly how adding machines were constructed. After two years of study, in 1908 Davidson patented his first invention, a rewind device for adding machines.[27]

The government utilized his concept with many of its adding contraptions. Three years later, Davidson, captivated by mechanisms for tabulation, patented an automatic fee device.

William Douglass, born in Jefferson County, Pennsylvania, excelled in the trades of blacksmithing, carpentry, cabinet and implement making, and inventing. After moving to Chicago, he formed the Douglass Automatic Straw and Grain Binder Company. Backed by African American capitalists, the capital stock of the company was $20,000, divided into 2,000 shares with a par value of $10 each. Douglass invented a self-binding harvester, patented in 1905 with thirty-seven drawings and 166 patent claims. The document was the single largest patent grant issued at that time. The Douglass harvester made a twisted rope of the straw it cut, replacing the twine binder. Adjusting to any kind of reaper, it had a number of arms with which to gather the straw from the bundle and to tie the regulation knot of the old field hand.[28]

Sugarcane planter Leonard Julien of Modeste, Ascension Parish, Louisiana, patented a cane planter, the first major innovation in the sugarcane industry since its beginning. The planter drops the stalks into three rows simultaneously, outperforming the standard single-row mechanical apparatus. As owner of a seven-hundred-acre farm, Julien invented the machinery for the purpose of saving farmers money and labor costs.

St. Louis native William A. Roberson was the only person of color working as a U.S. inspector for the quartermaster service of the army in 1903.[29] Headquartered in Jeffersonville, Indiana, and residing in Louisville, Kentucky, Roberson invented and then patented a portable or field laundry in 1904, usable by troops in the field. The federal government ordered the unit for the Philippines and for Cuba. In 1905, Roberson took out a patent on a convertible cot, followed by his devising an identification button used by army officers and by general travelers, the sale of which made him a wealthy man.

Kelly Miller and Joseph R. Gay in their *Progress and Achievements of the Colored People* refer to the records of the U.S. Patent Office and reiterate that many of the inventions "among the Colored people" are of supreme quality and utility. The innovations are "for devices of every conceivable use . . . [including] a pencil sharpener [a type patented by John Lee Love in 1897] in common use today . . . [and] life saving guards for locomotives and street cars [invented by James H. Robinson in 1899]."[30] These worthy contrivances were improvements on past discoveries.

A black dentist made a singular achievement in 1899 and was rewarded for his creativity. Dr. George F. Grant of Boston, Massachusetts, patented the golf tee as we know it today. Previously, a golfer had used "conical mounds of sand or similar material" formed by the player's fingers "on which the ball is supported when driving off." Grant's historic invention comprises a wood base tapered "to a point" at the lower end which is inserted in the ground, and an upper end on which the ball rests "as in a cup." He filed the application about five months before the patent was issued in December 1899. This simple and cheaply produced article of manufacture was the first effective modern tee for use in the game of golf. Born in Oswego, New York, in 1849, Grant died in New Hampshire in 1905.[31]

Inventor and manufacturer A. C. Howard manufactured a shoe polish concocted by him. Given excellent comment for a practical innovation, Howard, a former Pullman porter and an early ruling member of the National Negro Business League, opened a factory in Chicago and one in New York, using his keen business acumen. In *Progress of a Race*, Howard declares:

As a railroad porter I had saved up something like $180; with that $180 I started a business. I began by selling my blacking to railroad porters. . . . I started preparing my goods in a woodshed, which was on the alley back of my home. I used to use an old tin box for mixing purposes; now we have a factory well equipped, and in all the big department stores of Chicago, Philadelphia and New York, Howard shoe polish has won its place in the standard stock.[32]

No. 638,920.

Patented Dec. 12, 1899.

G. F. GRANT.
GOLF TEE.
(Application filed July 1, 1899.)

(No Model.)

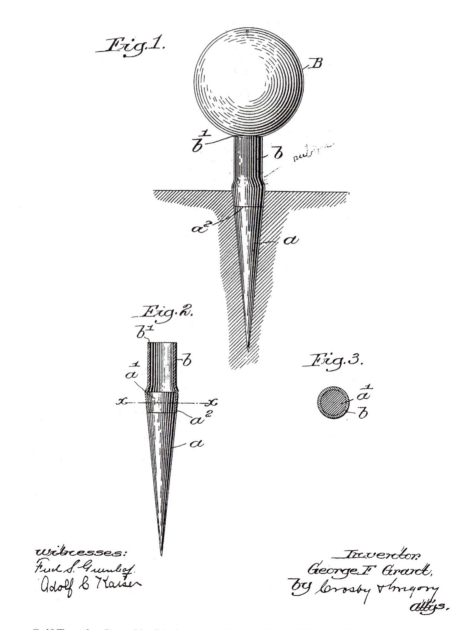

Fig.1.

Fig.2.

Fig.3.

Witnesses:
Fred S. Greenleaf.
Adolf B. Kaiser

Inventor:
George F. Grant,
by Crosby & Gregory
attys.

Golf Tee, the first of its kind, patented invention of George F. Grant.

George F. Grant.
From the IOKTS Archives,
courtesy of the Francis A.
Countway Library of Medicine.

Scholar and barehanded ball-catcher Moses Fleetwood Walker was the holder of four patents. In Syracuse, New York, Walker patented a cartridge that "will do deadly work claimed for the Justin gun in discharging dynamite," asserted an Ohio newspaper.[33] Sometime later he secured three patents within the same year, all in the field of motion-picture reels. When he was residing in Ohio, the ever-innovative Walker became the manager and lessee of an opera house in Candiz. After inventing the motion-picture film reel, Walker made an agreement with the Globe Machine and Stamping Company of Cleveland to make and sell his patented invention, which was regarded as the best available on the market. He held foreign patents as well on his discoveries.

In 1884, Moses Walker became the earliest African American major-league baseball player, some sixty-three years before Jackie Robinson's Brooklyn Dodgers debut. Walker, who played in Ohio for the Toledo team of the American Association, was regarded as the best catcher of that time. He had attended Oberlin College and the University of Michigan and had played baseball at both. Walker died in 1924 and is buried at Union Cemetery in Steubenville, Ohio.[34]

№

4011116

THE UNITED STATES OF AMERICA

TO ALL TO WHOM THESE PRESENTS SHALL COME:

Whereas, THERE HAS BEEN PRESENTED TO THE

Commissioner of Patents and Trademarks

A PETITION PRAYING FOR THE GRANT OF LETTERS PATENT FOR AN ALLEGED NEW AND USEFUL INVENTION THE TITLE AND DESCRIPTION OF WHICH ARE CONTAINED IN THE SPECIFICATIONS OF WHICH A COPY IS HEREUNTO ANNEXED AND MADE A PART HEREOF, AND THE VARIOUS REQUIREMENTS OF LAW IN SUCH CASES MADE AND PROVIDED HAVE BEEN COMPLIED WITH, AND THE TITLE THERETO IS, FROM THE RECORDS OF THE PATENT AND TRADEMARK OFFICE IN THE CLAIMANT(S) INDICATED IN THE SAID COPY, AND WHEREAS, UPON DUE EXAMINATION MADE, THE SAID CLAIMANT(S) IS (ARE) ADJUDGED TO BE ENTITLED TO A PATENT UNDER THE LAW.

NOW, THEREFORE, THESE **Letters Patent** ARE TO GRANT UNTO THE SAID CLAIMANT(S) AND THE SUCCESSORS, HEIRS OR ASSIGNS OF THE SAID CLAIMANT(S) FOR THE TERM OF SEVENTEEN YEARS FROM THE DATE OF THIS GRANT, SUBJECT TO THE PAYMENT OF ISSUE FEES AS PROVIDED BY LAW, THE RIGHT TO EXCLUDE OTHERS FROM MAKING, USING OR SELLING THE SAID INVENTION THROUGHOUT THE UNITED STATES.

In testimony whereof I have hereunto set my hand and caused the seal of the **Patent and Trademark Office** *to be affixed at the City of Washington this* eighth *day of* March *in the year of our Lord one thousand nine hundred and* seventy-seven, *and of the Independence of the United States of America the two hundredth and* first.

Attest:

Ruth C. Mason
Attesting Officer.

C. Marshall Dann
Commissioner of Patents and Trademarks.

A patent cover that depicts, at its top, the Patent Office at the end of the Herbert Hoover building.

4

PROGRESSIVE ACHIEVEMENT
Exposing Ebony Talent

But I have understanding as well as you;
I am not inferior to you: yea, who knowth
not such things as these?

Job 12:3

FAIRLY REPRESENTING

The creative mind of the African American brought a superior quality of life to mankind. In helping to build the country, these innovators, in turn, hoped for economic and social rewards. Their invention, or patent property if they were successful in traversing the federal patent system, was, however, practically worthless unless they found capital with which to exploit it. Knowing the risks, black Americans still had the zest and zeal to pursue a dream. In so doing, they greatly contributed to the nation's advancement. It is impossible to learn of America's development without knowing how minorities helped promote it.

Fairs and expositions were trendy in the 1800s and early 1900s, but a handy tool to expose and champion ebony talent. State and regional fairs set aside segregated sections for "colored" or "Negro" patrons. Creating additional venues, anniversaries celebrating the Emancipation Proclamation—the 1863 manifesto that liberated slaves—spawned shows called "emancipation expositions." In 1851, the Colored American Institute for the Promotion of the Mechanic Arts and Sciences promoted black inventive talent in Philadelphia. The Convention of the Colored Citizens of Massachusetts in 1858 identified two black inventors, Alexander (Aaron) Roberts of Philadelphia, the developer of an apparatus functional at fires, and William Deitz of Albany, New

York, who invented a steam-powered railway.[1] More than likely this is the William Abbott Deitz who received a patent in 1867 for a shoe upper (boot construction). Born in Albany, New York, on October 15, 1820, Deitz died on April 1, 1874.

RAIL-LINE FANFARE

Recognition of the technological advancements made by black inventors helped promote their industrial skills. During the decades of the industrial growth of the nation, a plethora of ideas relating to rails abounded as rail exhibitors used public venues to expose talent. Design and development of rail lines helped expand the growth of the nation, moving goods and people east to west. Rail-line companies, offering a source of transportation, were also gainful employers. More than 70,000 miles of rail lines were laid, mostly by desperate former slaves seeking a livelihood for themselves and their families.

The energy and perseverance of a black engineer revolutionized the country's transportation industry. Elijah McCoy (1843–1929), a son of fugitive slaves from Kentucky, conceived an automatic oiling process that became so well known that railroad personnel, industrial engineers, and mechanics would not use any new equipment or piece of machinery unless it contained the "real McCoy" device, an indication of the genuine apparatus.

According to his death certificate, Elijah McCoy was born on March 27, 1843, in Canada. He was the third of twelve children of George and Mildred Goins McCoy, living in Colchester, Ontario. His parents used the Underground Railroad to flee slavery in 1837, and settled in Canada, where his father became a member of the Canadian army. Honorably discharged, the elder McCoy was given 160 acres of farmland in Colchester, where Elijah attended school.[2] At age fifteen, his parents sent him to Edinburgh, Scotland, to study mechanical engineering. McCoy returned to his homeland five years later as a master mechanic, but had difficulty finding a job for which he was qualified. Finally he moved to Ypsilanti, Michigan, where he became a fireman on the Michigan Central Railroad. One of his duties was oiling steam engines. When a train stopped, McCoy walked around the engine squirting oil from a can onto the cylinders, levers, and connecting pins of the engine where friction and heat built up, causing premature failure of the parts. Because of many problems with the technique, McCoy began to design a device that would automatically lubricate. He discovered that canals with connecting units would distribute the oil throughout the machinery in calibrated amounts at regular intervals. As result of two years of experimentation, McCoy filed for patent rights and on July 23, 1872, received his first grant, patent number 129,843,

Elijah McCoy.
Courtesy of the Moorland-
Spingarn Research Center,
Howard University.

titled "Improvement in Lubricators for Steam Engines." Even though the device was the first of its kind to automatically lubricate, the term *improvement* in this instance was used to distinguish it from hand oiling. To make a profit and to gain capital for further research, McCoy assigned his patent rights to himself and S. C. Hamlin of Ypsilanti, a common practice among inventors, used often by McCoy.

Other improvements quickly followed. Less than a month later, McCoy received another patent on his improved original device. This patent was unassigned at the time it was issued. However, his 1873 patent providing for the escape of oil through a tube to the steam chest was assigned to Sullivan M. Cutcheon and Edward P. Allen.

By 1875, McCoy had moved to the county of Ionia in Michigan. He received two more patents on steam-cylinder lubricators in 1876, assigning half of his right to the first to William J. Stiff and assigning rights to the second grant to Ransom C. Luce and George S. Woodruff of Grand Rapids. Due to racial prejudice and bigotry, whites ridiculed his creation and dubbed it the "Nigger Oil Cup." However, the device spoke for itself, for it saved the enormous expense of periodically stopping trains to oil them. McCoy was hired to personally supervise the installation of his patented oil cup. Eventually the device became gen-

E. McCOY.

Improvement in Lubricators for Steam-Engines.

No. 130,305.   Patented Aug. 6, 1872.

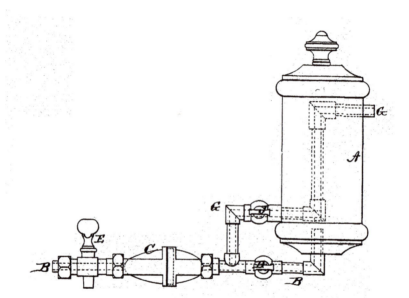

Witnesses:
Jas. H. Hutchinson
C. L. Evert.

Inventor.
Elijah McCoy.
per
Attorneys.

Improvement in Lubricators for Steam-Engines, patented invention of Elijah
McCoy, who was inducted into the National Inventors Hall of Fame in 2001.

erally used on railroads and steamers and widely used in industry because it extended the longevity of heavy industrial machinery.

After a hiatus and now in Detroit, McCoy patented two inventions on lubricator improvements that were assigned to Henry C. and Charles Hodges. McCoy then patented an invention specific to the use of the lubricator with air-brake pumps. Until 1888, McCoy assigned his patent to the Hodgeses; however, a year later, he teamed with inventor Clarence B. Hodges to patent an improvement on the lubricator. McCoy assigned this patent also to the previous Hodgeses, but McCoy was the sole inventor and owner of the 1891 lubricator patent on additional improvements. McCoy then focused on the problems of lubrication for railroad locomotives. He produced an independent steam pipe and overflow steam pipe to provide equalization of the steam pressure in the engine for its proper lubrication.

McCoy's strong interest in machines and tools led to twenty-three inventive oiling methods. This prodigious trend continued through each decade into the twentieth century. Between his inventions on lubricators, McCoy found time to patent other items such as a folding ironing table, a folding scaffold support, a gauge, a tread for tires, and three design patents for a lawn sprinkler, a rubber heel, and a vehicle wheel tire. He considered his best invention to be the graphite lubricator, patented in 1915. This apparatus, called "Locomotive Lubricator," had a means for suspending graphite or a similar solid lubricant in free-flowing oil so that it would not obstruct the chokeplug when lubricating superheated engines. Two years later the McCoy Manufacturing Company, assignee of Elijah McCoy, secured a Canadian patent, number 176,755, on a lubricator.

In 1920, McCoy set up his own development company, named the Elijah McCoy Manufacturing Company, in Detroit, Michigan, to make, use, and sell all his inventions. By 1923, McCoy had obtained patents in foreign countries as well, including Great Britain, France, Germany, Austria, and Russia. Frequently he was hired as a consultant and became an advisor to large corporations. His creative thinking covered a period of five decades. McCoy spent most of his life in Detroit and often counseled young boys, inspiring them to achieve as he had done.

Widower Elijah McCoy died at age eighty-six of senile dementia in 1929 in the Eloise Infirmary at Eloise, Michigan.[3] Although he sold many of his patent rights, he died relatively poor since many obstacles impeded his progress. Others, though, made millions on his inventions. McCoy was renowned for his brilliance and his contributions to mankind by patenting fifty-seven inventions, the last received on March 2, 1926, for the lubricator, his lifelong enterprise. The Henry Ford Museum at Dearborn, Michigan, exhibits a number of McCoy's inventions, some of which assisted the Henry Ford automobile industry. His

DESIGN.

No. 31,549.

Patented Sept. 26, 1899.

E. McCOY.
LAWN SPRINKLER.
(Application filed July 31, 1899.)

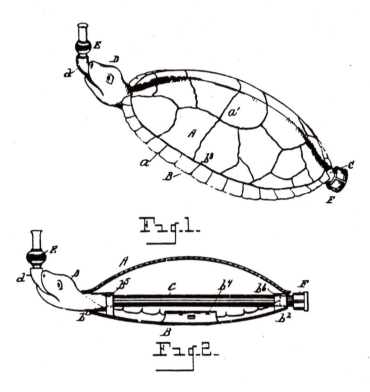

Fig. 1.

Fig. 2.

WITNESSES.
O. B. Barziger.
M. Hickey.

INVENTOR.
Elijah McCoy
By Morrell S. Wright
Attorney

Lawn Sprinkler, patented design of Elijah McCoy.

Granville T. Woods.
Courtesy of the Moorland-
Spingarn Research Center,
Howard University.

legacy is the famed expression "It's the real McCoy." The Smithsonian Institution titled its catalog *The Real McCoy* for the *African American Invention and Innovation, 1619–1930* exhibition of 1989, and the National Intellectual Property Law Association adopted "Illuminating the Real McCoy" as its motto. Elijah McCoy was inducted into the National Inventors Hall of Fame at Akron, Ohio, in September 2001.

Some African Americans opposed designated Negro sections at white national or regional exhibitions, which they considered discriminatory; however, others saw the separation as the only way to expose technological and artistic skill. The phenomenal inventiveness of Granville T. Woods (1856–1910) was showcased at world's fairs and at national displays. The 1900 Paris Exposition and the 1907 Jamestown Negro Exhibit were prime venues for Woods.

The rail companies, as kings of transportation, exploited unskilled and skilled workers alike. African Americans in the thousands worked as linemen and locomotive firemen. Many of them participated in the development of railways, offering solutions to help make the rail lines safer. The lines were extensive, and the engineer running the train on the tracks needed to know of hazards and the whereabouts of approaching trains to avoid accidents. Woods, a telegraphic and electrical wizard, solved numerous problems and eased a multitude of the engineer's concerns. Sometimes called the "Black Edison," a moniker created to equate him with the genius of Thomas Edison, Woods had a phenomenally gifted mind, triumphant in investigation into the field of electricity.

The electrical cleverness of Granville Woods might have budded at age ten when he started to work in a railroad equipment repair shop in Columbus, Ohio. He subsequently apprenticed with skilled tradesmen as a machinist and blacksmith during Reconstruction after the Civil War. At sixteen, he left Ohio for Missouri, where he got more knowledge of machinery by working as a fireman and then as an engineer on the Iron Mountain Railroad. At twenty, Woods moved east, became interested in the developing field of electrical engineering, and sustained a passion for reading any material he found on the subject while working part time. He enrolled in an eastern college in the evenings, studying electrical and mechanical engineering, but mostly he was self-educated.

Around 1880, after a short stint as an engineer aboard the British steamer *Ironsides*, he returned to Ohio imbued with a drive and determination to look for a challenge in his area of training and expertise. He found work as an engineer at the Danville and Southern Railroad Company. Fired with a desire to produce electrical, telephone, and telegraph equipment, Woods then established a factory to manufacture the devices in Cincinnati.[4] Woods was first rewarded for his creative talent in 1884 by receiving two patents in diverse fields in the same year. His initial invention was an improved steam boiler furnace patented on June 3, and the second invention was a telephone transmitter that sent sound over a distance by means of electric current, patented on December 2. The following year, nine years after the invention of the telephone by Alexander Graham Bell, Woods received a patent on an apparatus for transmission of messages by electricity where transmitters used either Morse code or voice messages. He coined the word *telegraphony* for this technology, which combined the telegraph with the telephone. This patent strongly competed with the earlier Bell patent, and Woods sold the rights to this invention to the Boston-based American Bell Telephone Company. When the entire rights are sold by the inventor, the innovator loses all claim to any profit. Sometimes the value of inventions is misjudged or undervalued, so the originator of the idea receives minimum compensation. Woods, however, was not in that category. A few inventors are rewarded handsomely, and some, like Woods, assign the patent to their own company for commercial exploitation.

In 1887, Woods and his brother Lyates founded the Woods Electric Company, which owned his early patents and manufactured telegraph and electrical equipment. This was the year Woods received a patent on one of his most important and controversial inventions. On November 15, 1887, he patented the induction telegraph system, a means for deterring accidents by keeping each train informed of the whereabouts of the one immediately ahead or following it and communicating with stations from moving trains as well, a phenomenal idea that companies quickly adopted in the industry. The inventor termed it the "Synchronous Multiplex Railway Telegraph," produced by Woods's company.

His inventions on electrical railway telegraph systems competed with inventions of Lucius Phelps and Thomas Edison. They invented similar telegraph procedures and litigated to decide who was first to invent the systems. Woods was victorious in the legal battle that put his inventions in the limelight, and he relished the celebrity, eclipsing that of Edison and other inventive luminaries. The *American Catholic Tribune* in 1888 lauded Woods as the greatest person knowledgeable in electricity in the world.

Woods's company never became a household name, but many corporations to which the Granville Woods patents were licensed or sold developed into gigantic conglomerates, famous for buying out competitors. Both the American Engineering Company and the General Electric Company of New York purchased or licensed Woods's patents. In 1890, Woods moved to New York City to find lucrative work for electrical engineers. He put into practice many ideas on the electric streetcar and obtained patent protection on them. He conceived "dynamotors" that significantly diminished the threat of fires on the streetcars. Additionally, he discovered a better system for transferring electric current to the electric cars and devised a grooved wheel, the troller, so the car could accept electric current, at the same time reducing friction. The common term *trolley car* is derived from the word *troller*. Granville Woods patented more than sixty inventions, thirty-five of which were on electrical innovations, and fifteen of which dealt exclusively with electric railways.

Probably his greatest single achievement in this field was his "third rail" innovation described in U.S. patent 667,110, issued in 1901, titled "Electric Railway." This technology for supplying electricity to trains is used today by many subway and commuter railroad systems, both in this country and abroad. Just after 1900, Woods conceived an automatic air-brake system patented in 1902, assigned to the Westinghouse Air Brake company. Lyates Woods and S. E. Woods (likely Susie Elizabeth Woods, allegedly his wife) were listed as witnesses on the patent drawings. One year later, Lyates joined with his brother as coinventor on the electric railway apparatus, assigned to the General Electric Company (GE). The brothers continued joint inventorship up until 1907, having their patents variously assigned to the Westinghouse Air Brake Company or to GE.

Wizard Granville Woods was responsible for modernizing transportation that made it easier, cheaper, cleaner, and more efficient. Few minds matched the brilliance of Woods. His inventive genius was widespread, branching to a patent for an egg incubator that supplied a balanced humidity and even temperature and was the prototype of the present machines, which can hatch 50,000 eggs at a time. Also, he received patents for an amusement device, a galvanic battery, and an automatic circuit-breaking apparatus. The amusement contraption had a series of tracks for motorized vehicles, located at resorts, and the safety contact circuits.

Granville Woods was born on April 23, 1856, a son of Tailer and Martha Woods. His death certificate identifies his place of birth as Australia even though other sources commonly give his origin at Columbus, Ohio.[5] He died of cerebral hemorrhage in New York City on January 30, 1910, in virtual poverty after protracted and costly legal battles. He is buried at St. Michael's Cemetery, Queens, New York City.[6] In 1974, both the White House and the state of Ohio saluted him posthumously for his brilliance as an inventor. City authorities named Public School 335 in Brooklyn, New York, for the esteemed Granville T. Woods.

The Atlanta Cotton States Exposition of 1895 featured Pullman-car porter Humphrey H. Reynolds's notion of a ventilator for railroad cars. Because of its popularity, his ideal screen to shut out cinders flying through car windows came to the attention of the Pullman Company, which adopted it after Reynolds explained the invention to the company's owner. However, the magnate ignored the patent claims, so Reynolds sued for infringement and netted a handsome $10,000 settlement.

The dedicated trainman Andrew Jackson Beard, born a slave on a Jefferson County farm in Alabama in 1849, was never formally taught to write, and this deficiency forced him to sign his papers with an "X." Freed at fifteen years of age by a family named Beard, he married at sixteen and supported his wife by farming near Birmingham. Beard tried operating a flour mill he built at Hardwicks, Alabama. The effort inspired him to invent various plows, one of which he sold for $4,000. He sold another plow for $5,200, then invested this money in the lucrative real estate business. Soon amassing $30,000, Beard moved in another inventive direction, developing and patenting a rotary steam engine. This concept prompted him to work in the rail yards. Tragic accidents of trainmen who earned wages by risking their lives to manually join rail cars as they came together inspired Beard, who lost a leg in a coupling mishap, to conceive a mechanism to join the cars auto-

G. T. WOODS.
ELECTRIC RAILWAY.

(Application filed Sept. 29, 1897. Renewed Oct. 15, 1898.)

(No Model.)

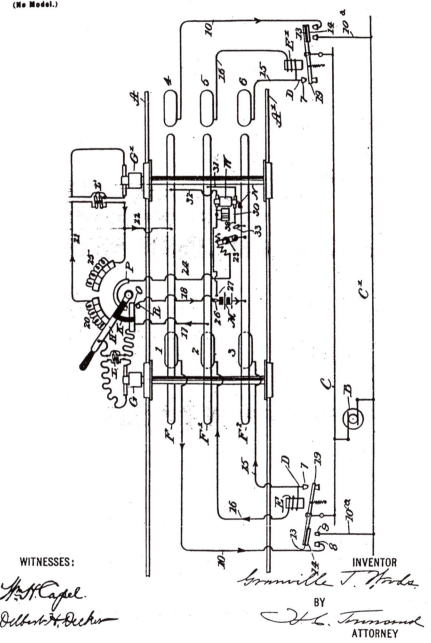

WITNESSES: INVENTOR

Wm H Capel.   Granville T. Woods.

Delbert H. Decker   BY

                                                   H. C. Townsend
                                                   ATTORNEY

Electric Railway, patented invention of Granville T. Woods.

matically. He was granted a patent on the car coupler just two months after filing the application in 1897. The device, called the "Jenny coupler," was sold by Beard to a firm in New York that year for $50,000. Beard died a wealthy man about 1921.[7]

The *Chicago Defender* in 1949 featured William Hunter Dammond (1874–1956) as a New York inventor who had made plans that would change the railroad industry.[8] The occasion was the Chicago Railroad Fair, and Dammond was a brilliant but ill-treated scientist. As the creator of the Dammond track circuit, the inventor conceived an outstanding means to prevent signal mishaps where electricity propelled trains (the complementing invention to the safer flanged wheel invented by another sable genius, Elbert R. Robinson). This was the only known way then to operate signals on the subway system. The U.S. Patent Office awarded him a patent in December 1903, titled simply "Signalling System."

Dammond worked for a railway system that owned lines running along the eastern seaboard from New York to Florida. Replacing manually controlled devices, Dammond's block signal system controlled things automatically on the sectional lines that ran from Manhattan to the nation's capital, the most heavily traveled corridor in the country, carrying the largest volume of passengers. In 1906, the inventor received a second patent on a safety system for operating railroads, similar to the conditions "clear," "caution," and "danger." With failure to receive adequate compensation for the knowledge and his refusal to teach rail experts the full working of the Dammond track circuit, or of a "metonymy of track circuit," Dammond never realized any reward and later was snubbed for his stance. A popular rumor circulated that his employers sent Dammond to England to stay long enough so that his patent rights could expire and come into the public domain, whereby anyone could make, use, or sell his inventions without legal reprisals.

Dammond was the first black graduate of the University of Pittsburgh. He died practically a pauper at age eighty-two on December 8, 1956, in Manhattan, New York. His nephew rather than his estranged son saved the genius from a pauper's burial.[9]

Chicago inventor Elbert R. "Doc" Robinson pioneered several of the finest inventions in the railroad industry. His clever inventions were on wide display at the 1907 Jamestown Negro Exhibit. He devised the flanged railway car wheel, an interlocking switch, and a track crossing, all useful on a system of street railways and steam trunk lines using steam or Diesel locomotives. His training and experience as a blacksmith and steelworker inspired him to make an inestimable contribution to railroading. "Doc" Robinson, as people popularly knew him, moved to Chicago after the 1893 World's Fair and found work with

No. 823,513.

823513

PATENTED JUNE 19, 1906.

W. H. DAMMOND.

SAFETY SYSTEM FOR OPERATING RAILROADS.

APPLICATION FILED FEB. 17, 1906.

2 SHEETS—SHEET 1.

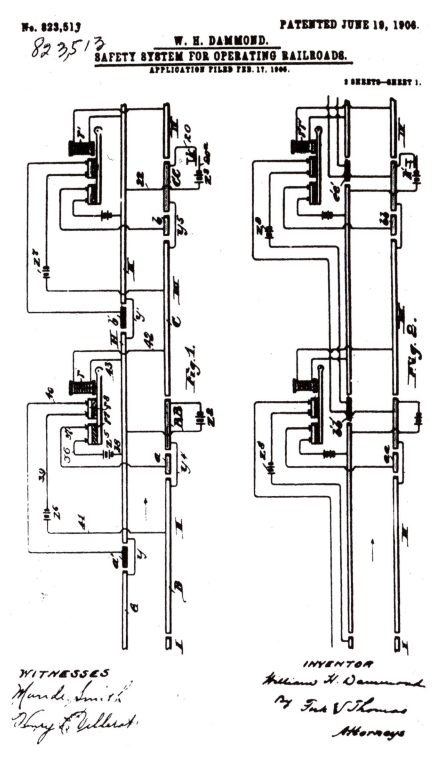

WITNESSES

Maude Smith

Henry F. Villerot.

INVENTOR

William H. Dammond

By Fred V. Thomas

Attorneys

Safety System for Operating Railroads, patented invention of William H. Dammond.

Railway Car Wheel and Track Crossing, patented inventions of Elbert R. Robinson.

the car-wheel-manufacturing facility in Pullman, Illinois.[10] There he patented his electric railway trolley, the first of several grants.

Robinson discovered that a mixture of a metal alloy and steel produced a lighter and cheaper product, and he received a patent on the composite casting. His most valuable and noteworthy conception, the composite involved a steel car wheel, so cast that it was perfectly round when it came out of the mold without being turned on the lathe, as happened with the standard wheel. Because of its retained hard surface, the wheel lasted five or six times the life of the ordinary wheel, which was difficult to maneuver and expensive. The track crossing had an extra tempered steel insertion where tracks intersected. This modification kept the crossing from wearing out so rapidly.[11]

Robinson's employers allegedly took possession of his ideas and the formula, which prompted a notorious lawsuit in the railroad industry. Robinson sued for $1,000,000, according to a 1949 edition of the *Chicago Defender*. After a supposed offer to settle for $300,000 that the inventor refused, it was rumored that the firm strung him along with paltry sums to drag out the case, which lingered for years in the court system. According to hearsay, Robinson would have become the world's wealthiest man if the rail company had paid him a penny for each of his formulated wheels. An organization gave money to support Robinson's suit, and its members, in return, were receiving all money transferred to him plus a pro rata allotment of the settlement; however, the lawyers netted the lion's share.[12]

"Doc" Robinson died a poor man in 1937. His last three grants, for a switch, a rail, and a cast-iron axle, were issued in 1907 and 1908. Subsequently, Robinson's heirs sued the Chicago Surface Lines for alleged violation of his patents. During the suit's twenty-five-year court life cycle, the family brought action against companies including the Ford Motor Company, the American Car Foundry Company, and the Chicago City Railway Company. The suits were eventually dropped or dismissed.[13]

FAVORITES

As time progressed, a variety of exhibition venues favored the black inventor. The Franklin Novel Institute in Philadelphia and the Agriculture Society Exhibition in Burlington, New Jersey, showcased the premier prizewinning patents of George M. Williams in 1885.[14] The New Orleans Cotton Centennial in 1884 and the Chicago World's Fair in 1893, along with the Southern Exposition in Atlanta in 1895, all exposed the great ingenuity of African American inventors. U.S. patent examiner Henry Baker uncovered inventions credited to blacks when interest in this ethnic group heightened.

As chief of the Department of Colored Exhibits for the upcoming New Orleans exposition, Blanche Kelso Bruce made an appeal to the Honorable Marcellus Gardner, who was a commissioner for the Interior Department, and requested patent artifacts of "colored men." In a letter he wrote:

Dear Sir:

Calling your attention to the fact that among the models representing the inventions of the Patent Office under your supervision at the World's Exposition, are some presented by colored men, and to the desirableness of having these models, designs and drawings placed where they will fairly represent the progress of this race in this scientific and industrial form, I respectfully request that you will take such steps as may be necessary to place said models, designs, etc, in the Dep't of Colored Exhibits, in the Exposition at New Orleans.[15]

Ten days later, Gardner, attaching a copy of Bruce's letter, wrote to the acting commissioner of patents, R. G. Dyrenforth, asking for clarity on the issue of custody:

Blanche K. Bruce, U.S.
Senator, 1875–1881.
From the Patricia Carter
Ives Sluby Collection.

Sir:

I have the honor to submit herewith a copy of a letter, addressed to me as Commissioner for the Interior Dept., for the World's Industrial and Cotton Exposition, New Orleans, La., and to request that I be furnished with such information as will enable me to reply thereto.

I would inform you, in this connection, that the models referred to were selected and forwarded to New Orleans, but, the question having been raised of the propriety of transferring them to the custody of persons not employe[e]s of the Patent Office, the placing of them in cases was deferred until a few weeks since.

They were arranged with other models forming a part of the Patent Office Exhibit.[16]

Dyrenforth was acting in place of the appointed commissioner, Benjamin Butterworth of Cincinnati, whom voters had just reelected to Congress. Bruce surely felt pleased at the success of his appeal. Born a slave in Virginia in 1841, Bruce organized and taught school in Hannibal, Missouri. After several political positions in Mississippi, he was elected to the U.S. Senate in 1875 and served in that legislative body until 1881. Afterward, he secured various political positions at Washington, D.C., and was a Howard University trustee. He died on March 17, 1898, and is interred at Woodlawn Cemetery in the nation's capital.[17]

Congressman, inventor, and former slave George Washington Murray (1853–1926) of South Carolina, on August 10, 1894, during the second session of the 53rd Congress, read the names of ninety-two black patentees and their inventions into the *Congressional Record* (curiously, the record does not list Jennings nor Blair, and it misidentifies Matzeliger as "Cuban"). In part, Murray passionately prefaces that "thirty or forty years ago our ability to even learn to read and write, or

M. A. CHERRY.
VELOCIPEDE.

No. 382,351.

Patented May 8, 1888.

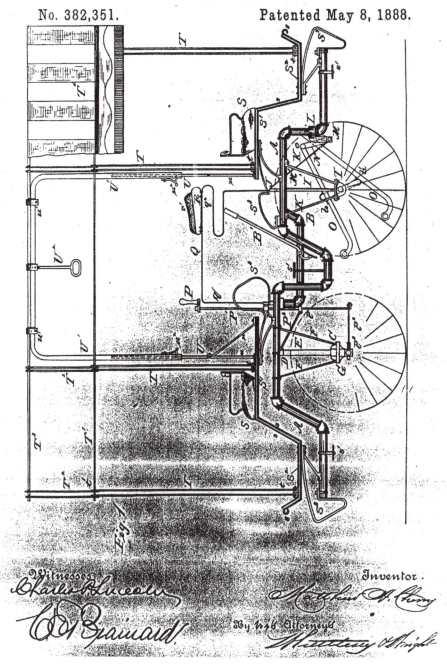

Velocipede, patented invention of Matthew A. Cherry.

J. LEE.
BREAD CRUMBING MACHINE.

No. 540,553.   Patented June 4. 1895.

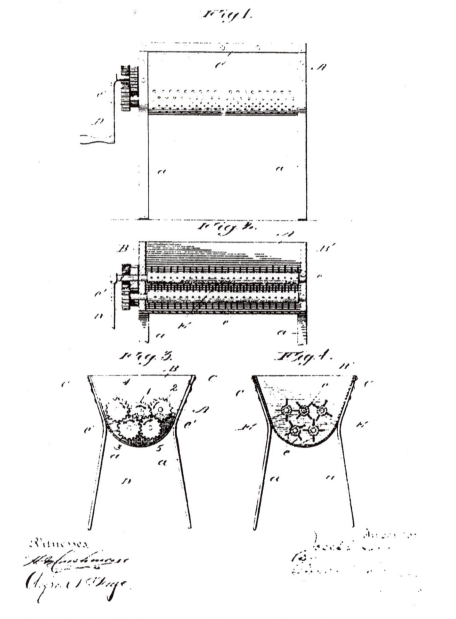

Bread Crumbing Machine, patented invention of Joseph Lee.

to learn ordinary arithmetic, was doubted . . . [There were] those who denied that we were a part of the Adamic creation, and assigned us a reason that we could not vie with the other members of the human family in producing what they produced, in making what they made, or in doing anything except the lowest order of manual labor. . . . [African Americans have] proven in almost every line that we are capable of doing what other people can do. . . . we will demonstrate to the satisfaction of everybody that we have made and are capable of making almost anything that other people can make or have made." Murray then announced, "I hold in my hand a statement . . . showing the inventions that have been made by colored men within the past few years."[18] The patents they took out were representative of everything produced at that time.

The roster of names, researched by Baker, listed Congressman Murray himself, who held eight patents on agricultural implements. The only African American in Congress from 1893 to 1897, Murray took long leaves of absence from his legislative duties, during which time he capitalized on his inventions. In the three-month period between April and June of 1894, Murray patented farm tools to cultivate, harvest, and fertilize southern crops.

Born near Rembert in Sumter County, South Carolina, Murray was orphaned in 1865. He became a teacher as a young man and at age twenty-one decided to attend South Carolina University, only to be expelled toward the end of Reconstruction. Afterward, Murray became a gentleman farmer and later enrolled at the State Normal Institute at Columbia. By 1888, Murray was chairman of the Sumter County Republican Committee and in 1890 became a customs inspector for the port of Charleston. Two years later, Murray was elected to a U.S. congressional seat from his legislative district. He took advantage of his position to fight against discrimination, continually delivering orations on the floor of the House of Representatives. After his congressional tenure, Murray moved his family to Chicago in 1905. A fighter for the realization of democratic and egalitarian ideals, Murray died on April 21, 1926, at the age of seventy-three and is buried in Lincoln Cemetery in Chicago.[19]

The Pennsylvania Exposition Society at Pittsburgh, around 1913, showcased the patented automated server of inventor James Doyle. Handy for restaurant, lunch-counter, and dining-room servers, the dispenser model, built at a cost of $2,000, received extensive attention from visitors and the press.[20]

Joint Resolution Designating March 27, 1988, as "National Black American Inventors Day"

Whereas inventions by black Americans range from items of vital importance to business and industry;

Whereas these inventions include the third rail system used in subways (1892), the radiator and steam furnace (1884), the traffic light (1923), the shoe lasting machine (1883), the gas mask (1914), the electric light bulb with a carbon filament (1881), the first practical refrigeration system for longhaul trucks (1942), the synchronous multiplex railway telegraph (1887), the lunar surface ultraviolet camera/spectrograph (1972), and the first working clock made in America (1753);

Whereas these inventions also include laborsaving devices such as the corn planter (1834), the cotton planter (1836), the hand corn shelling device (1884), the lawn mower (1899), the automatic lubricator for heavy machinery and trains (1872), and the railroad car coupler (1897);

Whereas many of these inventions revolutionized their respective industries;

Whereas, prior to the Civil War, many black Americans did not receive credit for their inventions because slaves could not receive patents and because masters often claimed credit for the inventions of their slaves;

Whereas the number of inventions that are indeed credited to black Americans is in the thousands;

Whereas the contributions of black American inventors have not received the national attention that they deserve:

Now, therefore, be it

Resolved by the Senate and House of Representatives of the United States of America in Congress assembled, That March 27, 1988, is designated as "National Black American Inventors Day" and the President is authorized and requested to issue a proclamation calling upon the people of the United States to observe the day with appropriate programs, ceremonies, and activities.

Source: Resolution introduced by Congressman Floyd Flake of New York City, U.S. House of Representatives, 100th Congress, First Session. Flake, an African American, coincidentally introduced this legislation nearly one hundred years after Congressman Murray's statement in Congress.

THE AMERICAN NEGRO EXHIBIT, PARIS, 1900

The International Exposition of 1900, held in Paris, France, displayed exemplary African American ingenuity. The exposition was a glorious introduction to the new century, and countries worldwide sent exhibits for display. The United States submitted a separate "Negro section" that the exhibit's special agent, Thomas J. Calloway, compiled.

Henry E. Baker, chronicler and patent examiner. From D. W. Culp, ed., *Twentieth-Century Negro Literature* (1902; Reprint, New York: Arno Press, 1969).

Its scene was set forth in "The American Negro at Paris," an article published in the *American Monthly Review of Reviews* and written by educator and founder of the *Crisis* magazine William E. B. Du Bois. In response to the U.S. Commission to the Paris Exposition, this was the first time the U.S. Patent Office methodically identified African American inventors. Henry Baker undertook the project to collect the data under the directive of the commissioner of patents. From his research, African Americans had patented 357 inventions by 1900. The display was indicative of black expertise in the mechanical, electrical, and chemical arts. Although many inventions in Baker's work credit coinventors, it is not readily ascertainable who they are. A team of inventors may comprise other ethnic groups besides African Americans, who often felt comfortable taking out patents in partnership with whites.

Baker patiently and painstakingly labored on two occasions to satisfy the pressing public inquiry for names of sable inventors. Official notice went out to patent attorneys, manufacturing establishments, newspaper editors, prominent persons, and inventors as well to collect "reliable data" for the Paris Exposition of 1900 and again for the 1913 Emancipation Exposition at Philadelphia. Baker sorted responses, most of them disheartening, and reported his conclusions in a voluminous collection of assembled patents. He gave an insightful account of the ordeal. Part of the effort to find black patentees involved correspondence with some 12,000 registered patent attorneys and agents "in this country who are licensed to prosecute applications for patents before the Patent Office."[21] It was a monumental task to uncover reliable statistics. There were two organized efforts to ferret out true information, one being the circular correspondence and the other the occasional visit to the patent office by the inventor, which left nothing to the imagination.

In his attempts to seek true information, Baker encountered racial bigotry, ignorance, and racism from the white community at large and especially from white lawyers and agents he contacted. He reported that "a leading newspaper in the city of Richmond, Virginia, made the bold statement that of the many thousands of patents annually granted by our government to the inventors of our country, 'not a single patent had ever been granted to a colored man.' " Amazed at attorneys, he remarked, "It is astonishing to have nearly 2,500 of them reply that they never heard of a colored inventor, and not a few of them add that they never expect to hear of one."[22] A practicing lawyer in Tennessee thought that the whole subject was a joke.

Baker was immensely successful in spite of seemingly grim circumstances. By 1913, the U.S. Patent Office had granted more than one million patents. Baker had discovered more than 1,200 "instances" of African American creative genius, but he "verified" only 800. He proclaimed, "We know that the colored man has accomplished something—indeed, a very great deal—in the field of invention, but it would be of the first importance to us now to know exactly what he has done."[23] More important, he felt that the commercial value of these inventions was of paramount importance to black inventors, but its full impact would never be known. Baker believed that the number of validated patents did not represent the full picture of those that had been granted because of uncertain records of patent attorneys and concluded that "the credit for these must perhaps forever lie hidden in the unbreakable silence of official records."[24] Some inventors also refused acknowledgment because they did not want the products of their creative genius recognized as coming from a minority, for they feared reprisals. Moreover, darker-hued inventors had applied to patent attorneys for help, but had been rebuffed for lack of funds. Accordingly, the inventors felt compelled to abandon their efforts to get patents.

After arduously gathering data that he expected would impress the publishers of science or social studies textbooks, Baker published his material in 1913 under the title *The Colored Inventor: A Record of Fifty Years.* The work represents the earliest and most comprehensive effort to uncover African American inventive genius. His list contains several erroneous dates and patent numbers, but this is of little consequence compared to the significance of the entire presentation. It was copied, reprinted, and extensively exploited after 1913, though Baker sold only a few copies of an effort that took enormous amounts of energy, time, patience, diligence, and perseverance.

Howard University is the caretaker of the massive compilation. Its Moorland-Spingarn Research Center proudly boasts in a circular that it has "the world's only copy of Baker's *Negro Patentees of the United States, 1834–1900*," one of its "most highly prized possessions," comprising patent drawings and specifications for awarded patents.

THE NEGRO EXHIBIT, JAMESTOWN, 1907

At the 1907 Jamestown Exposition, the Negro Exhibit featured evidence of the progress of African Americans, housed in the Negro Building. To show the skill of blacks as mechanics and inventors at the Jamestown Negro Exhibit, a department was set up to have mechanical devices, manufactures, and inventions by artisans of the minority group. Arthur C. Newman, the instructor in electricity and physics at Armstrong Manual Training School in the nation's capital, and Franklin N. Hilyer, a highly skilled trained assistant, were in charge of the department on the first floor. The total number of artifacts installed was a stupendous 9,926, submitted by artisans and students as well— then the largest display underscoring Negro attainment. The architectural plans of William Sidney Pittman of Washington, D.C., were accepted for the project. Pittman, who married the daughter of Booker T. Washington, was born in Montgomery, Alabama, and studied architecture and mechanical engineering at Tuskegee. He designed its Collis P. Huntington Memorial Building and later other structures in the South plus a few in the nation's capital and the couple's home in Fairmount Heights, a Maryland suburb of the capital city. Black contractors built the Negro Building, separated by some distance from other structures at the Jamestown Exposition. An auditorium on the second level was built to showcase African American musical and oratorical talent. The talent of the African American Lynchburg, Virginia, contracting firm of Bolling and Everett diligently followed the plans and specifications of the Negro Building of 1907, which called for a structure 213 feet long, 129 feet wide, and two stories high. The young black electrical contractor Arthur N. Johnson of Wytheville, Virginia, performed the highly technical task of wiring the huge structure, which required careful work.

This presentation of inventions and innovations reflected that minorities were not wanting in inventive spirit. Twelve hundred square feet were set aside for the display of these ingenious ideas and mechanical devices. About fifty models and the specifications and drawings of 341 U.S. patents issued to African Americans were exhibited.

The Negro Building, designed by Sidney Pittman.
In G. B. Jackson and D. W. Davis, *Industrial History of the Negro Race of the United States* (Richmond, Va.: Presses of The Virginia Press, 1908). From the Patricia Carter Ives Sluby Collection.

Cotton Planter, invention of Aiken C. Taylor.
In G. B. Jackson and D. W. Davis, *Industrial History of the Negro Race of the United States* (Richmond, Va.: Presses of The Virginia Press, 1908). From the Patricia Carter Ives Sluby Collection.

Inventions Listed in **The Industrial History,** *1908,* **by G. B. Jackson and**
D. W. Davis

Device	Inventor or Maker
Book or copy holder	B. T. Montgomery
Boat propeller	S. G. Crawford
Barber's sign [Design]	G.A.E. Banes
Cotton planter	Aiken C. Taylor
Coal and wood cabinet	Barton
Cigar maker's board (improved)	A. C. Cambridge
Chestnut gatherer	S. G. Crawford
Curtain support	Aiken C. Taylor
Duplex mouthpiece for telephone	Ira Ashe
Gun	Alfred McKnight
Horse over-boot	R. Coater
Horse over-shoe	William Hill
Hot air evaporator	Andrew F. Hilyer
Headlight	W. H. Montgomery
Harness buckle and strap	R. B. Benford
Incubator and bread raiser	G. F. Carr
Invalid's bed	A. C. Taylor
Musical clock	W. T. Davis

MINIATURE RAILROAD:

Block system	A. C. Newman
Trolley wheel	Elbert R. Robinson
Car fender	M. A. Cherry

Showing

Electric system	A. C. Newman
Spring seat for chair	A. B. Blackburn
Model battleship	W. W. Davis
Plough	E. Nelson
Plough and heel sweep (improved)	R. P. Rodgers
Patent models	U.S. Patent Office
Passenger register	William Lawrence
Ring puzzle	George Ellis
Track crossing and wheel	Elbert R. Robinson
Model steam engine	Eldridge Nichols
Wagon	J. W. Dorkins
Model battleship	Percy Smith
Model schooner	James Stanley
Model battleship	Willis Toliver
Horse shoe exhibit	John Showell
Horse shoe exhibit	Clarence Kittrell

Horse shoe exhibit	J. H. Stone
Engine and boiler	J. Moore
Pattern exhibit	G. A. Harrison

Three fine inventions by Aiken C. Taylor of Charleston, South Carolina were on display. He conceived a combined cotton planter and fertilizer distributor, an extension stepladder, and handy bedsprings that the turning of a lever could convert into a chair.

Philip B. Williams of Washington, D.C., patented an invention of an electric switch for a rail car that the operator controlled from within. This provided the motorman or engineer with a unit to move the vehicle at his discretion while in motion. A model actually operated at the Negro Exhibit.

A. C. Newman's displayed invention represented a block system for railroads, which operated by alternating currents. When two trains were in the same block at the identical time, red lights showed in the cabs of both engines. The apparatus was inexpensive and effective.

Most of the patent information for the Jamestown Negro Exhibit probably came from Baker's research, while the remainder apparently came from canvassing the African American national community. Colonel Giles B. Jackson (1873–1924), a former slave, businessman, confidant, and Virginia's early premier black attorney, conceived the Negro Exhibit. He organized the Negro Development and Exposition Company of the United States of America to promote the enormous undertaking and was appointed the exhibit's director general. The chairman of the executive committee was Thomas J. Calloway, of 1900 Paris Exposition fame, who was assisted by inventor Andrew F. Hilyer, the secretary-treasurer. Jackson appealed to the U.S. Congress for an appropriation of $1,200,000 and received $100,000 toward the enterprise, which needed additional funds to supplement the allocation.[25] After meeting all demands, the Negro Exhibit was realized.

President Theodore Roosevelt scheduled a trip to Virginia in 1907 to participate in the Georgia-day celebration at the exposition and to visit the Negro Exhibit as well on June 10. After viewing the collection with Mrs. Roosevelt, the president paid great tribute to Colonel Jackson, saying:

> My friend, I can simply say one word of greeting, it is a great pleasure to be here to go through this magnificent building and to see the unmistakable evidences of progress you are making, as shown by the exhibits I find here. I congratulate you upon it, may good luck be with you. Those who have argued from the outset that a high grade exposition of what the Negro has accomplished in his three centuries of struggle and achievement would go

Giles B. Jackson, Director General, Negro Development and Exposition Company, Jamestown, 1907.
From the Patricia Carter Ives Sluby Collection.

far to vindicate his title to the full panoply of citizenship, have unquestionably won their case.[26]

Roosevelt was ever the skilled politician, and his words were powerful and seductive. Thrilled after listening to the leader of their country, the crowd gave thunderous applause. In particular, Jackson and his colleagues beamed with unabashed pleasure at the success of their huge, arduous venture.

Because the Negro Exhibit was viewed by less than 1 percent of the race during the exhibit's three-month tenure, Jackson felt that most of his race should see evidence of their progress and the fruit of their labors in its three centuries of steady upward mobility. He campaigned diligently to have the Negro Exhibit moved to a permanent location where the public would know it as a "National Museum for Colored People." With the concept well thought out, Jackson approached city,

The Negro Development and Exposition Company of the United States of America, organizer of the Negro Exhibit at Jamestown, 1907.
From the Patricia Carter Ives Sluby Collection.

True Reformers Savings Bank exhibit, Jamestown, 1907.
In G. B. Jackson and D. W. Davis, *Industrial History of the Negro Race of the United States* (Richmond, Va.: Presses of The Virginia Press, 1908). From the Patricia Carter Ives Sluby Collection.

state, and federal authorities. However, he ran into political opposition and, sadly, abandoned the idea. Other examples of the ongoing trend of exposing black versatility in intellectual property were showcased at the Negro National Fair in 1908 in Mobile, Alabama, the Chicago Jubilee Exposition in 1915, and Jackson's later brainchild in Richmond, the Second National Negro Exposition in 1915.

People of color hoped that they were free of oppression, hatred, intolerance, bigotry, and other inequities, but this was not true, as they quickly learned. The deteriorating relations between blacks and whites in the country had been discussed for decades, especially by Frederick Douglass. Even though a number of inventors indeed pressed forward to protect their ideas, most of them, in all likelihood, were too fearful to be known independently. An alliance with a white person seemed a safe haven.

5

ONWARD, SOLDIERS OF FORTUNE

For what man knoweth the things of a man,
save the spirit of man which is in him?

1 Corinthians 2:11

SPRINGING INTO ACTION

At times of great military conflicts, creative thinkers sprang into action, producing a flurry of inventions. Americans hailed the banner of patriotism and sweated at inventive thought to develop devices for defense of their land. Various technologies surfaced, feeding the imagination of great minds. At the beginning of the last century, a special steel alloy, the radiotelephone, and the powered airplane were invented. In the following decades, Albert Einstein developed the theory of relativity and other theories through 1955. In 1909, the existence of electrons was confirmed, and the gun silencer was patented. Atomic theory and the understanding of atomic structure were basic scientific discoveries that fueled more developments for the defense of our nation.

Prior to World War I, patents were issued on a seaplane, the gyrocompass, ductile tungsten, the mercury vapor lamp, and the amplified telephone, along with cracked gasoline, the X-ray, the Browning gun, and the depth bomb, to list a few. African Americans in the decades of the 1900s contributed significantly toward the national defense and the quality of everyday life with inventions, concepts, and discoveries. During World War I, black combat troops were assigned for the most part to the French, rather than to American armies. Connected with the French army at the front, the 369th, 370th, and 371st Infantry

Garrett A. Morgan.
Courtesy of the Moorland-
Spingarn Research Center,
Howard University.

Regiments fought against the Germans. More than two hundred African American men received the Legion of Honor for outstanding bravery in action in 1918. Almost 200,000 black troops experienced action in France, where most served as stevedores, cooks, and laborers.

An outstanding inventor, Garrett Augustus Morgan (1877–1963) demonstrated diversified inventive genius during these early years of the twentieth century. Like many of his creative predecessors, he received very little formal training, having to look for work to sustain himself as a teenager in his native state of Kentucky. At age fourteen, Morgan went to Ohio and for four years worked in Cincinnati as a handyman and then as a machine worker in Cleveland, where he became talented as a sewing-machine adjuster for a clothier and eventually skilled at repairing mechanical devices.

Around 1907, Morgan opened an establishment that sold and fixed sewing machines. Two years later, he opened a large tailoring shop. Sewing needles at that time needed constant polishing to prevent certain fabrics, especially woolens, from scorching by friction heat as the needle moved rapidly through the fabric. Morgan began experimenting on a method to solve the problem and, quite accidentally, found a process for straightening human hair. Using various needle-polishing ingredients, he discovered that the mixture unwrinkled the fibers on the fur cloth used to wipe the needles.

A Few Successful Inventors

Joseph C. Bagley of Beloit, Alabama, invented a combination shovel torch and match tender. H. Robinson of Paris, Kentucky, invented and patented "The Robinson Mechanical Book," a dictionary designed to spell and define any word in the language by turning a crank. Allen Enon of Nashville, Tennessee, fashioned a rat trap from old baling wire, which he patented and for which he received $25,000. Charles E. Holmes of Newark, New Jersey, invented a new type oil burner. G. W. Turner of Washington, D.C., has been granted a patent for an improvement on incandescent light bulbs, so that the glass bulb can be used if broken. Churchill White of Junction, Kentucky, invented a new power hemp braking machine, which may revolutionize the hemp breaking business. Neola Moore of Kansas City, Kansas, patented a wheel design to be a perfection of the spring system upon which motor car engineers have been working for years. James A. Whittaker of Boston, Massachusetts, invented an engineering brake for automobiles.

Source: The Negro in Chicago, 1779–1927 (Chicago: Washington Intercollegiate Club of Chicago), vol. 1, p. 99.

Morgan recognized the potential value of his discovery and decided to introduce his hair-straightening cream to the public. In 1913, he established the G. A. Morgan Hair Refining Company that manufactured the first human hair straightener. The company quickly became a thriving business. Morgan prospered from his keen business sense, marketing also a black hair oil stain for men and a curved-tooth iron comb he invented in 1910 for women.

In 1912, Morgan developed another invention, for which he received a patent in 1914. His ingenious device protected rescuers, especially firemen, from breathing smoke and poisonous gas when entering dangerous rooms. The patent was titled "Breathing Device." Later known as a gas mask, the device was a gas inhalator. Its first operation received immense publicity when it was used by the inventor and his brother to rescue men trapped by an explosion in the gas- and smoke-filled Cleveland Water Works Tunnel under Lake Erie. Morgan was honored by the city of Cleveland and the International Association of Fire Engineers for his heroic efforts in saving the lives of several workers. An improved gas mask was purchased by the U.S. Army and was used extensively by troops during World War I and in following wars.

Morgan was constantly thinking of new ideas. He had witnessed a severe accident involving a horse with carriage and an automobile at an intersection. Morgan visualized that it was a good idea to use illuminated colored lights, visible during the day and at night, to control vehicular traffic at intersections, the first of such devices. He produced a three-way electric traffic signal that was awarded a U.S. patent in 1923 and later British and Canadian patents. He sold the rights to this invention to the General Electric Company for $40,000.[1]

Morgan, a man of many talents with a fertile mind, further devised a woman's hat fastener, a round belt fastener, and a friction drive clutch. Also, Morgan founded a newspaper, originally named the *Cleveland Call*, which later merged with the *Post* to become the *Call and Post*. He received many medals and national honors for his inventive efforts. Born on March 4, 1877, in Paris, Kentucky, to Sidney and Elizabeth Morgan, Morgan died after several years of illness on July 27, 1963, at age eighty-six in Cleveland, Ohio.[2]

In the second decade of the 1900s, the great Booker T. Washington died. Masses of Americans of color migrated to the North and to the Midwest and found menial work in factories. Apprehension about lynch mobs, destruction of the cotton crop from the Mississippi Delta floods, novel labor-saving machinery for planting and picking cotton, and the rapid spread of the boll weevil, an insect destructive to cotton, were compelling reasons to relocate from the Deep South. African Americans were farming at their peak when the dreaded insect struck. One-third of all southern farmers were black. In South Carolina and Mississippi, sable farmers outnumbered white farmers. The exodus from farm to urban sites, along with the military draft for defense of the nation at the onset of the U.S. entry into World War I in 1917, created a severe southern labor shortage that carried through to the next world war. Fleeing the South, African Americans from the rural areas met the demand of northern industries for unskilled laborers in the first half of the twentieth century, leaving the nation in dire need of labor in the production of food that was critical during the war conflicts. To study the problem and to help relieve the shortage, the federal government created a short-lived Department of Labor advisory bureau of Negro economics headed by economics professor George Edmund Haynes. Later, years after the war, the Department of Labor

G. A. MORGAN.
BREATHING DEVICE.
APPLICATION FILED AUG. 19, 1912.

1,113,675.

Patented Oct. 13, 1914.
2 SHEETS—SHEET 1.

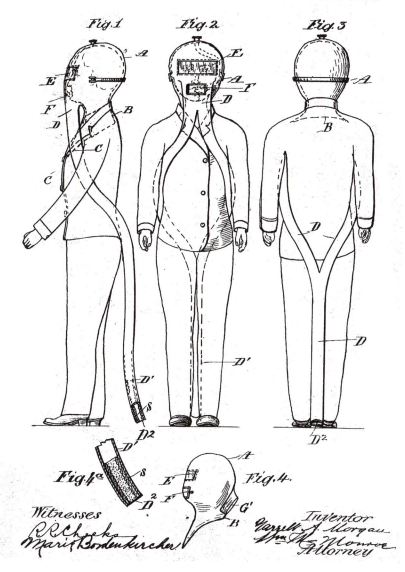

Breathing Apparatus (early type of gas mask), patented invention of Garrett A. Morgan.

Nov. 20, 1923.

G. A. MORGAN

TRAFFIC SIGNAL

Filed Feb. 27. 1922

1,475,024

2 Sheets—Sheet 1

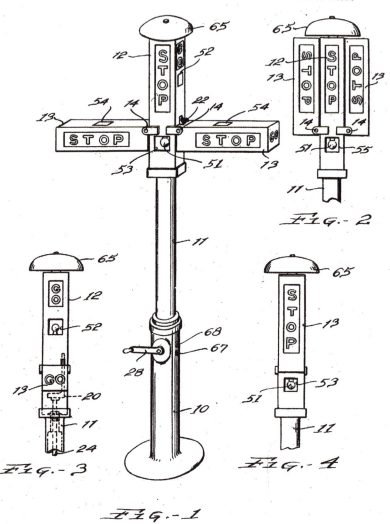

FIG.-2

FIG.-3

FIG.-4

FIG.-1

INVENTOR
Garrett A. Morgan,
By Baker & Macklin,
ATTORNEYS

Three-Way Traffic Signal, patented invention of Garrett A. Morgan.

George Washington Carver.
Courtesy of the Moorland-Spingarn Research Center, Howard University.

cited the departure of more than 500,000 African Americans from the South in a single twelve-month period. By the end of World War II, more than one million African Americans had fled the oppressive conditions.

The brilliant scientist and inventor George Washington Carver (1861?–1943), director of agriculture at Tuskegee from 1896 to 1943, worked unceasingly to aid southern agriculture in providing food for the country. He discovered a farming method that shifted southern farming of the risky cotton crop to a crop-rotation program that revitalized the decaying agriculture during this tumultuous period. In John Hope Franklin's speech "The Gift of Service," delivered at the enshrinement ceremony of George Washington Carver into the Hall of Fame for Great Americans in 1977, he remarked, in part:

> For a half-century following the Civil War the South groped to find its way. As it turned to industry and, for the first time, joined the mainstream of American economic life, it turned its back on the agricultural way of life that had always been the source of its strength and growth and on the masses of the people who, alas, remained on the farm. Then came George W. Carver who provided oil for the lamps by which average Southerners, black

and white, could see how to work themselves out of the corner into which staple-crop agriculture had painted then. He lighted the way by emancipating them from their dependence on cotton and tobacco and by showing them that peanuts, sweet potatoes and soybeans were at last as honorable and perhaps even more profitable than some traditional crops. In capturing the imagination of Southerners by providing them with many alternatives, he complemented the resources of the region by the resources of its residents.[3]

The force behind Carver's inventiveness was his determination to move southern agriculture away from cotton, which he perceived to be a risky crop and one that drained nutrients from the soil. He began experimentation with other crops that might have an affinity for southern soil, focusing on the peanut, the soybean, and the sweet potato. He was recognized for his work, which transformed southern agriculture from a single-crop economy based on cotton to a diversified one that did not deplete the land. He subsequently developed more than 300 uses for the peanut, 118 for the sweet potato, and did work with soybeans, pecans, goldenrod, edible grass, and pulp as alternative crops and agriculture products. As a consummate chemist, Carver synthesized organic dyes from the soils of Macon County, Georgia, superior to those imported from Germany.

For years it was incorrectly believed and published that George Washington Carver never received any patents. Carver did, in fact, secure three U.S. patent grants, the first on January 6, 1925, for a cosmetic and process of making it, and the second the same year on June 9, for a process of making paints and stains. The last patent was for another process of making paints and stains, issued June 14, 1927.

How and why Carver initially took the steps to use the patent system for protection of a few of his inventions is unknown. Perhaps others, more aware of the advantages of protecting some of his creativity, influenced him. Perhaps, too, specialists in the patent field solicited and encouraged him to use the system, no doubt mostly to their advantage, because Carver was a prolific inventor and they would benefit from fees as his legal representative.

His granted patents did not, and still do not, conflict with the widely held belief that Carver never cared for great wealth. Records do not reveal that he used the patents to make money. Obviously, Carver cared nothing for their value once the patents were issued, for he may have chosen several avenues. One, Carver might have sold his patents to someone; two, he could have licensed his patents to interested parties and received royalties; three, he may have assigned part or all of his patent rights to Tuskegee, the institution that courted him and enjoyed his intellect. Tuskegee, in turn, could have marketed the proc-

UNITED STATES PATENT OFFICE.

GEORGE W. CARVER, OF TUSKEGEE, ALABAMA.

PAINT AND STAIN AND PROCESS OF PRODUCING THE SAME.

No Drawing.   Application filed June 13, 1923.   Serial No. 645,199.

To all whom it may concern:

Be it known that I, GEORGE W. CARVER, a citizen of the United States, residing at Tuskegee, in the county of Macon and State of Alabama, have invented certain new and useful Improvements in Paints and Stains and Processes of Producing the Same, of which the following is a specification.

The invention relates to paints and stains, and has as an object the provision of a process for producing paints and stains from clays. Clays are found in many sections of the country of a variety of colors, and by a proper choice of color there may be produced by the process of the invention a large variety of colors of pigments, fillers and stains for treating wood or other materials.

To carry out the process of the invention the desired clay having a high percentage of iron is treated by any of the well known processes for refining the same and reducing it to a finely divided condition. A desirable composition for a clay to be treated by the process of the present invention is 5.6% peroxide of iron and 16.7% aluminum.

While a clay testing as above described and substantially free from lime or any similar alkali is suitable for the carrying out of the process, yet a higher iron content will vary the effect only by improving the result.

To reduce the clay to a gelatinous condition the same is treated with acid. For this purpose taking as a basis a quantity of 25 pounds of clay free from sand or other objectionable substances, 25 pounds of commercial sulphuric acid and 25 pounds commercial hydrochloric acid may be added to the clay, with three pounds of clean scrap iron of any kind, iron turnings being a desirable form for the iron. The clay and iron are put into an acid-proof vessel which is capable of withstanding heat, as for instance a porcelain vessel. The acids are added with enough water to make a thin paste. The substance is then boiled slowly, with frequent stirring, until the iron is dissolved, and the whole mass assumes a uniform color. Water free from alkali is then added sufficient to substantially double the volume, when the solution is well stirred and allowed to settle for about five minutes, for the purpose of settlement of coarser portions. The material remaining in suspension with the liquid is then decanted into shallow acid-proof vessels and the remaining coarse and insoluble material is thrown away.

The material thus secured is utilized as a base for subsequent steps, the nature of which, as well as the nature of the clay first taken for treatment may be chosen to vary the color of the resultant products.

As a variation of the above process the nitric acid may be added with the sulphuric and hydrochloric, but it is found that slightly inferior results are thus obtained. Moreover copperas may be substituted for the scrap iron with, however, probably not such fine results.

For use as a wood filler or stain, clay of a desired color may be treated with the acid as above described, and the thus secured gelatinous clay is found to strike into the wood fiber and to produce an exceedingly smooth surface, giving a color thereto dependent upon the color of clay chosen for treatment, thereby acting as a filler and stain with the single application. It is found that a filler made as thus described becomes very hard when dry and enables the wood to take a high polish. Moreover specimens of wood which have been thus treated are found, after twenty years, to be brighter and more beautiful than when first treated. For this use the iron scrap may be omitted if desired.

The material thus described as a compound filler and stain, may be dried and mixed with linseed oil or its equivalent as a pigment to provide a paint. If desired to be darkened to a slight extent some good grade of carbon or lamp black may be added.

When the above acid treatment is carried out utilizing a micaceous clay of the variety of shades which occur in the Southern States a sheen results that has not to my knowledge been secured by heretofore used artificial mixtures.

I claim:

1. The process of producing pigment or the like which comprises boiling clay and metallic iron with acid and separating the coarser particles therefrom.

2. The process of producing pigments or the like which comprises boiling a mixture of clay and scrap iron with a mixture of sulphuric and hydrochloric acid, and separating the coarser particles therefrom, the color of clay utilized being chosen in accordance with the color desired in the finished product.

GEORGE W. CARVER.

Paint and Stain and Process of Producing the Same, patented invention of George W. Carver, first African American inducted into the National Inventors Hall of Fame, Akron, Ohio, 1990.

esses and products, assuming, of course, that it would capitalize on its investment. One can safely assume that Carver had no wish to pursue these possibilities.

Born a slave about 1861 on a plantation near Diamond Grove, Missouri, Carver was the property of Moses Carver, a farmer in Newton County in the southwestern part of the state. He was kidnapped and then recovered by his owner, who raised George and his brother James after the Civil War. He learned a basic education in a one-room schoolhouse and then excelled in high school in Kansas.

Denied admission to church-supported Highland University because of his race, Carver in his late twenties finally succeeded in his quest for education. In 1890, he began his college education by studying art at Simpson College in Indianola, Iowa, but transferred to the Iowa State Agricultural College at Ames, earning his B.S. degree in 1894. He had a passion for painting and plants, but concentrated on mycology because of his hobby, collecting plant fungi. Two years later, he obtained an M.S. degree in agriculture. Afterward, in the fall of 1896, Carver accepted the positions of a teacher of natural sciences and head of agricultural research at Tuskegee Institute under the leadership of Booker T. Washington.[4]

He received the prestigious Spingarn Medal in 1923 from the National Association for the Advancement of Colored People. Institutions conferred many honorary degrees upon Carver, and he obtained the Franklin Delano Roosevelt Medal in 1939 "for distinguished research in agricultural chemistry." Also, he spoke before congressional leaders in Washington. Carver died at Tuskegee on January 5, 1943, and was buried on the grounds of Tuskegee Institute next to Booker T. Washington.[5]

The U.S. Postal Service issued a commemorative George Washington Carver postage stamp on January 5, 1948, and the U.S. Congress in 1953 enacted legislation to establish the George Washington Carver National Monument, now at his birth site in Missouri. Many public schools across the country carry Carver's name. Carver was the first African American inducted into the National Inventors Hall of Fame at Akron, Ohio, in 1990.

WAVE OF INNOVATIVE SPIRIT

Black inventors surfaced in quick succession between the great world conflicts. Often, success for the inventor has come from individual performance and lots of luck. Many are ordinary people who have a love for developing ideas, some of which became assets to merchant suppliers of goods. A few years before World War I, to help improve the routine humdrum of daily life, Boston Clay of Muscatine, Iowa, enhanced machines that made buttons and received proprietary rights on the apparatus in 1912. Inventor Henry H. Dyer of Massachusetts devised an improved pipe and cigar holder to cool the smoke and to collect the nicotine from the tobacco, patented in 1914.

In 1905, newspaperman Robert A. Pelham (1859–1943) received his grant for inventing a pasting apparatus and in 1913 developed a tallying machine. Professional dollhouse maker James W. Butcher (1875–1950) designed a truck and clamp, protected by a 1912 patent. Butcher, born in Washington, D.C., graduated from the famed M Street High School, where he marched in the select cadet corps that participated in President Grover Cleveland's second inaugural parade. He briefly sought a medical degree at Howard University, but a short loss of vision forced Butcher to choose another occupation. After retirement from designing covers for printing manuals at the Government Printing Office, Butcher designed and built dollhouses sold at premier local and out-of-state department stores. However, he failed to get federal protection for his folding desk, another of his inventions.[6]

Washingtonian Charles H. Carter obtained a patent in 1921 for an automatic fish cleaner designed to remove scales in addition to easy slicing and cleaning of the seafood under hygienic conditions. Carter spent time working along the Chesapeake Bay before employment as a U.S. Internal Revenue Service assessor in local Virginia environs.

After devising a timing mechanism, Charles Fred White secured a patent grant on the invention in 1912. Howard University law school graduate Albert P. Albert of New Orleans, Louisiana, was federally rewarded for his invention of a cotton-picking apparatus also in 1912. After successfully petitioning an unfavorable determination of his second cotton-picking apparatus invention, Albert was awarded the coveted grant.

Food inventor Oscar C. Carter was the black headwaiter of the Seminole Club in Jacksonville, Florida, who formulated a new type of sauce around the early 1900s that was favored by the famous Wall Street speculator Jesse Livermore. At a luncheon there, the speculator issued Carter a sizeable check to place the concoction, known as the Oscar Carter Sauce, on the market. Carter wanted to duplicate the success of the famous "Oscar of Waldorf" (who rose to fame by his own sauce) and possessed a hothouse where he grew some of the ingredients to make his sauce.[7]

Inventor Samuel J. Hines was inspired to protect his life-preserver invention with a patent in 1915. Eighteen years later he patented a lawn-mower attachment. Originator Walter H. Sammons developed a special comb, patented in 1920.

Many discoverers acquired multiple patents on diverse inventions.

Walter McClennan was mechanically inclined and secured patents on an automatic railway car, an actuating mechanism for the car door, and a coin device in the early 1920s. Chemist Jay H. Montgomery was a joint inventor who developed and patented a food product of honey and butter, then shifted his interest to aviation, individually acquiring a patent on an aeroplane aerofoil wing. Prolific innovator Samuel Moore conceived a variety of headlights and patented them between 1926 and 1928. A year later he patented a whimsical hobby horse and then, in 1935, he developed a fuel valve lock. Hassell D. Robinson developed an interest in traffic signals and designed a casing for them, then patented a type of automobile traffic signal.

Reverend Benjamin F. Thornton conceived two unique mechanisms for the telephone. While in the employ of his boss, Thornton often had to receive and to take messages over the telephone. Due to the sheer volume of note taking, he decided that there was a better way to handle the situation. In 1931, Thornton was issued a patent for an apparatus for automatically recording telephonic messages and a year afterward received a patent for a device that automatically transmitted messages over a telephone line.

In 1925, Clifton M. Ingram of Oklahoma was granted two patents the same year, one for a railroad-crossing flag and the other for a well-drilling tool. Inventor Charles M. Banks got a patent for a jack and another one for a release valve.

African Americans initiated advancements in aviation at its early stage of development. John F. Pickering of Gonaives, Haiti, West Indies, patented a dirigible-type airship three years before Orville and Wilbur Wright received intellectual property rights on their flying machine with a motor. Innovator Oscar R. Cassell successfully secured a grant in 1912 for a flying machine that utilized the buoying effect of a gas and the supporting effect of air as well. The contrivance of John E. McWorter of St. Louis, Missouri, met full patent requirements. He invented a flying contraption that "may ascend vertically from the ground," having propelling and sustaining wings with large blade surfaces.

Inventor James Sloan Adams was rewarded for his propelling means for aeroplanes in 1920, and the colorful Trinidadian Hubert Fauntleroy Julian (1897–1983), one of the earliest black aviators, known as "the Black Eagle," gained a patent in 1921 for an airplane safety appliance. Four years afterward, William Hale of Litwar, West Virginia, secured his grant for an improvement in aeroplanes whereby a type of helicopter could be made to hover, ascend, and descend vertically, as well as be propelled horizontally. According to patent attorney Charles E. Smith of North Carolina, Herman L. Grimes of California secured protection for his folding-wing aircraft in 1938.

Hubert F. Julian, *dark suit*, greeting friends.
From the IOKTS Archives, Courtesy of the National Archives.

In 1940, Leroy R. Posey, a professor of mathematics at Southern University in Scotlandville, Louisiana, received a patent on a combination slide board, an educational tool for instructing number facts and fundamental functions of mathematics. Posey composed a teacher's manual, which accompanied the mathematical device and gave instructions for its use and operation. The novel slide board was used with any text in arithmetic or with books handling the teaching of arithmetic. Due to his accomplishment, the American Association of Inventors received Posey into its membership.

Houston engineer, aviator, and inventor Frank C. Mann was an extraordinary individual. He had a keen sense for aviation and mechanics and met the enigmatic, eccentric Howard Hughes in his teen years when he was employed as an airplane mechanic. During his fifty-year

The Julian Flight Committee

requests the pleasure of your company at

a testimonial banquet in honor of

Col. Hubert Julian

the "Black Eagle"

in the

Little Theatre of the Y. M. C. A.

180 West 135th Street

Armistice Night, November 11, 1933

at 8 P. M.

Committee

Dr. Godfrey Nurse, Chairman
Judge James Watson
Mrs. Susan Meyers
Lemuel Foster
Geraldine Dismond
Charges d'affaires

Informal

M——

Mr. James Green

Testimonial banquet in honor of
Col. Hubert Julian

Invitation from Colonel Hubert F. Julian to James [John W.] Green[e], [Jr.], aviation pioneer and contemporary of Julian.
From the Patricia Carter Ives Sluby Collection.

friendship with Hughes and stints at Hughes Aircraft Company, Mann was involved with the design of the famous huge *Spruce Goose* wooden seaplane. His labor was kept secret because white engineers would not have worked for Hughes had they known about Mann's ingenuity. He died at age eighty-four on November 22, 1992.[8]

These names attest to the amazing ingenuity and fortitude of these persons who lived in a debilitating period for people of color. Race relations were poor. In spite of this bleakness, African Americans of creative skill were determined, industrious, and resourceful. The complete story of how they funded their inventions or how they paid for their protection can only be surmised. Certainly they wanted a return on their precious investment. Luckily a corps of African American geniuses worked as federal employees on special teams, as corporate personnel in special laboratories, or as scientists researching at institutions.

PLASMA FOR BRITAIN

During the early years of World War II, British troops critically needed blood transfusions. A "Plasma for Britain Project" was initiated in 1940 at eight New York City hospitals. The project's medical director and liaison officer at Presbyterian Hospital in New York City was Dr. Charles Richard Drew, the brilliant physician and researcher whose successful research modified and improved former mechanical methods used to mass-produce the plasma critically needed by the British troops. His innovative research on blood preservation and his achievements in the enormous production of blood plasma led to the formation of blood banks of stored blood plasma.

The discovery of plasma processing by Drew is monumentally significant because the number of lives saved as a direct result of his research is incalculable. In recent years, countless victims of automobile accidents have received emergency blood plasma treatment at the scene from the quick response of specially trained shock trauma technicians. This "within-minutes" emergency treatment has helped save their lives.

Charles Richard Drew was born on June 3, 1904, in Washington, D.C., the eldest of five children. His parents, Richard Thomas and Nora Burrell Drew, were of modest means, yet maintained a virtuous and dignified livelihood for their family. To provide income for his education and to fulfill his dream of becoming a medical doctor, Charles supplemented his parents' income by taking odd jobs. He attended Dunbar High School and exhibited great skill in athletics. Drew graduated with honors in 1922, then entered Amherst College, where he set an impressive athletic record during the next four years. To

Charles R. Drew.
From the Patricia Carter
Ives Sluby Collection.

raise the money for medical school, Drew worked for two years at Morgan State College (now Morgan State University) as the athletic director and a teacher of biology and chemistry. Afterwards, he was admitted to McGill University in Montreal, Canada, and graduated doctor of medicine and master of surgery, finishing second in a class of 137 students. There he received the Julius Rosenwald Fellowship, won the annual prize in neuroanatomy, and set track records that remained unbroken for several years.[9]

At McGill, Drew met an English doctor, John Beattie, who encouraged him to work on problems associated with blood transfusion. For many years in medicine, it had been the custom to inject donated blood into a patient's veins within a few minutes or hours after the blood was taken from the donor. If this was not done promptly, the blood quickly deteriorated unless it was properly preserved. Drew went into intensive research on the situation, seeking all information on the subject. He had a flair for detail and organization—a trait that became his hallmark and nurtured his creative talent.

In 1938, after teaching stints in pathology and surgery at Howard University and work at Freedman's Hospital, Drew did a residency in surgery at Presbyterian Hospital while he was General Education Board Fellow at Columbia University, where he received the doctor of medical science in 1940. He wrote a brilliant thesis titled "Banked Blood" that cast him as a pioneer. As a protégé of Dr. John Scudder, an assistant professor of clinical surgery at Columbia, Drew worked on Scudder's team, which was studying his particular interest, fluid balance, blood chemistry, and blood transfusion, especially the associated condition of surgical shock. Shock, common in cases involving severe wounds, may also occur after surgery where a patient loses a large amount of blood.

In February 1941, Charles Richard Drew was selected as the first director of the American Red Cross Blood Bank in New York City. In spite of Drew's years of research devoted to blood preservation and his credited accomplishments in that field, he never received a patent, as is commonly cited. However, Drew's professor, John Scudder, patented an apparatus for preserving blood in 1942. This device comprised a container that had two reservoirs. In the process of storing blood, the liquid plasma was retained in the top section, while blood-cell content was stored in the bottom reservoir. On October 13, 1942, Scudder assigned the entire title and interest in the invention to Charles Drew:

WHEREAS, JOHN SCUDDER, of New York, County and State of New York, . . . as ASSIGNOR, has invented certain improvements in Method of and Apparatus for Preserving Blood, for which he has made, on April 1, 1939, application . . . for letters patent of the United States and is desirous of assigning the entire right, title and interest in and to the inventions of and said application and any patent which may issue thereon, and

WHEREAS, CHARLES R. DREW of Howard University, Washington, D.C., . . . as ASSIGNEE, is desirous of obtaining the entire rights, title and interest in and to the inventions of and said application and any patent which may issue thereon.

NOW, THEREFORE, in consideration of One Dollar ($1.00) each to the other in hand paid, receipt of which is hereby acknowledged, and of other good and valuable consideration, it is mutually agreed.[10]

Thus Charles Drew became the legal owner of the blood-preservation apparatus that had been invented and then patented by Scudder. In the assignment document, Drew requested that any monies received from the use or sale of the device be applied by him for research in surgery at Howard University.

In 1944, Charles Richard Drew was awarded the Spingarn Medal of the National Association for the Advancement of Colored People for his outstanding contribution to human welfare. Two years later, he was elected a fellow of the International College of Surgeons.

On the morning of April 1, 1950, a tired physician was motoring to Alabama with three of his colleagues, through the Deep South during segregation. Doctors Samuel L. Bullock, Richard Ford, Walter Johnson, and Drew were journeying from Washington, D.C., to Tuskegee Institute (now Tuskegee University) to attend the annual John A. Andrews Memorial Hospital Clinic. The sky had been lit with stars and a bright

UNITED STATES PATENT OFFICE

2,301,710

APPARATUS FOR PRESERVING BLOOD

John Scudder, New York, N. Y., assignor to
Charles R. Drew, Washington, D. C.

Application April 1, 1939, Serial No. 265,560

4 Claims. (Cl. 167—78)

This invention relates to the method of and apparatus for preserving blood and more particularly human blood to be used for transfusions.

For a long time in medical and surgical practice it has been customary to inject blood into a patient's veins to take the place of his own which has either been lost or has become altered. Formerly this transfusion of the new blood was done within a few minutes or a few hours after the new blood had been taken from the person giving it. The reason for this prompt transfusion is that blood, when taken from one person soon becomes unfit for injection into another, since it quickly deteriorates unless properly preserved. So long as there is a donor ready to supply blood for injection into a patient or there is time to obtain a donor when needed, there is no special demand for a store or a bank of blood ready to be used. However, it is often the case that blood of the right type is needed immediately in order to save the patient's life. He may be brought into a hospital after losing blood in an accident or he may, being already in a hospital, take a sudden turn for the worse and can be saved only by prompt blood transfusion. In instances such as these it becomes imperative that a supply of typed blood be kept on hand for immediate use.

The larger hospitals have of late years been accustomed to keep a bank or store of blood, which has been typed or classified, on hand for emergency use. This has been accomplished by means of refrigeration, keeping the temperature at about four degrees centigrade. By this method human blood can be kept fit for use only a short period of time, after which it is discarded, as it has deteriorated so much as to be harmful for sick individuals if used.

It is an object of this invention to preserve blood much longer than formerly possible.

Blood is composed of red cells, white cells and plasma which latter is a liquid in which the blood cells, both red and white, are suspended. Blood contains potassium in the form of various salts of potassium and the plasma contains about 20 milligrams of potassium per hundred cubic centimeters of plasma, the red cells about 400 milligrams of potassium per hundred cubic centimeters of red cells and the white cells slightly more. The disintegration of blood, when stored in containers, which makes it dangerous for rapid transfusion into a living animal such as a human, is in part caused by the diffusion of the potassium salts from the cells, especially the red cells, into the plasma of the blood. There are so very few white cells in the blood that the small amount of potassium salts which is given off by their disintegration is negligible. Potassium, even in salt form, in the plasma is toxic to animals and humans and acts as a cardiac poison and also inhibits respiration when a certain concentration is exceeded. Potassium contained within the blood cells has little or no such effect upon the human system.

It is the object of this invention to retard this diffusion of potassium from the cells, especially from the red cells, into the blood plasma. I can retard this diffusion enough so that blood can be stored with the usual refrigeration, much longer than formerly.

It is to be understood that the length of time blood can be stored is comparative depending upon the amount to be used in the transfusion, the rapidity with which it is to be injected, and the condition of the patient into whose veins it is to be injected. As stated above, excessive amounts of potassium in the blood plasma acts as a poison, but the body normally maintains potassium concentration within certain limits, by eliminating the excess from the circulating body fluids. The danger lies, however, in increasing the potassium contained in the patient's blood plasma to such an extent and in such a short space of time that his body can not eliminate it fast enough. If this should occur, the patient's life would be endangered by the high content of potassium in the plasma. It has been estimated that about 3 to 4 grams of potassium is the utmost that may safely be given to an average healthy man by way of infusion in one rapid dose; factors such as the speed of the injection, resistance of the individual, efficiency of the excretory organs are, however, some of the limiting conditions. It is, however, the fact that this amount may be safely given if the injection is done very slowly or if injections are given with intervals of time between each. This is because the body is given an opportunity of eliminating the potassium from the circulating body fluids. It is thus apparent that small quantities of blood, the plasma of which is high in potassium content, can be given a patient from time to time without injurious effect, but large quantities of such blood cannot be given at one time without endangering his life. Thus, when large quantities of blood are to be injected rapidly, the plasma thereof must contain but small quantities of potassium; in other words, the diffusion of potassium from cells to plasma must be small.

Apparatus for Preserving Blood, patented invention of John Scudder; patent assigned to Charles R. Drew.

INVENTOR	ASSIGNORS	ASSIGNEES	DATE OF ASSIGNMENT	DATE OF RECORD	INVENTION
1 Smith, Hiram P.	Hiram P. Smith.	International Harvester Company, Corporation of N.J.	Oct. 2, 1942. (acknowledged)	Oct. 10, 1942. (B-4950)	Braking System. Appln. cxctd. Oct. 2, 1942. Pat. 2,353,540 July 19, 1944
2 Sir, Bernard F.	Bernard F. Sir.	David Williams, Fred Williams, Edwin N. Williams, John G. Williams, doing business as Williams Brothers, St. Joseph, Mich., a copartnership.	Oct. -, 1942	Oct. 12, 1942 (9556.)	Containers and End Closures Therefor and Method of Making. Specn. cxctd. Oct. 1, 1942. Pat. 2,357,861 Oct. 10-1944
3 Spilhaus, Athelstan F. (Great Britain)	Athelstan F. Spilhaus (Great Britain)	Submarine Signal Company, Boston, Mass, Corporation of Maine	Sept. 30, 1942. (acknowledged)	Oct. 12, 1942.	Sea Sampler. Filed Ap. 2, 18, 1941. Ser. No. 389,219. Pat. 2,314,312 Mar. 23, 1943
4 Same.	Same.	Same.	Sept. 30, 1942. (acknowledged)	Oct. 12, 1942	Bathythermograph and Sea Sampler. Filed Ap. 2, 18, 1941. Ser. No. 389,220 Pat. 2,346,124 - Mar. 19, 1946
5 Same.	Same.	Same.	Sept. 30, 1942. (acknowledged)	Oct. 12, 1942.	Bathythermograph. Filed Dec. 18, 1941. Ser. No. 423,402. Pat. 2,331,510 Oct. 12, 1943
6 Somers, Brock A. Rauley, D. McCoy James R. Lilienthal	Brock A. Somers Rauley D. McCoy James R. Lilienthal.	Sperry Gyroscope Company, Inc., Manhattan Bridge Plaza, Brooklyn, Corporation of N.Y.	Oct. 8, 1942. (acknowledged)	Oct. 12, 1942.	Follow-Up System. Filed Oct. 2, 1942. Ser. No. 460,730. Pat. 2,452,609 Nov. 2, 1948
7 Seib, Albert F.	Albert F. Seib.	Wilson Manufacturing Co., Boston, Mass.	Oct. 10, 1942. (acknowledged)	Oct. 12, 1942.	Combined Billfold and Pass Case. Appln. cxctd. even date herewith.
8 Smith, Neil V.	Neil V. Smith.	Smith-Johnson Corporation, Los Angeles Calif., Corporation of Calif.	acknowledged Oct. 7, 1942.	Oct. 3, 1942.	Feed for Drill Press and the like. appln. cxctd. Oct. 7, 1942.
9 Same.	Same.	Same.	acknowledged Oct. 7, 1942.	Oct. 13, 1942.	Live Means for Motors, etc. appln. Oct. 7, 1942.
10 Scudder, John	John Scudder.	Charles R. Drew, Howard University, Oct. 9, 1942.	acknowledged Oct. 9, 1942.	Oct. 13, 1942.	Method of and Apparatus for Preserving Blood. appln. cxctd. Apr. 9, 1942. Ser. No. 5,562

Digest of Assignments: John Scudder assigns his patent to Charles R. Drew of Howard University, October 9, 1942.

moon on the night of March 31 and April 1, 1950, as the four con-
genial physicians began their motorcar trip shortly after midnight to
render their services at the annual free medical clinics serving as diagnostic and treatment centers for black rural residents. Drew earlier
had attended a banquet that Friday night that ended at a late hour
and delayed the departure of the four men. They had planned to leave
early that night, drive to Atlanta, and relax before proceeding on to
Tuskegee.

Each took turns at the wheel. About 5:30 Saturday morning, the
physicians stopped for doughnuts near the North Carolina state line.
After the brief refreshments, they continued their journey with Charles
Drew at the wheel of the Buick Roadmaster motorcar. The men joked,
but soon grew sleepy. About ninety minutes later, Drew's fate was
sealed. The car veered off the road in Alamance County into a corn-
field on the left side of the highway. Johnson was the first to awaken
in the car. Injured, he freed Bullock, whom he found wedged under
the dashboard. Ford was found sitting in a daze on the ground nearby
holding his arm. Pale faced, Drew was lying on his back near the front
left wheel, breathing irregularly. The doctor was in shock. Bullock,
Johnson, and passing motorists did what they could to help before the
arrival of the ambulance.[11] Walter Johnson's report of the accident was
filed with officials at Howard University. News of Charles Richard
Drew's untimely death stunned the world.

Ironically, the injuries suffered by Drew as the result of the automobile accident duplicated conditions associated with the research to
which he had dedicated himself for many years. The following report
is a personal account by Walter R. Johnson, one of the passengers in
the automobile with Drew, chronicling his unfortunate death and the
circumstances that surrounded his medical treatment in a North Carolina hospital:

"What happened?" questioned an attending physician in a long, white coat
as he entered the emergency room at the Alamance County General Hospital of Burlington.

"We had an accident on the highway," replied Dr. Johnson, a passenger
in the automobile driven by the severely wounded patient.

"Is that Dr. Drew?" asked the astonished white physician after observing
the patient, recognizing his features.

"Yes," answered Dr. Johnson. The emergency room burst into a frenzy of
activity as the physician in a commanding voice ordered emergency meas-
ures in attempts to save the life of the famous, renowned patient. However,
the breath of life eluded Charles Drew. After two long hours in the emergency room the doctor returned to Drew's colleagues who anxiously were
awaiting news of his condition.

"We did the best we could. We started fluids but our efforts were unrewarding." The men were crushed by the devastating news.[12]

The cause of the accident was never determined, nor was there any evidence that Drew received less than acceptable emergency treatment.

FROM HEAT OF BATTLE TO COLD WAR

During the depression, jobs were hard to find for everyone, especially for blacks. President Franklin Roosevelt's New Deal improved the situation marginally, but it did not curb the depression. It was World War II that did the trick. Jobs then literally were going begging. Hence African Americans trained in the sciences got a foothold in the door in positions normally inaccessible to them. Even the lower-economic-level worker suddenly found employment everywhere.

By the early to mid-twentieth century, inventors of color had instituted changes in multimillion-dollar industries such as the food, shoe, hair, medical, chemical, refrigeration, aviation, and automotive, to cite a few. The record of their achievement is exceptional in the fields of electrical, mechanical, civil, electronic, metallurgical, structural, and chemical engineering, including telephony. This is especially true of those who labored on teams. Individually, many inventive careers spanned decade after decade.

As a student of famed inventor Enrico Fermi, physicist Lloyd Albert Quarterman was one of six African American scientists who helped develop the atomic bomb in the Manhattan Project at Columbia University. At Argonne National Laboratory in Chicago, Illinois, Quarterman was assistant to the associate research scientist and chemist from 1943 to 1949. He assisted with the first nuclear reactor for atomic-powered submarines.

Manhattan Project team member Robert Johnson Omohundro was a physicist fresh out of Howard University's master's program. During World War II, he served on the project as a mass spectroscopist who worked on the development of the atomic bomb. From 1948 to 1984, Omohundro applied the techniques of nuclear physics and technology to defense requirements at the Naval Research Laboratory. One of his projects included certain mechanisms at airfields used to prevent the propagation of plutonium. He helped design devices to measure and detect radiation emissions from nuclear warheads. Omohundro obtained two patents in the field of nuclear physics, one in 1963 and another in 1971. He passed away on May 4, 2000, at age seventy-eight.[13]

Another Manhattan Project team member was Dr. William Jacob Knox, Jr., a physical chemistry graduate of the Massachusetts Institute of Technology in 1935. He taught chemistry at five historically black col-

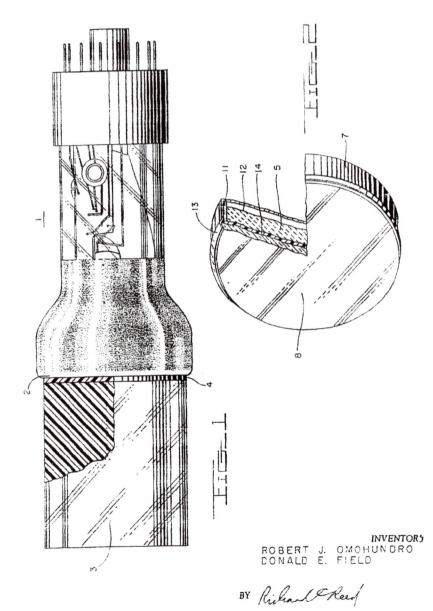

INVENTORS
ROBERT J. OMOHUNDRO
DONALD E. FIELD

BY *Richard C Reed*

ATTORNEY

Scintillation Counter, patented invention of Robert J. Omohundro et al.

leges and universities before his tenure on the project as research associate and as its first African American supervisor. After work on the atomic bomb, he became a research associate at Eastman Kodak Company from 1945 to 1970. Knox received about twenty patents on the application of surfactants in photographic processes.

James A. Parsons, Jr., was a chief metallurgist and director of the laboratories at the Durion Company in Dayton, Ohio, for thirty-one years. Parsons received patents from 1929 through 1949 on corrosion-resistant alloys and processes involving silicon compounds. His patents are all assigned to the Durion Company, a corporation of New York. He was the primary organizer of the metallurgy department at Tennessee Agricultural and Industrial State University, where he remained for thirteen years, retiring in 1966.

Physicist Louis W. Roberts was a pioneer in microwave and gaseous discharge electronics and labored on guidance systems for craft to land on the moon. Roberts taught physics at Howard University in 1943 after leaving a teaching position at St. Augustine's College in Raleigh, North Carolina. By 1946, he was at the Massachusetts Institute of Technology pursuing doctoral studies, where he later served on the research staff. During those years, Roberts managed tube development at Sylvania Electric Products and acquired several patents in 1954 on gaseous electronic devices, all assigned to Sylvania. Later, Roberts was awarded intellectual property rights on high-power microwave and gaseous discharge devices, respectively, which were assigned to Microwave Associates of Boston, Massachusetts, the company he founded. A few years afterward, he received more patent grants. Roberts then joined the staff at the National Aeronautics and Space Administration (NASA) on its inception, July 1, 1970, and became chief of the Optics and Microwave Laboratory at its Electronics Research Center. Later he was the director of the Office of Data Systems and Technology of the U.S. Department of Transportation.[14]

Electrical and mechanical engineer David Nelson Crosthwait, Jr., was born in Nashville, Tennessee. As a young student, Crosthwait demonstrated inventive skill when pursuing his master's degree from Purdue University. He merited his first patent on a thermostatic steam trap in 1919 and graduated in 1920. At that time he resided in Marshalltown, Iowa. He was a research engineer at C. A. Dunham Company and remained with the business (renamed Dunham-Bush) for more than forty years. An expert on heat transfer, ventilation, and air conditioning, Crosthwait designed the Radio City Music Hall heating system. Crosthwait was awarded thirty-nine patents during his outstanding career, primarily on heating and ventilation systems.

Inventor Robert F. Bundy of Yeadon, Pennsylvania, was a physicist on a team that perfected the man-portable radar device operated during World War II at the Normandy invasion. Additionally, Bundy produced the X-ray system used in scanning airline luggage. In 1960, he patented a signal generator. His scientific career was spent at Grumman Aerospace Corporation.

The brilliance of African American scientists was often ignored in the media; however, mainstream publications have begun to recognize their importance to the development of American technology. Minority journals and newspapers have continued to champion their contributions since the earliest of times. The *Philadelphia* (Pennsylvania) *Tribune* in February 1977 hailed the achievements of twenty-four black scientists and inventors honored at the unveiling of a permanent collection presented to the Afro-American Historical and Cultural Museum by the Philadelphia Electric Company. Moreover, *Jet* and *Ebony* magazines, along with individual publications by African Americans, acclaim the genius of their people. Films have been produced by the U.S. Patent and Trademark Office and by a variety of television news stations depicting the genius of blacks. Revered among other highly acclaimed scientists and innovators are scientists Spencer Robinson, Sr., Nathaniel John Mullen, Dr. Irving W. Jones, Carl English, Mrs. Katherine C. G. Johnson, Dr. Delon Hampton, Alfred L. Morris, J. Ernest Wilkins, Dr. Robert A. Thornton, and inventor O. S. "Ozzie" Williams. As time progresses, so does creativity. Hardly any form of commerce or commercial, industrial, or military products exists today without some input from the genius of African Americans. Innovators of color are without doubt in the mainstream of society.

All the aforementioned creative talents are examples of inventors solving problems in the wide spectrum of inventive subject matter. People of color have exercised untrammeled undertakings, evident in other extraordinary minds of the century.

PROGRESSIVE ACHIEVEMENT

From his early years, Percy Lavon Julian (1899–1975), son of a railway mail clerk and a schoolteacher, a grandson of slaves, seemed destined for greatness. He exhibited the positive attributes of courage, tenacity, scholarship, industry, and business keenness—characteristics that molded a pioneer and a role model for future researchers in chemistry.

For years, Julian was a research fellow and professor of chemistry at DePauw University before working as a director of research for the Glidden Company. He started in the Soya Products Division, where his research resulted in the development of a process to derive cortisone from a base of soybean oil. His pioneering research with the protein-rich soybean was of great use in seeking a solution to the worldwide problem of protein deficiency. Also, he isolated a soya protein that

Percy Lavon Julian, depicted on a U.S. postage stamp, was the second African American inducted into the National Inventors Hall of Fame, Akron, Ohio, in 1990.

could be used to coat and size paper and textiles and to create cold-water paints. The multitalented Julian discovered the base for a fire-fighting foam, called "Aero-Foam," to extinguish gasoline and oil fires, used during World War II.

Julian is highly acclaimed for his synthesis of cortisone from soybeans that provided affordable relief for millions of individuals suffering from rheumatoid arthritis and other inflammatory conditions. The drug previously had been extracted from particular animal organs and had been extremely expensive to manufacture, making it practically inaccessible to the average patient.

Moreover, Julian helped develop physostigmine from the Calabar bean for the treatment of glaucoma. He received many patents in the field of chemistry, including patent grants on the synthetic production of the male and female hormones testosterone and progesterone. As coinventor with two other colleagues, Julian was awarded his first patent on October 22, 1940, titled "Recovery of Sterols." The next four, all granted in 1941, concerned methods for making vegetable protein. Thereafter, the prolific inventor continually received patents until 1974. He further obtained patents from Switzerland, Great Britain, Mexico, France, Australia, Canada, Germany, and the Netherlands.

Julian, born on April 11, 1899, in Montgomery, Alabama, was one of six children. He attended DePauw University, where he majored in chemistry and graduated valedictorian and Phi Beta Kappa in 1920. He taught at Fisk University and at Howard University while pursuing postgraduate degrees. He achieved his M.A. degree in 1923 from Howard University and his Ph.D. in 1931 from the University of Vienna.[15]

Included in his many awards were eighteen honorary degrees and the NAACP Spingarn Award. In 1950, Julian was acclaimed "Chicagoan of the Year," but suffered discrimination the next year at Chicago's restricted Union League Club. He was elected to the National Academy

Percy Lavon Julian.
Courtesy of the Schomburg Center for Research in Black Culture, The New York Public Library, Astor, Lenox and Tilden Foundations.

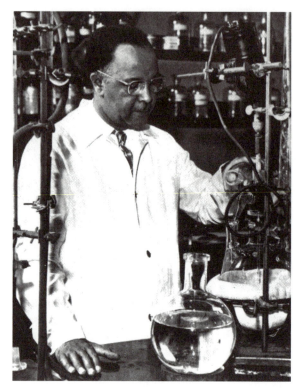

of Sciences and received the Proctor Prize of the Sigma Xi science research honor society.

Percy Lavon Julian passed away on April 19, 1975, at age seventy-six in a Waukegan, Illinois, hospital. He was survived by his wife, Dr. Anna J. Julian, a son and a daughter, and a grandchild.[16] In 1990, Julian became the second African American to be inducted into the National Inventors Hall of Fame at Akron, Ohio, at the time of Carver's induction.

An inventor who held more than sixty patents in various disciplines, having forty in the refrigeration field alone, Frederick McKinley Jones (1893–1961) was the first black member of the American Society of Refrigeration Engineers. Born in Cincinnati, Ohio, Jones made it possible for our lives to be more comfortable by developing means to preserve perishables during long truck hauls. He accepted employment at a motion-picture-equipment-manufacturing plant in 1930, a position that inadvertently began his diversified patent career. Jones received his first patent in 1939 for a ticket machine that dispensed movie-house tickets. His truck-refrigeration system, patented in 1942, began his long career in temperature-controlled vehicles' refrigeration that concluded in 1960, netting his business more than three million dollars annually. Jones received exclusive rights as well for a portable X-ray machine, for a military field kitchen refrigerator, and for military field hospital units. Frederick McKinley Jones served as a federal government consultant in the 1950s to the Department of Defense and the National Bureau of Standards. He died in Minneapolis in 1961.[17]

Mechanics became a lucrative field of endeavor as the county progressed into highly industrialized production of commerce. African Americans pursued that endeavor, but at great expense to their psyches.

Solomon Harper, born on October 8, 1895, was a brilliant electrical engineer and a prolific inventor from 1911 through the 1950s. The tall, ebony-hued Harper was a member of the American Association for the Advancement of Science and was lauded with an award from the NAACP. He argued on his own behalf for rights to patents for many of his applications, often making personal appeal in flamboyant style before the examiners handling the documents. He patented a triple-chamber airplane bomb, vibration- and shock-resistant thermostats, and relays useful on submarines, but most of his patents are on thermostatic-controlled hair combs, curlers, and heating devices like the type used today.

One of twelve children, Harper was precocious and magically gifted in mathematics. After receiving his degree from Syracuse University and following a course of inventiveness, he became frustrated with the routes to patent grants and the journeys through court procedures. Author Wil Haygood in his book on Adam Clayton Powell, Jr., *King of the Cats*, described Harper as becoming a "lost soul" who turned to communism and rummaged for a living. Powell befriended him and let Harper spend time at the newsroom of his journal, the *People's Voice.* Solomon Harper died poor on December 8, 1980, at age eighty-five in Harlem, New York.[18]

After employment of only a few months during World War II, Joseph Turner received the first award of its kind for individual production merit recognition from the Carnegie Illinois Steel Corporation at South Charleston, West Virginia.[19] The former hotel bellman and car washer discovered an improved system for removing scale from steel plates. The invention involves a cold-air distribution system that extends the life of the device employed in the removal process, which diminishes manual labor and saves time. Turner began as a common laborer, but quickly advanced.

Pugilist John Arthur Johnson, more popularly known as "Jack" Johnson, was a successful inventor. Amazingly, he filed two patent applications in 1921 while incarcerated in the federal penitentiary at Leavenworth, Kansas, because he had violated the Mann Act by transporting white women across a state line for immoral purposes. Johnson entered prison in the fall of 1920. The patents were issued after his early release for "good time" in the summer of 1921, engineered by either friends or his promoters, who wanted him to challenge the winner of the fight between Jack Dempsey and George Carpentier. The first patent was granted in April 1922 for an improved type of monkey wrench. The second patent, acquired in December 1922, was for an invention coengineered with white fellow prisoner James Pearl Thompson. The invention, of all things, is a theft-preventing device for vehicles.

Johnson was born in 1878 in Galveston, Texas, and began his boxing career in 1899. He became the first black heavyweight boxing champion of the world defeating Tommy Burns in 1908. Johnson, agreeing to lay down his title because of difficulties stemming from the Mann Act seven years later, lost the title to Jess Willard in Havana, Cuba, but appeared in boxing matches until he was sixty-seven years of age. He died on June 10, 1946, from injuries received in a car accident near Raleigh, North Carolina.[20]

The forty-five-year-old Thompson, born in Michigan, was convicted of "obstructing military service, seditious conspiracy, and conspiracy to injure civil rights." He was sent to Leavenworth in 1918 after his Chicago trial. Thompson was a member of the Industrial Workers of the World (the "Wobblies") who resisted the nation's entry into World War I. The Seattle, Washington, resident described himself as a "lecturer."[21]

Self-educated hairstylist Willie Lloyd Turner, a convicted murderer, although incarcerated for nearly six years, perfected a type of barbering shear for removing split ends, named "De-ending Shears" on his patent. Turner, the son of a Southampton County, Virginia, sharecropper, was scheduled for execution in Virginia's electric chair the following year in 1985, and he offered any proceeds gained from his invention to the victim's family. The proposal was rejected.[22]

Turner filed the patent application himself. In 1981, he appealed to the commissioner of patents and trademarks, stating that "while it is true that the fact that I am a death row prisoner is embarrassing enough, I must go on to explain that I am, and have been for all the days of my life, a poor person. Therefore, I am unable to pay for the assistance of a patent attorney in regard to the prosecution of . . . [my] application." He then thanked the official "for all possible guidance." Three years later he was successful at the patent and trademark agency, but not with his immediate circumstances. After seventeen years and numerous appeals, Turner was executed at Jarratt, Virginia, in 1995.[23]

Reverend John S. Thurman suffered years of anguish and pain at the loss of his first innovation, sent in good faith to a bogus invention agency in Washington, D.C. While employed at a North Carolina shin-

J. A. JOHNSON.

WRENCH.

APPLICATION FILED MAR. 22, 1921.

1,413,121.

Patented Apr. 18, 1922.

2 SHEETS—SHEET 1.

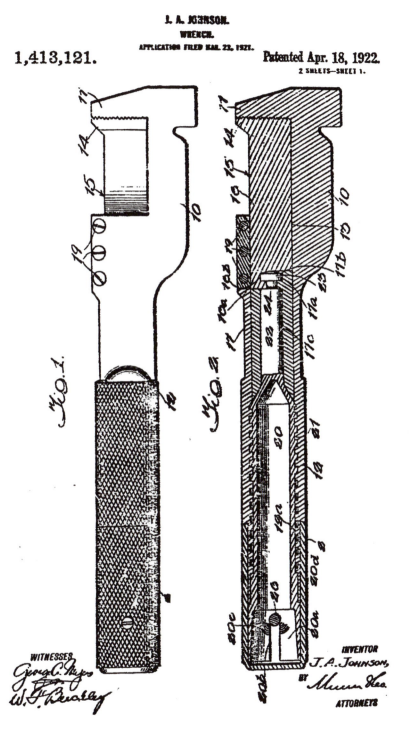

Wrench, patented invention of pugilist John Arthur "Jack" Johnson.

gle mill, the twenty-one-year-old Thurman, walking home from work, observed that there was a better way to give turning signals from automobiles other than by hand. He developed the "automobile signal," consisting of an electrically wired case with niches for "left," "right," and "stop." However, Thurman's documents were never filed at the Patent Office. Many believe that his invention was stolen, or maybe another notion merged with his unprotected design. In any instance, Thurman, who was suffering from a heart condition, came up with the new idea of a vehicle motion-signaling system fifty years later that matured into a patent in June 1986, one month after his demise. Inventors sometimes receive patents posthumously, and this was the circumstance with inventor Thurman. Reverend Thurman, however, learned just before he died that the coveted grant would be awarded to him at the future date of issue.[24]

For janitor Holcomb Hall, born in 1887 at Lynchburg, Virginia, the creative struggle never reached fruition. In tinkering with suspenders, or braces, Hall conceived an improved way to hold up pants. He designed a metal hook and buckle to join the upper and lower sections of the special back strap to help keep the rear suspenders hooked. The suspender of earlier time sported a modified Y design from two independent straps. Hall hired Attorney Victor J. Evans, a popular patent lawyer, in the hope of securing a patent; apparently, his invention went no further than some initial efforts at protecting it. Decades later Hall's daughter, Alice Hall Green of Stuart, Florida, drafted a story about her father's discovery of a finer set of suspenders and received a copyright registration for her initial efforts. Hall died in New York City in 1952.[25]

Struggling to make a success of his business, built on approximately eighty patents and several trademarks, Meredith C. Gourdine founded the company Gourdine Systems. Later he owned and headed the firm Energy Innovations, of East Orange, New Jersey, and then of Houston, Texas.

Gourdine won an Olympic silver medal for the broad jump in 1952 and later earned a Ph.D. in engineering from the California Institute of Technology. In the 1970s, he invented the Incineraid, a device that controls smoke pollution, and the Electradyne paint spray gun. Some patented products were licensed to Sherwin-Williams, and others were manufactured and sold by the Estey Corporation. Suffering from diabetes, Gourdine gradually lost his vision but continued his inventive streak regardless of the disability. He created a device to eliminate fog above airfields in 1984 to help pilots with a safer landing. Afterward he obtained numerous patents in the 1990s. Gourdine, a former navy officer, is one of the most prolific inventors of color. He died on November 20, 1998, in Texas at sixty-nine years of age.[26]

Inventor and computer analyst Kenneth Jerome Braxton, then of Springfield, Illinois, devised and patented a security system for centralized monitoring and selective reporting of remote alarm conditions. Circuit boards detect which window a trespasser violated or pinpoint the exact area of a fire. The computerized security system helped contribute toward a revolution in the home and commercial security industry. The uses of Braxton's system are nearly endless. Braxton was unlucky at selling, licensing, or marketing his concept and felt that his patent was being infringed upon. He worked for the Illinois Department of Conservation and at age thirty-nine moved to Cedar Rapids to work as a computer specialist at Collins. After a protracted lawsuit, Braxton became frustrated, distraught, and later ill. Retired from Philip Morris, the fifty-four-year-old senior systems analyst, born in Whitby, West Virginia, died of a heart attack in 1994 in Richmond, Virginia.[27]

ROLE PLAYED BY AFRICAN AMERICAN ACADEMIC INSTITUTIONS

During slavery, some held in bondage and a few free persons of color were self-taught. A number of other freed souls were apprenticed or were trained by missionaries and by benevolent citizens. Several managed to go abroad for their early education.

The educational background of the African American technologist has been varied. The minimally educated discoverer is a grade-school or high-school dropout; others are college graduates. The specialized innovator favored postgraduate work either abroad or in America at predominately white institutions.

The initial collegiate education began for most at minority institutions. Liberal arts, fine arts, and religion were the common curricula. These institutions had small but well-trained staffs in their natural science departments that featured mathematics, chemistry, biology, physics, and some geology and engineering. Training in various trades and instruction in remedial courses were available. Historically black colleges and universities such as Fisk University, Virginia Union University, Talladega College, Morehouse College, Howard University, and Clark University gave their students early training in the foundations they needed to pursue their careers. These creditable institutions graduated inventors Howard S. Jones, Jr., Darnley M. Howard, and M. Lucius Walker, Jr., who, collectively, hold forty U.S. patents and additional foreign grants. Physicist and electronics engineer Jones originated numerous discoveries in the field of microwave antennas while he was employed over a twenty-year span beginning in the 1960s at the

Harry Diamond Laboratories in Washington, D.C. Engineer and inventor Walker, later dean of the School of Engineering at Howard University, received a patent for creating a special laminar fluid element in 1969.

Selected Natural Science Graduates of Historically Black Colleges and Universities

Physicist Robert Powell
Mathematician Berthal Carmichael
Roentgenologist Cliland B. Powell
Dermatologist Theodore K. Lawless
Civil engineer Taft H. Broome
Clinical antibiotic researcher Louis T. Wright
Mathematician and educator Harriett G. Jenkins
Electrical engineer Katherine Clinton
Physicist and mathematician Norman T. Grier
Physician and pathologist Marion Mann
Mechanical engineer Yvonne Young Clark

These gifted college graduates surpassed their peers; however, creative genius does not require one to have a document certifying completion of any formal training. Inventors have an inherent quality and an Almighty-given talent. What the predominately African American higher education system did for these talents was to give them insight into various fields of study. Well-structured curricula required discipline and understanding. These training institutions are natural resources "since they provide a pool of expertise that enables students who have been educationally deprived prior to entering college to achieve a quality education," wrote patent attorney J. Richard Everett in his 1978 article "Patents: Potential Economic Benefits for Minority-Run Universities."[28] Accordingly, natural talent sprang forth with ease. But the most difficult struggle for the gifted was to reap benefits from their ideas and concepts, and no amount of instruction could ensure this economic success. Many talents were also denied jobs commensurate with their higher education. The barrier, though, did not still tinkering fingers. College graduates performing blue-collar jobs persevered and struggled to protect any breakthrough.

6

AMONG WOMEN AND FAMILY

Blessed art thou among women.

Luke 1:28

AFRICAN AMERICAN WOMEN

The famed Richmond, Virginia, banker and leader of the St. Luke Society, Maggie Lena Walker, addressing an assembly in 1909, stated, "Out of the wilderness, out of the night has the black woman crawled to the dawn of the night, beaten by lashes and bound by chains a beast of burden, with soul and brains. She has come thro' sorrow and need and woe and the cry of her heart is to know, to know."[1] Walker, a woman of conviction, self-reliance, spirit, courage, and indomitable willpower to rise out of the depth of human deprivation, knew first-hand how the "colored woman" could conquer obstacles and rise above limitations placed on womanhood by those of limited vision. As the first woman president of a bank anywhere in the world, she thoroughly understood that the mind of humans, no matter their background, was a precious commodity that could not be harnessed or leashed. Walker crawled out of the wilderness of ignorance and achieved in the mighty world of finance years before female suffrage and more than half a century before the decisive women's liberation of modern times.

Preceding the creation of the present patent systems of the world, women displayed creative genius. Thousands of years before the birth of Christ, Eastern women were thinkers and innovators. According to ancient tradition, the Chinese people had worshiped several empresses of China for their creativity. The invention of spinning was attributed to Yao, wife of the fourth emperor, and the discovery of silk, a precious commodity for centuries, to Si-Ling-Chi, wife of the Emperor Ch'in Shih Huang'ti.[2]

In the Western world in the thirteenth century, the invention of wood engraving is credited to a twin brother and sister team of Ravenna, Italy. In Great Britain, four centuries later, the record of its first woman patentee accords Sarah Jerom a patent for an engine that cut timber into thin pieces for making ban boxes. On May 5, 1809, the U.S. patent system rewarded Mary Kies, the first U.S. woman inventor to receive a patent, for her method of weaving straw with silk or thread.

African women suffered enormous hardship along with their male counterparts during the Middle Passage. The surviving women improvised to maintain some sense of life and struggled to endure. The talents they brought from their homeland to the colonies on a new continent were molded to shape a new existence in a strange culture. Grasses, herbs, flowers, and fauna became familiar tools for these women, providing baskets, remedies, clothing, and other necessities.

EARLY FEW

Several decades after the issuance of the Emancipation Proclamation, which brought freedom on this new continent, the earliest known woman of color to merit federal protection for an invention was Judy W. Reed of Washington, D.C., in 1884. Reed filed a patent application early that year and after passing patent standards received the grant nine months later. She conceived an improved dough kneader and roller that subjected "the mass of dough to a thorough and equable mixing" by passing it "between a pair of intermeshing corrugated rollers." A covered receiver protected the dough "from dust or impurities in the atmosphere throughout its working." An "X" marked her signature on the patent.

Previously Sarah E. Goode of Chicago, Illinois, was cited as the first black woman patentee; however, she received her patent on a folding "cabinet-bed" the year following Reed in 1885. It was witnessed by Archibald L. Goode, probably a relative. Her furniture combination, similar to the modern foldaway beds, folded up to "an ordinary office-desk" that contained sections for the bedding and office supplies. Three years later, in 1888, Miriam E. Benjamin (discussed later) received a patent for a gong and signal chair for hotels and like facilities while she was living in Washington, D.C.

African American exhibitions in the 1890s and later included practical and efficient inventions by women. These early pioneering, self-reliant women inventors, accustomed to heavy housework and to labor in the kitchen, naturally wanted tasks made easier and simpler. What is noteworthy is their ingenuity at getting letters patent for their cre-

J. W. REED.
DOUGH KNEADER AND ROLLER.

No. 305,474.

Patented Sept. 23, 1884.

Fig. 1.

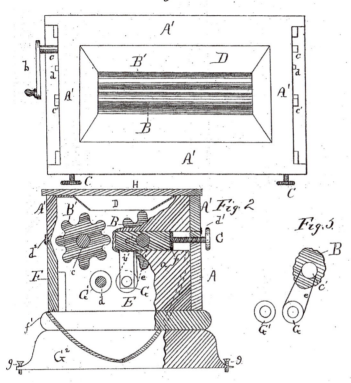

Inventor.
Judy W. Reed
By Edw. J. Underwood
attorney

Dough Kneader and Roller, patented invention of Judy W. Reed.

ative ability, especially during the anxious period of second-class citizenship. This was an achievement against the odds. Generally, women of color were fearful to be known as inventors. As reported in the *Woman Inventor*, published in Washington, D.C., in June 1891, domestic Ellen Elgin, also a government clerk and a member of the Woman's National Industrial League, devised a clothes wringer that she sold to a disreputable agent "for the sum of $18.00 in 1888," a paltry amount. The device was financially successful to the buyer, and when she was asked why she had sold the device so cheap after months of development, she replied, "You know I am black and if it was known that a [N]egro woman patented the invention, white ladies would not buy the wringer; I was afraid to be known because of my color in having it introduced in the market, that is my only reason." Afterward, she worked on another invention that she financed and for which she wanted a patent but did not want it to be known then as the result of a "black woman's" effort. Elgin participated in the Washington, D.C., Woman's International Industrial Inventors Congress in 1890, which was open to all regardless of color.[3]

The plight of Elgin, and numerous white women inventors as well, was unfortunate. Many hid their inventions under the names of males and thereby obscured their real identity, thus making it impossible to find their invention in patent files. *The Work of the Afro-American Woman*, written in 1894 by Mrs. N. F. Mossell (1855–1948) of Philadelphia, Pennsylvania, mentions inventions of several women, including those of Mossell herself, who claimed that she patented a camping table and portable kitchen. However, Nellie Mossell, wife of Dr. Nathan F. Mossell, appears to have no patent record, like the following women she mentioned: Mrs. C. Whetzel of St. John, New Brunswick, Canada, is asserted to have invented an ice house, "whereby meats and other provisions may be kept for months without losing their sweetness," and Mrs. M. E. Elliot reportedly "years ago [before 1894] secured a patent on several toilet articles and opened branch establishments in many cities."[4] The *Crisis* magazine of May 1913 reported that Mrs. Russell James had invented a "Portable Newsstand."

Mossell lamented that "many unique inventions are now in the possession of Afro-American women too poor to secure patents."[5] Many were unsophisticated or too destitute to take advantage of the federal patent system. Even if these early inventive women could finance their enterprise, a married woman's invention was the property of her husband until relief laws of the late nineteenth century relating to married women's property were enacted.

During this period, militant women asserted themselves and demanded equal status. They wanted to vote and campaigned in the fight for the privilege. Time was running out for husbands, fathers, uncles,

Mrs. N. F. Mossell and her daughters.
In G. F. Richings, *Evidences of Progress among Colored People* (Philadelphia: George S. Ferguson Co., 1905). From the Patricia Carter Ives Sluby Collection.

or sons to be in control of women's political and financial affairs. In 1890, one small achievement was made at the Convention of the Patent Centennial, where women inventors urged recognition and successfully received it.[6]

Two years later, in 1892, Anna M. Mangin of Woodside, New York, won a patent for a pastry fork. The device is the forerunner of some kitchen utensils of today. It pressed, cut, and pulverized dry pastry and also was useful as an egg whipper.

More than likely, Mangin was born in Louisiana in October 1854 and was the wife of a coal dealer, A. F. Mangin. She had two children, but only a son, Andrew, was alive at the time the 1900 federal census was taken, which noted that all in the family could read.[7]

The Mangin pastry fork was displayed at the 1893 World's Colombian Exposition at Chicago as part of the New York Afro-American Exhibit. Jeanne Madeline Weimann's *The Fair Women* described Mangin's device as "the only thing of its kind at the patent office."[8] The exhibit was in a diminutive corner space on the second floor of the women's exhibit building, assembled after protesters fought exclusion by fair organizers. The Chicago World's Fair was dubbed the White City, and in many ways it was. Across the nation, African American women vehemently objected to the treatment of requests by blacks to exhibit. Mrs. Anna J. Cooper, the corresponding secretary of the Colored Woman's League, protested at the Congress of Representative Women. In a lame effort to recover some modicum of decency, August 25 that year was designated "Colored People's Day." Frederick Douglas as envoy at the small Haitian pavilion was the sole significant black in White City.[9]

Another innovator surfaced in the spring of 1892. Sarah Boone of New Haven, Connecticut, received a patent grant for an ironing board that year. She tapered, padded, and curved a board to ease ironing the sleeves and bodice of fussy female garments. Six years later, Lyda D. Newman of New York, New York, merited her patent in 1898 for a hairbrush that permitted easy cleaning of the brush and bristles carried by a detachable unit. The list of "colored" inventors for the Paris Exposition of 1900 identified women inventors; oddly, only Goode, Benjamin, Boone, and Newman were specified.

The last decade of the nineteenth century chronicled momentous changes for African Americans. While lynching escalated during this period, Virginian John M. Langston was elected and seated in the U.S. Congress in 1890. Thomas E. Miller of South Carolina was reelected to Congress the same year, and people of color continued a path of progress despite serious setbacks. The national population was nearly sixty-three million, with about 12 percent African American. Blacks opened banks in the South, founded colleges, and established a myriad of businesses. T. Thomas Fortune organized the Afro-American League of the United States, the predecessor of the National Association for the Advancement of Colored People.

At the beginning of the new century, women were progressive and competed with their male counterparts in many fields of endeavor. The African American woman achieved shoulder to shoulder alongside her white sister. She applied her energy in education, law, science, art, business, politics, medicine, and invention. Nurse Clara Frye invented a surgical appliance, a device that "may be employed for obstetrical purposes, in cases of fever, or in any case of sickness." The mechanism, patented in 1907, consisted of a chair having a bedpan and capable of supporting extensions to provide a flat, bedlike position.

Born in Albany, New York, in 1872, Clara moved with her family to Montgomery, Alabama, where she grew up. In 1888, she married S. H. Frye at age sixteen and studied nursing in Chicago, where they moved. Twelve years later, the couple resided in Tampa, Florida, the locale in which she later developed her novel device. Frye turned her home into a substitute medical facility to aid the sick. Subsequently a black hospital constructed in West Tampa was named for her in the 1930s, but was later demolished. A wing at the Tampa city hospital now carries her name.[10]

FLOWING TRESSES

One of the earliest to conceive the idea of applying a softening pomade to hair and flattening out curled strands of hair, Madame C. J. Walker built a million-dollar business from the development of the

Madame C. J. Walker.
Courtesy of the Moorland-
Spingarn Research Center,
Howard University.

"Anti-Kink Walker System." Several African American women had developed hair preparations and established businesses at the century's turn in 1900, but Walker surpassed them. After trial and tribulation, Sarah Breedlove McWilliams Walker became the first woman of color to amass a million dollars through her personal struggles.

Born to former slave parents in Delta, Louisiana, and orphaned at seven years of age, Sarah married at age fourteen and was left a widow in Mississippi with a child at age twenty. She moved to St. Louis, Missouri, found work as a laundress, and eventually developed a formula to prevent her hair from continually falling out. In 1906, Sarah married newspaperman Charles Joseph Walker in Denver, Colorado, and embarked in business from the success of the hair product. Disagreements between the couple resulted in a divorce, and Sarah, inspired with the desire to help women with hair problems, was well on her way to financial freedom through her manufactured hair goods and various cosmetic preparations.[11]

Walker conceived the process of physically transforming resistant

Registered Jan. 13, 1953 **Registration No. 569,306**

AFFIDAVIT SEC. 8
ACCEPTED

RENEWED

SUPPLEMENTAL REGISTER
Trade-Mark

UNITED STATES PATENT OFFICE

The Mme. C. J. Walker Manufacturing Company, Inc., Indianapolis, Ind.

Act of 1946

Original filed, act of 1946, Principal Register, December 15, 1948; amended to application, Supplemental Register, May 31, 1951, Serial No. 570,597

Mme. C. J. Walker's
Satin Tress

STATEMENT

The Mme. C. J. Walker Manufacturing Company, Inc., a corporation duly organized under the laws of the State of Indiana, located at Indiana Avenue at West Street, Indianapolis 2, Indiana, and doing business at Indiana Avenue at West Street, Indianapolis 2, Indiana, has adopted and is using the trade-mark shown in the accompanying drawing, for a HAIR DRESSING USED FOR LONG-LASTING STRAIGHTENING, CURLING, WAVING AND STYLING HUMAN HAIR WITH EASE, in Class 51, Cosmetics and toilet preparations, and presents herewith five (5) specimens showing the trade-mark as actually used in connection with such goods, the trade-mark being shown on labels pasted on the container of the solution, and requests that the same be registered in the United States Patent Office on the Supplemental Register, in accordance with the act of July 5, 1946.

The trade-mark was first used on September 17, 1948, and first used in commerce among the several States which may lawfully be regulated by Congress on September 17, 1948, and has been in lawful use in such commerce upon or in connection with the goods for the year preceding the filing of this application.

Applicant is the owner of Trade-Mark Registrations Nos. 120,759 (Re.) and 153,556 (Re.).

THE MME. C. J. WALKER MANUFACTURING COMPANY, INC.,
By VIOLET D. REYNOLDS,
Secretary.

Madame C. J. Walker's Satin Tress, registered trademark of the Madame C. J. Walker Manufacturing Company, Inc.

curly hair to a smooth look by first applying petrolatum jelly to strands of hair, followed by hot pressing with a steel comb. In 1908, Walker moved to Pittsburgh, Pennsylvania, where she established Lelia College to train women in the Walker System and ultimately set up her headquarters in Indianapolis, Indiana, in 1910. She traveled extensively to promote her enterprise and continually trained agents who advanced her system worldwide.

Six years before the famous and wealthy Madame C. J. Walker succumbed to kidney failure, she filed an application to the U.S. Patent Office on February 3, 1913, for her invention, the "Hair Drying and Straightening Comb." She applied privately as Sarah Walker who lived at 640 North West Street, Indianapolis, Indiana, but the papers were incomplete, missing some formal requirements. After notification of the deficiencies in a letter dated April 12, 1913, signed by the patent office chief clerk, the application apparently was abandoned, because no further record has been found of the issuance of a patent. It is likely that Sarah Walker forsook the patent process for some unknown reason. It is usual for inventors to become frustrated with the system and to feel intimidated by procedure. However, the Madame C. J. Walker Company, at Indianapolis, successfully filed for the registration of trademarks. The company received its first trademark in 1917 for "The Madame C. J. Walker Wonderful Hair Grower." Madame Walker died at age fifty-two on May 25, 1919, at New York City.[12]

TWENTIETH-CENTURY OUTBURST

Madeline M. Turner of Oakland, California, received a patent in 1916 for an ingenious apparatus that pressed and extracted the juice from fruits. Three years later, Alice H. Parker of Morristown, New Jersey, acquired her patent rights for a heating furnace in late 1919. Parker's system provided a mechanism for regulated heat to be carried to various rooms of structures such as houses or buildings. The furnace, fueled by gas, was reliable and efficient.

Two women received patents a month apart in 1920. In April 1920, Mary Jane Reynolds of St. Joseph, Missouri, was awarded a patent on an improvement on a hoisting and loading gear mechanism for "heavy and bulky articles." In May 1920, Mary H. Toland of Chattanooga, Tennessee, appeared in the record for patenting her circuit closer, a "float operated alarm to be used in conjunction with refrigerators, so that the filling of the drip pan . . . may serve to operate a satisfactory signaling device." Also in that year, inventor Sacramenta G. Tankins acquired the right to exclude others from making and using her distinctive comb.

In 1928, another hair culturist took advantage of the patent system.

1,337,667.

Patented Apr. 20, 1920.

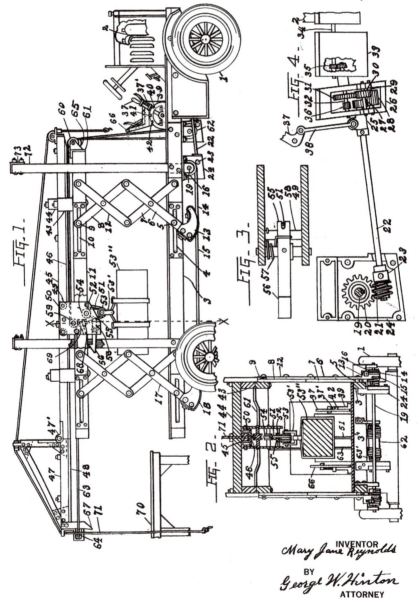

INVENTOR

Mary Jane Reynolds

BY

George W. Hinton

ATTORNEY

Hoisting and Loading Mechanism, patented invention of Mary Jane Reynolds.

Marjorie Stewart Joyner (1896–1994) of Chicago, Illinois, received a grant that year for a "permanent wave machine" that could wave the hair of minorities and whites alike. It consisted of sixteen thin rods electrically hooked to a hair-dryer hood. She might have missed the opportunity to get a patent grant if it had not been for two young attorneys who urged her to get government protection after seeing the contraption at her shop in 1928. Joyner had no idea what a patent was. She had opened her own shop, called Marjorie's Beauty Salon, in the basement of her home, where the idea struck her when she was cooking a pot roast using long, narrow rods that held the roast together and heated it internally. She reasoned that similar rods could "cook a permanent curl into the hair." Her second patent of 1929 on a "scalp protector" was a direct outgrowth of the first concept.[13]

Joyner assigned the patent rights of both inventions to the Madame C. J. Walker Manufacturing Company, where she became a member of the board of directors. As a novel idea to wave or curl hair and because of its use in the Walker chain of beauty salons, the machine was in great demand. However, Joyner personally accrued no financial benefit directly from her innovations. In 1945, Joyner established the United Beauty School Owners and Teachers Association (now Alpha Chi Pi Omega, a Greek-letter organization for beauticians) and later retired from the Walker Company. Now a wealthy Chicago patron and an avid volunteer, Joyner became a philanthropist, helping to foster the welfare of children and assisting the arts. In 1989, the Patent Law Association of Chicago at its ninety-fifth-anniversary dinner invited Joyner as guest of honor. She died at age ninety-eight in December 1994.[14]

While some women inventors were notably successful, others are still remarkable in a society biased against their talent. The *Negro Year Book, 1931–1932* cited the ability of Virginia Scharschmidt of Harlem, New York. Her patent of April 1929 identifies a safe window-washing apparatus that operated from inside a structure for cleaning the outside pane of windows. The ingenious gadget cleaned windows of multistoried office buildings and apartment structures without endangering the operator, who commonly labored from the exterior.

During the 1930s, patent grants were awarded to women who were triumphant inventors several times. Sacramenta G. Tankins received her second patent in 1932 for a method and means for treating human hair, three years before Margaret Cheetham's accomplishment of receiving a patent for a toy. Mary E. Jackson, as a coinventor with Harry Jackson (perhaps related) topped the charts with three innovations. Two protective appliance devices merited grants in 1936, and a burglar-alarm switch passed patent scrutiny in 1937.

Necessity was the mother of invention for these talented women and for some of those who followed. Patent attorney Lloyd McAulay of a

New York City law firm, in a February 24, 1982, letter to the author referring to the scope of female patent activity, "observed that the focus of innovation is on the activities of those who hold status in society . . . [and] there are a lot of inventions to aid the medical doctor but relatively few to aid the nurse." He commented that the "Shakers are responsible for many innovations to lessen the burden of house-hold care," such as the clothespin and the manually actuated washing machine, and he noted that the Shakers "were headed by a woman."

As the decades progressed, black women founded sororities, insti-tutions, and self-help organizations and began receiving doctorates in the liberal arts, followed by the sciences. The African American woman, diversified like other inventors, filled a void with a need to make things easier. She too perceived the question and the answer. She patented games, toys, household items, hair techniques and im-plements, women's apparel, and infant items, along with complex me-chanical, electrical, medical, and technical methods and apparatuses. Then and now, many of these women were and are aware of the ben-efits of the patent and trademark systems.

An example of diverse female ingenuity is the story of Henrietta Mahim Bradberry of Chicago, Illinois. Bradberry, born in Franklin, Kentucky, finished a secondary-school education and is credited with two patent documents. On May 25, 1943, she patented a bed rack that was an attachment that permitted air to pass through and refresh worn clothes. Two years later, during World War II, apparently motivated by patriotic feelings, her interest centered on, amazingly, a torpedo dis-charge means. Patented in 1945, the complex device operated pneu-matically and could discharge torpedoes below the water surface while located in submarines or in subterranean forts. It had three gears, giving the capability of firing multiple torpedoes rather than the stan-dard single charge. The discharge device prevented the water from penetrating into the effective mechanism. Before Bradberry's death in 1979, she told this author that "ideas just came" to her. As a home-maker, she had time to "work out the concepts to perfection" and, of course, to the satisfaction of the Patent Office.

For inventor Louise H. Williams of Los Angeles, California, the idea in 1946 was to provide a receptacle of different shapes and dimensions "adapted to accommodate a wide variety of articles." She patented a collapsible or foldable and transportable unit having a cloth or plastic body to contain the objects. When not in use, it simply folded for easy storage. That year Jessie T. Pope of Detroit, Michigan, received her notice of allowability for a patent on an electric curling or croquignole iron.

In the 1950s, more ebony women inventors took advantage of the patent system, such as Bertha Berman, Lydia M. Holmes, Irma G.

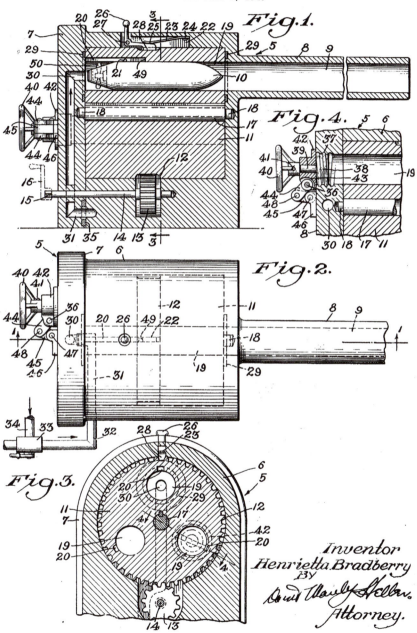

Torpedo Discharge Means, patented invention of Henrietta Bradberry.

Lydia M. Holmes with
husband Walter.
From the Patricia Carter
Ives Sluby Collection,
courtesy of granddaughter
Glennette Tilley Turner.

Dixon, and M. Beatrice Kenner. For Christina M. Jenkins of Cleveland, who married orchestra leader Duke Jenkins of Malvern, Ohio, the story of success was fortuitous. In 1952, Jenkins patented a process of permanently attaching commercial hair to live hair. Although her patent was held invalid in 1965, she had profited from the invention before the litigation. Jenkins owned beauty shops in six U.S. cities and owned an oil well in Louisiana valued, it is said, at more than one million dollars.[15]

Certified physiotherapist Bessie Griffin, also known as Bessie J. Blount, invented an invalid feeder, patented in 1951 as a portable receptacle support. Inspired by a physician's offhand remark to "make something by which they can feed themselves," Griffin envisioned the invalid feeder.

Born in Hickory, Virginia, at age seven Bessie went to New Jersey, where she completed high school and studied psychology at Union Junior College. She explored physiotherapy in Chicago and became an industrial designer in 1944. Later she took courses in educational therapy at Bronx Hospital, where she was helping to rehabilitate disabled veterans. Griffin offered the invention, which she valued at $100,000, to the Hospital Operation Service of the Veterans' Administration. After its rejection, Griffin gave the French government her patented receptacle support apparatus following its request for the loan of her feeder for experimentation and use in French military hospitals.[16] Griffin also conceived other inventions to assist hospital patients. Her son, representing his mother, visited the author at the Patent Office and recounted many stories of her.

The 1960s marked a dramatic period in America. The African American median income rose to 63 percent of white family income. In the Vietnam era, discontent, protests, and violence erupted; W.E.B. Du Bois, a founder of the NAACP, moved to Ghana in West Africa; schools desegregated in Atlanta, Georgia; and the Southern Christian Leadership Conference helped organize the 1963 March on Washington. The spirit of ingenuity among African Americans was undaunted, though. It was at this period that employment barriers against blacks began to crumble; thus the patent, trademark, and copyright systems yielded their grip on selective hiring practices and began to earnestly employ African Americans in the ranks of intellectual property examiners.

Dr. Ida Gray of Cincinnati, Ohio, is reputed to have been the first African American female dentist. She received her dental degree from the University of Michigan in 1890.

Dr. Hallie Tanner Johnson is the earliest woman to practice medicine in Alabama. Her husband was the president of Allen University, and she is the sister of famed painter Henry O. Tanner.

Dr. Jennie R. Patrick is the first African American woman to obtain a Ph.D. in chemical engineering. In 1983, she was honored in Ciba-Geigy's Exceptional Black Scientists Poster Series while a senior research engineer at the Philip Morris Research Center in Virginia.

Teresa Duncan Cox of Plainfield, New Jersey, is the first African American woman to earn a degree in nuclear engineering.

Sources: Washington *Afro-American*, July 30, 1983; Bertina Hunter and Mabel B. Perry, "Achievements of Black Woman, 1600–1900's," Newark, New Jersey, Alpha Kappa Alpha Sorority, February, 1988; letter from Dr. Patricia Crawford Dunn to author, 1991.

During these turbulent yet hopeful years, housewife Iula Carter of Ohio, hematological technician Reatha L. Wiggins of New York, and

Iula O. Carter.
From the Patricia Carter
Ives Sluby Collection.

the security conscious Marie Van Brittan Brown (with Albert Brown), also of New York, each filed for and received a patent grant. Respectively, they met all government requirements for a portable nursery chair, a portable plurality of aspirators for collecting liquid samples, and a home security system using television surveillance. In 1991, Carter established and headed in Ohio the Dayton–Miami Valley Educational Affiliate of the National Intellectual Property Law Association.

Numerous technological advances were being made that turned entire industries around. The classic upright typewriter was fading along with reel-to-reel recording tapes, Beta video recording, and the corner telephone booth, to name a few items. Computers, synthetics, and laser technology coupled with space stations and satellites began to rule

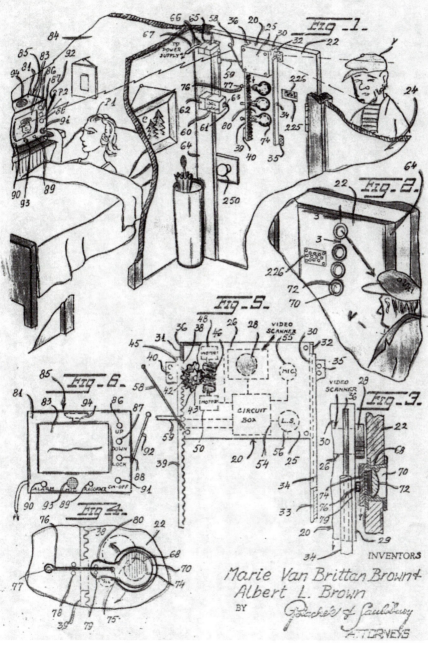

Home Security System Utilizing Television Surveillance, patented invention of Marie Van Brittan Brown and Albert L. Brown.

Valerie Thomas.
From the Patricia Carter
Ives Sluby Collection.

everyday life. Nonetheless, the patent and trademark systems embraced the highly technical innovations side by side with the mundane.

A flurry of female ingenuity closed out the last three decades of the twentieth century. The 1970s produced patentees Olivia Saxton, Gertrude Downing, Leonora Rocke, Virgie Ammons, Dorothy Hayes, Evelyn Carmon Nicol, coinventors Beatrice L. Cowans and Virginia E. Hall, Debrilla Ratchford, and Mary A. Moore. Their inventions, decorative or utilitarian in nature, range from cleaning devices, fireplace tools, three-dimensional architectural panels, and wall hangings to a security anchor, a transporting luggage hook, pharmaceuticals, and chemical processes. Some women teamed with family or associates; others labored independently. Still others worked at corporate or educational laboratories.

The 1980s highlight patentees Mildred Austin Smith for a game, Maxine W. Snowden for a rain hat, NASA physicist Valerie Thomas for independently patenting an illusion transmitter, Donna Richards for a file-folder retainer, and Deanna R. Meredith for a skateboard. Moreover, vacuum-cleaner-attachment producer Claudette D. Hill and air

Patricia E. Bath.
From the IOKTS Archives,
photographer, G. Theo-
dore Catherine.

freshener innovator Yvonne Bolling received grants. This decade show-cased also a number of design patent holders. Prolific inventor Jacquelyn A. Briggery Myles of Dayton, Ohio, received twelve design patents on ornamental swimwear from 1981 through 1986, and Joan Clark obtained a design patent on a medicine tray. The design of Ann A. Moore's infant carrier was assigned to the Snugli Company. Ruane Sharon Jeter is the sole designer of a toaster and of a cabinet and, with relative Sheila Lynn Jeter, designed a handheld multifunctional office device as well. Additionally, Ruane Jeter and colleagues at Graphic Control Corporation patented a serviceable medical waste disposal container. Lawyer Amy R. Goldson co-invented a baby bib, discussed later, with her husband.

Renowned professor emeritus Dr. Patricia E. Bath, nominated to the National Inventors Hall of Fame by the National Intellectual Property Law Association, is an internationally acclaimed ophthalmologist who has revolutionized surgical techniques for restoring vision to those blinded by eye diseases like glaucoma. Commonly, in delicate eye surgery, a mechanical drill-like tool is employed to grind away the cataract, a cloudiness of the lens of the eye. Bath's innovation, patented in 1988,

United States Patent [19]

Bath

[11] Patent Number: **4,744,360**

[45] Date of Patent: **May 17, 1988**

[54] **APPARATUS FOR ABLATING AND REMOVING CATARACT LENSES**

[76] Inventor: **Patricia E. Bath,** 4554 Circle View Blvd., Los Angeles, Calif. 90024

[21] Appl. No.: **943,098**

[22] Filed: **Dec. 18, 1986**

[51] Int. Cl.⁴ A61B 17/36
[52] U.S. Cl. 128/303.1; 128/397; 604/20; 604/35; 604/43
[58] Field of Search 128/303.1, 395, 397, 128/398; 604/22, 20, 35, 43

[56] **References Cited**

U.S. PATENT DOCUMENTS

3,460,538	8/1969	Armstrong	128/303.1
3,971,382	7/1976	Kransov	
3,982,541	9/1976	L'Esperance, Jr.	128/303.1
4,024,866	5/1977	Wallach	604/22
4,320,761	3/1982	Haddad	604/22
4,538,608	9/1985	L'Esperance, Jr.	128/395
4,580,559	4/1986	L'Esperance .	
4,583,539	4/1986	Karlin et al.	128/395

OTHER PUBLICATIONS

"Heatless Laser Etching" by John Free; Popular Science 12/83.
Serial No. 702,569 filed 2-19-85 to Gruen et al.

Primary Examiner—Lee S. Cohen
Assistant Examiner—David Shay
Attorney, Agent, or Firm—Cushman, Darby & Cushman

[57] **ABSTRACT**

A method and apparatus for removing cataracts in which a flexible line preferably 1 mm or less in diameter is inserted through an incision into the anterior chamber until its end is adjacent the cataract. Coherent radiation, preferably at a frequency between 193 and 351 nm, is coupled to the cataract by an optical fiber in the line. An irrigation sleeve provided about the fiber and an aspiration sleeve extending partially around the irrigation sleeve conduct irrigating liquid to and remove ablated material from the anterior chamber and form with the optical fiber the flexible line.

7 Claims, 1 Drawing Sheet

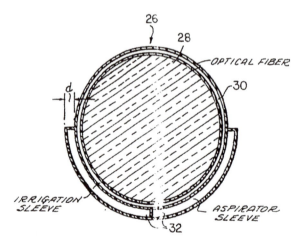

Apparatus for Ablating and Removing Cataract Lenses, patented invention of Patricia E. Bath, M.D.

uses a laser-powered probe that vaporizes and fragments the cataract in minutes.

Bath was born in 1942 in Harlem and attended public schools in New York City. Her father was an immigrant from Trinidad, British

West Indies, and her mother was the descendant of African slaves and Cherokee Indians. In 1964, she graduated from Hunter College in New York and in 1968 earned her M.D. degree with honors at the Howard University School of Medicine. Bath performed eye surgery offshore in Tunisia, Nigeria, Pakistan, China, and Yugoslavia.[17] Owner of several patents, she received her latest in 2000 on an improved eye surgery technique.

Like business entrepreneur Madame Walker, Dr. Frances Christian Gaskin of Albany, New York, founded a firm in her name after discovering new products to protect African Americans. Gaskin, a clinical nurse for three decades, earned a doctorate from Fordham University for research on melanin. Frances Christian Gaskin, Inc., an outgrowth of Gaskin's dissertation, produced the first patented melanin-based sun-care and hair-care products in the United States. The company successfully manufactured novel products to shield African Americans from harmful sun rays. As a by-product of her 1989 patent, Gaskin's progressive business persevered against all comers. Continuing her innovative trend, Gaskin is taking advantage of all elements of intellectual property.

The closing decade of the twentieth century ushered in previously mentioned patent holder Bath, sisters Bertha B. Cook and Betty J. Smith, Janice Goffney, and Levonia Jones along with Carol Randall, Dawn Francis, and Jean M. Gatling. Included in the 1990s are Emeline Stevens and Joanna Hardin, both of New York City; Natalie R. Love of Baltimore; designer Brothella Quick of Evanston, Illinois; and Natalie Robinson of Bowie, Maryland, and Connie D. Blair of Indiana.

For the Monsanto Agricultural Company, Virginian Dannette Connor-Ward, formerly of St. Louis, Missouri, cleaned out obstacles that ruined crops by developing a nonselective herbicide marketed as Roundup. Connor-Ward, a senior research biologist, coengineered a method for transferring herbicide-resistant genes into soybeans that are spliced with a certain gene. As a significant invention for farm production, the sprayed chemical assists the survival of the engineered soybean by destroying weeds deficient in the spliced gene. The dedicated inventor works at the company in an unprecedented area of agricultural biotechnology.

The singular career of Lynne T. McGuire of Washington, D.C., inspired creative thought in mortuary science. She was successful at patenting a self-contained viscera treatment unit, a device that treats, stores, and drains the internal organs of the body. Young Tahira Reid of New York City envisioned a double dutch jump rope when she was a third grader.[18] After several prototype revisions, the college-age inventor received a patent on her eventual double dutch machine.

Most African American women inventors are unknown in the mainstream of intellectual data. Others have made an imprint in the minds of authors and their readers. Some women took out patents on their hobbies, avocations, and sundry interests, and various ones obtained grants via their vocation, employment, and educational training. Given the increase of women in the workforce and the shifts in the workplace paradigm coupled with economic, cultural, and global changes, the new century promises more diverse feminine ingenuity.

Little known is the governmental participation of African American women in an allied field of invention and creative talent. As U.S. patent, trademark, and copyright examiners, they are specialized, professionally trained scientists or jurists who place the official stamp of approval on applications that mature into a patent, trademark, or copyright. A number of African American female examiners sign and issue the federal grants to minority inventors or writers worthy of the distinction. In the private sector, the talent of black female intellectual property attorneys is quite evident as well. They are law-firm members or partners, sole owners of their practices, and university professors of intellectual property.

FAMILIAL INVENTIVENESS

... and thou shalt spread abroad to the west,
and to the east, and to the north, and to the south:
and in thee and in thy seed shall all the families
of the earth be blessed.

Genesis 28:14

The word *family*, a collective noun, means relations, in particular, a group of people having common ancestry or ties that bind one to another. Family lines follow many trails peppered with winding paths. From one such trail springs familial inventiveness. Hobbies and varied interests beacon family members toward reward for creative thinking, each member encouraging the other. At times these inventive relations are sisters, brothers, or brother and sister. Other times the creative combination includes husband and wife, acting as coinventors or independently, or the combination of father and son or mother and son or daughter. On occasion cousins become patent holders jointly or independently.

During the ugly days of slavery, families deliberately were torn apart. Sons and daughters were sold off from arms of loving mothers, fathers were split from families, and mothers were separated from the nest. Afterward, families reunited as best they could and stayed together in black enclaves in the North and in the segregated South seeking to improve their welfare. Families moved from place to place to aspire toward a better life, finding temporary lodging, at times, with relatives until they could get on their feet.

Similarity of habits, traits, and interests will likely influence thinking processes because of close proximity of family members and relations. Solving problems and working out solutions increase skills. African Americans participated in these processes to achieve comfortable homes and an improved environment. Moreover, improved business practices bring promises of a better livelihood. In spite of terrorism, peonage, and the prohibition against joining trade unions, blacks managed to provide for their families, exhibiting the ability to triumph over all comers and difficulties.

SISTER ACTS

Inventors Mary Beatrice Davidson Kenner and her sister Mildred Davidson Austin Smith blossomed from one family. Their unusual creative abilities illustrate the extraordinary talent of women. Both were born in Charlotte, North Carolina, Mary Beatrice on May 17, 1912, and Mildred on January 31, 1916. They believed that their natural talent for discovery came from their nurturing, inventive father, Sidney Nathaniel Davidson, who was born in June 1890 and died in November 1958. When Beatrice was just a toddler, he began working on an invention for a pants presser that was patented in 1914. Their maternal grandfather, Robert Phromeberger, of German and Irish extraction, tinkered with objects to make them work better. He invented many devices, including a tricolor light signal for trains.[19]

This family's ingenuity formed a pattern that the two sisters followed. Beatrice was the first to exhibit exceptional female intuitiveness. She has received patents in diverse areas and continues to think of new ideas while retired from active work as a professional floral arranger who operated her own business. Beatrice has utility patents on catamenial devices (two), an invalid walker, a toilet-tissue holder, and a back washer mounting on a shower wall and bathtub.

When Mildred was a young, married woman with two young sons, she was stricken with multiple sclerosis and was incapacitated. During her lengthy illness, she had lots of time to think. Eventually she thought of a game to teach family relationships, so she filed for a patent. The game is for young people to help them understand their place in the extended family. After receiving the "Family Relationships Card Game" patent in 1980, Mildred protected her brainchild, getting a trademark on the game's name, "Family Treedition." She manufactured it in Braille as well. After a long illness Mildred passed away on

Mary Beatrice Kenner.
From the Patricia Carter
Ives Sluby Collection.

July 30, 1993, in Washington, D.C.[20] Her marketing and distribution strategies did not make her rich, but she was able to recover some money that she spent to market the enterprise.

Sisters Bertha B. Cook and Betty J. Smith, both of Southfield, Michigan, explored the idea of a multiple-character doll to keep a child's interest and avoid boredom while making it convenient to carry around one doll rather than to store or transport multiple dolls. Draping more than three of the four "simulated figures" to hide them, a fabric covers the figures and the center body section such that the doll element exposes one figure for view. The sisters received a patent grant in 1990.

United States Patent [19]

Kenner

[11] **3,957,071**

[45] **May 18, 1976**

2,887,348	5/1959	Sadowsky	108/124
3,596,668	8/1971	Tosto	135/45 A
3,625,237	12/1971	Wertz	135/45 A

[54] **CARRIER ATTACHMENT FOR INVALID WALKERS**

[76] Inventor: **M. Beatrice Kenner**, 6300 Linway Terrace, McLean, Va. 22101

[22] Filed: **Sept. 10, 1975**

[21] Appl. No.: **612,037**

[52] U.S. Cl. .... 135/47; 108/115; 135/45 A
[51] Int. Cl.² A45B 3/00
[58] Field of Search .... 108/13, 14, 15, 25, 108/115, 124; 135/45 A, 47; 297/5, 6; 224/46 T

[56] **References Cited**

UNITED STATES PATENTS

2,430,235　11/1947　Mendenhall .... 135/45 A

Primary Examiner—James T. McCall
Assistant Examiner—Darrell Marquette
Attorney, Agent, or Firm—William J. Daniel

[57] **ABSTRACT**

A carrier attachment including a rigid tray section and a pocket section is suspended by connecting straps from one side of the top frame member of an invalid walker. The tray section can be swung to operative position above and supported by the top frame member.

7 Claims, 6 Drawing Figures

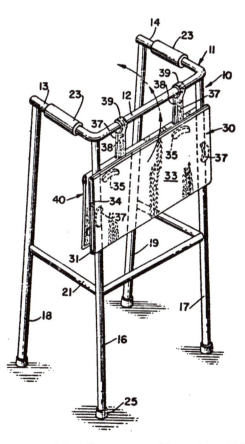

Carrier Attachment for Invalid Walkers, patented invention of M. Beatrice Kenner.

Mildred Austin Smith.
From the Patricia Carter
Ives Sluby Collection.

BROTHER, BROTHER

John Beckley and Charles Beckley, both born in the 1930s in Washington, D.C., followed different paths as young adults, but later found common ground as creative thinkers and tinkerers. John, a retired pharmacist and a full-time artist, is two years senior to Charles, a retired Department of Labor attorney. Their paternal ancestors were from Beckley, West Virginia, one of whom, John Beckley, signed the U.S. Bill of Rights. Edgar Randolph Beckley, their father and a Howard University Medical School graduate in 1889, married Gabrielle Dorothy Pelham of Washington, D.C. Three sons were born to the couple.[21] Gabrielle Dorothy's father, editor and publisher Robert Pelham (1859–1943) of Michigan, moved to Washington, D.C., in 1900, and worked for the U.S. Census Bureau for thirty-seven years, where he developed and patented a pasting apparatus and engineered a tallying machine. His newspaper, the *Plain Dealer* in Detroit, was a premier African American Midwest journal. The Pelhams were industrious and enterprising. Fred Pelham, uncle of John and Charles, installed the first talking

MILDRED A. SMITH
Family Relationships CardGame

U.S. Patent   Oct. 28, 1980   4,230,321

FIG. 1.

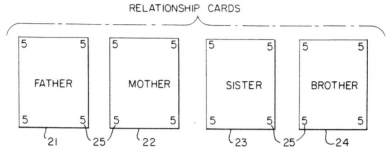

FIG. 2.

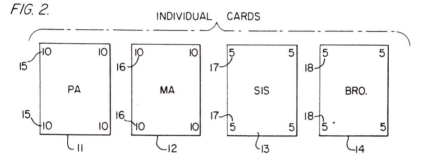

FIG. 3.

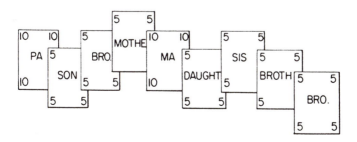

Family Relationships Card Game, patented invention of Mildred A. Smith.

motion-picture system at one of the large, white movie theaters in Washington, D.C., but was denied entry to see movie productions.[22]

The sons were encouraged to tinker and explore the unknown. This stimulated independent thinking, fueling interest in doing things a different way. Charles, a graduate of Mount Herman School, was the first to receive patents. On December 24, 1974, he obtained a grant for a folding chair. The folding seat "includes a web which is supported between a pair of folding frames by three detachable cross members extending between the frames." Charles received four more patents on the folding or "knockdown" furniture from 1977 to 1979.

After attending Tilton Preparatory School in New Hampshire and Champlain College in Plattsburg, New York, John completed pharmacy school at Howard University. Following a full career in the medical profession, John became a renowned metalsmith and sculptor. Several U.S. galleries showcase his extraordinary talent. John acquired his first, second, and third patents in 1996 (two) and in 1998, all for a "Vertical Lifted Portable Electric Furnace." His registered trademark for the device is "the Melting Pot."

Gloster J. Garrett and Herbert C. Garrett, brothers of Richmond, Indiana, filed a patent application in 1912 for a vehicle wheel. Their objective was to provide a resilient wheel for automobiles or other vehicles that was "strong and durable in construction, neat and attractive in appearance," lightweight, and economical. The construction dispensed with the "use of the ordinary pneumatic tires." A year later, they received a U.S. patent grant.

Brothers William Jacob Knox, Jr., Ph.D., and Lawrence Howland Knox, Ph.D., were knowledgeable professors on the academic scene and accomplished scientists at various chemical companies. Born in New Bedford, Massachusetts, these achievers, who both attended Harvard University, had careers in physical chemistry and in organic chemistry, respectively, and acquired nearly three dozen patents between them.

Born in 1903, William (discussed previously) had the greater number of grants, concentrating on inventions relating to photography, before retiring. After leaving as head of the department of chemistry at North Carolina College, younger brother Lawrence pursued a lengthy vocation in synthetic organic chemistry at several research centers. Both siblings were members of the American Chemical Society among other professional organizations, and both received numerous awards.

BROTHERS AND SISTERS

One of the early African American women to receive a U.S. letters patent was Miriam E. Benjamin. In 1888, Miriam received a patent on a gong and signal chair for hotels and other places. The chair was used in the U.S. House of Representatives to get the attention of pages during House proceedings. Interestingly, her invention was witnessed by chronicler Henry E. Baker at the time of her filing the application in 1887. The *Colored American* on November 14, 1903, reported that yet another invention on a pinking device useful in dressmaking was patented by Miriam.[23]

Born in 1861 in Charleston, South Carolina, Miriam, the oldest of four children, spent her high school years with her family in Boston, Massachusetts. Between 1888 and 1895, she was in Washington, D.C., where she taught school and lived in the northwest section of the city at 1736 New York Avenue. Between 1894 and 1895 Miriam attended medical school at Howard University, matriculating there for a session as a student in her early thirties. By 1900, she was back in Boston, proclaiming herself as a "solicitor of patents." Her address is given as 34 School Street, room 28.[24]

The inventive bug in her family was not limited to just Miriam. A younger brother, Lyde W. Benjamin of Boston, Massachusetts, patented a broom moistener and bridle on May 16, 1893. The object of the invention was "to keep the broom moist while sweeping without being so wet as to drip, and to prevent the dust from rising." The bridle of the broom helped to bind together the straws to prevent them from spreading. What is most engaging on his patent drawing is that Miriam, given that she is M. E. Benjamin, is identified as the attorney! Miriam Benjamin, in addition to being one of the earliest black female inventors, *could* be the earliest known African American woman patent attorney, but there is no definitive proof. (The register for patent attorneys and agents commenced in 1883 and she is not listed among the registrants.) At a period when few women, black or white, were practicing law, this would be a rare attainment. The place and date she received her legal training is unknown. It is possible that she "read the law" under the tutelage of one of her brothers, who was a lawyer, or under the instruction some other attorney. Perhaps, too, she graduated from a law school. Additionally, some technical or scientific background is an asset to someone practicing patent law, but where Miriam may have attained this instruction is also unknown. (Her attendance at medical school was subsequent to the year 1883.) In any case, Miriam Benjamin's name is recorded in history as an "attorney" on an official government document.

Irma G. Dixon and her brother, Reverend Benjamin F. Thornton, Jr., both of Washington, D.C., invented an underarm perspiration pad that is "readily" flexible to the body contour besides absorbing underarm perspiration. A U-shaped wire frame provides flexibility for the antiperspirant shield and forms a pocket for the arm to fit. The couple applied for a patent on the notion in October 1957 and received it in 1959.

OTHER INVENTIVE COUPLETS

Husband and Wife

Olivia Saxton of Indianapolis, Indiana, invented a theft-deterrent anchor for securing furniture such as television sets, chairs, and tables in the home or office. A chain is welded to a rod mounted to the furniture and then anchored to the floor or wall structure. Her patent for an "Anchor for Furniture Including Television Sets with Telescopic Insert Rod" was issued in 1978.

Olivia's husband, Richard L. Saxton, had his own idea. In 1983, he patented a "Pay Telephone with Sanitized Tissue Dispenser." After the user deposits a coin, a tissue dispenses from the telephone unit for "each consumer to wipe the pay telephone before using it." This refreshes the telephone, giving the consumer "some protection from germs."

The husband and wife team of Dr. Alfred L. Goldson and attorney Amy R. Goldson of Washington, D.C., developed a unique device to benefit them and their infant child as well. When "worn by either parent, the device improves bonding between the child and parent, especially for the male, by anatomically simulating the female." The Goldsons came up with a "bib-like device for assisting in nursing a child" that enhances bonding between the male parent and infant.

The unit, preferably made from fabric, has a pair of pouches called "the bonder," with an opening "sized to permit" a bottle nipple to extend through it. The Goldsons received a patent in 1988 for their "Parent-Child Bonding Bib," which they marketed. They appeared on television and in the print media promoting their invention.

Mother and Son

Levonia Jones of Suitland, Maryland, and her son, Bruce K. Smith of Landover, Maryland, ingeniously produced a method and apparatus for recycling soap by combining its segments. Jones and Smith, one of a set of identical twins, provide a configured soap mold inside a canister to construct the final product. The inventors promote the idea as putting "an end to the problems and inconvenience of having to deal with remaining slivers of soap." They obtained a patent in 1991 for their "Soap Saving Method and Apparatus," featured as the "Soap Buster" on the television series *Why Didn't I Think of That?* in 1992.

United States Patent [19]

Goldson et al.

[11] Patent Number: 4,776,546

[45] Date of Patent: Oct. 11, 1988

[54] **PARENT-CHILD BONDING BIB**

[76] Inventors: **Alfred L. Goldson; Amy R. Goldson**, both of 4015 28th Pl., NW., Washington, D.C. 20008

[21] Appl. No.: **47,101**

[22] Filed: **May 8, 1987**

[51] **Int. Cl.⁴** **A47D 15/00**
[52] **U.S. Cl.** **248/102; 224/148**
[58] **Field of Search** .... 248/102, 104, 103; 2/75, 49 R; 224/148, 251, 258, 901

[56]   **References Cited**

U.S. PATENT DOCUMENTS

1,987,132	1/1935	Shine	248/104
2,494,632	1/1950	Rodin	224/148 X
2,577,849	12/1951	Henry	248/102 X
3,065,944	11/1962	Liebendorfer	224/148 X
3,085,612	4/1963	Gobel	248/102 UX
4,220,302	9/1980	Hampton	224/148 X
4,498,613	2/1985	Donahue	248/102 X
4,537,341	8/1985	Kelly	224/148 X

FOREIGN PATENT DOCUMENTS

| 678702 | 1/1964 | Canada | 248/105 |

OTHER PUBLICATIONS

The Washington Post, J. Street, Sep. 27, 1987.
The Right Start Catalog p. 14, Spring/Summer 1987.
Life Span Development, Martin Blook, New York, Mac-Millan Pub. 1980, "How Love Begins Between Parent and Child".

Primary Examiner—J. Franklin Foss
Attorney, Agent, or Firm—Vorys, Sater, Seymour and Pease

[57]   **ABSTRACT**

A bib-like device for assisting in nursing a child and improving bonding between a parent and the child. The device includes a bib-like member made from a fabric, such as terry cloth, comfortable for the child. The device defined includes a generally mammary-shaped area defining a pouch therein for retaining a container of liquid, such as formula, milk, juice, or water for the child. The pouch is sized to receive the container therein and communicates with an opening in the fabric for permitting a nipple on the container to protrude therefrom. When worn by either parent, the device improves bonding between the child and parent, especially for the male, by anatomically simulating the female.

28 Claims, 1 Drawing Sheet

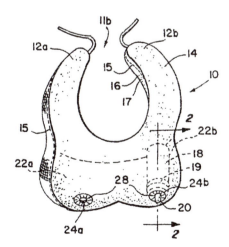

Parent-Child Bonding Bib, patented invention of Alfred L. Goldson and Amy R. Goldson.

Albert W. Turner, Sr.
From the Patricia Carter
Ives Sluby Collection,
courtesy of Glennette
Tilley Turner.

Father and Son

Howard University dean of the School of Engineering and professor Darnley E. Howard developed an apparatus for a milling machine where the machine operator knows the position of a tool with respect "to the work being acted upon." His "Optical Apparatus for Indicating the Position of a Tool" was patented in 1939.

Exactly thirty years and five months later, in 1969, his son, Darnley Moseley Howard of College Park, Maryland, along with Irving Mathis, secured a patent for a "Method of Making Radome with an Integral Antenna" while working for the U.S. Department of the Navy. The radome has a "separate antenna positioned inside the reflector" that eliminates "microphonics due to relative motion between the antenna and radome." Born in Brooklyn, New York, Howard graduated from Howard University in 1947 after completing mechanical engineering requirements and went to serve as an engineer at the National Bureau of Standards. He became a department head at Litton Systems and was senior mechanical engineer at Johns Hopkins University Applied Physics Laboratory. Later he achieved the position of executive officer at the U.S. Postal Service.

Albert W. Turner of Wheaton, Illinois, born in 1927 in New Orleans, Louisiana, says that he "set a goal early on to be an inventor." In senior high school at the time of World War II, he studied automotive mechanics. After graduation, he joined the navy to fulfill his military obligation, and two years later he attended Tuskegee Institute, where he received a degree in commercial industries-automotive mechanics.[25]

Thus Turner was prepared to make discoveries and to tinker. This experience netted him a patent on "lever assemblies for augmenting prime mover power" in 1978. The lever actuates an alternator that generates electrical power for vehicles tilted on irregular roadbeds.

His son, Cyril Turner of Stone Mountain, Georgia, nineteen years after his father, patented a "Sloped Gutter Assembly" in 1997. The device provides for the "controlled discharge of runoff water" from roofs to prevent the collection of leaves and debris.

Besides an inventive father, Cyril's maternal great-grandmother, Lydia M. Holmes, was an early black woman inventor, born in 1881 in Illinois and raised in Nebraska. She received her patent when a resident in St. Augustine, Florida, in 1950, on a knockdown wheeled toy for use "in homes, nursery schools and the like, to encourage the ability of concentration in young children."

Cousins

Inventors Estelle W. Sanders of Washington, D.C., and attorney Lawrence J. Goffney, Jr., formerly of Detroit, Michigan, now a resident of Alexandria, Virginia, are cousins who linked together on a "Scalp Massaging Implement," patented in 1982. Estelle, former owner of Georgetown Women's Club, and her cousin devised a device for use with human fingers to agitate and massage the scalp and hair during shampoos. The nails of the human hand tend unnecessarily to abrade the scalp to loosen dirt and dandruff, and the nails often are damaged. With the cousins' appliance, the fingers are oriented "in a way that allows only the tips of the fingers" to be in contact with the scalp. A rubber fingertip covering provides desired results. In 1990, Janice F. Goffney of Detroit, Michigan, teamed with her coinventor Maurice T. Gray, a tennis professional and also of Detroit, to receive a grant on a tennis racquet with a detachable handle for storing in a small suitcase or travel bag. She hired her former spouse, Lawrence Goffney, a patent attorney, to handle the prosecution of the patent application.

Attorney John R. Moses of Annapolis, Maryland, is filled with inventive spirit. He has received patents as the sole inventor and as joint inventor as well. Moses and Adolph Fram obtained a patent in 1981 on a lubricating oil filter-refiner for internal combustion engines, and two years later in 1983, Moses alone succeeded in getting a patent on a flat emergency exit sign using an electro-illuminescent lamp. After attending Mount Herman School for Boys, Moses graduated from Yale University and later received a law degree from Catholic University. Presently he is a partner at the intellectual property law firm of Millen, White, Zelano, and Branigan.

Robert P. Moses of Cambridge, Massachusetts, John's cousin, was

John R. Moses.
From the Patricia Carter
Ives Sluby Collection.

granted his coveted document in 1996 for games to enhance mathematical understanding. Known as "Flagways," the game is designed to bring math literacy to every schoolchild. Afterward, he was awarded a patent for the method of playing the games. Bob Moses, a legend in civil rights action, developed the Algebra Project that uses the product. In 2000, the National Intellectual Property Law Association nominated Moses to the National Inventors Hall of Fame at Akron, Ohio. The Algebra Project received $12.9 million from the George Soros Foundation to expand and develop further its meritorious work aimed nationwide. *Smithsonian* and *Reader's Digest* have lauded his accomplishments.[26]

Relations, Perhaps

It is highly likely that inventors John Albert Burr and William F. Burr were related. Each hailed from Agawam, Massachusetts, assigned patent rights to the same individual, Oscar L. King, and employed the same patent attorney in 1898 and 1899. The two patent holders also had the drawings of their inventions witnessed by the same persons.

John Burr, the earlier patentee, conceived an improved lawn mower

United States Patent [19]

Moses

[11] **Patent Number:** **5,520,542**

[45] **Date of Patent:** **May 28, 1996**

[54] **GAMES FOR ENHANCING MATHEMATICAL UNDERSTANDING**

[76] Inventor: **Robert P. Moses**, 73 School St., Cambridge, Mass. 02139

[21] Appl. No.: **371,074**

[22] Filed: **Jan. 10, 1995**

[51] Int. Cl.⁶ **G09B 1/00**; G09B 19/00; G09B 23/02

[52] U.S. Cl. **434/209**; 434/207

[58] Field of Search 434/207, 209, 434/205, 188; 273/299, 302

[56] **References Cited**

U.S. PATENT DOCUMENTS

1,415,019	5/1922	Crossland	434/209
1,694,405	12/1928	Troidl	434/207
2,839,844	6/1958	Lahnkering	434/209
4,512,746	4/1985	Turner	434/209
5,083,793	1/1992	Sanford	434/207
5,242,171	9/1993	Hata	434/207
5,318,447	6/1991	Mooney	434/209

Primary Examiner—Paul J. Hirsch
Attorney, Agent, or Firm—Millen, White, Zelano, & Branigan

[57] **ABSTRACT**

A game for enhancing mathematical skills is played in the a classroom with teams of players or individual players. The game utilizes a branched lattice having a central starting point and a plurality of terminal points. The lattice is placed on the floor of a classroom. In playing the game, students select three numbers from a location on the classroom wall and factor those three numbers to find the prime factors of the numbers, which prime factors are then recorded in input/output tables. The tables have an output line or column in which the output value "−1" is written if the number of factors is odd; the output value "0" is written if the output value includes repeated primes, indicating raising a prime to a power; and the output value "+1" is written if the number of prime factors is even. The output values are used to locate the input/output tables, which are on slips of paper, at correct terminal points of the lattice. The path to each of the terminal points comprises three legs of the lattice, with each of the legs being defined by one of the output values "−1," "0" and "+1." A frequency table is provided to retire the number chips in columns in accordance with their output values. In accordance with additional embodiments of the invention, the game is played in combination with a Venn diagram puzzle having color chips which are assembled in accordance with the results of casting color-coded dice. In accordance with still further embodiments of the invention, the lattice is configured as a three-dimensional, color-coded array, with legs extending parallel to one another being of the same color.

16 Claims, 20 Drawing Sheets

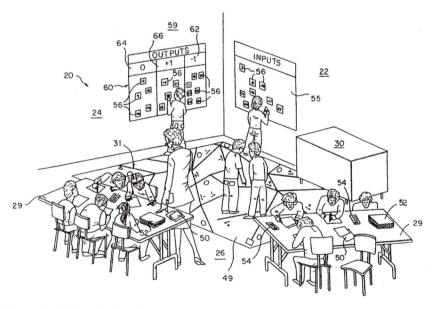

Games for Enhancing Mathematical Understanding, patented invention of Robert P. Moses.

"of the most common type comprising traction wheels and a rotary cutter or shear operating in conjunction with a fixed bar." The invention provided for a "casing which wholly incloses the operating gear" to prevent choking by grass or clogging by obstructions, therefore making it possible to cut grass closer to a building.

The railway switching device of William Burr improved the performance of street railways. The automatic action of the switching device switched the car to the siding or branch. Also, it ensured the running of the car on the main track. The contraption included a casing that enclosed an upright support and a section of a roller.

The Burr patents were issued within six months of each other in 1899. No models were submitted for the ingenious devices, as that requirement had been lifted by the Patent Office a few years earlier.

When the creative juices flow to help solve a problem in family circles, many times another family member will produce a unique idea to improve on the original concept. Family members also share resources and information, teaming toward a common goal. In the midst of a friendly environment, relations feel comfortable and can think or tinker without interruption. This support system fosters creative thinking that advances science and the useful arts.

7

THE NEW AGE
The Leading Edge of Technology

We have decided to write a full history . . . to inspire the youth
of this land to high endeavor, to encourage them in every laudable attempt to rise, and let them see what has already been
accomplished, and thus give hope for the years to come.
  Giles B. Jackson and D. Webster Davis, *Industrial History*, 1908

EQUAL EMPLOYMENT

Racial equality, the dream, the hope, is the laudable attempt of mankind to rise above past inequities. In spite of insidious actions against
this equality, African Americans sharpened their technological tools.
They invented means to change their way of life, and they pushed the
federal government into providing civil, social, and economic relief.

A balm came in the form of numerous federal acts—the Civil Rights
Act, the Economic Opportunity Act, and the Fair Housing Act. It took
the special Equal Employment Opportunity Act of 1981 to prohibit the
use of numerical quotas in hiring or in school enrollment of minorities
and of women, which amended the deficiencies of the Civil Rights Act
of 1964.

The turbulent civil rights years were, however, colored with outstanding achievements. Doors opened for people of hue, now hired to
fill openings in positions formerly closed to them. Lieutenant Com-
mander Samuel L. Gravely of Richmond, Virginia, became the first of
his race to command a U.S. war vessel the year following the appoint-
ment of Robert Weaver as administrator of the Housing and Home

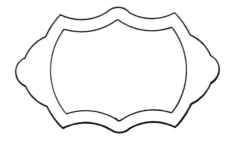

Fig. 1.

Fig. 2.

INVENTOR

Dennis A. Forbes,

BY

N. Ralph Burdon

ATTORNEY

Card for Chemistry Games, patented invention of Dennis A. Forbes.

Finance Agency and the selection of Whitney Young as executive director of the National Urban League. African Americans graduated from the Air Force Academy, Sidney Poitier became the first black to receive an Academy Award for best actor, and journalist Carl T. Rowan was hired as the head of the U.S. Information Service. Edward W. Brooke became the first of his color to be elected to the U.S. Senate since Reconstruction near the time civil rights attorney Constance Baker Motley was appointed the first African American woman federal judge, and Solicitor General Thurgood Marshall was the first black appointed to the U.S. Supreme Court.

The four decades of the 1960s through the 1990s heralded a shift of the black population from rural areas to inner cities, then to urban communities. The income margin of African Americans and of whites decreased due to the increase of black family incomes. The number of black women in the workforce escalated as well as their presence as heads of households. Although blacks made substantial gains, the gap between the haves and the have-nots widened. Civil rights and affirmative action policies made decades earlier were disassembled by directives of two presidential administrations in the late 1980s and early 1990s.

Against this background of the last four decades is a picture of unprecedented achievement among African American creative thinkers. Most of them took advantage of intellectual property in the popular form of a patent grant (utility and design types), but others sought the protection of registered trademarks, and a mass of creative minds gained federal copyright protection on the written word. The 1895 patented spoon design of coinventors William H. Purdy and Leonard C. Peters, both of Providence, Rhode Island, merits special mention. The designers sketched a portrait bust of the leading African American figure, Frederick Douglass, surmounted by laurel branches, on the upper portion of the spoon's handle. In the spoon's bowl or ladle is the representation of a typical southern log cabin located in a clearing and the figure of a boy carrying across his shoulder a stick from which is suspended a bundle. On the narrow portion of the spoon's handle is the representation of a ladder that symbolically depicts that the boy is setting out to step up and climb to the height of a great figure. The imagery is profound, figuratively showing deprivation, but also hope to reach beyond disadvantaged beginnings.

United States Patent Office

Des. 223,086
Patented Mar. 7, 1972

223,086

ROTATABLE SURVEILLANCE CAPSULE FOR BUILDINGS

Ronald B. Royster, Sr., 1705 Belle Haven Drive, Apt. 203, Landover, Md. 20785

Filed Jan. 15, 1970, Ser. No. 20,943

Term of patent 14 years

Int. Cl. D25—03

U.S. Cl. D13—1

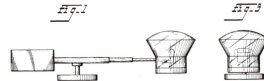

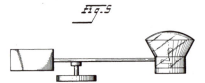

FIG. 1 is a front elevational view of the rotatable surveillance capsule for buildings showing my new design;

FIG. 2 is a top plan elevational view thereof;

FIG. 3 is a right side elevational view thereof;

FIG. 4 is a left side elevational view thereof;

FIG. 5 is a front elevational view of a modified form of the rotatable surveillance capsule for buildings described in FIG. 1 showing my new design.

The right side elevational view of FIG. 5 is identical to FIG. 3. The left side elevational view of FIG. 5 is identical to FIG. 4.

I claim:

The ornamental design for a rotatable surveillance capsule for buildings, as shown and described.

References Cited

UNITED STATES PATENTS

D. 99,613	5/1936	Sweet	D34—5
D. 186,524	11/1959	Bowers	D34—5
1,432,746	10/1922	Downey.	

A. HUGO WORD, Primary Examiner

Rotatable Surveillance Capsule for Buildings, patented invention of Ronald Royster.

United States Patent

Des. 237,022
Patented Oct. 7, 1975

237,022

BARBER'S APRON

Nathaniel Mathis, 4014 Vine St.,
Bradbury Heights, Md. 20027

Filed Mar. 8, 1973, Ser. No. 337,861

Term of patent 14 years

Int. Cl. D2—*02*

U.S. Cl. D2—229

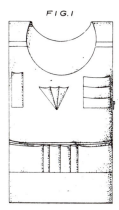

FIG. 1

FIG. 2

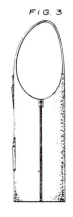

FIG. 3

FIG. 1 is a front elevational view of a barber's apron showing my new design;

FIG. 2 is a rear elevational view thereof; and

FIG. 3 is a side elevational view.

I claim:

The ornamental design for a barber's apron, as shown.

References Cited

UNITED STATES PATENTS

| D. 135,712 | 5/1943 | King | D2—229 |
| 2,066,072 | 12/1936 | Powell | 2—51 |

OTHER REFERENCES

Simplicity Patterns, January 1971, p. 813, pattern 8976.

LOIS S. LANIER, Primary Examiner

Barber's Apron, patented design of Nathaniel Mathis.

Patentee	Title	Number	Date
Allen, Johnny G.	Garbage Can Rack	Des. 320,104	September 17, 1991
Baker, Franklin W.	Antitheft Steering Wheel Restrictor	Des. 350,274	September 6, 1994
Barnes, George A.	Sign	Des. 29,193	August 9, 1898
Booker, Louis Fred	Rubber Scrap. Knife	Des. 30,404	March 28, 1899
Brown, Paul L., et al.	Gyro Top	Des. 322,100	December 3, 1991
Brown, Paul L., et al.	Spinning Musical Toy Top	Des. 331,082	November 17, 1992
Clark, Joan	Medicine Tray	Des. 283,249	April 1, 1986
Clark, Wardell F.	Cart for Pots, Pans	Des. 285,852	September 23, 1986
Forbes, Dennis A.	Card Game	Des. 91,996	April 17, 1934
Harper, David	Mobile Utility Rack	Des. 187,654	April 12, 1960
	Bookcase	Des. 190,500	June. 6, 1961
Harvey, Franklin	Comb	Des. 229,583	December 11, 1973
Hess, Constance R.	Combined Table & Cabinet	Des. 192,689	May 1, 1962
Jeter, Ruane, et al.	Toaster	Des. 289,249	April 14, 1987
	Hand-held Device	Des. 383,783	September 16, 1997
	Cabinet	Des. 411,008	June 15, 1999
Jeter, Sheila, et al.	Hand-held Device	Des. 383,783	September 16, 1997
Jones, Frederick M.	Air Conditioning Unit	Des. 132,182	April 28, 1942
	Air Conditioning Unit	Des. 159,209	July 4, 1950
Jordan, John H., Jr.	Divan	Des. 219,735	January 19, 1971
	Headboard for Bed	Des. 219,904	February 16, 1971
	Dresser	Des. 219,927	February 16, 1971
	Cocktail Table	Des. 220,768	May 18, 1971
	Combined Clock and Wall Plaque	Des. 220,965	June 22, 1971
Lovelady, Herbert G.	Sound Emitting Bobber	Des. 314,417	February 5, 1991
Lovell, Henry R.	Door Check	Des. 87,753	September 13, 1932
Mathis, Nathaniel	Barber's Apron	Des. 237,022	October 7, 1975
McCoy, Elijah	Rubber Heel	Des. 68,725	November 10, 1926
McDonald, Peter	Tire	Des. 270,723	September 27, 1983
	Tire	Des. 278,228	April 2, 1985
Moody, William U.	Game Board	Des. 27,046	May 11, 1897
Moore, Ann A.	Infant Carrier	Des. 277,811	March 5, 1985
Myles, Jacquelyn	Swimwear	Des. 259,821	July 14, 1981
	Swimwear	Des. 275,476	October 9, 1984
	Swimwear	Des. 278,472	April 23, 1985

Patentee	Title	Number	Date
	Swimwear	Des. 278,473	April 23, 1985
	Swimwear	Des. 278,474	April 23, 1985
	Swimwear	Des. 278,475	April 23, 1985
	Swimwear	Des. 278,476	April 23, 1985
	Swimwear	Des. 278,568	April 30, 1985
	Swimwear	Des. 278,569	April 30, 1985
	Swimwear	Des. 279,936	August 6, 1985
	Swimwear	Des. 280,252	August 27, 1985
	Swimwear	Des. 282,116	January 14, 1986
Oliphant, Adam L.	Portable Grill	Des. 301,106	May 16, 1989
Pickett, James, Jr.	Combined Lamp, Ornament & Container	Des. 289,694	May 5, 1987
Purdy, William H., et al.	Spoon	Des. 24,228	April 23, 1895
Quick, Brothella	Pocketed Underwear	Des. 341,470	November 23, 1993
Robinson, Hassell	Traffic Signal Casing	Des. 66,703	February 24, 1925
Rocke, Leonora	Corner Cleaning Brush	Des. 235,942	July 22, 1975
Royster, Ronald B.	Rotatable Surveillance Capsule	Des. 223,086	March 7, 1972
	Plate for Chain Door Locks	Des. 230,009	January 22, 1974
Scott, J. C.	Shadow Box	Des. 212,334	October 1, 1968
Still, Donald E.	Telephone Set	Des. 294,496	March 1, 1988
Taylor, Don A.	Toy Play Table	Des. 176,740	January 24, 1970
	Heater Adaptor	Des. 244,450	May 4, 1991
	Combined Display Counter	Des. 244,570	June 7, 1991
Taylor, Richard	Leaf Holder	Des. 105,037	June 22, 1937
Turner, Ronald L.	Eating Container	Des. 428,767	August 1, 2000
Wilson, Donald C.	Simulative Toy Vehicle	Des. 261,291	October 13, 1981
Wood, Robert	Wheeled Trundle Toy	Des. 270,847	October 4, 1983
Young, Joseph	Stimulant Massager	Des. 404,139	January 12, 1999

A trademark identifies the source of a product. It represents value, uniform quality, and the integrity of the owner and can be an arbitrary word, name, symbol, device, or slogan that is used by a manufacturer, seller, or other outlet for goods or for services. A small TM or ® identifies a registered trademark.

Like Madame C. J. Walker, who received full benefit from the protection the registered trademark offered her company, Henry G. Parks of Baltimore, Maryland, also utilized this process to cover his diligent, hardworking efforts. His firm, H. G. Parks, Inc., producer of meat products, obtained trademarks on the word "Parks." Parks's products—sausages are probably the best known—were found in most supermarkets across the country. A meat product, pork sausage, was registered under the mark in 1961, and refrigerated and/or frozen food products, such as pork and fresh, smoked, and cooked sausages, along with scrapple, cooked chitterlings, barbecue sauce, chili, chopped beef, and pork were registered under another mark in 1970. Directed by the leadership of Parks, the company was continually cited by *Black Enterprise* as one of the top one hundred black firms in the nation. Eventually the company was sold to another enterprise after Henry Parks's death.

The world-famous Motown Record Corporation, founded by Berry Gordy, Jr., in 1959, obtained numerous registered marks from the 1960s through decade after decade. In 1960, the black-owned company received its first gold record, *Shop Around* by Smokey Robinson (William Robinson, Jr.), a vice president of the corporation. Originally of Detroit, Michigan, and then of Los Angeles, California, the corporation acquired the principal mark "Motown" and "The Motown Sound" along with various designs on these marks for products such as phonograph records, popular musical entertainment, tape cartridges, tapes, cassettes, and audiovisual reproducing devices. Early Detroit recording artists who used the Motown label included the Temptations, the Supremes, the Four Tops, the Jackson Five, Mary Wells, and Martha and the Vandellas. After invading the recording industry, Gordy's company rose to the heights of a multimillion-dollar venture.

A particular mark, called a service mark, was granted in 1981 to Thomas Lewis of Washington, D.C., on the words "The 150th Psalms" for performing gospel music as a group. Renamed Capital Community Singers, his gospel assembly services congregations and other gatherings. "The Shirelles," a widely popular rock and roll vocal and instrumental group, is the service mark for their musical entertainment

Int. Cl.: 29

Prior U.S. Cl.: 46
Under Section 2 (f)

United States Patent Office

Reg. No. 1,063,449
Registered Apr. 12, 1977

TRADEMARK
Principal Register

H. G. Parks, Inc. (Maryland corporation)
501 W. Hamburg St.
Baltimore, Md. 21230

For: MEAT, in CLASS 29 (U.S. CL. 46).
First use as early as 1955; in commerce as early as 1955.
Owner of Reg. Nos. 897,005 and 722,658.

Ser. No. 99,733, filed Sept. 13, 1976.

C. R. BUSH, Examiner

Parks Famous Flavor, registered trademark of H. G. Parks, Inc., maker of sausages and other meats.

United States Patent Office
858,961
Registered Oct. 22, 1968

PRINCIPAL REGISTER
Trademark

Ser. No. 277,686, filed Aug. 7, 1967

THE MOTOWN SOUND

Motown Record Corporation (Michigan corporation)
2648 W. Grand Blvd.
Detroit, Mich. 48208

For: PHONOGRAPH RECORDS AND TAPE CARTRIDGES, in CLASS 36 (INT. CL. 9).
First use Aug. 25, 1966; in commerce Aug. 25, 1966.
No claim is made to the exclusive use of the word "Sound" separately and apart from the mark.
Owner of Reg. No. 800,977.

C. A. MARLOW, Examiner.

The Motown Sound, registered trademark of Motown Record Corporation.

Int. Cl.: 41

Prior U.S. Cl.: 107

United States Patent and Trademark Office
Reg. No. 1,297,015
Registered Sep. 18, 1984

SERVICE MARK
Principal Register

THE SHIRELLES

Beverly Lee (United States citizen)
Apt. D-14
77 Brook Ave.
Passaic, N.J. 07055

For: MUSICAL ENTERTAINMENT SERVICES RENDERED BY A VOCAL AND IN-STRUMENTAL GROUP, in CLASS 41 (U.S. Cl. 107).
First use Jan. 1, 1958; in commerce Jan. 1, 1958.

Ser. No. 438,849, filed Aug. 11, 1983.

R. M. FEELEY, Examining Attorney

The Shirelles, registered service mark of Beverly Lee for musical entertainment services rendered by a vocal and instrumental group.

registered by cofounder Beverly Lee of Passaic, New Jersey, in 1984. "Dedicated to the One I Love," "Soldier Boy," and "Will You Still Love Me Tomorrow?" are a few of their renowned hits. The Hanover Group, Inc., a Florida corporation, received a service mark for "Ink Spots" in 1985 for providing entertainment services by the vocal doo-woop group famous for songs such as its signature song "If I Didn't Care," "My Prayer," and "I'll Never Smile Again." The name for the group, which has more than eighty hit records and many million sellers, was first used in 1945, according to member Bill Kenny, who replaced Jerry Daniels. The original members, Daniels, Ivory "Deek" Watson, Orville Jones, and Charles Fuqua, formed a quartet in the 1930s.

Gourdine Systems, the corporation of Dr. Meredith Gourdine, mentioned earlier, holds numerous trademarks on the name "Incineraid," a smoke-pollution-control device known as an electrostatic smoke precipitator. Likewise, attorney Charles Beckley acquired a registered trademark simply on his surname for furniture that he manufactured. William C. Lee's Acme Boot Company, a New York corporation located in Clarksville, Tennessee, registered a mark in 1968 for leather boots that included a large letter "A" encircled nearly 360 degrees with the word "Acme" written underneath to close the circle.

Int. Cl.: **41**

Prior U.S. Cl.: **107**

United States Patent and Trademark Office

Reg. No. **1,361,085**

Registered Sep. 17, 1985

SERVICE MARK
PRINCIPAL REGISTER

INK SPOTS

HANOVER GROUP, INC., THE (FLORIDA CORPORATION), DBA INK SPOTS
SUITE 202
5300 POWERLINE ROAD
FORT LAUDERDALE, FL 33309

FIRST USE 9-15-1945; IN COMMERCE 9-15-1945.

SER. NO. 496,616, FILED 8-27-1984.

FOR: PROVIDING ENTERTAINMENT SERV-ICES—NAMELY, PERFORMANCES BY A VOCAL GROUP, IN CLASS 41 (U.S. CL. 107).

JEANNETTE M. LOPEZ, EXAMINING ATTOR-NEY

Ink Spots, registered trademark for providing musical entertainment services by a vocal group.

CORPS OF INGENUITY

African Americans in science and technology generally faced many problems. Their advancement in that field has been painstaking. Unfortunately, the transition of ideas from dreams to reality was often blocked; however, some persistent minorities endured, and their contributions were highlighted and recorded with a flair. Statistics show that technological careers have attracted more and more minorities at all job levels. However, by the late 1970s, the earnings of African American employees took a dramatic turn for the worse. The administration of President Ronald Reagan is accused of a national economic divide. Charles M. Christian attests that the "number of well-educated Black men receiving wages below the poverty line had grown faster than the number earning more than $36,000 a year."[1]

For the many unrewarded geniuses of color, financing of ideas has been and still remains a monumental problem. They generally cannot find willing risk takers. Seeking the money to back their concepts is an exhausting process. Many inventors resort to using their life savings, which expire long before they are able to realize a profit, and those in small businesses are particularly hard hit. White financial institutions

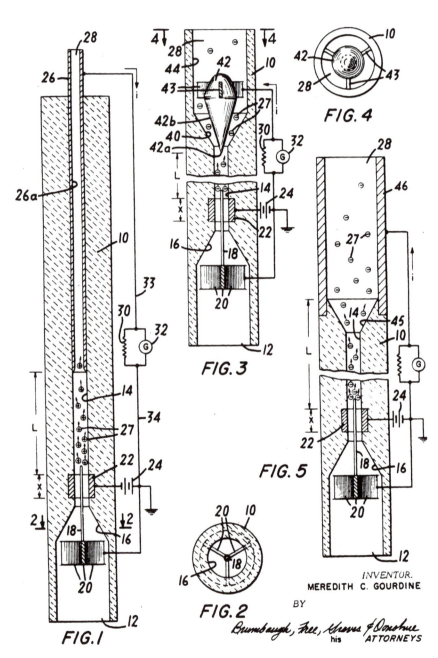

FIG. 4

FIG. 3

FIG. 5

FIG. 2

FIG. 1

INVENTOR.
MEREDITH C. GOURDINE
BY
Brumbaugh, Free, Graves & Donohue
his   ATTORNEYS

Electrogasdynamic Method and Apparatus, patented invention of Meredith C. Gourdine.

are unwilling to jeopardize money that might help these innovators succeed. The early czars of the banking world had racist attitudes, with no intention of letting African Americans get a foothold on the economy through credit. Seeing people of color as irresponsible, these power brokers surmised that minorities were unable to handle their affairs and were a thriftless, indigent lot—a policy formulated in the early years of the American government and presently unchanged to any significant degree.

Second, those stalwart African Americans who are able to labor through the complexities of the patent and trademark systems find difficulty protecting their intellectual property from powerful large companies or conglomerates. The corporations sniff out potential competitors and make offers to them that appear lucrative but, in reality, have a minimum chance of success.

Additionally, the minority innovator is frustrated by the federal bureaucracy in the areas of contracts, licensing, grants, and programs, ostensibly set forth to support and to assist the applicant. It is the very astute person, the sophisticated minority, who initially perceives problems or roadblocks and prepares for any setbacks, if necessary. This individual cannot be shortsighted in attempts to profit from his or her creativity, a very difficult task. Some individuals who took advantage of "offers" to participate in the research and development departments of large corporations immediately found that they were not a part of the climate. Promises were unfulfilled; lies and deceit were abundant. On occasion, minority inventors were placed in profitable innovative departments and encouraged to invent, but subsequently had their names removed from the list of inventors named on applications filed for patents. Various reasons were put forth, adroitly phrased in legal jargon. Unwittingly, they had consented to sign papers that would eliminate their name from the list of other inventors, thereby losing credit for any creativity.

A long-standing issue in the inventive arena concerns the rights of inventive employees, particularly those innovators in the private sector and in federal employment. The question is, who owns the rights of the inventions? This is a problem common to all inventors, whether of darker hue or white.

For the creative talent hired in the private sector, the question has been answered by legislation, the judicial system, and employee invention agreements with the employer. In the latter instance, the ingenuity of the inventor plays an important role in the final decision. In the absence of an express agreement, common law determines ownership rights such that the employer owns any invention developed on company time with company money and equipment that results from specific inventive employment. In other words, the employee assigns the invention over to the employer, including the proprietary rights derived from the fruits of his or her creative thinking. The employee in return might receive an award, a salary increase, or a letter of commendation, should the employer be so inclined.

Some relief from this frustrating circumstance comes in the form of the inventor making agreements with the employer where the employee and the employer determine their respective rights by contract. Other relief comes in the form of state legislation, such as that mandated by Minnesota, Washington, and California, for example, or challenging this discretionary practice in the courts of law.

NASA and Military Teams: Selected Patentees

Name	Branch
George E. Alcorn	NASA
Benjamin Bluford	Army
Robert P. Bundy	Army
George R. Carruthers	NASA
John L. Carter	Army
Winston Cavell	Army
Emmett W. Chappelle	NASA
John B. Christian	Air Force
Samuel Clark	Army
Samuel Dixon, Jr.	Army
Howard S. Jones, Jr.	Army
John Perry	Army
Robert E. Shurney	NASA
Bernard Smith	Army
William L. Wade, Jr.	Army

Those who are hired or employed by the federal government to "invent" receive patents that are issued in their name but are exclusively assigned to the United States of America in the name of the employee's agency of that particular branch of the federal government. The inventor in this case is rewarded with a small cash award for each effort. Often it is only a few hundred dollars or less, regardless of the projected value of the invention.

On the other hand, it is very difficult to assess the full monetary value of the patent grant. The federal government has the option of using the patent itself or licensing the patent grant to others who use the patent to their best advantage. In doing so, the licensee receives rewards at whose value one can only speculate. Such rewards could be in the millions of dollars, of which the government receives little and the inventor—the federal employee—none. Such is the penalty for the inventive public servant.

Independent African American creative talent is also frustrated by seemingly disinterested prospective backers once the patent is received. In hopes for financial backing, minority patent holders approach various companies that might have an interest in the concept. The responses are various, often covering a myriad of explanations why the venture is unfruitful or expressing amazement at the scope and talent of the minority inventor followed by the old unwelcome cliché "Don't call us, we'll call you." Other times prospective developers inquire as to how the invention operates, and the inventor unintentionally supplies valuable information about the nature of the concept. Eventually, the inventor finds that seventeen years later (under the previous expiration time before the new 1995 law) his or her invention appears on the market produced by someone else. At this point, the patent is in the public domain, and the inventor has no legal recourse. This clandestine method of operation is a classic story recounted by countless African American innovators.

The African American scientist is involved in the thirst for knowledge, as is the majority counterpart. However, the black scientist rather than his or her counterpart is set back by procedure, prejudicial feelings, and discrimination that permeate an entire existence, especially while seeking employment. Though his or her incentive is not crushed because of the inherent nature of scientific development vis-à-vis intellectual pursuit, problems arise when the African American attempts to implement concepts or reduce creativity to practice. Assignments and choices decided by supervisors exclude the person of color because of white subjective attitudes and perceptions that lead to discriminatory practices.

The social stigma of being other than white is a serious problem in the workforce. It permeates every element of life, resulting in a lack of general acceptance. Consequently, African Americans are often excluded from social intercourse among whites during social affairs. This practice damages career opportunities at best. Many minorities find cloaked racism intolerable despite federal and state laws and regulations, affirmative action, and diversity programs. Politics and the economics of the 1980s left African Americans with poor earning advantages and low ability to secure justice and amends for discrimination.

IDEAS ABOUND

Pioneer food chemist and prolific inventor Dr. Lloyd Arthur Hall was born in Elgin, Illinois, in 1894. Hall began his interest in chemistry in high school when chemistry was almost an enigmatic science. Eventually, he met chemist Carroll L. Griffith at Northwestern University, where he received his higher education. This relationship netted him the position of chief chemist and technical director at Griffith Laboratories after a stint as chemist in the Chicago Department of Health Laboratories. Achieving striking success during a brilliant career in the preservation of food products, Hall remained with Griffith Laboratories in Chicago for thirty-six years. During these years, he obtained more than one hundred domestic and foreign grants, primarily as the sole inventor. A few patented concepts on sterilizing and protecting foodstuffs were coauthored with his employer.[2]

Hall's patented sterilization method of commercial products like drugs, food, medicines, cosmetics, and hospital supplies with ethylene oxide to kill germs revolutionized these businesses. His experimentation with various kinds of antioxidants used to avoid food spoilage or rancidity led to patents on their novel preparation. Spanning two world wars, Hall served as science advisor in the U.S. Army from 1917 to 1919 and as a member of the Scientific Advisory Board for the War Department from 1943 to 1948. Recipient of many honors and awards throughout a meritorious career, Hall retired in 1959 and moved to California, where he died in 1971.[3]

Fort Monmouth, New Jersey, a major center of electronic developments for the U.S. Army, was and still is fertile territory for a corps of minority scientists, engineers, and technologists, present there since World War II in the 1940s. As an employer of African Americans with scientific backgrounds, the army post offered career opportunities for the men, but particularly gave women of color openings as technicians, draftspersons, and engineers as well. This high technology complex is the nexus of electronic concepts for the U.S. Army.

Some ingenious African Americans in high technology have been cited in national publications such as *National Technical Journal*, the *Black Collegian, Black Enterprise,* and the *National Society of Black Engineers (NSBE) Journal,* to list a few. It is a challenge to detect who they are and how many inventions there are. A clear definition of "high technology" is helpful, given the fact that science and the study of technology advance rapidly in the fields of practical or industrial arts. Writer Carl Spight in a 1986 *NSBE Journal* article titled "High Technology" says that the language must have "as its central theme a concern with the production and exploitation of innovation." He concludes that " 'high tech' refers to productive, innovation-intense and innovation-based techniques and tools. That which was 'high tech' for an earlier historical (industrial) period typically becomes the conventional (low) technology of the following period."[4]

A glance at the yearly changes in academic requirements for students pursuing degrees in computer science, engineering, mathematics, or physics furnishes a clue. Graduates of only a few years may need refresher courses to keep up in their respective arts. The field of bioengineering, for example, has erupted into the disciplines of biomechanical, biomedical, bioelectrical, and biochemical engineering. Deans of schools of engineering at historically black colleges and universities such as Morgan State University and Howard University, among others, have been administering courses in these disciplines for several decades, preparing minority students for future applications of the high-technology workings. The science of biomechanical engineering, for example, may be applied to the plans for prostheses or artificial limbs or to the production of mechanical human hearts, and, additionally, to sports medicine. One means of learning about new developments is to peruse the weekly *Official Gazette* of the U.S. Patent and Trademark Office, which reveals the latest patented innovations in engineering, physics, chemistry, medicine, and other fields.

By the 1990s, nearly all workforces used computers. This phenomenon spurred one of the most rapid employment growths in the job market. As a part of high technology, computer science, certainly an innovation-based technology, introduced computer methods and tools. It follows, then, that high technology provided a multitude of new positions.

A number of inventors of color are new patent holders in these fields. Corporations such as IBM tout luminary talents who are architects in the computer industry. Dr. Mark Dean, a native of Jefferson City, Tennessee, helped generate the advancements in computer architecture that allow IBM and compatible PCs to utilize high-performance software and to work in tandem with auxiliary apparatuses. Dean, an electrical engineer, is the recipient of more than twenty domestic patents, three of which encompass IBM's original nine personal computer grants. He joined the corporation in 1980 and received his Ph.D. from Stanford University in 1992. The first African American to hold an IBM fellowship, Dean is vice president of performance for the RS/6000 division in Austin, Texas.[5]

Seven years after the first two African Americans were inducted into the National Inventors Hall of Fame, Mark Dean became the third to claim the prestigious distinction in 1997 at Akron, Ohio. He and coinventor Dennis Moeller were inducted for the work that allows IBM and IBM-compatible computer elements to communicate with each other in a fast and efficient way.[6]

Lucent Technology (previously Bell Labs) in New Jersey has some gifted thinkers whose discoveries place them on the frontiers of high technology. Dr. James E. West, an experimental physicist who received his first patent in 1964, is a coinventor of foil-electret transducers—devices employed to change sound into electrical signals, the founda-

James E. West, 1999
inductee into the
National Inventors
Hall of Fame.
From the Patricia Carter
Ives Sluby Collection.

tion of today's telecommunications and broadcasting businesses that annually produce a billion microphones—another African American reforming a multimillion-dollar industry.

West, who was born in Prince Edward County, Virginia, in 1931, is deeply committed to his field. He used foil-electret microphones, a high-quality but inexpensive product, to discover secrets of directional sound perception. To pursue this, he sojourned to "halls of sound" such as concert auditoriums and jazz clubs, where he remained motionless for long stretches of time, wearing microphones to gather information.[7]

This quest for data further has taken West to the Cornell University Medical Center to monitor blood pressure. A foil-electret transducer is employed to read the changes in the intricate rhythmic flow of blood through the arteries of patients suffering from hypertension. The transducer is manufactured in the form of an electrically charged thin plastic with one surface metallized and the other held to a metal plate

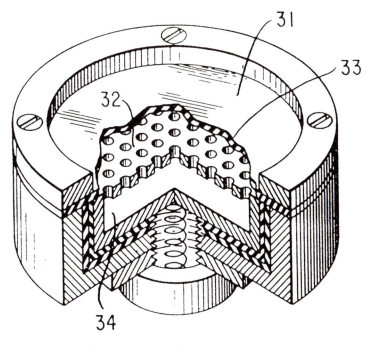

Technique for Fabrication of Foil Electrect, patented invention of James E. West.

with an air gap between. West has more than a hundred U.S. and foreign patents. He received six U.S. patents in 1984 alone.

West was the fourth African American to be inducted into the National Inventors Hall of Fame, achieving the distinction in 1999 at Akron, Ohio. He and his colleague, Gerard M. Sessler, a German native, were awarded the basic patent on foil electrets that are functional in serviceable and popular consumer items like hearing aids, portable tape recorders, and lapel microphones, and for the Bell System phone-with-a-memory. The honor was shared with Wessler. West, an attendee of Hampton and Temple Universities, presently resides with his family in New Jersey.[8]

Inventor Earl D. Shaw, who started at Bell Labs in 1969, works with the executive director of the physics division and is exceptional in laser technology. He coinvented the spinflip Raman laser that has the capability of being tunable at all wavelengths, similar to the ability to change radio frequencies. These lasers change optical energy wavelengths and find great utility in molecular measurements, especially for air pollution. To build tuning lasers, it is necessary to change the electronic behavior of molecules. Shaw discovered that he could stimulate light at extremely long wavelengths, well above the one-hundred-micron region.[9]

Other brilliant minds at the corporation include Dr. George H. Simmons, who began at AT&T Bell Labs during his final summer at Michigan State University and fully joined the company after graduation. His first patent was awarded for a circuit design to eliminate spurious pulses in a dial pulse stream. After receiving his Ph.D. in computer science, Simmons in 1987 conceived a fiber-optic extension of an optic local area network (LAN) that merited him his second patent. Taking on a supervisory position, he was responsible for design and development of the Intercept Computer Main Memory Unit and a component of the 3B computer. Afterward Simmons ascended to a director's position.[10]

Another African American scientist who found a promising career at Bell Labs is Dr. James W. Mitchell, an administrator of analytical chemistry. Upon receiving his Ph.D. in analytical chemistry, Mitchell became a member of the technical staff at Bell Labs, where he remained for more than twenty years. Safety in science and the desire to minimize risk in handling toxic chemicals spurred Mitchell to keep semiconductors super clean. During his outstanding, meritorious career he acquired numerous patents.[11]

The cable engineering career of Alfred G. Richardson started with the Bell System's Cable Ship Long Lines. As an authority on cable mechanics and cable-laying techniques, Richardson understands the requisite procedures for producing and for laying specially engineered transatlantic cable. Undersea cable requires sophisticated manufacturing design. Richardson and his coinventors received a patent in 1984 for their method of making optical-fiber cable for telecommunications systems. The glass optical fibers are embedded in a core that is adhesively bonded to a layer of steel wire and is then sheathed with a copper tube and protected by a polyethylene thermoplastic resin insulator. Richardson also discovered a solution to the problem of detecting breaks in optical-fiber cable. He developed a laser alarm system that detects twists in the fiberglass.[12]

For Dr. Samuel P. Massie, professor emeritus of chemistry at the U.S. Naval Academy, creative brainstorming in compositions useful in the treatment of gonorrhea, malaria, or bacterial infections merited him and his coinventors a patent in 1984, assigned to the United States of America as represented by the secretary of the army. During World War II, Massie was a member of the team that worked on the atomic bomb and on chemical warfare agents along with antimalarial agents. Over the years he investigated various processes of making drugs to fight tuberculosis, malaria, cancer, sickle-cell anemia, and other debilitating human conditions.[13]

Ideas flourished in the mind of academician Dr. Isiah M. Warner, a chemistry professor at Emory University who received two patents one year apart. In 1985, he merited a grant for his innovation on a process and apparatus for chemical removal of oxygen in luminescence measurements. The following year, Warner was issued a patent for a procedure and apparatus for the stabilization of a direct-current arc lamp. A year later, the distinguished professor became the Samuel Chandler Dobbs Professor of Chemistry at Emory.[14]

On the research team at Eastman Kodak Research Laboratories, Dr. Walter Cooper became devoted to solid-state chemistry and molecular spectroscopy. He specialized in photographic dyes. Within the two years 1970 and 1971, Cooper was issued two patents for his polymerization processes. His patent grant reciting ways of using metallized dyes was employed in graphic arts and printing around the world.[15]

The Letton name is legendary at Procter & Gamble. James C. Letton, given his first corporation job at the renowned Julian Laboratories in Chicago owned by prolific inventor Percy L. Julian, worked in steroid processing and manufacturing. After a teaching stint followed by receipt of his Ph.D. in chemistry in 1970, Letton later moved to Procter & Gamble to become a member of its packaged soap division and originated biodegradable soap agents. He earned his first patent from that development and went on to receive another patent on enzyme stabilization for the detergent Era. Later, he moved to a process-development team exploring a fat substitute named Olestra. From this innovative ingredient, useful in cooking oil, shortening, or almost any similar composition, Letton obtained a number of patents.[16]

As a recipient of numerous awards, Letton has inspired African Americans to enter scientific fields, especially his sons. James A. Letton followed his father at Procter & Gamble to work as a chemist. Another son, Alan Letton, acquired a doctorate in chemical engineering, was previously employed at the Dow Chemical Company, but is now with AlliedSignal, Inc.[17]

Aerospace engineer Lonnie Johnson was an astute, clever thinker. When he was working on a team at the Jet Propulsion Laboratory at Pasadena, California, in 1982, Johnson tinkered at home with a new heat pump that could use water instead of freon as the cooling or heating means. When he was experimenting with vinyl tubing and a self-made nozzle, a powerful jet of water erupted across the bathroom, flinging the shower curtain aside. From that day forward, Johnson's creative juices flowed until he made his first powerful water gun from the breakthrough discovery that kids could pressurize the water by forcing air, and later water, into the mechanism.

Johnson was born and raised in Mobile, Alabama, and received a bachelor of science degree in mechanical engineering followed by a

United States Patent [19]

Johnson

[11] Patent Number: 4,509,361

[45] Date of Patent: Apr. 9, 1985

[54] **SOIL MOISTURE POTENTIAL DETERMINATION BY WEIGHT MEASUREMENT**

[76] Inventor: **Lonnie G. Johnson,** 12503 S. 31st St., Omaha, Nebr. 68123

[21] Appl. No.: **556,276**

[22] Filed: **Nov. 30, 1983**

[51] **Int. Cl.³** G01N 5/02
[52] **U.S. Cl.** 73/73; 73/335
[58] **Field of Search** 73/73, 335

[56] **References Cited**

U.S. PATENT DOCUMENTS

1,765,816 6/1930 Allen .... 73/73 X
2,060,957 11/1936 Tarvin et al. 73/73
2,073,611 3/1937 Dunlap .... 73/73 X
3,520,476 7/1970 Schmid .... 73/73 X
4,269,060 5/1981 Kethley .... 73/335 X

Primary Examiner—Daniel M. Yasich

[57] **ABSTRACT**

An instrument for measuring soil moisture potential comprising a moisture absorber movably coupled to the soil being measured by means for maintaining said absorber in moisture potential equilibrium with said soil and permitting weight measurement of said absorber. The instrument includes scale means for weighing said absorber to determine moisture content thereof and provide an indication of soil moisture potential. The instrument includes adjustable controls for calibration.

12 Claims, 5 Drawing Figures

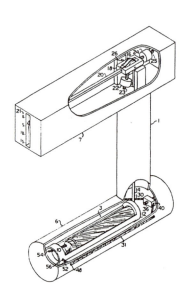

Soil Moisture Potential, patented invention of Lonnie Johnson.

Lonnie Johnson, enjoying his Super Soaker squirt gun invention with NIPLA national secretary, Pat Sluby. From the Patricia Carter Ives Sluby Collection.

master of science degree in nuclear engineering from Tuskegee University. He then became an air force officer and worked on space systems such as Galileo before joining the technical staff at the Jet Propulsion Laboratory. In 1991, he founded the Johnson Research and Development Company to promote and sell his successful invention, the Super Soaker. The unit, which has taken modified forms such as a water-powered airplane and a robot, became an instant hit with kids. He also patented a measuring instrument, a smoke-detecting timer, a sensor, an automatic sprinkler control, a squirt gun, a pinch-trigger pump water gun, a wet-diaper detector, and a hair-curler drying apparatus, to list a few items.[18]

OUT OF THE BOX

The breakthroughs in science and technology are startling and breathtaking. Amazing "out-of-the-box" ideas appear from new discoveries in aviation, the world's manipulation and production of energy, the explosion of access to information, whether for entertainment, education, or industry, and novel medical concepts that impact the living and those who will come to live.

The by-products of the creative genius of African American space scientists on the team at NASA play a critical role in space programs.

United States Patent [19]

Johnson

[11] Patent Number: **4,591,071**

[45] Date of Patent: **May 27, 1986**

[54] **SQUIRT GUN**

[76] Inventor: **Lonnie G. Johnson,** 1463 E. Barkley Dr., Mobile, Ala. 36606

[21] Appl. No.: **541,898**

[22] Filed: **Oct. 14, 1983**

[51] Int. Cl.⁴ **B67D 5/32**
[52] U.S. Cl. .... **222/39;** 222/79; 222/401; 340/384 E; 340/406; 116/137 R
[58] Field of Search .... 340/384 E, 406; 116/137 R, 139; 222/39, 79, 323, 324, 401

[56] **References Cited**

U.S. PATENT DOCUMENTS

1,333,704	3/1920	Brinks	340/406
2,249,608	7/1941	Greene	222/79
2,302,963	11/1942	Lefever	222/39
2,589,977	3/1952	Stelzer	222/79
3,202,318	8/1965	Black	222/39
4,086,589	4/1978	Cieslak et al.	340/384 E
4,214,674	7/1980	Jones et al.	222/401
4,239,129	12/1980	Esposito	222/79

Primary Examiner—H. Grant Skaggs
Attorney, Agent, or Firm—John A. Beehner

[57] **ABSTRACT**

A toy squirt gun which shoots a continuous high velocity stream of water. The squirt gun is configured as a structure facilitating partial filling with water leaving a void for compressed air. The squirt gun includes a nozzle for ejecting water at high velocity, a pressurization pump for compressing air into the gun to pressurize water contained therein, and a trigger actuated flow control valve for shooting the gun by controlling flow of pressurized water through the nozzle. A battery-powered oscillator circuit and a water flow powered sound generator produce futuristic space ray gun sound effects when the gun is shooting.

9 Claims, 7 Drawing Figures

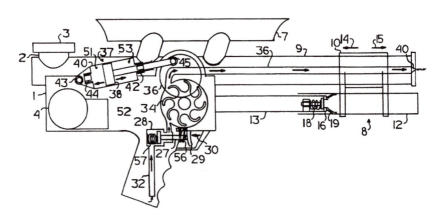

Squirt Gun, patented invention of Lonnie Johnson, Super Soaker developer.

George R. Carruthers, 2003 inductee into the National Inventors Hall of Fame, with his Image Converter invention.
From the IOKTS Archives, courtesy of the National Aeronautics and Space Administration.

When we think of the specially designed wheels on the "Moon Buggy" and of the waste-management system for the Skylab, we should know of the inventive ability of Dr. Robert E. Shurney. He developed metal chevrons for wheels to divert moon dust away from the astronauts in the lunar landing of Apollo 15. Shurney, an A&I State University graduate, also planned the refuse disposal units on board Skylab, designing eating utensils and lavatory facilities. Dr. George Carruthers's patented Far Ultraviolet Camera and Spectrograph for viewing the earth's upper atmosphere, stars, and interstellar space was rewarded with the prestigious NASA Exceptional Scientific Achievement medal, and the camera traveled to the moon aboard the 1982 Apollo 16 lunar mission. Inventor Carruthers was a 2003 inductee into the National Inventors Hall of Fame.

Artist and designer David Gittens invented and designed an innovative gyroplane named *Ikenga 530Z*, promoted as a "future link" air-

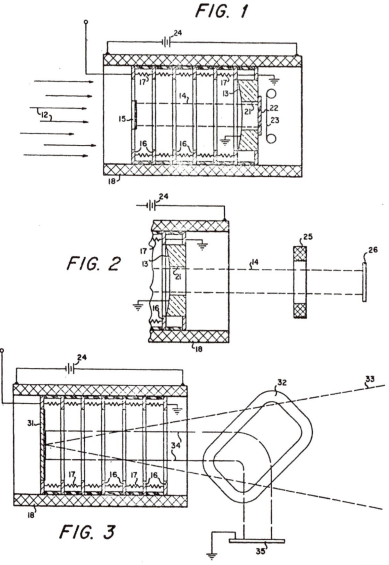

FIG. 1

FIG. 2

FIG. 3

INVENTOR

GEORGE R. CARRUTHERS

BY *Melvin L. Crane* AGENT

R. S. Sciascia ATTORNEY

Image Converter, patented invention of George R. Carruthers.

Robert E. Shurney, in weightless atmosphere of space, at NASA.
From the IOKTS Archives, courtesy of the National Aeronautics and Space Administration.

craft. The novel, promising design won the Grand Champion Prize at the 1988 Albuquerque International Airshow, was Best New Rotocraft Idea for the Popular Rotocraft Convention, and became the first home-built autogyro in the National Air and Space Museum collection.[19]

Visionary and futurist Dr. Marc Hannah helped make box-office hits of *Jurassic Park, Terminator 2, The Hunt for Red October,* and *Beauty and the Beast,* to cite just a few. As a special-effects wizard, he developed sophisticated three-dimensional graphics software for high-powered computers in the laboratories of his Silicon Graphics company head-quartered in Mountain View, California. Hannah and six other company founders turned around the entire computer industry, revolutionizing it with a dynamic workstation having enormous storage capability and mainframe computing power.[20]

Founded in 1982, Silicon Graphics set out to create extremely powerful workstations useful to industrial customers. Hannah, a brilliant electrical engineer, received his doctorate while on sabbatical from the company in 1984. Upon his return, he became chief scientist and worked on his vision of a universal, high-performance desktop style that was affordable to the average consumer. The innovative technology paid off for the publicly traded company, which now employs thousands worldwide.[21]

Inventors Francis S. Bernard and Kirk Law are also on the team at Silicon Graphics. With more than eight patents between these electrical engineers, whose creative careers began earlier at other large companies such as RCA, General Electric, and David Sarnoff Labs, Silicon Graphics appears a fertile setting for professional advancement of African American scientists.[22]

Amid the medical explosion is the hope that in this new millennium, with the help of African American innovators, the trend toward alternative approaches to wellness along with medical breakthroughs will correct, cure, or present new treatments for all disorders. Even on space flights to the International Space Station, black astronauts alongside others perform designated experiments to seek causes and to find cures.

Monthly or weekly, the news seems to bombard us with some innovation or discovery about such things as genes, whose genetic code was cracked in 1966. Thus genetics seems to be the key factor to life and to longevity as well. What is in our genes? What can we do about it? How can we stave off a shortened life span because of a genetic quirk in an ancestor? These are hard questions.

Dr. J. Clay Smith, Jr., dean of the Howard University School of Law in 1986, fortuitously published a bibliographic index (1981–1986) entitled *The Genetic Engineering Revolution: A New Century Reality*. Two years earlier, biologist Kary Mullis had invented a novel technique of sequencing DNA that accelerated all genetic research. Envisioning future scenarios, trends, and impacts, Smith surmised that "genetic engineering and the technology associated with it are an area of great importance to all people on this planet. However, only a few people on this planet really understand the issues associated with the gene cascade of deoxyribonucleic acid (DNA)." He issued the listing "to spur the interest of leaders, scientists, lawyers, political and social scientists and students on the subject, especially in minority communities, before the policy issues and rules regulating this industry become irrevocably fixed." Smith suspected correctly that a movement was afoot to create and duplicate all life forms, inclusive of humans. He realized that to no small degree, the science-fiction notion of cloning was highly probable.[23] The movement, of course, is the gene movement, in which many African American scientists are involved as researchers, administrators, and specialists.

Following four years of debate, the U.S. Patent and Trademark Office approved patent number 4,736,866, on April 12, 1988, for "transgenic non-human mammals," assigned to the President and Fellows of Harvard College, the first patent on an animal. Biotechnology then exploded, and the office set aside a separate section to handle the multitude of applications that poured in. This new invention of transforming a mouse through genetic engineering met the legal requirements for a patent. Just as plants are living organisms and a new variety that fits the plant patent regulations can be patented, it was reasoned that transgenic engineering of animals presents a similar case. Manipulating genes to make novel forms of life, drugs, and other biological matter is very difficult; however, once the process is known, duplication of the outcome is fairly easy.

Innovations by Selected Health Science Practitioners

Name	Invention
Dr. Neville A. Baron (ophthalmologist)	Method that recurves the cornea of the eye
Dr. Patricia Bath (ophthalmologist)	Apparatus for ablating and removing cataract lenses
Dr. Andrew Burton (physician)	Infusion of liquid into tissue Adjustable spectacles
Dr. Andre Jackson (veterinary medicine)	Urinary cup for animal testing
Dr. William B. Jones (dentist)	Improved dental impression tray
Dr. Kermit J. Mallette (dental surgeon)	Sensitive condom
Dr. V. Lopez Rowe (physician)	Bicycle drinking apparatus
Dr. Robert Williams (dentist)	Surgical glove sterilizing agent
Dr. Robert E. Willis (physician)	Orthopedic apparatus
Dr. Louis T. Wright (surgeon)	Novel method for smallpox vaccination Design of a brace for broken necks First to use Aureomycin in humans

---

Alert to the enormous ethical and legal issues connected with patenting transgenic animals, Congress inflicted moratoriums on the promising domestic biotechnology industry. It needed time to conduct

a congressional review of the new technology and devise suitable procedures to move cautiously on the touchy, thorny concerns relating to
ethics, religion, legalities, the environment, and other matters. A fire-
storm ensued. Delays were harmful for smaller biotechnology companies who sought to get proprietary rights, hesitant to publicize their
products on the market without patent protection.

Experiments continued on plant and animal life. In 1997, news reports flashed the startling tidings that the first mammal cloned from
an adult cell had been born in Scotland. The birth of the lamb Dolly
set off intense ethical controversy.

A November 1999 *Chemical and Engineering News* article reported that
researchers had "developed a technique that identifies genes associated with specific biological active proteins much more quickly than
previously possible."[24] Sickle-cell disease, prevalent in African Americans and thought to be incurable a few decades ago, is now thought
curable, at least from a hint in the *New England Journal of Medicine*
suggesting a cure using bone-marrow transplant.[25]

Decades ago there were no synthesized drugs of the caliber we have
today, or replacement parts from other humans. Home therapy, brews,
and concoctions were, and perhaps still are for a few, the formative
solutions to hold on to what God gave us. But what the new practitioner, specialist, or surgeon is witnessing are ready-to-wear implants
such as ears, noses, and eyes; heart valves grown from blood-vessel cells;
bone substitutes made from foreign substances; or restoration of damaged brain tissue via implanted cells or growth factors—all these and
many more startling innovations in view of the latest scientific and
medical sources. As a case in point, specialists at the University of Massachusetts and at the Massachusetts Institute of Technology have already accomplished the unbelievable feat of growing a human ear on
a mouse. Additionally, *in vivo* and *in vitro* fertilization procedures have
leaped new boundaries. Inevitably, as amazing as it may seem, scientists
finally have achieved the ultimate controversial move—the cloning of
a human embryo.

The pharmaceutical industry, boosted by its approval procedure for
biotechnology, geared up the manufacture of innovative medicines ge-
netically engineered. Major strides have been realized in the contest
against vexatious diseases such as cancer, acquired immune deficiency
syndrome (AIDS), and forms of hepatitis. Flourishing worldwide are
firms that market supplements that boost testosterone levels up to
three times higher than normal or prescribed pharmaceuticals that
increase sex drives. Prescription drugs invented to reverse natural hair
loss on the human head were developed to offset baldness. These and
other pharmaceuticals, promoted to massage the egos of aging adults,
surfaced at the threshold of this new century.

United States Patent [19]

Baron

[11] Patent Number: 4,461,294

[45] Date of Patent: Jul. 24, 1984

[54] **APPARATUS AND PROCESS FOR RECURVING THE CORNEA OF AN EYE**

[76] Inventor: Neville A. Baron, Medical Plaza - #66 Rte. 46, Dover, N.J. 07801

[21] Appl. No.: 340,978

[22] Filed: Jan. 20, 1982

[51] Int. Cl.³ A61B 17/36
[52] U.S. Cl. 128/303.1; 128/395
[58] Field of Search 128/303.1, 395-398

[56]   **References Cited**

U.S. PATENT DOCUMENTS

3,703,176 11/1972 Vassiliadis et al. 128/395
3,783,874 1/1974 Koester et al. 128/395
3,900,034 8/1975 Katz et al. 128/395

FOREIGN PATENT DOCUMENTS

563751 12/1977 U.S.S.R. 128/303.1

Primary Examiner—Lee S. Cohen

[57]   **ABSTRACT**

The cornea of an eye is recurved by disposing therein light-absorbing color bodies and thereafter vaporizing such color bodies according to a pre-selected design to form corneal-recurving scars.

6 Claims, 1 Drawing Figure

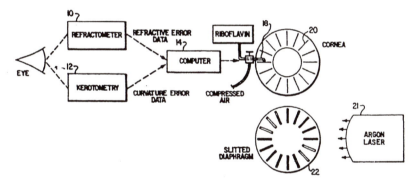

Apparatus and Process for Recurving the Cornea of the Eye, patented invention of Neville A. Baron.

The field of dermatology exploded with the manufacture of ointments and creams designed to help beautify mankind along with novel compounds and compositions that aid burn victims and patients suffering a multiplicity of skin ailments. In fact, a few biotech companies successfully have achieved the growth of human skin in laboratory dishes.

Remote surgical procedures have already taken a foothold in the medical field. Surgeons can operate from a far-off city or country and perform surgery on patients in a distant location without being physically present. Through the use of satellites, robots, and sophisticated medical machines and instruments, the patient can experience surgery minus the traditional operating-room teams of nurses and doctors at his or her side.

For answers to the immense legal, social, moral, or ethical questions concerning these innovative procedures, one has to look to ethicists or specialists in other disciplines. The Human Genome Project, set forth to identify and treat illnesses, revolutionized mankind. However, the global pestilence of AIDS and the reappearance of diseases once thought eradicated now cause immense concern.

Other technological wonders surfaced in tandem with ones previously mentioned. The novel technology associated with superconductivity is mind boggling. Laser science, itself a fresh development, impacted a plethora of scientific fields over the past decade, accomplishing dramatic results. The application of lasers in proficient weaponry, in the transmission and distribution of information, in treatment of cardiovascular diseases, and in photopharmacology, for instance, has altered essentially the way we eat, work, and live—nearly our entire existence.

The remarkable science associated with the microprocessor in telecommunications has turned upside down the one-way and two-way shift of information, whether voice, data, video signals, text, or imaging. Futurist John L. Petersen in his 1994 book *The Road to 2015* avers that in the "same way that Gutenberg's movable type multiplied the spread of information during the Enlightenment, so the microprocessor-based computer is exponentially expanding the human ability to collect, analyze, manipulate and communicate information."[26] The microprocessor is driving the developed world. Petersen asserts that "we are actively exploring new disciplines and sciences that became feasible only in the last few years, with the advent of the interactive capabilities of the desktop computer."[27]

Massive forces such as population growth, new technologies, and business practices are redesigning the world as we now know it. The visionary and imaginative cartoonists of the early and mid-1900s entertained us with gadgets and space notions, but little did we realize just how "on target" their ideas were.

African American creative thinkers and innovators discovered that their skills were useful in all the major industries, revolutionizing many from the early nineteenth century to the present. These scientists, engineers, and specialists were designers of the future as we knew it in an earlier historical time and are designers of the future as we experience and forge new frontiers. Their work on teams or individually at

United States Patent [19]

Dillon et al.

[11] **Patent Number:** 4,800,263

[45] **Date of Patent:** Jan. 24, 1989

[54] **COMPLETELY CROSS-TALK FREE HIGH SPATIAL RESOLUTION 2D BISTABLE LIGHT MODULATION**

[75] Inventors: **Robert F. Dillon**, Stoneham; **Cardinal Warde**, Newtonville, both of Mass.

[73] Assignee: **Optron Systems, Inc., Waltham,** Mass.

[21] Appl. No.: **160,185**

[22] Filed: **Feb. 25, 1988**

Related U.S. Application Data

[62] Division of Ser. No. 15,055, Feb. 7, 1987.

[51] Int. Cl.⁴ H01J 40/14
[52] U.S. Cl. .... 250/213 R; 313/103 CM
[58] Field of Search .... 250/213 R, 213 VT; 313/103 R, 103 CM, 105 CM, 334, 523

[56] **References Cited**

U.S. PATENT DOCUMENTS

2,495,697	1/1950	Chilowsky	250/213 VT
2,907,886	10/1959	Willard et al.	250/213 R
2,929,934	3/1960	Nicoll	250/213 R
2,972,803	2/1961	Koury et al.	250/213 R
2,973,436	2/1961	Koury	250/213 R
3,085,159	4/1963	McNaney	250/213 R
3,243,642	3/1966	Gebel	313/103 CM
3,459,946	8/1969	Lahr et al.	250/213 R
3,543,034	11/1970	Finkle	250/213 VT

Primary Examiner—David C. Nelms
Assistant Examiner—Stephone B. Allen
Attorney, Agent, or Firm—Weingarten, Schurgin, Gagnebin & Hayes

[57] **ABSTRACT**

In one voltage-driven embodiment, a high spatial resolution two-dimensional array of bistable completely cross-talk free light modulation elements is constituted as a lamination of an input two-dimensional photoconductor thin film layer and an output two-dimensional electroluminescent phosphor thin film layer disposed in etched wells individually defined in corresponding cores of the optical fibers of a fiber optic face plate. In another voltage-driven embodiment, a very low cost high spatial resolution 2-D array of bistable substantially cross-talk free light modulation elements is constituted as a lamination of a photoconductor thin film layer, a selectively dimensioned and apertured opaque masking thin film layer, and an electroluminescent phosphor thin film layer. In an electron-driven embodiment, a high spatial resolution two-dimensional array of substantially cross-talk free bistable light modulating elements is constituted as an assembly of a two-dimensional input window having a deposited photocathode thin film layer, a two-dimensional output window having a deposited cathodoluminescent phosphor, and a two-dimensional glass capillary array defining plural charge feed forward and light feedback channels mounted therebetween in a vacuum tight enclosure. In a further electron driven embodiment, a microchannel plate subassembly is mounted in the vacuum-tight enclosure in the place of the glass capillary array. In the several embodiments, voltages are applied via transparent conductors to the photoconductor and phosphor layers.

5 Claims, 4 Drawing Sheets

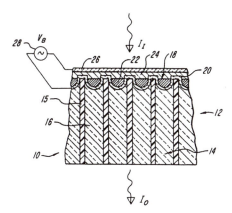

Bistable Light Modulation, patented invention of Cardinal Warde.

manufacturing, pharmaceutical, and aerospace firms as well as at federal facilities, universities, and colleges is of immense value. For instance, the approval for the marketing of pharmaceuticals for decades has been given, in part, by African American specialists and practitioners at the Food and Drug Administration. Their presence in the overseeing of the much sought-after requests is inspiring to the younger generation of African Americans who are new entrants into the scientific and medical realms. For many inventors, the lure of launching private businesses proves fruitful after gaining experience in government or in industry. Always inspired by high endeavor, African Americans of this great land have gone beyond limitations imposed upon them time and again for centuries, encouraged by mentors to rise above all demands, to see what was already accomplished, and thereby to give hope for future generations.[28]

CONCLUSION

The history of invention is an absorbing theme. Inventions and their improvements have been around for eons. Creative *Homo sapiens* developed the physical world around us, and this report of African American inventiveness gives perspectives on the changing needs of mortals. Prehistoric man survived, undoubtedly, through an abundance of motivation and persistence, necessary ingredients to provide necessities and conveniences. Ideas for the wheel, metal tools, moveable type, the wooden clock, crop rotation, or the computer came from remarkable minds. These mystical individuals sustained themselves on determination, fortitude, and courage, qualities needed for reinforcement against the slings and arrows of those who do not understand them or their ideas.

We have examined how the creative genius of African Americans has changed or altered our living habits by bringing us a better quality of life. Additionally, we have observed how valuable patents and trademarks are to inventors who feel a sense of reward when the consumer benefits from the officially protected product or process. It is unfortunate indeed that before emancipation the colored (enslaved) inventor was not privy to proprietary rights. Given control over a slave chattel, the master constrained the inventive slave to assign all rights for the invention to him, thus seizing control of the discovery. Subsequently the master patented the invention in his own name as if he invented the article of manufacture or process and then pocketed any proceeds coming from its sale. After white masters took advantage of slave-inspired innovations, their kind, in the latter half of the nineteenth century, insidiously decried whether the Negro had inventive genius, discarding this notion as wild speculation.

Since 1821, and perhaps earlier in America, free inventors of color have participated in the process in which they took out patents solely in their name or as a partner of a white person. Moreover, manufacturers, marketers, and employers have benefited from African American innovations through increased earnings from greater production and distribution of products or goods. Without protection of intellectual property rights, many developments would not have occurred because entrepreneurs or investors would be reluctant to spend money on a product lacking the monopoly protection of a patent.

The impact of black intellect is found in many corners of the Earth. At the end of the nineteenth century, the U.S. Congress enacted the Federal Safety Appliance Act, directly related to Andrew J. Beard's automatic rail car coupler, patented in 1897. It was unlawful for a railroad to issue rail cars that did not automatically couple to each other. Then Congress passed the Federal Employers Liability Act in 1908, which gave railroad employees suing rights in federal courts. Similar acts of legislation concerning the safety and welfare of employees in other trades and industries followed the concepts outlined in the 1908 legislation.

A more direct impact of minority influence upon Americans is witnessed by the shrewdness with which George Washington Carver delivered his brilliant address before Congress in 1921 that promptly resulted in a tariff mandate. The Hawley-Smoot Tariff Act contained language weighted to protect the peanut from foreign competition.

The brilliance of human beings whose skin color branded them is immeasurable, whether they worked, for instance, in newspaper publishing, like Robert Pelham, or in dermatological processes, like millionaire skin specialist Theodore K. Lawless, who has a clinic named for him in Israel, or in a three-million-dollar annual refrigeration business like that of Frederick M. Jones. In the free-enterprise world, commerce and trade are embodied around the survival of the fittest, and minority business is no exception. Black enterprises, founded on the principle of capitalism, many encouraged by the regulations resulting from intellectual property ownership, surmount economic frustrations and a multitude of other barriers in a struggle to maintain a station in national and world marketplace. Withstanding and overcoming a myriad of hardships, the fittest outlast spiraling inflationary trends that impact profits and earnings. Difficult, yes. Many entrepreneurs are haunted by old trends compounded with a lack of diversified skills such as serious planning, accounting, marketing, and general business insight. But, to put it simply, survival means plain, old luck.

In a letter, Conrad Groves, a black patentee who had observed my earlier book, *Creativity and Inventions*, concludes that "in a society where money is considered to be the only standard of achievement, it is wonderful to know that creativity is beginning to be appreciated." He adds,

"Creativity is important because, although rarely appreciated for being practical, it is the very foundation of the science and industry upon which our economic prosperity is based. Individuals such as myself are strongly motivated by the fact that patent royalties from a major discovery can finance social programs which can result in vast improvements in the standard of living of so many underprivileged people."[1]

As with any endeavor, there are success stories and reports of the unfortunate. The field of intellectual property is no exception. Heartbreaking accounts of any inventor who struggled to make a difference are overwhelming, and those of African American inventors, women alongside men, are particularly devastating. The chronicle of domestic Ellen Elgin's plight in 1888 at the sale of her invention for a paltry sum or of Reverend Herman Douglas's lengthy legal adventures with his innovative disposable training pants/diapers that he hoped would make him the first black diaper manufacturer rouses the pangs of one's heart, but penetrates into the bosom of that diligence. Any trial or tribulation experienced by the seeker of federal protection is difficult to avoid at best and impossible to overcome at worst.

Black talent in the field of intellectual property, specifically patents, circumvents age, gender, education, religion, station in life, or any other category. As ordinary humans who worked in fields, factories, government, schools, hospitals, homes, or elsewhere, some began inventing as youths. As youngsters or as adults, they found a way to guard their discoveries in this field of usefulness. Highly trained African American innovators began careers in scientific laboratories; many then founded their own companies or migrated into the legal profession. The move from being employed by others to self-employment was irresistible for various creative thinkers.

The presence of black women as patent holders steadily accelerated from less than a dozen by 1900 to nearly two dozen just in a decade. Their experience ranges from housewife and teacher to the highly trained a scientist and scholar. In the latter part of the 1970s, there were more women than men attending colleges in the United States for the first time since World War II, according to a 1980 U.S. census report. More older women were seeking higher education. The enrollment of African Americans as teens or young adults remained steady after doubling in the early 1970s. During the women's liberation years of the 1960s and 1970s, employment doors opened, and black women moved through for a share of the opportunity.

The American innovator of color leaves an impressive legacy for future generations. Begun during the founding and growth of our great nation, the legacy continues through educational achievement and scientific prowess at the hands of mathematical, mechanical, medical, chemical, and engineering wizards. Present African American instructors, scholars, and scientists labor to educate youth through a variety of educational and religious programs and strategies set by professional associations and civic groups dedicated to move forward what forebears gained. Historically, unawareness of black accomplishments and innovations has affected the white mind-set toward parity for Americans of African descent; nonetheless, this book, hopefully, will do more than educate them.

This new decade, century, and millennium will explode with ideas, concepts, and mechanisms that will challenge science writers. Science changes so rapidly that it almost makes tomorrow's news obsolete. Less than seventy years ago, there were no blood banks, penicillin, truck refrigeration, polio inoculations, frozen food, contact lenses, or contraceptive pills. Credit cards, newfangled microwave appliances, cell phones, telescopes and cameras to take pictures of new stars, laser beams, or radar equipment were unknown. A fierce race is on, spurring big business in virtually all sectors. Scientific and engineering discoveries mainly have moved from university laboratories under the supervision of academe to the private sector spawned by ambitious technology and drug companies. Expectedly, successes have affected current business practices and economic trends while setting off political debates and immense moral controversies.

Humankind wants to survive as long as it can, in the healthiest fashion. African Americans assuredly are a part of that drive for well-being and for a better quality of life. A new pattern has emerged, affecting a growing portion of developed society. An accounting will reveal changes occurring in everything from technology to production to banking, and black American inventors will be in the number of those bringing about these changes. One example is the bright, intuitive, and gifted young teen Shannon Crabill of Maryland, a 2000 invention contest winner who conceived a unique clock, now on the open world market.[2]

Creative youth, such as Crabill, represent African American talent coming into the workforce, bursting with new ideas. Many programs are afoot to encourage young African Americans to pursue careers in science, mathematics, engineering, computer technology, banking, and business so that they can keep pace with fast-moving global changes. Through activities such as science fairs and competitions, students are being inspired to explore technical ideas that may, at some future date, alter our lifestyle.

Appendix I

MINORITIES IN THE PRACTICE OF INTELLECTUAL PROPERTY LAW

African Americans have served as government patent examiners in the United States since the latter part of the nineteenth century, but their work as intellectual property law (IPL) practitioners in corporations and in private law firms is of a more recent vintage. The history of African American intellectual property law practitioners is representative of the struggles minorities faced in science and technology and in the legal profession. Insight into the emergence of this specialized practice reflects a microcosm of the powerful civil rights movement. The number of these attorneys grew substantially in the early 1960s, primarily as a result of large corporations hiring African American engineers. In a short time, a few major corporations began recruiting African American attorneys for their IPL departments, and patent law firms began to add minority patent attorneys to their staffs.

It is believed that the first African American corporate IPL practitioner was John Peele, whom Bell and Howell recruited about 1962 in the Chicago, Illinois, area. Beginning in 1966, companies like Eastman Kodak, Upjohn, Xerox Corporation, Bell Laboratories, and Polaroid and the U.S. Department of Defense began recruiting and hiring minority specialists. These included James E. Carson, Fred L. Denson, John Richard Everett, Jerome J. Norris, Joseph A. Finlayson, Jr., Richard A. Gaither, John R. Moses, Bernard Bettis, Sidney B. Williams, Jr., Willie Leftwich, and Lawrence A. Wright. It was this assembly of attorneys, most of whom were former patent examiners, who rallied to organize the National Patent Law Association in Washington, D.C., in 1970.

The group, later renamed the National Intellectual Property Law Association (NIPLA), recognized that minorities were participating in all facets of intellectual property, which involves patents, copyrights, trademarks, and trade secrets. The association is the first and most prestigious organization devoted to representing and assisting African American inventors; patent, trademark, and copyright law practitioners; patent examiners; trademark- and copyright-examining attorneys; scientists; business leaders; and medical professionals. To more fully participate in the nation's economic mainstream, NIPLA also encourages employment of minorities in the intellectual property systems.

NIPLA sees the U.S. patent, trademark, and copyright systems as a keystone supportive of the country's economy. It seeks to ensure that growth of black participation there keeps pace with the increasing inclusions of minorities in other areas such as research and international trade. The association operates exclusively for charitable and educational purposes and publishes and disseminates relevant information concerning intellectual property to disadvantaged persons.

Various programs, seminars, workshops, and periodic membership meetings are held to foster the development, training, and education of African American business persons and others having an interest in intellectual and industrial property. Headquartered near the nation's capital at Arlington Virginia, NIPLA has successfully had three nominees inducted into the renowned National Inventors Hall of Fame at Akron, Ohio. Through the continual persistence of one of its officers, then a patent examiner at the U.S. Patent and Trademark Office, the organization survives today.

After the founding of the association, the members who were also members of the bar began the Patent Section of the National Bar Association (NBA), which later was renamed the Intellectual Property Section of the NBA. Their thrust is toward educational forums and seminars coupled with review and analysis of intellectual property legislation that affects intellectual property law practices.

Nearly all of the early professionals received their initial IPL training as U.S. patent examiners who were sponsored by the agency through evening law school programs. More corporations and federal agencies began recruiting African Americans for their IPL departments after the initial wave in the late 1960s and early 1970s. Some recruits were James A. Crawford, Philip Dalton, Carrie Walthour Williams, Charles E. Smith, Sandra M. Nolan, Samuel R. Williamson, Wendell Fredericks, Leonard Williamson, Lawrence Harbin, Clarence F. Stanback, and Charles A. Malone. Various companies hired many African Americans as scientists and engineers who subsequently shifted their employment position to the company's legal/IPL offices while attending law school, for which the employer often paid the tuition.

Private practice was the last area of intellectual property law practice where barriers to African American practitioners started to crumble, but linger as bulwarks in need of change. African American IPL attorneys first appeared in law firms in the late 1970s and the early 1980s. John Moses was probably the first partner at an intellectual property law firm, having become one at Quaintance and Murphy in 1982. Presently, more than two dozen African American IPL attorneys are partners in these specialized firms. Probably some general law firms that litigate patent and other IPL matters also have minority attorneys as practicing partners.

In the past decade, including entry into the new millennium, even more minority IPL practitioners have entered corporations and firms directly from law schools. U.S. government agencies like the Department of Defense, the U.S. Patent and Trademark Office (USPTO), and the Library of Congress during the latter decades of the last century hired African IPL professionals who serve as patent and trademark administrators and counsels, as administrative judges, and as copyright counsels. USPTO careerist and attorney Lutrelle F. Parker, Jr., in 1975 was the first minority to achieve the status of deputy commissioner of patents and trademarks and subsequently became acting commissioner. In 1993, Lawrence J. Goffney, Jr., formerly of the law firm Dykema Gossett, was appointed assistant commissioner for patents, and Philip G. Hampton II, previously with the law firm Kenyon and Kenyon, was designated assistant commissioner for trademarks. Goffney a few years later was selected to the higher position of acting deputy commissioner. It is a historic milestone in the annals of the U.S. Patent and Trademark Office to have two African American IPL attorneys serve as administrators concurrently. Timely coinciding, even most rare, is the fact that an African American husband and wife serve concurrently as an administrative patent judge and as an administrative trademark judge, respectively. They are Judge Kenneth W. Hairston and Judge Paula T. Hairston.

Appendix II

ROSTER OF AFRICAN AMERICAN PATENTEES
Utility Grants from 1821

The listed African American inventors have solely owned patent grants and/or grants that are jointly owned. A number of the inventors cited have numerous U.S. patents and foreign grants as well, which are not presented herein. The patents designated "Reissue" are those patents that have been reissued under a special ruling. In some lengthy titles an abbreviated entry has been used.

PATENTEE	TITLE OF INVENTION	PATENT NUMBER	ISSUE DATE
Abbott, Liston, et al.	System for Passing Two Color TV Signals	4,120,001	October 10, 1978
Abbott, Liston, et al.	System for Transmitting Two Color TV Signals	4,179,703	December 18, 1979
Abbott, Liston	Cancelling Cross Modulation in Two Color TV Signals	4,264,919	April 28, 1981
Abbott, Liston	TV Privacy System Using Gray Sync	4,454,544	June 12, 1984
Abbott, Liston, et al.	Reducing Video Crosstalk in a Data Carrier	5,909,253	June 1, 1999
Abbott, Liston, et al.	Recovering Data from a Vestigial Sideband	6,046,775	April 4, 2000
Ables, Charles A.	Electric Bow for the Electric Bass Guitar	4,526,082	July 2, 1985
Abrams, William B.	Hame Attachment	450,550	April 14, 1891
Adams, James Sloan	Propelling Means for Aeroplanes	1,356,329	October 19, 1920
Albert, Albert P.	Cotton Picking Apparatus	851,475	April 23, 1907
Albert, Albert P.	Cotton Picking Apparatus	1,031,902	July 9, 1912
Alcorn, George Edward, et al.	Method for Forming Dense Dry Etched Multi-level Metallurgy	4,172,004	October 23, 1979
Alcorn, George Edward, et al.	Hardened Photoresist Master Image Mask	4,201,800	May 6, 1980
Alcorn, George Edward, et al.	Dense Dry Etched Multi-level Metallurgy	4,289,834	September 15, 1981
Alcorn, George Edward, et al.	Imaging X-ray Spectrometer	4,472,728	September 18, 1984
Alcorn, George Edward, et al.	GaAs Schottky Barrier Photo-Responsive Device	4,543,442	September 24, 1985
Alcorn, George Edward, et al.	Method of Fabricating an Imaging X-ray Spectrometer	4,618,380	October 21, 1986
Alcorn, George Edward, et al.	Cold Drink Vending Machine with Window Front Panel	5,392,953	February 28, 1995
Alexander, Benjamin H., et al.	Process for Preparation of D-Glucosaccharic Acid	2,472,168	June 7, 1949
Alexander, Benjamin H., et al.	6-Bromopiperonyl and 6-Chloropiperonyl Esters	2,886,485	May 12, 1959
Alexander, Benjamin H., et al.	Process for Preparing Mixed Piperonyl Acetals of Acetaldehyde	3,070,607	December 25, 1962
Alexander, Eugene D.	Geographic Cultural and Economic Board Game	5,292,133	March 8, 1994
Alexander, Nathaniel	Folding Chair	997,108	July 4, 1911
Alexander, Winser Edward	System for Enhancing Fine Detail in Thermal Photographs	3,541,333	November 17, 1970

Author	Title	Number	Date
Allain, Joseph L., Jr.	Portable Life Monitor, Medical Instrument	4,350,164	September 21, 1982
Allen, Charles William	Self-Leveling Table	613,436	November 1, 1898
Allen, Floyd	Telemeter for Battery	3,919,642	November 11, 1975
Allen, James B.	Clothes Line Support	551,105	December 10, 1895
Allen, James Matthew	Remote Control Apparatus	2,085,624	June 29, 1937
Allen, John S.	Package Tie	1,093,096	April 14, 1914
Allen, Johnny G.	Ring Assemblies for Supporting Refuse Bags	5,033,703	July 23, 1991
Allen, Tanya R.	Undergarment with Pocket	5,325,543	July 5, 1994
Alleyne, Ernest P.	Obstetrical Instrument	2,323,183	June 29, 1943
Ambrose, Ronald R., et al.	Thermosetting High Solids Solvent-Based Polyester Polyol Coating	4,535,132	August 13, 1985
Ambrose, Ronald R., et al.	Thermosetting High Solids Solvent-Based Polyester-Urethane	4,540,766	September 10, 1985
Ambrose, Ronald R., et al.	High Solids Polyester Polyols and Resinous Polyols	4,540,771	September 10, 1985
Ambrose, Ronald R., et al.	High Solids Polyurethane Polyols and Coating	4,543,405	September 24, 1985
Ambrose, Ronald R., et al.	Color Plus Clear Application of High Solids Thermosetting Coating Composition Containing Epoxy-Functional Polyrethanes	4,699,814	October 13, 1987
Ambrose, Ronald R., et al.	Color Plus Clear Application of Thermo High Solids Coating Composition of Hydroxy-Functional Epoxies and Anhydrides	4,732,790	March 22, 1988
Ambrose, Ronald R., et al.	Epoxy-Functional Polyurethanes and High Solids Thermosetting Coating	4,749,743	June 7, 1988
Ammons, Virgie M.	Fireplace Damper Actuating Tool	3,908,633	September 30, 1975
Amos, Carl R.	Method and Apparatus for Manipulating Phenomenon	5,369,511	November 29, 1994
Anderson, Alan, et al.	Zodiac Designer Jeans	4,513,454	April 30, 1985
Anderson, Vance J.	Safety Streetcar Fender	1,102,563	July 7, 1914
Anthony, John A.	System for Conserving Energy and Washing Agents in a Dishwasher	4,357,176	November 2, 1982
Armstead, Kenneth W., et al.	Pop-up Artificial Christmas Tree	4,847,123	July 11, 1989
Artis, Derrick L.	Contact Lens Case with Automatic Counter	5,699,900	December 23, 1997

PATENTEE	TITLE OF INVENTION	PATENT NUMBER	ISSUE DATE
Ashbourne, Alexander P.	Improvement in Processes for Preparing Cocoanut for Domestic Use	163,962	June 1, 1875
Ashbourne, Alexander P.	Improvement in Processes of Treating Cocoanut	194,287	August 21, 1877
Ashbourne, Alexander P.	Biscuit Cutters	170,460	November 30, 1875
Ashbourne, Alexander P.	Improvement in Processes of Treating Cocoanut	194,287	August 21, 1877
Ashbourne, Alexander P.	Refining Cocoanut Oil	230,518	July 27, 1880
Askew, Ben	Cotton Chopper	1,174,538	March 7, 1916
Austin, Theodore Dunbar	Desensitization of Liquid Explosives	3,116,188	December 31, 1963
Austin, Theodore Dunbar	Radar Reflecting Electrolytes	4,638,316	January 20, 1987
Bailey, Byron H.	Preparation of Liquid Liniment	4,582,706	April 15, 1986
Bailey, Clarence R.	Automatic Switch	982,410	January 24, 1911
Bailey, Leonard C.	Combined Truss and Bandage	285,545	September 25, 1883
Bailey, Leonard C.	Folding Bed	629,286	July 18, 1899
Bailey, Ronald Irwin	Swivel Electrical Receptacle	5,967,836	October 19, 1999
Bailey, Samuel G.	Talking Marionette with Theatre	4,690,655	September 1, 1987
Bailiff, Charles Orren	Shampoo Head Rest	612,008	October 11, 1898
Bailis, William	Ladder Scaffold-Supports	218,154	August 5, 1879
Baker, Bertram F.	Automatic Cashier	1,582,659	April 27, 1926
Baker, David	Railway Signal Apparatus	1,054,267	February 25, 1913
Baker, David	Signal Apparatus High Water Indicator for Bridges	1,154,162	September 21, 1915
Baker, David	Interliners to Prevent Tire Punctures	1,620,054	March 8, 1927
Baker, Jackson R.	Car Brake	314,417	March 24, 1885
Ballow, William J.	Combined Hat Rack and Table	601,422	March 29, 1898
Bankhead, Charles A.	Assembled Composition Printing	3,097,594	July 16, 1963
Banks, Charles M.	Hydraulic Jack	1,758,640	May 13, 1930
Banks, Charles M.	Jack	1,774,693	September 2, 1930

Name	Title	Patent No.	Date
Banks, Charles M.	Release Valve	1,893,757	January 10, 1933
Barnes, Ned E.	Sand Band for Wagon	792,109	June 13, 1905
Barnes, Ned E.	Rail and Tie Brace	815,059	March 13, 1906
Barnes, Ned E.	Hot Box Cooler and Oiler	899,939	September 29, 1908
Barnes, Ned E.	Indicator or Bulletin	969,592	September 6, 1910
Barnes, Ned E., et al.	Automatic Film Mover	1,124,879	January 12, 1915
Barnes, Ned E.	Tie Plate for Railway	1,180,467	April 25, 1916
Barnes, Ned E.	Rail Brace	1,446,957	February 27, 1923
Barnes, Ned E.	Tie Plate and Joint Brace	1,655,305	January 3, 1928
Barnes, Ned E.	Pole, Post, and Tree Protector	1,673,729	June 12, 1928
Barnwell, Irving	Air Valve Guard for Radiators	2,476,578	July 19, 1949
Baron, Neville A.	Method and Apparatus for Sterilizing and Storing Contact Lenses	4,063,890	December 20, 1977
Baron, Neville A.	Apparatus and Process for Recurving the Cornea of an Eye	4,461,294	July 24, 1984
Baron, Neville A.	Process for Recurving the Cornea of an Eye	4,712,543	December 15, 1987
Baron, Neville A.	Ophthalmic Liquid Sunglasses	4,765,977	August 23, 1988
Barton, Lyndon O.	Dual Timer Device	4,236,242	November 25, 1980
Barton, Lyndon O.	Timing Device	4,238,846	December 9, 1980
Bath, Patricia E.	Apparatus for Ablating and Removing Cataract Lenses	4,744,360	May 17, 1988
Bath, Patricia E.	Method and Apparatus, Ablating and Removing Cataract Lenses	5,843,071	December 1, 1998
Bath, Patricia E.	Laser Apparatus for Surgery for Cataractous Lenses	5,919,186	July 6, 1999
Bath, Patricia E.	Pulsed Ultrasound Method for Cataractous Lenses	6,083,192	July 4, 2000
Battle, James	Variable Resistance Resistor Assembly	3,691,503	September 12, 1972
Bauer, James A.	Coin Changer Mechanism	3,490,571	January 20, 1970
Bayless, Robert Gordon, et al.	Encapsulation Process and Its Product	3,565,818	February 23, 1971
Bayless, Robert Gordon, et al.	Encapsulation Process and Its Product	3,574,133	April 6, 1971
Bayless, Robert Gordon, et al.	Pressure-Sensitive Record Sheet and Coating Composition	3,576,660	April 27, 1971

PATENTEE	TITLE OF INVENTION	PATENT NUMBER	ISSUE DATE
Bayless, Robert Gordon, et al.	Water Solubilization of Vanadyl-Hardened Poly (vinylalcohol) Films	3,629,140	December 21, 1971
Bayless, Robert Gordon, et al.	Process of Forming Minute Capsules	3,674,704	July 4, 1972
Bayless, Robert Gordon, et al.	Capsule Wall Treating Process	3,726,803	April 10, 1973
Bayless, Robert Gordon, et al.	Capsule Manufacture	3,755,190	August 28, 1973
Bayless, Robert Gordon, et al.	Continuous Encapsulation and Device	3,816,331	June 11, 1974
Bayless, Robert Gordon	Solid Microglobules Containing Dispersed Materials	3,922,373	November 25, 1975
Bayless, Robert Gordon	Process of Feeding Larval Marine Animals	4,073,946	February 14, 1978
Bayless, Robert Gordon	Method of Producing Microcapsules and Product	4,107,071	August 15, 1978
Bayless, Robert Gordon, et al.	Tobacco-Substitute Smoking Material	4,195,645	April 1, 1980
Bayless, Robert Gordon, et al.	Hydrolyzed Ethylene Vinyl Acetate Encapsulating Coating	4,377,621	March 22, 1983
Bayless, William E. and Frank B.	Blackboard Eraser	1,214,411	January 30, 1917
Baylis, Robert M.	Aerial Toy	2,105,579	January 18, 1938
Bean, Lloyd F.	Multiple Layer Migration Imaging System	3,966,465	June 29, 1976
Bean, Lloyd F.	Multiple Layer Migration Imaging System	3,982,939	September 28, 1976
Bean, Lloyd F.	Single Component Color Development System	4,057,340	November 8, 1977
Bean, Lloyd F., et al.	Toner Combination for Carrierless Development	4,142,981	March 6, 1979
Bean, Lloyd F., et al.	Tribo Induction Toner Combination	4,457,996	July 3, 1984
Bean, Lloyd F.	Multi-Reflection Scanner	5,136,415	August 4, 1992
Bean, Lloyd F.	Single Pass Duplexing Method and Apparatus	6,345,167	February 5, 2002
Beard, Andrew Jackson	Double Plow	240,642	April 26, 1881
Beard, Andrew Jackson	Plow or Cultivator	347,220	August 10, 1886
Beard, Andrew Jackson	Rotary Engine	478,271	July 5, 1892
Beard, Andrew Jackson	Car Coupling	594,059	November 23, 1897
Becket, George E.	Letter Box	483,525	October 4, 1892
Beckley, Charles Randolph	Folding Chair	3,856,345	December 24, 1974
Beckley, Charles Randolph	Folding Seat	4,006,910	February 8, 1977

209

PATENTEE	TITLE OF INVENTION	PATENT NUMBER	ISSUE DATE
Bethea, Clyde George, et al.	Quantum-Well Radiation-Interactive Device, and Methods	5,023,685	June 11, 1991
Bethea, Clyde George	Making a Semiconductor Device Including Infrared Imaging, and Apparatus for Use in Imaging	5,396,068	March 7, 1995
Bethea, Clyde George, et al.	Laser Transmitter for Reduced SBS	5,991,061	November 23, 1999
Bethea, Clyde George, et al.	Laser Transmitter for Reduced Signal Distortion	5,991,323	November 23, 1999
Bethea, Clyde George, et al.	Sub-carrier Multiplexing in Broadband Optical Networks	6,081,361	June 27, 2000
Bethea, Clyde George, et al.	Broadband Tunable Semiconductor Laser Source	6,108,362	August 22, 2000
Bethea, Clyde George, et al.	WDM System for Reduced SBS	6,166,837	December 26, 2000
Bethea, Clyde George, et al.	Optical System for Reduced SBS	6,331,908	December 18, 2001
Bethea, Clyde George, et al.	Method and Apparatus for Suppressing Interference	6,564,038	May 13, 2003
Binga, M. William	Street-Sprinkling Apparatus	217,843	July 22, 1879
Bishop, Alfred A., et al.	Nuclear Reactor with Self-Orificing Radial Blanket	4,077,835	March 7, 1978
Blackburn, Albert B.	Railway Signal	376,362	January 10, 1888
Blackburn, Albert B.	Spring Seat for Chairs	380,240	April 3, 1888
Blackburn, Albert B.	Cash Carrier	391,577	October 23, 1888
Blackburn, Charles M., et al.	Electronic Counting Apparatus	3,618,819	November 9, 1971
Blair, Connie D.	Enclosure for Curling Iron and Similar Device	5,062,529	November 5, 1991
Blair, Henry	Seed Planter	8447X	October 14, 1834
Blair, Henry	Cotton Planter	15	August 31, 1836
Blanton, John W.	Hydromechanical Rate-Damped Servo System	3,101,650	August 27, 1963
Blenman, Orman L.	Variable Pressure Fuel Generator and Method	4,054,423	October 18, 1977
Blue, Lockrum	Hand Corn Shelling Device	298,937	May 20, 1884
Bluford, Guion S., Sr., et al.	Artillery Ammunition Training Round	2,541,025	February 13, 1951
Bolling, Yvonne	Doorbell Actuated Air Freshener	4,570,824	February 18, 1986
Booker, Peachy	Flying Landing Platform	3,003,717	October 10, 1961
Boone, Sarah	Ironing Board	473,653	April 26, 1892
Boston, Russell E., et al.	Thermosetting Compositions Comprising Acrylic Polymers	4,864,000	September 5, 1989

Name	Title	Patent No.	Date
Boston, Russell E., et al.	Coatings for the Protection of Products in Light-transmitting Containers	5,085,903	February 4, 1992
Boston, Russell E., et al.	Coatings and Method for Coloring Light-transmitting Containers	5,182,148	January 26, 1993
Bowman, Henry A.	Method of Making Flags	469,395	February 23, 1892
Boyd, Henry, III, et al.	Syringe Holder with Retractable Needle Assembly	5,360,409	November 1, 1994
Boykin, Otis F.	Wire Type Precision Resistor	2,891,227	June 16, 1959
Boykin, Otis F.	Electrical Resistor	2,972,726	February 21, 1961
Boykin, Otis F.	Electrical Capacitor and Method of Making	3,191,108	June 22, 1965
Boykin, Otis F.	Electrical Resistance Element and Method of Making	3,271,193	September 6, 1966
Boykin, Otis F.	Method of Making a Thin Film Capacitor	3,348,971	October 24, 1967
Boykin, Otis F.	Thin Film Capacitor	3,394,290	July 23, 1968
Bradberry, Henrietta	Bed Rack	2,320,027	May 25, 1943
Bradberry, Henrietta	Torpedo Discharge Means	2,390,688	December 11, 1945
Bradley, Alex	File	1,709,654	April 16, 1929
Braxton, Kenneth Jerome	Security System for Centralized Monitoring and Selective Reporting	4,141,006	February 20, 1979
Briscoe, James R.	Building Blocks with Sides Converging Upwardly	3,376,682	April 9, 1968
Brittain, Thomas H.	Level	940,671	November 23, 1909
Brooks, Charles B.	Punch	507,672	October 31, 1893
Brooks, Charles B.	Street Sweeper	556,711	March 17, 1896
Brooks, Charles B., et al.	Street Sweepers	558,719	April 21, 1896
Brooks, Charles B.	Dust Proof Bag for Street Sweepers	560,154	May 12, 1896
Brooks, Eddie L.	Gear Reduction Multiplier	5,913,938	June 22, 1999
Brooks, Eddie L.	Gear Ratio Multiplier	6,244,126	June 12, 2001
Brooks, James M.	Envelope Moistener	1,092,688	April 7, 1924
Brooks, Phil	Disposable Syringe	3,802,434	April 9, 1974
Brooks, Robert Roosevelt	Line Blanking Apparatus for Bar Generating Equipment	3,334,178	August 1, 1967
Brooks, Robert Roosevelt	Preset Sensitivity and Amplification Control System	3,518,371	June 30, 1970

PATENTEE	TITLE OF INVENTION	PATENT NUMBER	ISSUE DATE
Brooks, Robert Roosevelt	Vertical and Horizontal Aperture Equalization	3,546,372	December 8, 1970
Brown, Charles W., et al.	Water Closets for Railway Cars	147,363	February 10, 1874
Brown, Firmin Charles	Self-feeding Attachment for Furnaces	1,719,258	July 2, 1929
Brown, Henry	Receptacle for Storing and Preserving Papers	352,036	November 2, 1886
Brown, Henry T.	Combined Isomerization and Cracking Process	3,000,995	September 19, 1961
Brown, Henry T.	Reactivating Hydroforming Catalysts	3,407,135	October 22, 1968
Brown, Jacob Theodore	Specimen Collection Kit for Mailing	4,949,840	August 21, 1990
Brown, Lincoln F.	Bridle Bit	484,994	October 25, 1892
Brown, Marie V. B. and Albert L.	Home Security System	3,482,037	December 2, 1969
Brown, Oscar E.	Horseshoe	481,271	August 23, 1892
Brown, Paul L.	Spinnable Stringless Top	3,523,386	August 11, 1970
Brown, Paul L.	Gyroscopic Top	3,945,146	March 23, 1976
Brown, Paul L.	Spinnable Object on a Length-Adjustable Tether	4,086,722	May 2, 1978
Brown, Paul L.	Levitation Toy and Method of Operation	4,109,413	August 29, 1978
Brown, Paul L.	Toy Balloon Closure Device	4,428,149	January 31, 1984
Brown, Paul L.	Toy for Electrically Playing Rhythmical Melody	4,568,303	February 4, 1986
Browne, William H., Jr., et al.	Air-Sea Rescue Device with Floatation Collar	3,444,569	May 20, 1969
Browne, Hugh M.	Sewer or Other Trap	426,429	April 29, 1890
Browne, Hugh M.	Damper Regulator	886,183	April 28, 1908
Bryan, Joseph D.	Scrubbing Brush	1,041,011	October 15, 1912
Bundy, Robert F.	Signal Generator	2,922,924	January 26, 1960
Burgin, Paul D.	Head Lamp Rim Remover	1,788,507	January 13, 1931
Burkins, Eugene	Breech Loading Cannon	649,433	May 15, 1900
Burnham, Gerald O.	Direction Coded Digital Stroke Generator	3,938,130	February 10, 1976
Burr, John Albert	Lawn Mower	624,749	May 9, 1899
Burr, William F.	Switching Device for Railways	636,197	October 31, 1899

Name	Invention	Serial Number	Date
Burridge, Lee S., et al.	Type Writing Machine	315,366	April 7, 1885
Burton, Andrew F.	Infusion of Liquids into Tissue	4,159,720	July 3, 1979
Burton, Gus	Emergency Landing Runway	2,351,002	June 13, 1944
Burwell, Wilson	Boot or Shoe	638,043	November 28, 1899
Butcher, James W.	Truck Handle Clamp	573,334	March 26, 1912
Butler, Francis Edward	Audible Underwater Signal	2,803,807	August 30, 1957
Butler, Francis Edward	Drill Mine	2,912,929	November 17, 1959
Butler, Francis Edward	Watertight Electrical Connector	2,991,441	July 4, 1961
Butler, Francis Edward	Detachable Practice Mine Selector	3,086,464	April 23, 1963
Butler, Richard A.	Train Alarm	584,540	June 15, 1897
Butts, John W.	Luggage Carrier	634,611	October 10, 1899
Byrd, Turner, Jr.	Improvement for Holders of Reins for Horses	123,328	February 6, 1872
Byrd, Turner, Jr.	Apparatus for Detaching Horses from Carriages	124,790	March 19, 1872
Byrd, Turner, Jr.	Improvements in Neck Yokes for Wagons	126,181	April 30, 1872
Byrd, Turner, Jr.	Improvement in Car Couplings	157,370	December 1, 1874
Caliver, Ambrose	Work Cabinet	1,568,498	January 5, 1926
Campbell, Peter R.	Screw Press	213,871	April 1, 1879
Campbell, Robert Leon	Valve Gear for Steam Engines	728,364	May 19, 1903
Campbell, William S.	Self Setting Animal Trap	246,369	August 30, 1881
Cannon, Thomas C., Jr.	Remote Controlled Vehicle Systems	3,926,434	December 16, 1975
Cargill, Benjamin F.	Invalid Cot	629,658	July 25, 1899
Carrington, Alfred C.	Aerodynamic Device	4,433,819	February 28, 1984
Carrington, Alfred C.	Aerodynamic Device	5,072,892	December 17, 1991
Carrington, Thomas A.	Ranges	180,323	July 25, 1876
Carruthers, George R.	Image Converter for Detecting Electromagnetic Radiation	3,478,216	November 11, 1969
Carter, Charles H.	Automatic Fish Cleaner	1,394,711	October 25, 1921
Carter, Iula A.	Nursery Chair	2,923,950	February 9, 1960
Carter, John L., et al.	Equivalent High-Power Pulsed Microwave Transmitter	3,078,424	February 19, 1963

PATENTEE	TITLE OF INVENTION	PATENT NUMBER	ISSUE DATE
Carter, John L., et al.	Technique for Shaping Crystalline Spheres	3,103,770	September 17, 1963
Carter, John L., et al.	Electron Discharge Device	3,112,426	November 26, 1963
Carter, John L., et al.	Ferrite Power Limiter Duplexer	3,183,457	May 11, 1965
Carter, John L., et al.	Waveguide Power Limiter	3,629,735	December 21, 1971
Carter, John L., et al.	Power Dividing and Combining Techniques for Microwave Amplifiers	3,928,806	December 23, 1975
Carter, John L., et al.	Passive Microwave Power Distribution Systems	3,953,853	April 27, 1976
Carter, John L., et al.	Passive Microwave Power Distribution Systems	3,969,693	July 13, 1976
Carter, John L., et al.	Power Divider and Power Combiner	3,986,147	October 12, 1976
Carter, John L., et al.	Power Dividing and Combining Techniques for Microwave Amplifiers	4,028,632	June 7, 1977
Carter, John L.	Constant Current Charging Circuits for High Energy Modulators	4,090,140	May 16, 1978
Carter, John L., et al.	Distributed Pulse Forming Network	4,612,455	September 16, 1986
Carter, Thomas J.	Apparatus for Water Penetration Testing of Sole Leather	3,028,755	April 10, 1962
Carter, William C.	Umbrella Stand	323,397	August 4, 1885
Carver, George Washington	Cosmetic and Process of Producing	1,522,176	January 6, 1925
Carver, George Washington	Paint and Stain and Process of Producing	1,541,478	June 9, 1925
Carver, George Washington	Process of Producing Paints and Stains	1,632,365	June 14, 1927
Cashaw, Allen, et al.	Operating Room Gown and Drape Fabric with Improved Repellent Properties	4,705,712	November 10, 1987
Cassell, Oscar Robert	Bedstead Extension	990,107	April 18, 1911
Cassell, Oscar Robert	Flying Machine	1,024,766	April 30, 1912
Cassell, Oscar Robert	Angle Indicator	1,038,291	September 10, 1912
Cassell, Oscar Robert	Bedstead Extension	1,105,487	July 28, 1914
Cassell, Oscar Robert	Flying Machine	1,406,344	February 14, 1922
Cavell, Winston W., et al.	Smoke Tracer Composition	2,823,105	February 11, 1958

214

Author	Title	Number	Date
Cavell, Winston W., et al.	Spotter-Tracer Projectile	3,013,495	December 19, 1961
Cavell, Winston W., et al.	Electrically Initiated Spotter Tracer Bullet	3,101,054	August 20, 1963
Certain, Jerry M.	Parcel Carrier for Bicycles	639,708	December 26, 1899
Chappelle, Emmet W.	Light Detection Instrument	3,520,660	July 14, 1970
Chappelle, Emmet W., et al.	Method of Detecting and Counting Bacteria in Body Fluids	3,745,090	July 10, 1973
Chappelle, Emmet W., et al.	Method of Detecting and Counting Bacteria	3,971,703	July 27, 1976
Chappelle, Emmet W.	Rapid, Quantitative Determination of Bacteria	4,385,113	May 24, 1983
Cheetham, Margaret	Toy	1,998,270	April 16, 1935
Cherry, Matthew A.	Velocipede	382,351	May 8, 1888
Cherry, Matthew A.	Street Car Fender	531,908	January 1, 1895
Christian, John B.	Ion-Incorporation of Polar Solids as Lubrication Stabilizers	3,201,347	August 17, 1965
Christian, John B.	Multipurpose Grease Composition	3,314,889	April 18, 1967
Christian, John B.	Evaporation Loss Determination Apparatus and Method	3,360,985	January 2, 1968
Christian, John B.	Grease Compositions for Use at High Temperature and High Speed Applications	3,518,189	June 30, 1970
Christian, John B.	Grease Composition	3,525,690	August 25, 1970
Christian, John B.	Grease Composition for Vacuum and High Temperature Applications	3,536,621	October 27, 1970
Christian, John B.	Grease Compositions of Fluorocarbon Polyethers Thickened with Polyfluoro-Phenylene Polymers	3,536,624	October 27, 1970
Christian, John B.	Grease Composition	3,563,894	February 16, 1971
Christian, John B.	Grease Compositions of Polyol Aliphatic Esters	3,622,512	November 23, 1971
Christian, John B.	Grease Composition Comprising Polyfluoroakyl-Polysiloxane	3,642,626	February 15, 1972
Christian, John B.	Grease Composition of Perfluoroolefin Epoxide Polyethers	3,658,709	April 25, 1972
Christian, John B.	Grease Composition	3,725,273	April 3, 1973
Christian, John B.	Polyfluoroalkyl-Dimethyl Poly-siloxane/Polyol Aliphatic Ester Greases	3,814,689	June 4, 1974
Christian, John B.	Fluorine-containing Benzimidazoles	4,269,348	May 12, 1981
Christian, John B.	Polyfluoroakylether Substituted Phenyl Phosphines	4,454,349	June 12, 1984
Christmas, Charles T.	Hand Power Attachment for Sewing Machines	226,492	April 13, 1880

PATENTEE	TITLE OF INVENTION	PATENT NUMBER	ISSUE DATE
Christmas, Charles T.	Baling Press	228,036	May 25, 1880
Christmas, Charles T.	Bale Band Tightener	231,273	August 17, 1880
Church, Titus S.	Carpet Beating Machine	302,237	July 29, 1884
Clare, Obadian B.	Trestle	390,753	October 9, 1888
Clark, Ceffus, Jr.	Trash Container	4,823,979	April 25, 1989
Clark, Erastus	Nut Lock	308,876	December 9, 1884
Clark, Samuel A., Jr.	Protective Metal Cap for Plastic Fuze Radomes	3,780,661	December 25, 1973
Clark, Samuel A., Jr., et al.	Protective Metal Shield for Plastic Fuze Radomes	3,971,024	July 20, 1976
Clay, Boston	Button Making Machine	1,105,757	August 4, 1914
Clay, Percy	Signal Lantern	1,035,420	August 13, 1912
Clemens, Tony	Vehicle Running-Gear	1,174,392	March 7, 1916
Coates, Robert	Overboot for Horses	473,295	April 19, 1892
Cobb, Melvin	Electrical Power Conservation Circuit	4,687,947	August 18, 1987
Cobbs, William N.	Locomotive Headlight	1,780,865	November 4, 1930
Colbert, Douglas W.	Pallet Construction	4,145,975	March 27, 1979
Coles, James J.	Cap and Collar Case	1,577,632	March 23, 1926
Coles, Leander M.	Mortician's Table	3,799,534	March 26, 1974
Collic, Edward H., Sr.	Clamp and Hook Arrangement and Attachment	4,261,280	April 14, 1981
Collins, Phillip	Bubble Machine	4,775,348	October 4, 1988
Conner-Ward, Dannette V., et al.	Method for Soybean Transformation	5,416,011	May 16, 1995
Conner-Ward, Dannette V., et al.	Method for Soybean Transformation	5,569,834	October 29, 1996
Conner-Ward, Dannette V., et al.	Method for Soybean Transformation	5,824,877	October 20, 1998
Conner-Ward, Dannette V., et al.	Method for Transforming Soybeans	5,959,179	September 28, 1999
Cook, Bertha, et al.	Multicharacter Doll	4,921,449	May 1, 1990
Cook, George	Automatic Fishing Device	625,829	May 30, 1899
Coolige, Joseph Sidney	Harness Attachment	392,908	November 13, 1888

Cooper, Albert R.	Shoemaker's Jack	631,519	August 22, 1899
Cooper, James	Elevator Safety Device	536,605	April 2, 1895
Cooper, James	Elevator Safety Device	590,257	September 21, 1897
Cooper, John Richard	Two-Stage Phosgenation	3,234,253	February 8, 1966
Cooper, John Richard	Process for Isolating a Fluorine-Containing Polymer	3,536,683	October 27, 1970
Cooper, John Richard	Separation of Distillable Isocyanates	3,694,323	September 26, 1972
Cooper, Jonas	Shutter and Fastening	276,563	May 1, 1883
Cooper, Walter	Polymerization by Contact with Materials	3,532,680	October 6, 1970
Cooper, Walter	Polymerizable Composition, Ferrocene Dye	3,551,153	December 29, 1970
Cornwell, Phillip W.	Draft Regulator	390,284	October 2, 1888
Cornwell, Phillip W.	Draft Regulator	491,082	February 7, 1893
Cosby, Thomas L.	Rotary Machine	3,456,594	July 22, 1969
Cosby, Thomas L.	Closed Cycle Energy Conversion System	3,826,092	July 30, 1974
Cosgrove, William Francis	Automatic Stop Plug for Gas and Oil Pipes	313,993	March 17, 1885
Cotton, Donald J.	Vertical Liquid Electrode in Electrolytic Cells	4,040,932	August 9, 1977
Cotton, Donald J.	Capillary Liquid Fuel Nuclear Reactor	4,327,443	April 27, 1982
Covington, Joseph C.	Snow Chain	4,265,399	May 5, 1981
Cowans, Beatrice L., et al.	Embroidered Fruit Bowl Wall Hanging	4,016,314	April 5, 1977
Cox, David Wesley, Jr.	Manual Tool for Preparing Tube Ends for Jointure	4,899,409	February 13, 1990
Cox, Elbert L., et al.	Presettable Bistable Circuits	3,334,245	August 1, 1967
Craig, Arthur U.	Cushion Support for Vehicles	1,258,748	March 12, 1918
Cralle, Alfred L.	Ice Cream Mold	576,395	February 2, 1897
Crawford, Dale K.	Remote Controlled Moveable Fan	5,256,039	October 26, 1993
Crawford, Samuel T.	Comb	1,381,804	June 14, 1921
Creamer, Henry	Steam Feed Water Trap	313,854	March 17, 1885
Creamer, Henry	Steam Feed Water Trap	358,964	March 8, 1887
Creamer, Henry	Steam Trap	376,586	January 17, 1888
Creamer, Henry	Steam Trap and Feeder	394,463	December 11, 1888
Crichton, Francis D.	Flag Staff	1,855,824	April 26, 1932

PATENTEE	TITLE OF INVENTION	PATENT NUMBER	ISSUE DATE
Croslin, Michael E.	Method and Apparatus for Performing Non-Invasive Blood Pressure and Pulse	4,271,844	June 9, 1981
Croslin, Michael E.	Method and Apparatus for Performing Non-Invasive Blood Pressure and Pulse	4,326,537	April 27, 1982
Croslin, Michael E.	Method and Apparatus for Performing Non-Invasive Blood Pressure and Pulse	4,338,949	July 13, 1982
Croslin, Michael E.	Method and Apparatus for Performing Non-Invasive Blood Pressure and Pulse	4,407,297	October 4, 1983
Crossley, Frank A.	Titanium Base Alloy	2,798,807	July 9, 1957
Crossley, Frank A.	Grain Refinement of Beryllium with Tungsten Carbide and Titanium Diboride	3,117,001	January 9, 1964
Crossley, Frank A.	Grain Refinement of Titanium Alloys	4,420,460	December 13, 1983
Crosthwait, David N., Jr.	Thermostatic Steam Trap	1,315,596	September 9, 1919
Crosthwait, David N., Jr.	Apparatus for Returning Water to Boilers	1,353,457	September 21, 1920
Crosthwait, David N., Jr.	Method and Apparatus for Setting Thermostats	1,661,323	March 6, 1928
Crosthwait, David N., Jr.	Differential Vacuum Pump	1,755,430	April 22, 1930
Crosthwait, David N., Jr.	Steam Trap	1,797,258	March 24, 1931
Crosthwait, David N., Jr.	Automatic Discharge Valve	1,871,044	August 9, 1932
Crosthwait, David N., Jr.	Freezing Temperature Indicator	1,874,911	August 30, 1932
Crosthwait, David N., Jr.	Refrigerating Method and Apparatus	1,874,912	August 30, 1932
Crosthwait, David N., Jr.	Exhausting Mechanism	1,893,883	January 10, 1933
Crosthwait, David N., Jr.	Bucket Trap	1,930,224	October 10, 1933
Crosthwait, David N., Jr.	Vacuum Pump	1,946,524	February 13, 1934
Crosthwait, David N., Jr.	Method of Steam Heating from Central Station Mains	1,963,735	June 19, 1934
Crosthwait, David N., Jr.	Refrigeration Apparatus and Process	1,972,704	September 4, 1934
Crosthwait, David N., Jr.	Refrigeration Apparatus and Process	1,972,705	September 4, 1934

Crosthwait, David N., Jr.	Steam Heating System	1,977,303	October 16, 1934
Crosthwait, David N., Jr.	Steam Heating Apparatus	1,977,304	October 16, 1934
Crosthwait, David N., Jr.	Vacuum Heating System	1,986,391	January 1, 1935
Crosthwait, David N., Jr.	Remote Control Proportional Movement Motor	2,007,240	July 9, 1935
Crosthwait, David N., Jr., et al.	Heating	2,064,197	December 15, 1936
Crosthwait, David N., Jr.	Effective Temperature Thermostat	2,086,258	July 6, 1937
Crosthwait, David N., Jr., et al.	Effective Temperature Control Apparatus	2,094,738	October 5, 1937
Crosthwait, David N., Jr.	Exhausting Method and Apparatus	2,096,226	October 19, 1937
Crosthwait, David N., Jr.	One Pipe Heating System Regulating Plate	2,102,197	December 14, 1937
Crosthwait, David N., Jr.	Regulating Radiator Valve	2,114,139	April 12, 1938
Crosthwait, David N., Jr.	Generating Mixed Fluid Heating Medium	2,169,683	August 15, 1939
Crosthwait, David N., Jr., et al.	Heat Balancer	2,185,500	January 2, 1940
Crosthwait, David N., Jr., et al.	Unit Heater and Air Conditioner	2,205,716	June 25, 1940
Crosthwait, David N., Jr., et al.	Unit Heater and Air Conditioner	2,263,074	November 18, 1941
Crosthwait, David N., Jr., et al.	Resistance Type Temperature Controlling System	2,263,977	November 21, 1941
Crosthwait, David N., Jr., et al.	Discharge Valve	2,275,132	March 3, 1942
Crosthwait, David N., Jr., et al.	Window Thermostat	2,346,560	April 11, 1944
Crosthwait, David N., Jr., et al.	Balanced Resistance Type Temperature Control	2,431,790	December 2, 1944
Crosthwait, David N., Jr.	Float Operated Mechanism	2,384,536	September 11, 1945
Dacons, Joseph Carl	Process for the Manufacture of Nitroform	3,125,606	March 17, 1964
Dacons, Joseph Carl	Dodecanitroquaterphenyl	3,450,778	June 17, 1969
Dacons, Joseph Carl	Recrystallization of Hexanitrostilbene	4,260,847	April 7, 1981
Dammond, William Hunter	Signalling System	747,949	December 29, 1903
Dammond, William Hunter	Safety System for Operating Railroads	823,513	June 19, 1906
Darkins, John Thomas	Ventilator	534,322	February 19, 1895
Davidson, Shelby J.	Paper Rewind Mechanism for Adding Machines	884,721	April 14, 1908
Davidson, Sidney N.	Pants Presser	1,088,329	February 24, 1914
Davidson, Sidney N.	Body Lifter	2,607,103	August 19, 1952

PATENTEE	TITLE OF INVENTION	PATENT NUMBER	ISSUE DATE
Davis, Israel D.	Tonic	351,829	November 2, 1886
Davis, Stephen H.	Load Weighing and Totaling Device for Cranes, Hoists	2,324,769	July 20, 1943
Davis, William D.	Riding Saddles	568,939	October 6, 1896
Davis, William R., Jr.	Library Table	208,378	September 24, 1878
Davis, William R., Jr.	Game Table	362,611	May 10, 1887
Dean, Mark E., et al.	Color Video Display System Having Programmable Border Color	4,437,092	March 13, 1984
Dean, Mark E., et al.	Composite Video Color Signal Generation from Digital Color Signals	4,442,428	April 10, 1984
Dean, Mark E., et al.	Microcomputer System with Bus Control Means for Peripheral Processing Devices	4,528,626	July 9, 1985
Dean, Mark E.	Refresh Generator System for a Dynamic Memory	4,575,826	March 11, 1986
Dean, Mark E., et al.	Data Processing System	4,598,356	July 1, 1986
Dean, Mark E., et al.	Computer System Including a Page Mode Memory	5,034,917	July 23, 1991
Dean, Mark E., et al.	Method and Apparatus for Selectively Posting Write Cycles	5,045,998	September 3, 1991
Dean, Mark E., et al.	Bidirectional Buffer with Latch and Parity Capability	5,107,507	April 21, 1992
Dean, Mark E., et al.	Control of Pipelined Operation in a Microcomputer System	5,125,084	June 23, 1992
Dean, Mark E., et al.	System Bus Preempt for 80886 When Running in an 80386/82385 Microcomputer System with Arbitration	5,129,090	July 7, 1992
Dean, Mark E., et al.	Microprocessor Hold and Lock Circuitry	5,170,481	December 8, 1992
Dean, Mark E., et al.	Delayed Cache Write Enable Circuit for a Dual Bus Microcomputer System	5,175,826	December 29, 1992
Dean, Mark E., et al.	Data Processing Apparatus for Selectively Posting Write Cycles	5,327,545	July 5, 1994
Dean, Mark E., et al.	Connecting a Short Word Length Non-volatile Memory to a Long Word Length Address Data Multiplexed Bus	5,448,521	September 5, 1995

Author	Title	Number	Date
Dean, Mark E., et al.	Microcomputer System Employing Address Offset Mechanism	5,450,559	September 12, 1995
Dean, Mark E.	System and Method for Prefetching Information	5,544,342	August 6, 1996
Dean, Mark E., et al.	Non-contiguous Mapping of I/O Addresses to Use Page Protection of a Process	5,548,746	August 20, 1996
Dean, Mark E.	Self-Time Processor with Dynamic Clock Generator	5,553,276	September 3, 1996
Dean, Mark E., et al.	Method and System for Reading from M-byte Memory	5,603,041	February 11, 1997
DeCosta, John, et al.	Dynamic Position Locating System	4,340,777	July 20, 1982
DeCosta, John, et al.	Mounting Arrangement for Position Locating System	4,355,202	October 19, 1982
Dedmon, Robert	Combined Sleigh and Boat	1,716,230	June 4, 1929
Deitz, William A.	Improvement in Shoes	64,205	April 30, 1867
Delfyett, Peter J., Jr., et al.	Method and Apparatus for Generating Ultrashort Light Pulses	4,972,423	November 20, 1990
Delfyett, Peter J., Jr., et al.	Optical Pulse-Shaping Device and Method	5,166,818	November 24, 1992
Delfyett, Peter J., Jr.	Broadband Absorber Having Multiple Quantum Wells	5,265,107	November 23, 1993
Delfyett, Peter J., Jr.	Self Starting Femtosecond Ti Sapphire Laser with Intracavity	5,434,873	July 18, 1995
Delfyett, Peter J., Jr.	Mode Locked Laser Diode in a High Power Solid State Regenerative Amplifier and Mount Mechanism	5,469,454	November 21, 1995
Delfyett, Peter J., Jr., et al.	High Speed Pulse Slicer/Demultiplexer with Gain for Use in Solid State Regenerative Amplifier Systems	5,546,415	August 13, 1996
Delfyett, Peter J., Jr.	Mode Locked Laser Diode in a High Power Solid State Regenerative Amplifier and Mount Mechanism	5,652,763	July 29, 1997
Delfyett, Peter J., Jr., et al.	Three Dimensional Optical Imaging Colposcopy	5,921,926	July 13, 1999
Delfyett, Peter J., Jr., et al.	Optical Disk Readout Method Using Optical Coherence Tomography and Spectral Interferometry	6,072,765	June 6, 2000
Delfyett, Peter J., Jr., et al.	Three Dimensional Optical Imaging Colposcopy	6,141,577	October 31, 2000
Delfyett, Peter J., Jr., et al.	Multiwavelength Modelocked Semiconductor Diode Laser	6,256,328	July 3, 2001
Delfyett, Peter J., Jr., et al.	Hybrid WDM-TDM Optical Communication and Data Link	6,314,115	November 6, 2001
Delfyett, Peter J., Jr., et al.	Hybrid WDM-TDM Optical Communication and Data Link	6,647,031	November 11, 2003

221

PATENTEE	TITLE OF INVENTION	PATENT NUMBER	ISSUE DATE
Deloatch, Essex	Motor Control System for Self-Serving Table	1,466,890	September 4, 1923
Denson, Costel D.	Particulate Filled Coating Composition of Hydroxyl Polyester Cured with Pyromellitic Acid and Anhydride	3,205,192	September 7, 1965
Denson, Costel D.	Apparatus for Measuring the Thickness of a Liquid Draining from a Vertically Disposed Surface	3,569,722	March 9, 1971
Dent, Anthony L., et al.	Rehydrated Silica Gel Dentifrice Abrasive	4,346,071	August 24, 1982
Dent, Anthony L., et al.	Toothpaste Containing pH-adjusted Zeolite	4,349,533	September 14, 1982
Dent, Benjamin A.	Procedure Entry for a Data Processor Employing a Stack	3,548,384	December 15, 1970
Dickenson, Robert C.	Trolley Guard	1,314,130	August 26, 1970
Dickerson, Leary	Oyster Punching Machine	2,444,636	July 6, 1948
Dickinson, Joseph H.	Reed-Organ	624,192	May 2, 1899
Dickinson, Joseph H.	Pedal Housing for Pianos	770,563	September 30, 1904
Dickinson, Joseph H.	Music Sheetfeed Controlling Mechanism	772,225	October 11, 1904
Dickinson, Joseph H.	Means for Controlling Tension, Musical Players	780,411	January 17, 1905
Dickinson, Joseph H.	Mechanical Musical Apparatus	819,985	May 8, 1906
Dickinson, Joseph H.	Puppet-Valve	886,357	May 5, 1908
Dickinson, Joseph H.	Adjustable Tracker for Pneumatic Playing Attachments	915,942	March 23, 1909
Dickinson, Joseph H.	Player-Piano	1,028,996	June 11, 1912
Dickinson, Joseph H.	Phonograph and the Like	1,242,155	October 9, 1917
Dickinson, Joseph H.	Phonograph	1,252,411	January 8, 1918
Dickinson, Joseph H.	Brake	1,253,475	January 15, 1918
Dickinson, Joseph H.	Talking-Machine	1,279,522	September 24, 1918
Dickinson, Joseph H.	Record-Repeating Device for Phonographs	1,300,135	April 8, 1919
Dickinson, Joseph H.	Combined Talking-Machine and Piano	1,314,578	September 2, 1919
Dickinson, Joseph H.	Automatic Musical Instrument	1,359,040	November 16, 1920

Dickinson, Joseph H.	Rewind Device for Phonographs	1,395,802	November 1, 1921
Dickinson, Joseph H.	Motor Drive for Phonographs	1,405,572	February 7, 1922
Dickinson, Joseph H.	Automatic Musical Instrument	1,444,832	February 13, 1923
Dickinson, Joseph H.	Sound Box for Sound Reproducing Machines	1,446,886	February 27, 1923
Dickinson, Joseph H.	Multiple Record Magazine Phonograph	1,448,733	March 20, 1923
Dickinson, Joseph H.	Player Piano and the Like	1,502,618	July 22, 1924
Dickinson, Joseph H.	Automatic Musical Instrument	1,547,645	July 28, 1925
Dickinson, Joseph H.	Automatic Piano	1,732,879	October 22, 1929
Dickinson, Joseph H.	Automatic Piano	1,734,717	November 5, 1929
Dickinson, Joseph H.	Music Roll Magazine	1,808,808	June 9, 1931
Dickinson, Samuel L.	Player Piano	1,059,123	April 15, 1913
Dickinson, Samuel L.	Recording Attachment for Pianos	1,126,724	February 2, 1915
Dickinson, Samuel L.	Apparatus for Use in Making Music Sheets	1,126,725	February 2, 1915
Diggs, Thomas M.	Small Portable Universal Spark Plug Cleaner	3,604,156	September 14, 1971
Diggs, Thomas M.	Centrifugal Clutch	3,656,599	April 18, 1972
Diggs, Thomas M.	Plural Motor Drive Including a Servo Control System	3,911,336	October 7, 1975
Diuguid, Lincoln Isaiah	Burning Efficiency Enhancement Method	4,539,015	September 3, 1985
Dixon, Irma G., et al.	Underarm Perspiration Pad	2,911,647	November 10, 1959
Dixon, Samuel, Jr.	Gyromagnetic Waveguide Power Limiter	3,131,366	April 28, 1964
Dixon, Samuel, Jr.	Microwave Power Limiter Utilizing a Planar Ferrite Sphere	3,319,191	May 9, 1967
Dixon, Samuel, Jr.	Microwave Power Limiter Comprising Abutting Semiconductor and Ferrite	3,426,299	February 4, 1969
Dixon, Samuel, Jr.	RF Power Limiter Comprising Irradiated Semiconductor Block	3,465,266	September 2, 1969
Dixon, Samuel, Jr.	Ferrite Power Limiter Comprising Synchronously Tuned, Resonant Cavities	3,906,404	September 16, 1975
Dixon, Samuel, Jr.	Low Level Broadband Limiter Having Ferrite Rod Extending through Dielectric Resonators	4,027,256	May 31, 1977

PATENTEE	TITLE OF INVENTION	PATENT NUMBER	ISSUE DATE
Dixon, Samuel, Jr.	Electronically Tuned Gunn Oscillator and Mixer	4,342,009	July 27, 1982
Dixon, Samuel, Jr., et al.	Dielectric Waveguide Power Limiter	4,342,010	July 27, 1982
Dixon, Samuel, Jr.	Millimeter-Wave Power Limiter	4,344,047	August 10, 1982
Dixon, Samuel, Jr., et al.	Single Device for Measurement of Infrared or Millimeter Wave Radiation	4,509,009	April 9, 1985
Dixon, Samuel, Jr.	Millimeter Wave Signal Limiter	4,511,865	April 16, 1985
Dixon, Samuel, Jr.	Millimeter Wave Image Guide Band Reject Filter and Mixer Circuit	4,545,073	October 1, 1985
Dixon, Samuel, Jr., et al.	Three Diode Balanced Mixer	4,554,680	November 19, 1985
Dixon, Samuel, Jr., et al.	Monolithic Planar Doped Barrier Subharmonic Mixer	4,563,773	January 7, 1986
Dixon, Samuel, Jr., et al.	Dual Gunn Diode Self-Oscillating Mixer	4,573,213	February 25, 1986
Dixon, Samuel, Jr., et al.	Monolithic Planar Doped Barrier Limiter	4,654,609	March 31, 1987
Dorcas, Lewis B.	Combination Stove, Wood, Gas, or Coal	868,417	October 15, 1907
Dorman, Linneaus Cuthbert, et al.	3,5 Dihalo-4-Cyanoalkoxy Phenols	3,468,926	September 23, 1969
Dorman, Linneaus Cuthbert, et al.	Absorbents for Airborne Formaldehyde	4,517,111	May 14, 1985
Dorman, Linneaus Cuthbert, et al.	Composites of Unsintered Calcium Phosphates	4,636,526	January 13, 1987
Dorman, Linneaus Cuthbert, et al.	Composites of Unsintered Calcium Phosphates	4,698,375	October 6, 1987
Dorman, Linneaus Cuthbert, et al.	Composites of Unsintered Calcium Phosphates	4,842,604	June 27, 1989
Dorsey, Osbourn	Improvement in Door-Holding Device	210,764	December 10, 1878
Dorticus, Clatonia Joaquin	Device for Applying Coloring Liquids to Sides of Soles or Heels of Shoes	535,820	March 19, 1895
Dorticus, Clatonia Joaquin	Machine for Embossing Photos	537,442	April 16, 1895
Dorticus, Clatonia Joaquin	Photographic Print Washer	537,968	April 23, 1895
Dorticus, Clatonia Joaquin	Hose Leak Stop	629,315	July 18, 1899

Name	Invention	Patent Number	Date
Douglas, Fred J.	Valve Block	1,087,354	February 17, 1914
Douglas, Herman, Sr.	Child's Toilet Training Pants	4,909,804	March 20, 1990
Douglass, William	Self-Binding Harvester	789,010	May 2, 1905
Douglass, William	Band Twister	789,120	May 2, 1905
Douglass, William	Carrier Chain	789,122	May 2, 1905
Downing, Gertrude E., et al.	Reciprocating Corner and Baseboard Cleaning Auxiliary Attachment	3,715,772	February 13, 1973
Downing, Philip B.	Street Railway Switch	430,118	June 17, 1890
Downing, Philip B.	Street Letter Box	462,093	October 27, 1891
Doyle, James	Serving Apparatus for Dining Rooms	659,057	October 2, 1900
Doyle, James	Automatic Serving System	1,019,137	March 5, 1912
Doyle, James	Server for Automatic Serving System	1,098,788	June 2, 1914
Dugger, Cortland Otis	Method for Growing Oxide Single Crystals	3,595,803	July 27, 1971
Dugger, Cortland Otis	Solid-State Laser Produced by Chemical Reaction between a Germinate and an Oxide Dopant	3,624,547	November 30, 1971
Dugger, Cortland Otis	Aluminum Nitride Single Crystal Growth from a Molten Mixture with Calcium Nitride	3,933,573	January 20, 1976
Dunnington, James Henry	Horse Detacher	578,979	March 16, 1897
Dyer, Henry H.	Pipe, Cigar Holder, or the Like	1,090,036	March 10, 1914
Eaton, Harold, Jr., et al.	Detection System for Monitoring Gaseous Components in Air	3,617,734	November 2, 1971
Eaton, Harold, Jr., et al.	Method of Removing Deposits on Refrigeration System Surfaces	4,124,408	November 7, 1978
Edelin, Benedict F.	Pneumatic Toy Pistol	1,441,975	January 9, 1923
Edmonds, Joseph	Utility Carrier	4,790,559	December 13, 1988
Edmonds, Thomas Henry	Separating Screens	586,724	July 20, 1897
Edmonds, Willie L.	Collapsible Fishing Gear and Load Bearing Carriage	4,749,209	June 7, 1988
Elder, Clarence L.	Timing Device	3,165,188	January 12, 1965

PATENTEE	TITLE OF INVENTION	PATENT NUMBER	ISSUE DATE
Elder, Clarence L.	Non-capsizeable Container	3,367,525	February 6, 1968
Elder, Clarence L.	Sweepstake Programmer	3,556,531	January 19, 1971
Elder, Clarence L.	Bidirectional Monitoring and Control System	4,000,400	December 28, 1976
Elkins, Thomas	Dining, Ironing Table and Quilting Frame Combined	100,020	February 22, 1870
Elkins, Thomas	Chamber Commode	122,518	January 9, 1872
Elkins, Thomas	Refrigerating Apparatus	221,222	November 4, 1879
Emile, Philip E.	Transistorized Gating Circuit	2,982,868	May 2, 1961
Emile, Philip E.	Transistorized Multivibrator Circuit	3,005,963	November 24, 1961
Evans, James C., et al.	Airplane Appliance	1,749,858	March 11, 1930
Evans, John H.	Convertible Settee and Bed	591,095	October 5, 1897
Faulkner, Henry	Ventilated Shoe	426,495	April 29, 1890
Ferrell, Frank J.	Steam Trap	420,993	February 11, 1890
Ferrell, Frank J.	Apparatus for Melting Snow	428,670	May 27, 1890
Ferrell, Frank J.	Valve	428,671	May 27, 1890
Ferrell, Frank J.	Valve	450,451	April 14, 1891
Ferrell, Frank J.	Valve	462,762	November 10, 1891
Ferrell, Frank J.	Valve	467,796	January 26, 1892
Ferrell, Frank J.	Valve	468,242	February 2, 1892
Ferrell, Frank J.	Valve, Gate, or Similar Device	468,334	February 9, 1892
Ferrell, Frank J.	Valve	490,227	January 17, 1893
Ferrell, Frank J.	Valve	501,497	July 18, 1893
Fisher, David A., Jr.	Improvement in Joiners' Clamp	162,281	April 20, 1875
Fisher, David A., Jr.	Improvement in Furniture Caster	174,794	March 14, 1876
Fitzgibbon, Chester Manfield	Method and Machine for Making Bamboo Veneer and Products Thereof	3,643,710	February 22, 1972

Name	Title	Number	Date
Fitzgibbon, Chester Manfield	Component Type Building Construction System	4,165,591	August 28, 1979
Flemmings, Robert F., Jr.	Guitar	338,727	March 30, 1886
Flipper, Henry Ossian	Tent	615,544	December 6, 1898
Florence, Saulia O.	Mail Box	2,164,855	July 4, 1939
Flowers, Danny J.	Body Mountable Carrier	5,433,359	July 18, 1995
Ford, Curtis A.	Method of and Apparatus for Testing Internal Combustion Engines	4,702,620	October 27, 1987
Ford, Curtis A.	Methods and Apparatus for Identifying Faults in Internal Combustion Systems	6,389,889	May 21, 2002
Frame, George L., et al.	Genealogy Apparatus	4,201,386	May 6, 1980
Francis, Dawn E.	Organic Fertilizer and Production Thereof	4,957,534	September 18, 1990
Frazier, Orville Z.	Humidifier for Internal Combustion Engines	1,542,999	June 23, 1925
Freelain, Kenneth W.	Water Pipe	4,682,610	July 28, 1987
Freeman, Louis W.	Cuff of Trousers	1,805,577	May 19, 1931
Frye, Clara C.	Surgical Appliance	847,758	March 19, 1907
Frye, Irvin S.	Adjustable Shackle	3,468,123	September 23, 1969
Gamell, Joseph A.	Power Generating System	3,800,528	April 2, 1974
Gamell, Joseph A.	Ignition System for Engine	3,861,371	January 21, 1975
Gamell, Joseph A.	Internal Combustion Engine Having Coaxially Mounted Compressor Combustion Chamber, and Turbine	3,886,732	June 3, 1975
Gamell, Joseph A.	Radiant Heat Boiler	3,906,188	September 16, 1975
Gamell, Joseph A.	Combined Supercharger and Carburetion System	3,935,847	February 3, 1976
Gamell, Joseph A.	Supercharger System for Internal Combustion Engine	3,935,848	February 3, 1976
Gamell, Joseph A.	System for Utilizing Waste Heat of an Internal Combustion Engine	3,948,053	April 6, 1976
Gamell, Joseph A.	System for Utilizing Waste Heat of an Internal Combustion Engine	3,948,235	April 6, 1976

227

PATENTEE	TITLE OF INVENTION	PATENT NUMBER	ISSUE DATE
Gamell, Joseph A.	Power Generating System	3,967,914	July 6, 1976
Gamell, Joseph A.	Internal Combustion Engine	4,003,672	January 18, 1977
Gamell, Joseph A.	Rotary Motor	4,232,991	November 11, 1980
Gamell, Joseph A.	Turbo-electric Power Plant and Process	4,293,777	October 6, 1981
Gamell, Joseph A.	Air Compressing System and Process	4,307,574	December 29, 1981
Gamell, Joseph A.	Turbo-Flywheel-Powered Vehicle	4,336,856	June 29, 1982
Gamell, Joseph A.	Pressure Fluid Motor	4,378,195	March 29, 1983
Gamell, Joseph A.	Turbine Generator	5,118,961	June 2, 1992
Gant, Virgil A.	Method for Treating Hair	2,643,375	June 23, 1953
Gant, Virgil A.	Hair Treating Composition and Method of Use	2,750,947	June 19, 1956
Gant, Virgil A.	Ammonium Polysioxanolate Hair Treating Composition	2,787,274	April 2, 1957
Garner, Albert Y.	Novel Phosphonyl Polymers	3,127,357	March 31, 1964
Garner, Albert Y.	Process for Making Flame Retardant Material	3,955,029	May 4, 1976
Garner, Albert Y.	Flame Retardant	3,989,702	November 2, 1976
Garrett, Gloster J. and Herbert C.	Vehicle Wheel	1,055,029	March 4, 1913
Gaskin, Frances C.	Sun Protectant Composition and Method	4,806,344	February 21, 1989
Gaskin, Frances C.	Compositions and Methods of Strengthening Hair	5,006,331	April 9, 1991
Gaskin, Frances C.	Compositions and Method for Protecting the Skin from UV-Rays	5,256,403	October 26, 1993
Gaskin, Frances C.	Methods and Composition for Reducing Pyrimidine Photo-products	5,629,314	May 13, 1997
Gatling, Jean M.	Adjustable Garment Hanger	4,905,877	March 6, 1990
Gay, Eddie C.	Cathode for a Secondary Electrochemical Cell	3,907,589	September 23, 1975
Gay, Eddie C.	Method of Preparing Electrodes	3,933,520	January 20, 1976
Gay, Eddie C.	Compartmented Electrode Structure	4,029,860	June 14, 1977

Gill, Vincent A.	Quick Disconnect Valved Coupling	2,948,553	August 9, 1960
Gilliard, Joseph	Car Park	2,771,200	November 20, 1956
Goffney, Janice F., et al.	Racquet with Reinforced Throat	4,906,002	March 6, 1990
Goffney, Lawrence J., Jr., et al.	Scalp Massaging Implement	4,308,860	January 5, 1982
Goffney, Lawrence J., Jr., et al.	Self-Generated Lighted Hubcap	4,893,877	January 16, 1990
Golding, Russell J., Sr.	Motor Vehicle Camper	4,279,440	July 21, 1981
Goldson, Alfred L. and Amy R.	Parent-Child Bonding Bib	4,776,546	October 11, 1988
Goode, Sarah E.	Cabinet Bed	322,177	July 14, 1885
Gourdine, Meredith C.	Electrogasdynamic Method and Apparatus for Detecting Properties of Particulate Matter	3,449,667	June 10, 1969
Gourdine, Meredith C.	Electrogasdynamic Systems	3,452,225	June 24, 1969
Gourdine, Meredith C.	Electrogasdynamic Systems	3,519,855	July 7, 1970
Gourdine, Meredith C.	Electrogasdynamic Generating Systems	3,551,710	December 29, 1970
Gourdine, Meredith C.	Electrogasdynamic Precipitator	3,558,286	January 26, 1971
Gourdine, Meredith C.	Electrogasdynamic Systems Adapted for Circuit Breaking	3,562,585	February 9, 1971
Gourdine, Meredith C.	Improved Acoustic Image Reproduction System	3,573,845	April 6, 1971
Gourdine, Meredith C., et al.	Turbulence Inducing Electrogasdynamic Precipitator	3,581,468	June 1, 1971
Gourdine, Meredith C.	Electrogasdynamic Systems and Methods	3,582,694	June 1, 1971
Gourdine, Meredith C., et al.	Electrogasdynamic Particle Disposition System	3,585,060	June 15, 1971
Gourdine, Meredith C.	Alternating Current Systems	3,585,420	June 15, 1971
Gourdine, Meredith C.	Copying System Using Electrogasdynamics	3,592,541	July 13, 1971
Gourdine, Meredith C.	Image Reproduction Using Electrogasdynamics	3,606,531	September 20, 1971
Gourdine, Meredith C.	Electrogasdynamic Converter with Resisting Channel	3,612,923	October 12, 1971
Gourdine, Meredith C., et al.	Electrostatic Painting Method and Apparatus	3,613,993	October 19, 1971
Gourdine, Meredith C., et al.	Electrogasdynamics Precipitator Utilizing Retarding Fields	3,650,092	March 21, 1972
Gourdine, Meredith C.	Method and Apparatus for Electrogasdynamic Coating	3,673,463	June 27, 1972
Gourdine, Meredith C., et al.	Electrostatic Precipitator System	3,704,572	December 5, 1972
Gourdine, Meredith C., et al.	Electrostatic Mass per Unit Volume Dust Monitor	3,718,029	February 27, 1973
Gourdine, Meredith C.	Apparatus for Suppressing Airborne Particles	3,757,491	September 11, 1973

PATENTEE	TITLE OF INVENTION	PATENT NUMBER	ISSUE DATE
Gourdine, Meredith C.	Methods for Electrogasdynamic Coating	3,853,580	December 10, 1974
Gourdine, Meredith C.	Electrogasdynamic Production Line Coating System	3,991,710	November 16, 1976
Gourdine, Meredith C.	Electrogasdynamic Coating System	4,433,033	February 21, 1984
Gourdine, Meredith C.	Electrogasdynamic Coating System	4,498,631	February 12, 1985
Gourdine, Meredith C.	Method and Apparatus for Improved Cooling of Hot Materials	4,555,909	December 3, 1985
Gourdine, Meredith C.	Electrogasdynamic Coating System	4,574,092	March 4, 1986
Gourdine, Meredith C.	Method for Airport Fog Precipitation	4,671,805	June 9, 1987
Gourdine, Meredith C.	Apparatus and Method for Cooling Heat Generating Electronic Components in a Cabinet	5,297,005	March 22, 1994
Gourdine, Meredith C.	Apparatus and Method for Cooling Heat Generating Electronic Components in a Cabinet	5,422,787	June 6, 1995
Gousouland, Henry P.	Water Heating Apparatus	1,178,445	April 4, 1916
Gousouland, Henry P.	Water Heating Apparatus	1,198,344	September 12, 1916
Graham, Lonzell	Liquid Laundering Detergent and Softener	3,984,356	October 5, 1976
Graham, Lonzell, et al.	Moisturizing Body Soap and Shampoo	5,658,868	August 19, 1997
Graham, Lonzell	Settled Solids Process of Preparing Polyester Copolymer Resin	5,789,479	August 4, 1998
Graham, Lonzell	Continuous Process of Preparing Polyester Copolymer Resin	5,891,982	April 6, 1999
Grant, George F.	Golf Tee	638,920	December 12, 1899
Grant, William S.	Curtain Rod Support	565,075	August 4, 1896
Graves, Kurt M.	Infant Walker	4,773,639	September 27, 1988
Gray, Maurice T., et al.	Racquet with Reinforced Throat	4,906,002	March 6, 1990
Gray, Robert H.	Bailing Press	525,203	August 28, 1894
Gray, Robert H.	Cistern Cleaner	537,151	April 9, 1895
Green, Harry James, Jr.	Method of Making a Striated Support for Filaments	3,548,045	December 15, 1970
Green, Harry James, Jr.	Substrate for Mounting Filaments	3,584,130	June 8, 1971

Name	Invention	Number	Date
Green, Harry James, Jr.	Method for Sealing Microelectronic Device Packages	3,648,357	March 14, 1972
Green, James P.	Health Food Composition	4,806,354	February 21, 1989
Greene, Ervin G.	Guard for Downspouts	1,930,354	October 10, 1933
Greene, Frank S., Jr.	Use of Faulty Storage Circuits by Position Coding	3,654,610	April 4, 1972
Gregg, Clarence	Machine Gun	1,277,307	August 27, 1918
Gregory, James	Motor	361,937	April 26, 1887
Grenon, Henry	Razor Stropping Device	554,867	February 18, 1896
Griffin, Bessie V.	Portable Receptacle Support	2,550,554	April 24, 1951
Griffin, Thomas W.	Pool Table Attachment	626,902	June 13, 1899
Groves, Thomas Conrad	Hydraulic Timing Device	3,822,544	July 9, 1974
Gunn, Selim W.	Shoe	641,642	January 16, 1900
Gurley, Clyde Edward, et al.	Automatic Telephone Alarm Apparatus	3,505,476	April 7, 1970
Gurley, Clyde Edward, et al.	Programmable External Dial Operating Device	3,505,483	April 7, 1970
Haines, James Henry	Portable Shampooing Basin	590,833	September 28, 1897
Hale, William	Aeroplane	1,563,278	November 24, 1925
Hale, William	Motor Vehicle	1,672,212	June 5, 1928
Hall, Andrew	Garment with Indicia	4,991,233	February 12, 1991
Hall, Lloyd A., et al.	Asphalt Emulsion and Manufacture	1,882,834	October 18, 1932
Hall, Lloyd A., et al.	Protective Coating	1,914,351	June 13, 1933
Hall, Lloyd A., et al.	Solid Seasoning Composition Containing Capsicum and Chloride	1,995,119	March 19, 1935
Hall, Lloyd A., et al.	Nonbleaching Solid Seasoning Composition	1,995,120	March 19, 1935
Hall, Lloyd A., et al.	Stabilized Solid Seasoning Composition	1,995,121	March 19, 1935
Hall, Lloyd A.	Vitamin Concentrate	2,022,464	November 26, 1935
Hall, Lloyd A., et al.	Solid Seasoning Composition Containing Lecithin	2,032,612	March 3, 1936
Hall, Lloyd A.	Manufacture of Bleached Pepper Products	2,097,405	October 26, 1937
Hall, Lloyd A., et al.	Sterilizing Foodstuffs	2,107,697	February 8, 1938
Hall, Lloyd A.	Curing of Meats and the Like	2,117,478	May 17, 1938

PATENTEE	TITLE OF INVENTION	PATENT NUMBER	ISSUE DATE
Hall, Lloyd A., et al.	Alkaline Detergent Compound	2,142,870	January 3, 1939
Hall, Lloyd A., et al.	Homogeneous Alkaline Detergents and Producing Same	2,142,871	January 3, 1939
Hall, Lloyd A., et al.	Edible Dusting Powder	2,144,371	January 17, 1939
Hall, Lloyd A.	Stabilized Nitrite Salt Compound	2,145,417	January 31, 1939
Hall, Lloyd A., et al.	Inhibited Detergent Composition	2,155,045	April 18, 1939
Hall, Lloyd A., et al.	Inhibited Detergent Composition	2,155,046	April 18, 1939
Hall, Lloyd A., et al.	Composition of Matter	2,171,428	August 29, 1939
Hall, Lloyd A., et al.	Sterilization Process	2,189,947	February 13, 1940
Hall, Lloyd A., et al.	Sterilization of Pancreatin	2,189,948	February 13, 1940
Hall, Lloyd A., et al.	Sterilizing Colloid Materials	2,189,949	February 13, 1940
Hall, Lloyd A.	Protein Composition of Matter	2,251,334	August 5, 1941
Hall, Lloyd A., et al.	Seasoning Material Derived from Red Peppers and the Derivatives	2,260,897	October 28, 1941
Hall, Lloyd A., et al.	Sterilization Process	Reissue 22,284	March 9, 1943
Hall, Lloyd A.	Yeast Food	2,321,678	June 15, 1943
Hall, Lloyd A.	Puncture-Sealing Composition and Manufacture	2,357,650	September 5, 1944
Hall, Lloyd A.	Manufacture of Nitrogen-Fortified Whey Concentrate	2,363,730	November 28, 1944
Hall, Lloyd A.	Capsicum-Containing Seasoning Composition	2,385,412	September 25, 1945
Hall, Lloyd A.	Production of Protein Hydrolysate Flavoring Material	2,414,299	January 14, 1947
Hall, Lloyd A.	Manufacture of Stable Dry Papain Composition	2,464,200	March 15, 1949
Hall, Lloyd A., et al.	Antioxidant	2,464,927	March 22, 1949
Hall, Lloyd A.	Phosphoipoid Carrier for Antioxidant	2,464,928	March 22, 1949
Hall, Lloyd A.	Gelatin-Base Coating for Food	2,477,742	August 2, 1949
Hall, Lloyd A.	Synergistic Antioxidant and Methods of Preparing the Same	2,493,288	January 3, 1950

Hall, Lloyd A.	Antioxidant	2,500,543	March 14, 1950
Hall, Lloyd A.	Synergistic Antioxidant	2,511,802	June 13, 1950
Hall, Lloyd A.	Antioxidant Flakes	2,511,803	June 13, 1950
Hall, Lloyd A.	Antioxidant Salt	2,511,804	June 13, 1950
Hall, Lloyd A.	Synergistic Antioxidant Containing Amino Acids	2,518,233	August 8, 1950
Hall, Lloyd A.	Antioxidant	Reissue 23,329	January 16, 1951
Hall, Lloyd A., et al.	Production of Protein Hydrolysate	2,536,171	February 2, 1951
Hall, Lloyd A., et al.	Curing Process for Bacon	2,553,533	May 15, 1951
Hall, Lloyd A., et al.	Spice Extraction and Product	2,571,867	October 16, 1951
Hall, Lloyd A., et al.	Spice Extract and Product	2,571,948	October 16, 1951
Hall, Lloyd A.	Manufacture of Meat-Curing Composition	2,668,770	February 9, 1954
Hall, Lloyd A.	Stable Curing Salt Composition and Manufacture	2,668,771	February 9, 1954
Hall, Lloyd A.	Synergistic Antioxidants Containing Antioxidant Acids	2,677,616	May 4, 1954
Hall, Lloyd A.	Antioxidant Composition	2,758,931	August 14, 1956
Hall, Lloyd A.	Reaction Product of Poly-oxyethylene Derivative	2,761,784	September 4, 1956
Hall, Lloyd A., et al.	Meat-Curing Salt Composition	2,770,548	November 13, 1956
Hall, Lloyd A.	Meat-Curing Salt Composition	2,770,549	November 13, 1956
Hall, Lloyd A., et al.	Meat-Curing Salt Composition	2,770,550	November 13, 1956
Hall, Lloyd A., et al.	Meat-Curing Salt Composition	2,770,551	November 13, 1956
Hall, Lloyd A.	Antioxidant Material and Use of Said Material in Treating Meats	2,772,169	November 27, 1956
Hall, Lloyd A.	Antioxidant Composition	2,772,170	November 27, 1956
Hall, Lloyd A.	Fatty Monoglyceride Citrate and Antioxidant Containing Same	2,813,032	November 12, 1957
Hall, Lloyd A., et al.	Method of Preserving Fresh Pork Trimmings	2,845,358	July 29, 1958
Hall, Lloyd A.	Sterilization of Hospital and Physician's Supplies	2,938,766	May 31, 1960
Hall, Lloyd A.	Antioxidant Composition	2,981,628	April 25, 1961
Hall, Norman R.	Convertible Mat and Carrying Bag Combination	4,375,111	March 1, 1983

PATENTEE	TITLE OF INVENTION	PATENT NUMBER	ISSUE DATE
Hall, Virginia E., et al.	Embroidered Fruit Bowl Wall Hanging	4,016,314	April 5, 1977
Hammond, Benjamin F.	Inhibition of Plaque-Forming Bacteria	4,579,736	April 1, 1986
Hammonds, Julia Terry	Apparatus for Holding Yarn Skeins	572,985	December 15, 1896
Hannah, Marc R.	Pixel Mapping Apparatus for Color Graphics	4,772,881	September 20, 1988
Hannah, Marc R.	Interleaved Pipeline Parallel Processing Architecture	4,789,927	December 6, 1988
Hannah, Marc R.	Method for Updating Pipelined, Single Port Z-Buffer	4,951,232	August 21, 1990
Hannah, Marc R.	Method and Apparatus for Clearing a Region of Z-Buffer	5,038,297	August 6, 1991
Hannah, Marc R.	Integrated Apparatus for Displaying a Plurality of Modes of Color Information on a Computer Output Display	5,847,700	December 8, 1998
Harbin, Lawrence	Screen Saver for Exhibiting Artists and Artworks	5,680,535	October 21, 1997
Hardin, Joanna	Keyboard Stand	5,188,321	February 23, 1993
Harding, Felix Hadley	Extension Banquet Table	614,468	November 22, 1898
Harney, Michael C.	Lantern or Lamp	303,844	August 19, 1884
Harper, Solomon	Electric Hair Treating Implement	1,663,078	March 20, 1928
Harper, Solomon	Electrical Hair Treating Implement	1,772,002	August 5, 1930
Harper, Solomon	Thermostatic Controlled Hair Curlers, Combs, and Irons	2,648,757	August 11, 1953
Harper, Solomon	Thermostatic Controlled Fur and Material Dressing Equipment	2,711,095	June 21, 1955
Harper, Solomon	Mercury Switch-Indicator Thermostat Controlled Electric Hair Treating Implement	2,748,782	June 5, 1956
Harris, Betty Wright	Spot Test for TATB	4,618,452	October 21, 1986
Harris, Don Navarro, et al.	Inhibition of Blood Platelet Aggregation	4,051,236	September 27, 1977
Harris, Don Navarro, et al.	Inhibition of Thromboxane Synthetase Formation and A-rachidonic Acid-induced Platelet Aggregation and Broncho-constriction	4,243,671	January 6, 1977
Harrison, Emmett Scott	Gas Turbine Air Compressor and Control	3,606,971	September 21, 1971

Name	Title	Number	Date
Harrison, Emmett Scott	Turbojet Afterburner Engine with Exhaust Nozzle	4,242,865	January 6, 1981
Harrison, Jesse	Combination Tooth Brush and Paste Holder	1,844,036	February 9, 1932
Haskins, William B.	Shoulder Pad	378,394	February 21, 1888
Hawkins, Joseph	Gridiron	3,973	March 26, 1845
Hawkins, Mason A.	Music Cabinet	1,135,281	April 13, 1915
Hawkins, Mason A.	Box for Player Piano Music Rolls	1,309,030	July 8, 1919
Hawkins, Randall	Harness Attachment	370,943	October 4, 1887
Hawkins, Walter Lincoln	Preparation of 1,2 Di-Primary Amines	2,587,043	February 26, 1952
Hawkins, Walter Lincoln, et al.	Stabilized Straight Chain Hydrocarbons	2,889,306	June 2, 1959
Hawkins, Walter Lincoln, et al.	Alpha Olefin Hydrocarbons Stabilized with Carbon Black and Carbocyclic Thioether	2,967,845	January 10, 1961
Hawkins, Walter Lincoln, et al.	Alpha Olefin Hydrocarbons Stabilized with a Fused Ring Sulfide Compounds	2,967,846	January 10, 1961
Hawkins, Walter Lincoln, et al.	Alpha Olefin Hydrocarbons Stabilized with Carbon Black and a Compound Having R-S-S-R Structure	2,967,847	January 10, 1961
Hawkins, Walter Lincoln, et al.	Stabilized Straight Chain Hydrocarbons	2,967,849	January 10, 1961
Hawkins, Walter Lincoln, et al.	Compositions of Stabilized Straight Chain Hydrocarbons	2,967,850	January 10, 1961
Hawkins, Walter Lincoln, et al.	Compositions Including Saturated Hydrocarbons	3,042,649	July 3, 1962
Hawkins, Walter Lincoln, et al.	Polyolefin Stabilized with Sulfides and Thiobisphenols	3,216,967	November 9, 1965
Hawkins, Walter Lincoln, et al.	Stabilized Long-Chain Polymers	3,259,604	July 5, 1966
Hawkins, Walter Lincoln, et al.	Stabilized Alpha-Mono-Olefinic Polymers	3,304,283	February 14, 1967
Hawkins, Walter Lincoln	Multiconductor Communications Cable	3,668,298	June 6, 1972
Hawkins, William S.	Auto Seat Cape	1,899,327	February 28, 1933
Hayes, Dorothy E.	Translucent Structural Panels	3,904,866	September 9, 1975
Hayes, Harry C.	Condenser	1,826,540	October 6, 1931
Hayes, Rufus	Baseball Gloves	4,891,845	January 9, 1990
Hayes, Rufus	Baseball Gloves and Attachments	4,937,882	July 3, 1990
Hayes, Rufus	Baseball Gloves and Attachments and Methods	5,031,238	July 16, 1991
Headen, Minnis	Foot Power Hammer	350,363	October 5, 1886

PATENTEE	TITLE OF INVENTION	PATENT NUMBER	ISSUE DATE
Hearns, Robert	Sealing Attachment for Bottles	598,929	February 15, 1898
Hearns, Robert	Detachable Car Fender	628,003	July 4, 1899
Hearns, William	Device for Removing and Inserting Taps and Plugs	1,040,538	October 8, 1912
Helm, Tony W., et al.	Universal Joint	2,760,358	August 28, 1956
Helm, Tony W.	Universal Joint	2,895,314	July 21, 1959
Henderson, Henry F., Jr.	Weight Loss Control System	4,111,336	September 5, 1978
Henderson, Leonard L.	Ignition System	2,121,385	June 21, 1938
Henderson, Robert M.	Collapsilde Valet	5,022,617	June 11, 1991
Hendrix, Willie J.	Three-Wheel Vehicle	4,373,740	February 15, 1983
Hicks, Benjamin	Machine for Stemming and Cleaning Peanuts or Green Peas	688,519	December 10, 1901
Hill, Claudette D.	Magnetic Pick Up Attachment for Vacuum Cleaners	4,300,260	November 17, 1981
Hill, Henry Aaron	Manufacture of Azodicarbonamide	2,988,545	June 13, 1961
Hill, Henry Aaron	Foamable Composition Comprising a Thermoplastic Polymer and a Barium Azocarbonate and Method of Foaming	3,141,002	July 14, 1964
Hill, Henry Aaron	Curing Furfuryl-Alcohol-Modified Urea Formaldehyde Condensates	3,297,611	January 10, 1967
Hill, Walter A., et al.	Movable Root Contact-Pressure Plate Assembly for Hydroponic System	4,860,490	August 29, 1989
Hilyer, Andrew F.	Water Evaporator Attachment for Hot Air Registers	435,095	August 26, 1890
Hilyer, Andrew F.	Evaporator for Hot Air Registers	438,159	October 14, 1890
Hines, Samuel J.	Life Preserver	1,137,971	May 4, 1915
Hines, Samuel J.	Lawn Mower Attachment	1,911,278	May 30, 1933
Hinton, Albert R.	Mechanism for Automatically Applying Bags to Filling Machines	1,190,898	July 11, 1916
Hodge, John E.	Novel Reductones and Methods of Making	2,936,308	May 10, 1960
Hodge, John E.	Glucose-amine Sequestrants	2,996,449	August 15, 1961

Name	Title	Patent No.	Date
Hodge, John E.	Substituted Benzodioxan Sweetening Compound	4,146,650	March 27, 1979
Hollins, James E.	Carburetor Automatic Choke Construction	4,050,427	September 27, 1977
Holmes, Elijah H.	Gauge	549,513	November 12, 1895
Holmes, Lydia M.	Knockdown Wheeled Toy	2,529,692	November 14, 1950
Hooper, Francis L.	Bed Attachment	1,100,303	June 16, 1914
Hopkins, Harry C.	Preparation of Epoxy Resin-Rubber-Glass Mixture and Mixture Produced	4,256,612	March 17, 1981
Hopkins, Harry C., et al.	Ground Effect Flying Platform	4,290,500	September 22, 1981
Hopkins, Harry C.	Swimming Simulator	4,422,634	December 27, 1983
Hopkins, Harry C.	Microwave Agricultural Drying and Curing Apparatus	4,430,806	February 14, 1984
Hopkins, Harry C.	Power Controller	4,704,570	November 3, 1987
Horad, Sewell D.	Adjustable Valve for Controlling the Amount of Water Refilling a Toilet Bowl after Flushing	5,715,860	February 10, 1998
Howard, Darnley E.	Optical Apparatus for Indicating the Position of a Tool	2,145,116	January 24, 1939
Howard, Darnley Moseley, et al.	Method of Making Radomes with an Internal Antenna	3,451,127	June 24, 1969
Hughes, Isaiah D.	Combined Excavator and Elevator	687,312	November 26, 1901
Hull, Wilson E., et al.	Sublimation Timing Switch	3,286,064	November 15, 1966
Hull, Wilson E.	Mass Release Mechanism for Satellites	3,424,403	January 28, 1969
Hunter, John W.	Portable Weighing Scale	570,553	November 3, 1896
Hunter, Raymond	Shower Bath Economizer	4,372,372	February 8, 1983
Huntley, James B.	Emergency Fire Escape Mechanism	3,880,255	April 29, 1975
Hutchings, Richard S., et al.	Process for the Manufacture of Surfactant Cleaning Blocks and Compositions	4,722,802	February 2, 1988
Hutchings, Richard S.	Aqueous Alkali Metal Halogenite Compositions	4,790,950	December 13, 1988
Hutchings, Richard S.	Compositions Containing Chlorine Dioxide and Their Preparation	4,861,514	August 29, 1989
Hutchings, Richard S.	Aqueous Alkali Metal Halogenite Compositions Containing a Cobrant	4,880,556	November 14, 1989
Hyde, Robert N.	Composition for Cleaning and Preserving Carpets	392,205	November 6, 1888

PATENTEE	TITLE OF INVENTION	PATENT NUMBER	ISSUE DATE
Ingram, Clifton M.	Railroad Crossing Flag Signal	1,526,215	February 10, 1925
Ingram, Clifton M.	Well Drilling Tool	1,542,776	June 16, 1925
Ivory, Brian K.	Self-Adjusting Bag Support	4,702,445	October 27, 1987
Jackson, Aaron C.	Football Board Game	5,039,107	August 13, 1991
Jackson, André J.	Apparatus and Methods of Collecting Urine from Lab Animals	4,476,879	October 16, 1984
Jackson, Benjamin F.	Heating Apparatus	599,985	March 1, 1898
Jackson, Benjamin F.	Matrix Drying Apparatus	603,879	May 10, 1898
Jackson, Benjamin F.	Gas Burner	622,482	April 4, 1899
Jackson, Benjamin F.	Electrotyper's Furnace	645,296	March 13, 1900
Jackson, Benjamin F.	Automobile	672,941	April 30, 1901
Jackson, Benjamin F.	Steam Boiler	690,730	January 7, 1902
Jackson, Benjamin F.	Trolley-Wheel Controller	771,206	September 27, 1904
Jackson, Benjamin F.	Tank Signal	773,747	November 1, 1904
Jackson, Benjamin F.	Burner	836,883	November 27, 1906
Jackson, Benjamin F.	Gas Furnace	837,571	December 4, 1906
Jackson, Benjamin F.	Hydrocarbon Burner System	857,808	June 25, 1907
Jackson, Benjamin F.	Advertising Apparatus	1,865,374	June 28, 1932
Jackson, Harry	Protective Appliance	2,038,491	April 21, 1936
Jackson, Harry and Mary E.	Protective Appliance	2,053,035	September 1, 1936
Jackson, Harry and Mary E.	Burglar Alarm Switch	2,071,343	February 23, 1937
Jackson, Harry and Mary E.	Method and Composition for Automatically Depositing Copper	3,436,233	April 1, 1969
Jackson, Henry			
Jackson, Henry A.	Kitchen Table	569,135	October 6, 1896

Jackson, Jerome D.	Systems and Methods Employing a Plurality of Signal Amplitudes	5,864,301	January 26, 1999
Jackson, Joseph N.	Programmable Television Receiver Controllers	4,081,754	March 28, 1978
Jackson, Joseph N.	Programmable Television Receiver Controllers	4,228,543	October 14, 1980
Jackson, Joseph N., et al.	Video Viewing Censoring Supervision System	5,548,345	August 20, 1996
Jackson, Norman	Pneumatic Tire	1,384,134	July 12, 1921
Jackson, William H.	Railway Switch	578,641	March 9, 1897
Jackson, William H.	Railway Switch	593,665	November 16, 1897
Jackson, William H.	Automatic Locking Switch	609,436	August 23, 1898
Jefferson, Donald E.	Forming 2-Hydroxyethyl Methacrylate Foam	3,172,868	March 9, 1965
Jefferson, Donald E., et al.	Interpolymer Comprising Acrylic, Acid, and Acrylic Acid Ester	3,184,440	May 18, 1965
Jefferson, Donald E., et al.	Triggered Exploding Wire Device	3,288,068	November 29, 1966
Jefferson, Donald E.	Foamed Products and Process Thereof	3,293,198	December 20, 1966
Jefferson, Donald E., et al.	Polyesters, Polamides, and Polyesteramide	3,567,694	March 2, 1971
Jefferson, Donald E., et al.	Polymers from Diesters of N-Acrylyliminodiacetic Acids	3,598,792	August 10, 1971
Jefferson, Donald E., et al.	Increasing the Wet Strength of Cellulosic Materials	3,629,178	December 21, 1971
Jefferson, Donald E.	Preparation of N-Allyliminodiacetimide Dioxine	3,639,364	February 1, 1972
Jefferson, Donald E., et al.	Digital Data Storage System	3,678,468	July 18, 1972
Jefferson, Donald E., et al.	Increasing the Wet Strength of Cellulosic Materials	3,681,131	August 1, 1972
Jefferson, Donald E., et al.	Data Processing System	3,701,972	October 31, 1972
Jenkins, Christina M.	Permanently Attaching Commercial Hair to Live Hair	2,621,663	December 16, 1952
Jenkins, George A.	Semibuoyant Aircraft	1,821,061	September 1, 1931
Jennings, Thomas L.	Dry Scouring of Clothes	3306X	March 3, 1821
Jetter, Milton W.	Remote-Controlled Alarm Clock	4,316,273	February 16, 1982
Jetter, Milton W.	Alarm Deactivation System	4,352,170	September 28, 1982
Jetter, Milton W.	Clock Alarm-Deactivating System	4,352,171	September 28, 1982
Jetter, Milton W.	Clock Alarm Control System	4,426,157	January 17, 1984
Jetter, Milton W.	Random Multiple Push Button Clock Alarm Deactivation System	4,430,006	February 7, 1984

PATENTEE	TITLE OF INVENTION	PATENT NUMBER	ISSUE DATE
Johns, James A., et al.	Liniment	437,728	October 7, 1890
Johnson, Andrew R.	Precision Digital Delay Circuit	3,376,436	April 2, 1968
Johnson, Daniel	Rotary Dining Table	396,089	January 15, 1889
Johnson, Daniel	Lawn Mower Attachment	410,836	September 10, 1889
Johnson, Daniel	Grass Receiver for Lawn Mowers	429,629	June 10, 1890
Johnson, George M.	Automatic Stopping and Releasing Device for Mine Cars	1,249,106	December 4, 1917
Johnson, Isaac R.	Bicycle Frame	634,823	October 10, 1899
Johnson, John Arthur "Jack"	Wrench	1,413,121	April 18, 1922
Johnson, John Arthur "Jack," et al.	Theft Preventing Device for Vehicles	1,438,709	December 12, 1922
Johnson, Lonnie G., et al.	Digital Distance Measuring Instrument	4,143,267	March 6, 1979
Johnson, Lonnie G.	Variable Resistance Type Sensor Controlled Switch	4,181,843	January 1, 1980
Johnson, Lonnie G.	Smoke Detecting Timer Controlled Thermostat	4,211,362	July 8, 1980
Johnson, Lonnie G.	Automatic Sprinkler Control	4,253,606	March 3, 1981
Johnson, Lonnie G.	Thermal Energy Accumulation	4,476,693	October 16, 1984
Johnson, Lonnie G.	Soil Moisture Potential Determination by Weight	4,509,361	April 9, 1985
Johnson, Lonnie G.	Squirt Gun	4,591,071	May 27, 1986
Johnson, Lonnie G.	Johnson Tube, a Thermodynamic Heat Pump	4,724,683	February 16, 1988
Johnson, Lonnie G.	Flow Actuated Pulsator	4,757,946	July 19, 1988
Johnson, Lonnie G., et al.	Pinch Trigger Pump Water Gun	5,074,437	December 24, 1991
Johnson, Lonnie G., et al.	Double Tank Pinch Trigger Pump Water Gun	5,150,819	September 29, 1992
Johnson, Malcolm L., et al.	Cover Garment with Inner Garment Access Option	4,709,419	December 1, 1987
Johnson, Malcolm L., et al.	Protective Covering for a Mechanical Linkage	4,904,514	February 27, 1990
Johnson, Malcolm L., et al.	Melt Blown Nonwoven Wiper	4,904,521	February 27, 1990
Johnson, Malcolm L., et al.	Melt Blown Nonwoven Wiper	5,039,431	August 13, 1991
Johnson, Paul E.	Lamp	1,403,119	January 10, 1922
Johnson, Paul E.	Therapeutic Lamps	1,842,100	January 19, 1932

Name	Invention	Number	Date
Johnson, Payton	Swinging Chairs	249,530	November 15, 1881
Johnson, Powell	Eye Protector	234,039	November 2, 1880
Johnson, Wesley	Velocipede	627,335	June 20, 1899
Johnson, William A.	Paint Vehicle	393,763	December 4, 1888
Johnson, Willie Harry	Mechanism for Overcoming Dead Centers	554,223	February 4, 1896
Johnson, Willie Harry	Overcoming Dead Centers	612,345	October 11, 1898
Johnson, Willis	Egg Beater	292,821	February 5, 1884
Jones, Albert A., et al.	Caps for Bottles, Jars, etc.	610,715	September 13, 1898
Jones, Clinton	Electric Release for Toy Guns	2,474,054	June 21, 1949
Jones, Felix B.	Firearm	1,685,673	September 25, 1928
Jones, Frederick M.	Ticket Dispensing Machine	2,163,754	June 27, 1939
Jones, Frederick M.	Air Conditioner for Vehicles	2,303,857	December 1, 1942
Jones, Frederick M.	Removable Cooling Unit for Compartments	2,336,735	December 14, 1943
Jones, Frederick M.	Means for Automatically Stopping and Starting Gas Engines	2,337,164	December 21, 1943
Jones, Frederick M.	Two Cycle Gas Engine	2,376,968	May 29, 1945
Jones, Frederick M.	Two Cycle Gas Engine	2,417,253	March 11, 1947
Jones, Frederick M.	Removable Cooling Unit for Compartments	Reissue 23,000	May 11, 1948
Jones, Frederick M.	Preventing Frosting of Evaporator Heat Exchangers	2,471,692	May 31, 1949
Jones, Frederick M.	Air Conditioning Unit	2,475,841	July 12, 1949
Jones, Frederick M.	Starter Generator	2,475,842	July 12, 1949
Jones, Frederick M.	Means Operated by a Starter Generator for Cooling Gas Engines	2,475,843	July 12, 1949
Jones, Frederick M.	Means for Thermostatically Operating Gas Engines	2,477,377	July 26, 1949
Jones, Frederick M.	Rotary Compressor	2,504,841	April 18, 1950
Jones, Frederick M.	System for Controlling Operation of Refrigeration Units	2,509,099	May 23, 1950
Jones, Frederick M.	Engine Actuated Ventilating System	2,523,273	September 26, 1950
Jones, Frederick M.	Apparatus for Heating or Cooling Atmosphere	2,526,874	October 24, 1950

PATENTEE	TITLE OF INVENTION	PATENT NUMBER	ISSUE DATE
Jones, Frederick M.	Prefabricated Refrigerator Construction	2,535,682	December 26, 1950
Jones, Frederick M.	Refrigeration Control Device	2,581,956	January 8, 1952
Jones, Frederick M.	Locking Mechanism	2,647,287	August 4, 1953
Jones, Frederick M.	Methods and Means for Defrosting a Cold Diffuser	2,666,298	January 19, 1954
Jones, Frederick M.	Methods and Means for Air Conditioning	2,696,086	December 7, 1954
Jones, Frederick M.	Methods and Means for Preserving Perishable Foodstuffs in Transit	2,780,923	February 12, 1957
Jones, Frederick M.	Control Device for Internal Combustion Engine	2,850,001	September 2, 1958
Jones, Frederick M.	Thermostat and Temperature Control System	2,926,005	February 23, 1960
Jones, Howard S., Jr., et al.	Variable Waveguide Coupler	2,898,559	August 4, 1959
Jones, Howard S., Jr., et al.	Antenna Testing Shield	3,029,430	April 10, 1962
Jones, Howard S., Jr., et al.	Waveguide Components	3,046,507	July 29, 1962
Jones, Howard S., Jr., et al.	Magneto-Mechanical Waveguide Line Stretcher	3,268,837	August 23, 1966
Jones, Howard S., Jr., et al.	Electrically Scanned Microwave Antenna	3,268,901	August 23, 1966
Jones, Howard S., Jr.	Step Twist Diode Microwave Switch	3,314,027	April 11, 1967
Jones, Howard S., Jr.	Slot Antenna Built into a Dielectric Radome	3,346,865	October 10, 1967
Jones, Howard S., Jr.	Multifrequency Common Aperture Manifold Antenna	3,482,248	December 2, 1969
Jones, Howard S., Jr.	Radome Antenna	3,509,571	April 28, 1970
Jones, Howard S., Jr.	Dielectric-Loaded Antenna with Matching Window	3,518,683	June 30, 1970
Jones, Howard S., Jr.	Projectile with Incorporated Dielectric Loaded Cavity Antenna	3,518,685	June 30, 1970
Jones, Howard S., Jr.	Slotted Waveguide Antenna Array	3,524,189	August 11, 1970
Jones, Howard S., Jr.	Method and Apparatus for Joining Waveguide Components	3,577,105	May 4, 1971
Jones, Howard S., Jr.	Dual Waveguide Horn Antenna	3,611,396	October 5, 1971
Jones, Howard S., Jr., et al.	Re-entry Vehicle Nose Cone with Antenna	3,680,130	July 25, 1972
Jones, Howard S., Jr.	Base-Mounted Re-entry Vehicle Antenna	3,739,386	June 12, 1973

Name	Title	Patent No.	Date
Jones, Howard S., Jr., et al.	Super Lightweight Microwave Circuit	3,768,048	October 23, 1973
Jones, Howard S., Jr.	Cavity Excited Conical Dielectric Radiator	3,798,653	March 19, 1974
Jones, Howard S., Jr.	Rearmounted Forward-Looking Radio Frequency Antenna System	3,845,488	October 29, 1974
Jones, Howard S., Jr.	A Monolithic, Electrically Small, Multi-frequency Antenna	3,858,214	December 31, 1974
Jones, Howard S., Jr., et al.	Nose Cone Capacitively Tuned Wedge Antenna	3,914,767	October 21, 1975
Jones, Howard S., Jr., et al.	Low-Profile Quadrature-plate UHF Antenna	3,943,520	March 9, 1976
Jones, Howard S., Jr., et al.	Conformal Radome-Antenna Structure	3,987,458	October 19, 1976
Jones, Howard S., Jr.	Multi-function Integrated Radome Antenna System	3,975,737	August 17, 1976
Jones, Howard S., Jr., et al.	Conformal Edge-Slot Radiators	4,010,470	March 10, 1977
		4,051,480	September 27, 1977
Jones, James C.	Mailbag Transferring Device	1,227,914	May 29, 1917
Jones, John Leslie	Preparation of Substituted Phenols	2,497,503	February 14, 1950
Jones, John Leslie	Personnel Restraint System for Vehicular Occupants	3,690,695	September 12, 1972
Jones, John Leslie	Smokeless Slow Burning Cast Propellant	4,112,849	September 12, 1978
Jones, Levonia, et al.	Soap Saving Method and Apparatus	5,030,405	July 9, 1991
Jones, Marshall Gordon, et al.	Industrial Hand Held Laser Tool and Laser System	4,564,736	January 14, 1986
Jones, Marshall Gordon	Underwater Laser Welding Nozzle	6,060,686	May 9, 2000
Jones, Sylvester S.	Manicuring Device	1,742,862	January 7, 1930
Jones, Wilbert Leroy, Jr.	Duplex Capstan	3,258,247	June 28, 1966
Jones, William B.	Dentist Apparatus	2,096,375	October 19, 1937
Jones, Willie G., Sr.	Basketball Rim and Net Structure	3,948,516	April 26, 1976
Joyce, James A.	Coal or Ore Bucket	603,143	April 26, 1898
Joyner, Marjorie Stewart	Permanent Wave Machine	1,693,515	November 27, 1928
Joyner, Marjorie Stewart	Scalp Protector	1,716,173	June 4, 1929
Julian, Hubert	Airplane Safety Appliance	1,379,264	May 24, 1921
Julian, Percy L., et al.	Recovery of Sterols	2,218,971	October 22, 1940
Julian, Percy L., et al.	Production of a Derived Vegetable Protein	2,238,329	April 15, 1941
Julian, Percy L., et al.	Process of Preparing Vegetable Protein	2,246,466	June 17, 1941

PATENTEE	TITLE OF INVENTION	PATENT NUMBER	ISSUE DATE
Julian, Percy L., et al.	Preparation of Vegetable Phosphatides	2,249,002	July 15, 1941
Julian, Percy L., et al.	Protein-Urea Complex	2,249,003	July 15, 1941
Julian, Percy L., et al.	Process for the Recovering of Sterols	2,273,045	February 17, 1942
Julian, Percy L., et al.	Process for Recovering of Sterols	2,273,046	February 17, 1942
Julian, Percy L., et al.	Preparation of a Soybean Plastic	2,281,584	May 5, 1942
Julian, Percy L., et al.	Preparing Material Having Physiological Activity of Corpus Luteum Hormone	2,296,284	September 22, 1942
Julian, Percy L., et al.	Process for Isolating Vegetable Proteins	2,304,099	December 8, 1942
Julian, Percy L., et al.	Preparation of Tertiary Carbinols	2,304,100	December 8, 1942
Julian, Percy L., et al.	Protein Composition for Paints and Paint Clears	2,304,102	December 8, 1942
Julian, Percy L., et al.	Preparing Ketones of Cyclopentohydrophenanthrene	2,341,557	February 15, 1944
Julian, Percy L., et al.	Preparation of Etio-Cholenic Acid Derivatives	2,342,147	February 22, 1944
Julian, Percy L., et al.	Preparation of Oil-Soluble Phosphatide Composition	2,355,081	August 8, 1944
Julian, Percy L., et al.	Protein Composition Resistant to Formaldehyde Coagulation	2,363,794	November 28, 1944
Julian, Percy L., et al.	Methylation of Phospholipid, Cephalin	2,373,686	April 17, 1945
Julian, Percy L., et al.	Alteration and Control of Viscosity of Chocolate	2,373,687	April 17, 1945
Julian, Percy L., et al.	Increasing Oil Solubility of Phospholipids	2,374,681	May 1, 1945
Julian, Percy L., et al.	Dehalogenation of Halogenated Steroids	2,374,683	May 1, 1945
Julian, Percy L., et al.	Conversion of Soybean Globulin into Egg Albumin–Like Protein	2,381,407	August 7, 1945
Julian, Percy L., et al.	Effecting Phospholipid Solubility by Acid Treatment	2,391,462	December 25, 1945
Julian, Percy L., et al.	Refining Vegetable Oils	2,392,390	January 8, 1946
Julian, Percy L., et al.	Unsaturated Ketones of the Cyclopentanophenanthrene	2,394,551	February 12, 1946
Julian, Percy L., et al.	New Quaternary Compounds from Phospholipids	2,400,120	May 14, 1946
Julian, Percy L., et al.	Process for Canning Soybeans and Product	2,400,123	May 14, 1946
Julian, Percy L., et al.	Amines in the i-Steroid Series	2,428,368	October 7, 1947

Julian, Percy L., et al.	Preparation of 3-Amino-Derivatives of Steroids	2,430,467	November 11, 1947
Julian, Percy L., et al.	Procedure for Preparation of Progesterone	2,433,848	January 6, 1948
Julian, Percy L., et al.	Preparing 3-Amino-Steroids from i-Steroids	2,446,538	August 10, 1948
Julian, Percy L.	Oxidation of Soya Sitosteryl Acetate Dibromide	2,464,236	March 14, 1949
Julian, Percy L., et al.	6-Alkoxy-i-Androstene-17-ols	2,484,833	October 18, 1949
Julian, Percy L., et al.	Rearrangement of Steroid Oximes	2,531,441	November 28, 1950
Julian, Percy L., et al.	Steroid Dimethylamines and Their Quaternary Halides	2,561,378	July 24, 1951
Julian, Percy L., et al.	Steroid Mannich Amines	2,562,194	July 31, 1951
Julian, Percy L., et al.	Steroidal Ketones Containing Amino Groups	2,566,336	September 4, 1951
Julian, Percy L., et al.	Preparation and Degradation of Steroid Amines	2,582,258	January 15, 1952
Julian, Percy L., et al.	16-Alkyl Steroids and Process of Preparing	2,588,391	March 11, 1952
Julian, Percy L., et al.	Improving Alkali-Soluble Acid-Precipitable Vegetable Protein	2,588,392	March 11, 1952
Julian, Percy L., et al.	Preparation of Etio-Steroid Acids	2,606,911	August 12, 1952
Julian, Percy L., et al.	The Hydroxylation of Phospholipids	2,629,662	February 24, 1953
Julian, Percy L., et al.	Preparation, 3,20-Diketo-17 Alpha-Hydroxy-Steroids	2,648,662	August 11, 1953
Julian, Percy L., et al.	Preparation of 17 Alpha-Hydroxy-Steroids	2,648,663	August 11, 1953
Julian, Percy L., et al.	Preparation of 17 Alpha-Hydroxy Steroids	2,662,904	December 15, 1953
Julian, Percy L., et al.	Selective Dehalogenation of Certain Halogenated Ketones	2,667,498	January 26, 1954
Julian, Percy L., et al.	Degradation of Steroid Quaternary Ammonium Salts	2,670,359	February 23, 1954
Julian, Percy L., et al.	Procedure for Delta 16-20-Keto-Pregnanes	2,671,794	March 9, 1954
Julian, Percy L., et al.	Preparation of 16,17-Oxido-5-Pregnenes	2,686,181	August 10, 1954
Julian, Percy L., et al.	Preparation of Steroids of the C_{19} Series	2,696,490	December 7, 1954
Julian, Percy L., et al.	16,17-Oxido-pregnane-3 alpha ol-11,20-dione	2,705,233	March 29, 1955
Julian, Percy L., et al.	Steroid-Dimethylamines and Their Quaternary Halides	2,705,238	March 29, 1955
Julian, Percy L., et al.	Improved Margarine	2,724,649	November 22, 1955
Julian, Percy L., et al.	Preparation of Cortisone	2,752,339	June 26, 1956
Julian, Percy L., et al.	Hydroxylation of Vegetable Oils	2,752,376	June 26, 1956
Julian, Percy L., et al.	Separating Sterols from Vegetable Oils by Hydration	2,752,378	June 26, 1956

PATENTEE	TITLE OF INVENTION	PATENT NUMBER	ISSUE DATE
Julian, Percy L., et al.	Synergistic Compositions of Matter	2,773,771	December 11, 1956
Julian, Percy L., et al.	Process of Dehalogenating Steroids	2,773,867	December 11, 1956
Julian, Percy L., et al.	Preparation of 21-Bromo and 21-Iodo-Steroids	2,789,989	April 23, 1957
Julian, Percy L., et al.	Method for Introducing a 21-Hydroxy Group into 17-Oxygenated Steroids	2,816,108	December 10, 1957
Julian, Percy L., et al.	Certain 16,17-Oxido-Steroids of the C_{21} Series	2,820,030	January 14, 1958
Julian, Percy L., et al.	5,7-Pregnadiene-3-ol-one and Esters Thereof	2,876,237	March 3, 1959
Julian, Percy L., et al.	4,5-Epoxy Derivatives of 17Alpha-Alkyltestosterones	2,885,398	May 5, 1959
Julian, Percy L., et al.	Novel Method of Preparing Androstendione	2,887,478	May 19, 1959
Julian, Percy L., et al.	Substituted 2,5-Androstadienes	2,891,974	June 23, 1959
Julian, Percy L., et al.	2,5-Pregnadiene Derivatives	2,891,975	June 23, 1959
Julian, Percy L., et al.	Androstan-3,17-diol-4-one Derivatives	2,900,399	August 18, 1959
Julian, Percy L., et al.	Process for Preparation of 2-Acetoxy-Steroids	2,910,487	October 27, 1959
Julian, Percy L., et al.	3-Keto-4-Halo-Delta^{4,5} Steroids	2,933,510	April 19, 1960
Julian, Percy L., et al.	Method of Epimerizing 11-Bromo-Steroids	2,940,991	June 14, 1960
Julian, Percy L., et al.	Novel Epoxy-Pregnanes	2,944,052	July 5, 1960
Julian, Percy L., et al.	Preparation of the 12-Keto Isomer of Cortisone	2,947,765	August 2, 1960
Julian, Percy L., et al.	Shortening Composition and Emulsifier System	3,004,853	October 17, 1961
Julian, Percy L.	Isolation of Sapogenine	3,019,220	January 30, 1962
Julian, Percy L., et al.	12-Alkyl-12-Hydroxyprogesterone Derivatives	3,052,694	September 4, 1962
Julian, Percy L., et al.	Reduction of an Epoxy Group	3,055,918	September 25, 1962
Julian, Percy L., et al.	17-Substituted 2,5-Pregnadiene Derivatives	3,153,061	October 13, 1964
Julian, Percy L., et al.	Process for 11Beta, 12Beta-Epoxypregnane-3,20-dione	3,153,646	October 20, 1964
Julian, Percy L., et al.	Process for Preparing Compound "S"	3,187,025	June 1, 1965
Julian, Percy L., et al.	Preparing 16Alpha-Methyl Corticoids	3,231,568	January 25, 1966
Julian, Percy L., et al.	Method for Preparing 16Alpha-Hydroxypregnenes	3,274,178	September 20, 1966

Author	Title	Number	Date
Julian, Percy L.	Composition with Low Cholesterol Content	3,711,611	January 16, 1973
Julian, Percy L., et al.	Process for Introducing a Delta 5,6-Double Bond into a Steroid	3,759,899	September 18, 1973
Julian, Percy L.	Process for Manufacture of Steroid Chlorohydrins	3,761,469	September 25, 1973
Julian, Percy L.	Process for Conversion of a 3-Hydroxy-5,6-Oxido Group of a Steroid	3,784,598	January 8, 1974
Julian, Percy L.	Preparation, Wool Wax Alcohol of Low Cholesterol Content	3,821,121	June 28, 1974
Julien, Leonard	Cane Planter	3,286,858	November 22, 1966
Keelan, Harry S.	Colloidal Silver Iodide Compound and Method	1,783,334	December 2, 1930
Kelley, George W.	Steam Table	592,291	October 26, 1897
Kelly, Kenneth C.	Linearly Polarized Monopulse Lobing Antenna	3,063,049	November 6, 1962
Kelly, Lawrence R.	Automatic Telephone Alarm Apparatus	3,505,476	April 7, 1970
Kelly, Lawrence R.	Programmable External Dial Operating Device	3,505,483	April 7, 1970
Kenner, Mary Beatrice	Sanitary Belt	2,745,406	May 15, 1956
Kenner, Mary Beatrice	Sanitary Belt with Moisture Proof Pocket	2,881,761	April 14, 1959
Kenner, Mary Beatrice	Carrier Attachment for Invalid Walkers	3,957,071	May 18, 1976
Kenner, Mary Beatrice	Bathroom Tissue Holder	4,354,643	October 19, 1982
Kenner, Mary Beatrice	Shower Wall and Bathtub Mounted Back Washer	4,696,068	September 29, 1987
King, James	Combination Cotton Thinning and Cultivating Machine	1,661,122	February 28, 1928
Knox, Lawrence Howland	Production of Arecoline	2,506,458	May 2, 1950
Knox, Lawrence Howland	Photochemical Preparation of Tropilidenes	2,647,081	July 28, 1953
Knox, William Jacob, Jr.	Coating Aids for Gelatin Compositions	3,038,804	June 12, 1962
Knox, William Jacob, Jr.	Gelatin Coating Compositions	3,306,749	February 28, 1967
Knox, William Jacob, Jr.	Coating Aids for Hydrophilic Colloid Layers	3,539,352	November 10, 1970
Lancaster, Cleo, et al.	Cytoprotective Use of Oxamate Derivatives	4,439,445	March 27, 1984
Lancaster, Cleo, et al.	Method of Preventing Pancreatitis	4,891,382	January 2, 1990
Latimer, Lewis Howard, et al.	Water Closets for Railway Cars	147,363	February 10, 1874

Letton, James C.	Biodegradable Cationic Surface-Active Agents	4,228,042	October 14, 1980
Letton, Alan, et al.	Polyether-Polycarbonate-Polyether Triblock Copolymers	4,812,530	March 14, 1989
Letton, Alan, et al.	Crystallization Agent for Bisphenol-A Polycarbonate	5,248,756	September 28, 1993
Letton, Alan, et al.	Composition Containing Novel Modifier	6,214,908	April 10, 2001
Letton, Alan, et al.	Composition Containing Novel Modifier	6,414,066	July 2, 2002
Letton, James C.	Detergent Composition	4,260,529	April 7, 1981
Letton, James C.	Stabilized Aqueous Enzyme Composition	4,318,818	March 9, 1982
Letton, James C.	Process for Preparing Alkyl Glycosides	4,713,447	December 15, 1987
Letton, James C., et al.	Compositions Containing Solid, Nondigestible Compounds	4,797,300	January 10, 1989
Letton, James C., et al.	Improved Margarine Compositions	5,017,398	May 21, 1991
Letton, James C., et al.	Reduced Calorie Potato Chips	5,085,884	February 4, 1992
Letton, James C., et al.	Preparation of Mono-Condensation Derivatives	5,286,879	February 15, 1994
Letton, James C., et al.	Solid, Nondigestible, Fat-like Compound and Food Compositions	5,306,514	April 26, 1994
Letton, James C., et al.	Reduced Calorie Pourable Shortening, Cooking Oils	5,306,515	April 26, 1994
Letton, James C., et al.	Shortening Compositions Containing Polyol Polyesters	5,306,516	April 26, 1994
Letton, James C.	Synthesis of Sulfated Polyhydroxy Fatty Acid Amide Sufactants	5,312,934	May 17, 1994
LeVert, Francis Edward	Threshold Self-Powered Gamma Detector	4,091,288	May 23, 1978
LeVert, Francis Edward	Monitor for Deposition on Heat Transfer Surfaces	4,722,610	February 2, 1988
LeVert, Francis Edward	Continuous Fluid Level Detector	4,805,454	February 21, 1989
Lewis, Anthony L.	Window Cleaner	483,359	September 27, 1892
Lewis, Charles W.	Plant Supporting	4,318,247	March 9, 1982
Lewis, Edward R.	Spring Gun	362,096	May 3, 1887
Lewis, James E.	Antenna Feed for Two Coordinate Tracking Radars	3,388,399	June 11, 1968
Linden, Henry	Piano Truck	459,365	September 8, 1891
Little, Ellis	Bridle Bit	254,666	March 7, 1882
Loftman, Kenneth A.	Drying Agent and Process of Making	2,774,651	December 18, 1956
Loftman, Kenneth A.	Aqueous Dispersions of Pyrogenic Silica	2,984,629	May 16, 1961
Logan, Emanuel L., Jr.	Door Bar Latch	3,592,497	July 13, 1971

PATENTEE	TITLE OF INVENTION	PATENT NUMBER	ISSUE DATE
Logan, Emanuel L., Jr.	Magnetic Emergency Exit Door Lock	4,257,631	March 24, 1981
Logan, Emanuel L., Jr.	Timing Apparatus for Delaying Opening of Doors	4,314,722	February 9, 1982
Logan, Emanuel L., Jr.	Point-of-Egress Control Device	4,324,425	April 13, 1982
Logan, Emanuel L., Jr.	Retrofitted Point-of-Egress Control Device	4,354,699	October 19, 1982
Logan, Emanuel L., Jr., et al.	Emergency Exit Sign Utilizing Electroluminescent Lamp	4,466,208	August 21, 1984
Logan, Emanuel L., Jr., et al.	Emergency Exit Door Latch	4,470,625	September 11, 1984
Logan, Emanuel L., Jr., et al.	Emergency Exit Indicators	4,489,308	December 18, 1984
Logan, Emanuel L., Jr., et al.	Point-of-Egress Control Device	4,540,208	September 10, 1985
Logan, Emanuel L., Jr.	Apparatus for Securing a Pivoted Member	4,651,358	March 24, 1987
Long, Amos E., et al.	Caps for Bottles, Jars, etc.	610,715	September 13, 1898
Loudin, Frederick J.	Sash Fastener	510,432	December 12, 1893
Loudin, Frederick J.	Key Fastener	512,308	January 9, 1894
Love, John Lee	Plasterer's Hawk	542,419	July 9, 1895
Love, John Lee	Pencil Sharpener	594,114	November 23, 1897
Love, Natalie R.	T-Top Roof Cover	5,110,178	May 5, 1992
Love, Samuel D.	Fireplace Draft Adapter	4,399,806	August 23, 1983
Love, Samuel D.	Fireplace Grate Adapter	4,429,681	February 7, 1984
LuValle, James E.	Photographic Process	3,219,445	November 23, 1965
LuValle, James E.	Photographic Medium and Methods of Preparing	3,219,448	November 23, 1965
LuValle, James E.	Sensitizing Photographic Media	3,219,451	November 23, 1965
Lyons, Arthur W.	Oil Stove	1,730,224	October 1, 1929
Lyons, Donald R., et al.	Methods and Apparatus for Calibrating Gratings	5,552,882	September 3, 1996
MacDonald, Hugh D., Jr., et al.	Rocket Catapult	3,447,767	June 3, 1969
Mack, John Leslie	Participant Identification Recording and Playback System	4,596,041	June 17, 1986
Madison, Shannon L.	Refrigeration Apparatus	3,208,232	September 28, 1965

Madison, Shannon L.	Electrical Wiring Harness Termination System	4,793,820	December 27, 1988
Madison, Walter G.	Flying Machine	1,047,098	December 10, 1912
Magee, Charles	Hand Table and Carrying Rack	5,104,168	April 14, 1992
Mallette, Kermit J.	Sensitive Condom	5,284,158	February 8, 1994
Maloney, Kenneth Morgan	Alumina Coatings for Electric Lamp	3,868,266	February 25, 1975
Maloney, Kenneth Morgan	Alumina Coatings for Mercury Vapor Lamps	4,079,288	March 14, 1978
Mangin, Anna	Pastry Fork	470,005	March 1, 1892
Marshall, James E.	Flying Machine	1,038,168	September 10, 1912
Marshall, Randall S.	Articles for Cooling Beverages	4,554,189	November 19, 1985
Marshall, Randall S.	Articles for Cooling Beverages	4,761,314	August 2, 1988
Marshall, Willis	Grain Binder	341,589	May 11, 1886
Martin, Thomas J.	Fire Extinguisher	125,063	March 26, 1872
Martin, Washington A.	Lock	407,738	July 23, 1889
Martin, Washington A.	Lock	443,945	December 30, 1890
Massie, Samuel P., et al.	2-Acetyl Quinoline Thiosemicarbazones	4,440,771	April 3, 1984
Matzeliger, Jan Earnst	Lasting Machine	274,207	March 20, 1883
Matzeliger, Jan Earnst	Mechanism for Distributing Tacks, Nails	415,726	November 26, 1889
Matzeliger, Jan Earnst	Nailing Machine	421,954	February 25, 1890
Matzeliger, Jan Earnst	Tack Separating and Distributing Mechanism	423,937	March 25, 1890
Matzeliger, Jan Earnst	Lasting Machine	459,899	September 22, 1891
May, Edgar H.	Carpet-Cutting Machine	1,096,733	May 12, 1914
Mays, Alfred T., et al.	Patterned Densified Fabric Comprising Conjugate Fiber	4,774,124	September 27, 1988
Mays, Alfred T., et al.	Method and Apparatus for Patterned Belt Bonded Material	4,787,941	November 29, 1988
McClennan, Walter N.	Automatic Railway Car	1,333,430	March 9, 1920
McClennan, Walter N.	Car Door Actuating Mechanism	Reissue 15,338	April 18, 1922
McClennan, Walter N.	Coin Mechanism	1,518,208	December 9, 1924
McCoy, Admiral H., et al.	Torpedo Arrester or Insulator	2,348,094	May 2, 1944
McCoy Elijah	Lubricator for Steam Engines	129,843	July 23, 1872

PATENTEE	TITLE OF INVENTION	PATENT NUMBER	ISSUE DATE
McCoy, Elijah	Lubricator for Steam Engines	130,305	August 6, 1872
McCoy, Elijah	Lubricator	139,407	May 27, 1873
McCoy, Elijah	Steam Lubricator	146,697	January 20, 1874
McCoy, Elijah	Ironing Table	150,876	May 12, 1874
McCoy, Elijah	Steam Cylinder Lubricator	173,032	February 1, 1876
McCoy, Elijah	Steam Cylinder Lubricator	179,585	July 4, 1876
McCoy, Elijah	Lubricator	255,443	March 28, 1882
McCoy, Elijah	Lubricator	261,166	July 18, 1882
McCoy, Elijah	Lubricator	270,238	January 9, 1883
McCoy, Elijah	Steam Dome	320,354	June 16, 1885
McCoy, Elijah	Lubricator	320,379	June 16, 1885
McCoy, Elijah	Lubricator	357,491	February 8, 1887
McCoy, Elijah	Lubricator Attachment	361,435	April 19, 1887
McCoy, Elijah	Lubricator for Safety Valves	363,529	May 24, 1887
McCoy, Elijah	Lubricator	383,746	May 29, 1888
McCoy, Elijah, et al.	Lubricator	418,139	December 24, 1889
McCoy, Elijah	Drip Cup	460,215	September 29, 1891
McCoy, Elijah	Lubricator	465,875	December 29, 1891
McCoy, Elijah	Lubricator	472,066	April 5, 1892
McCoy, Elijah	Lubricator	610,634	September 13, 1898
McCoy, Elijah	Lubricator	611,759	October 4, 1898
McCoy, Elijah	Oil Cup	614,307	November 15, 1898
McCoy, Elijah	Lubricator	627,623	June 27, 1899
McCoy, Elijah	Lubricator	646,126	March 27, 1900
McCoy, Elijah	Lubricator	663,976	December 18, 1900
McCoy, Elijah	Journal Lubricator	783,382	February 21, 1905

Name	Invention	Number	Date
McCoy, Elijah	Scaffold Support	856,084	June 4, 1907
McCoy, Elijah	Lubricator	890,295	June 9, 1908
McCoy, Elijah	Lubricator	890,787	June 16, 1908
McCoy, Elijah	Lubricator	903,306	November 10, 1908
McCoy, Elijah	Lubricator	911,669	February 9, 1909
McCoy, Elijah	Gauge	1,021,255	March 25, 1912
McCoy, Elijah	Lubricator	1,031,948	July 9, 1912
McCoy, Elijah	Locomotive Lubricator	1,097,134	May 19, 1914
McCoy, Elijah	Valve and Plug Cock	1,101,868	June 30, 1914
McCoy, Elijah	Tread for Tires	1,127,789	February 9, 1915
McCoy, Elijah	Locomotive Lubricator	1,136,689	April 20, 1915
McCoy, Elijah	Lubricator	1,192,083	July 25, 1916
McCoy, Elijah	Air-Brake Pump Lubricator	1,338,385	April 27, 1920
McCoy, Elijah	Lubricator	1,499,468	July 1, 1924
McCoy, Elijah	Lubricator	1,558,266	October 20, 1925
McCoy, Elijah	Lubricator	1,574,983	March 2, 1926
McCree, Daniel	Portable Fire Escape	440,322	November 11, 1890
McDonald, Peter	Pneumatic Tire	3,610,308	October 5, 1971
McDonald, Peter	All-Season Pneumatic Tire Tread	4,278,121	July 14, 1981
McDonald, Peter	Addition Members for Rubber Articles	4,317,479	March 2, 1982
McDonald, Peter	Unified Modular Indicia Marking for Rubber Articles	4,343,342	August 10, 1982
McGuire, Lynn	Self Contained Viscera Treatment Unit	5,093,969	March 10, 1992
McIlwain, Ivy	Rat Trap	3,872,619	March 25, 1975
McKindra, Clayton D., et al.	Aircraft Rocket Firing System	3,712,170	January 23, 1973
McNair, Luther	Sanitary Mouth Attachment	1,034,636	August 6, 1912
McWhorter, John E.	Flying machine	1,114,167	October 20, 1914
Mendenhall, Albert	Holder for Driving Reins	637,811	November 28, 1899
Meredith, Deanna R.	Skateboard	4,458,907	July 10, 1984
Miles, Alexander	Elevator	371,207	October 11, 1887

253

PATENTEE	TITLE OF INVENTION	PATENT NUMBER	ISSUE DATE
Millington, James E.	Thermostable Dielectric Material	3,316,178	April 25, 1967
Millington, James E.	Method of Making Expandable Styrene-type Beads	4,286,069	August 25, 1981
Millington, James E.	Method of Making Styrene-type Polymer	4,730,027	March 8, 1988
Mitchell, Charles Lewis	Device for Aid in Vocal Culture	291,071	January 1, 1884
Mitchell, James M.	Check Row Corn Planter	641,462	January 16, 1900
Mitchell, James W., et al.	Deposition of Diamond Films	5,128,006	July 7, 1992
Mitchell, James W., et al.	Method of Growing Continuous Diamond Films	5,441,013	August 15, 1995
Mitchell, James W., et al.	Process and Apparatus for Generating Precursor Gases	5,474,659	December 12, 1995
Molaire, Michel F.	Binder Mixture/Optical Recording Layer and Elements	4,626,361	December 2, 1986
Molaire, Michel F., et al.	Photoelectrographic Elements and Imaging Method	4,661,429	April 29, 1987
Molaire, Michel F., et al.	Nonpolymeric Amorphous Developer Compositions	5,176,977	January 5, 1993
Molaire, Michel F., et al.	Photoelectrographic Elements	5,204,198	April 20, 1993
Molaire, Michel F., et al.	Photoconductive Element and Method	5,240,802	August 31, 1993
Montgomery, B. S. T.	Device for Holding Books, Papers, etc.		(Before 1903)
Montgomery, Jay H., et al.	Food Product and Process of Producing	1,694,680	December 11, 1928
Montgomery, Jay H.	Aeroplane Aerofoil Wing	1,910,626	May 23, 1933
Moore, Charles C.	Toilet	1,439,748	December 26, 1922
Moore, Mary Ann	Pain Relief Composition and Method of Preparing	4,177,266	December 4, 1979
Moore, Roy J.	Clamp Arrangement for Track Lifting and Aligning	4,565,133	January 21, 1986
Moore, Roy J., et al.	Split Workhead	4,899,664	February 13, 1990
Moore, Roy J., et al.	Split Tool Mechanism Vibrator	5,584,248	December 17, 1996
Moore, Samuel	Self-Directing Headlight	1,608,903	November 30, 1926
Moore, Samuel	Vehicle Headlight Mechanism	1,658,534	February 7, 1928
Moore, Samuel	Locomotive Headlight	1,659,328	February 14, 1928
Moore, Samuel	Hobby Horse	1,705,991	March 19, 1929
Moore, Samuel	Fuel Valve Lock for Motor Vehicles	2,006,027	June 25, 1935

Morehead, King	Reel Carrier	568,916	October 6, 1896
Morgan, Garrett A., Sr.	Breathing Device	1,090,936	March 24, 1914
Morgan, Garrett A., Sr.	Breathing Device	1,113,675	October 13, 1914
Morgan, Garrett A., Sr.	Traffic Signal	1,475,024	November 20, 1923
Morgan, Garrett A., Sr.	De-curling Comb	2,762,382	September 11, 1956
Morgan, Jerome	Mechanism Display Device	4,070,973	January 31, 1978
Morris, Joel Morton	Switching System Charging Arrangement	3,688,047	August 29, 1972
Moses, John R., et al.	Lubricating Oil Filter	4,272,371	June 9, 1981
Moses, John R.	Flat Emergency Exit Sign	4,420,898	December 20, 1983
Moses, Robert P.	Games for Enhancing Mathematical Understanding	5,520,542	May 28, 1996
Muckelroy, William L., et al.	Leadless Microminiature Inductance Element	3,691,497	September 12, 1972
Muckelroy, William L., et al.	Ceramic Inductor	3,812,442	May 21, 1974
Muckelroy, William L.	Microminiature Monolithic Ferroceramic Transformer	3,833,872	September 3, 1974
Muckelroy, William L.	Handling Beam-Lead and Odd-Shaped Semiconductor Devices	3,731,377	May 8, 1973
Muckelroy, William L., et al.	Microminiature Leadless Inductance Element	3,585,553	June 15, 1971
Muckelroy, William L.	Sintering Thick-Film Oxidizable Silk-screened Circuitry	3,726,006	April 10, 1973
Muckelroy, William L., et al.	Three Dimensional Circuit Modules	3,755,891	September 4, 1973
Mullen, Nathaniel John	Asphalt Paving Vehicles	3,880,542	April 29, 1975
Murray, George W.	Combined Furrow Opener and Stalk Knocker	517,960	April 10, 1894
Murray, George W.	Cultivator and Marker	517,961	April 10, 1894
Murray, George W.	Planter	520,887	June 5, 1894
Murray, George W.	Cotton Chopper	520,888	June 5, 1894
Murray, George W.	Fertilizer Distributor	520,889	June 5, 1894
Murray, George W.	Planter	520,890	June 5, 1894
Murray, George W.	Combined Cotton Seed Planter and Fertilizer Distributor	520,891	June 5, 1894
Murray, George W.	Planter and Fertilizer Distributor Reaper	520,892	June 5, 1894
Murray, William	Attachment for Bicycles	445,442	January 27, 1891

PATENTEE	TITLE OF INVENTION	PATENT NUMBER	ISSUE DATE
Nance, Lee	Game Apparatus	464,035	December 1, 1891
Napier, Dennis K.	Earth Splitter	5,109,930	May 5, 1992
Nash, Henry H.	Improvement in Life Preserving Stools	168,519	October 5, 1875
Nauflette, George W.	Synthesis of 2-Fluoro-2,2-Dinitroethanol	3,652,686	March 28, 1972
Nauflette, George W., et al.	Plasticizer for Nitropolymers	4,457,791	July 3, 1984
Nauflette, George W., et al.	Preparation of 2,4-Dinitro-2,4-Diazapentane	4,469,888	September 4, 1984
Neal, Lonnie George	Electromagnetic Gyroscope Float Assembly	3,475,975	November 4, 1969
Neal, Theophilus Ealey	Automatic Blow-off	1,885,466	November 1, 1932
Neal, Theophilus Ealey	Shower Bath Spray	1,893,435	January 3, 1933
Neblett, Richard Flemon	Gasoline Composition	2,955,928	October 11, 1960
Neblett, Richard Flemon	Motor Fuel Composition	3,054,666	September 18, 1962
Neblett, Richard Flemon	Oil-Soluble Ashless Dispersant-Detergent-Inhibitors	3,511,780	May 12, 1970
Newman, Lyda D.	Brush	614,335	November 15, 1898
Newson, Simeon	Oil Heater or Cooker	520,188	May 22, 1894
Nicholson, Jerome	Bags	5,913,606	June 22, 1999
Nicholson, Jerome	Toothpick Holder	6,076,658	June 20, 2000
Nicholson, Jerome	Mini-Blind/Curtain Rod Bracket	6,382,295	May 7, 2002
Nickerson, William J.	Mandolin and Guitar Attachment for Pianos	627,739	June 27, 1899
Nicol, Evelyn C.	Urokinase Production	3,930,944	January 6, 1976
Nix, Ceoma	Mobility Aid	4,451,080	May 29, 1984
Nokes, Clarence David	Venetian Blind Restringer	2,836,882	June 3, 1958
Nokes, Clarence David	Lawn Mower	3,077,066	February 12, 1963
Nokes, Clarence David	Programmed Steering Means for Moving Apparatus	3,650,097	March 21, 1972
Nokes, Clarence David	Lawn Mower Apparatus	4,354,339	October 19, 1982
Nokes, Clarence David	Snap-off Key	4,402,201	September 6, 1983
Norwood, James P.	Bread Wrapping, Labeling, and Sealing Machine	1,191,029	July 11, 1916

Name	Invention	Patent No.	Date
Nwoko, Luck	Enhanced Speed Lacing Device	4,916,833	April 17, 1990
Nwoko, Luck	Hook-Type Speed Fastening Device	4,970,763	November 20, 1990
Nwoko, Luck	Spring Actuated Fastening Device	5,050,915	September 24, 1991
Oliphant, Adam L.	Portable Barbeque Grill Assembly	4,876,476	November 7, 1989
Oliphant, Adam L.	Portable Cooking Grill	4,646,711	March 3, 1987
Oliver, Lee Grant	Auto Accessories	4,915,274	April 10, 1990
Omohundro, Robert Johnson, et al.	Scintillation Counter	3,087,060	April 23, 1963
Omohundro, Robert Johnson, et al.	Selective Detector for Fission Neutrons	3,612,872	October 12, 1971
Onley, John H.	Method and Apparatus for Removal of Carbon Monoxide	4,464,349	August 7, 1984
Outlaw, John W.	Horse Shoes	614,273	November 15, 1898
Overstreet, Tannis L.	Security Mail Receptacle	5,071,063	December 10, 1991
Parker, Alice H.	Heating Furnace	1,325,905	December 23, 1919
Parker, Alonzo E., Jr.	Passive Exercising Apparatus	4,723,537	February 9, 1988
Parker, Alonzo E., Jr.	Passive Exercising Apparatus	4,827,913	May 9, 1989
Parker, Alonzo E., Jr.	Oscillating Reclining Chair	4,860,733	August 29, 1989
Parker, Denson	Fluid Velocity Actuated Structure for a Wind Mill/Water Wheel	4,276,481	June 30, 1981
Parker, Denson	Centrifugal Force Magnetic Field Variator	5,053,659	October 1, 1991
Parker, George A.	Multipurpose Light Duty Garden Tool	4,334,583	June 15, 1982
Parker, John Percial	Portable Screw Press	318,285	May 19, 1885
Parsons, James A., Jr.	Iron Alloy	1,728,360	September 17, 1929
Parsons, James A., Jr.	Method of Making Silicon Iron Compounds	1,819,479	August 18, 1931
Parsons, James A., Jr.	Process for Treating Silicon Alloy Castings	1,972,103	September 4, 1934
Parsons, James A., Jr.	Corrosion Resisting Ferrous Alloys	2,134,670	October 25, 1938
Parsons, James A., Jr.	Corrosion Resisting Ferrous Alloy	2,185,987	January 2, 1940
Parsons, James A., Jr.	Corrosion Resisting Ferrous Alloy	2,200,208	May 7, 1940

PATENTEE	TITLE OF INVENTION	PATENT NUMBER	ISSUE DATE
Parsons, James A., Jr., et al.	Cementation Process of Treating Metal	2,318,011	May 4, 1943
Parsons, James A., Jr., et al.	Nickel Base Alloy	2,467,288	April 12, 1949
Pelham, Robert	Pasting Apparatus	807,685	December 19, 1905
Perry, John, Jr., et al.	Biochemical Fuel Cell	3,284,239	November 8, 1966
Perry, John, Jr.	Method of Making Fuel Cell Electrode and Fuel Cell	3,464,862	September 2, 1969
Perry, John, Jr.	Fuel Cell Anode Electrode, Method of Making and Fuel Cell	4,141,801	February 27, 1979
Perryman, Frank R.	Caterers' Tray Table	468,038	February 2, 1892
Peterson, Charles A., Jr.	Power Generating Apparatus	3,391,903	July 9, 1968
Peterson, Charles A., Jr.	Method and Apparatus for Generating Power by Sea Wave Action	4,086,775	May 2, 1978
Peterson, Henry	Attachment for Lawn Mowers	402,189	April 30, 1889
Phelps, William Henry	Apparatus for Washing Vehicles	579,242	March 23, 1897
Philips, Raymond P.	Radiotelephone System Featuring Switching Circuit	2,894,121	July 7, 1959
Pickering, John F.	Air Ship	643,975	February 20, 1900
Pickett, Henry	Improvement in Scaffolds	152,511	June 30, 1874
Pickett, James Henry, Jr.	Trophy Lamp	4,059,752	November 22, 1977
Pinn, Traverse B.	File Holder	231,335	August 17, 1880
Polk, Austin J.	Bicycle Support	558,103	April 14, 1896
Poole, Leonard	Donkey Calf Exercising Machine	4,346,887	August 31, 1982
Pope, Jessie T.	Croquignole Iron	2,409,791	October 22, 1946
Porter, James H.	Gas Well Sulfur Removal by Diffusion through Polymer Membranes	3,534,528	October 20, 1970
Posey, Leroy R.	Educational Device	2,188,723	January 30, 1940
Powell, Aaron	Illuminating Dancing Shoes	4,130,951	December 26, 1978
Powell, Manual, et al.	Self-Generated Lighted Hubcap	4,893,877	January 16, 1990

Prather, Alfred G. B.	Moveable Prefabricated Fireplace and Handling Hanger Attachment	3,289,666	December 6, 1966
Prather, Alfred G. B.	Method and Means for Instantly Filling and Sealing an Envelope	3,623,820	November 30, 1971
Prather, Alfred G. B.	Gravity Escape Means	3,715,011	February 6, 1973
Prather, Alfred G. B.	Man-Powered Glider Aircraft	3,750,981	August 7, 1973
Prather, Alfred G. B.	Collapsible Propeller for Man-Powered Glider Aircraft	3,811,642	May 21, 1974
Prather, Alfred G. B.	Fan-like Tail Section for Man-Powered Glider Aircraft	3,813,062	May 28, 1974
Price, Frank Osalo	Quarterback Draw Football Device	4,706,959	November 17, 1987
Prince, Frank R.	Production of 2-Pyrrolidones	3,637,743	January 25, 1972
Pugsley, Abraham	Blind Stop	433,306	July 29, 1890
Pugsley, Samuel	Gate Latch	357,787	February 15, 1887
Purdy, John E. and Sadgwar, Daniel A.	Folding Chair	405,117	June 11, 1889
Purdy, Walter	Device for Sharpening Edged Tools	570,337	October 27, 1896
Purdy, Walter	Device for Sharpening Edged Tools	609,367	August 16, 1898
Purdy, Walter	Device for Sharpening Edged Tools	630,106	August 1, 1899
Purvis, William B.	Bag Fastener	256,856	April 25, 1882
Purvis, William B.	Hand Stamp	273,149	February 27, 1883
Purvis, William B.	Paper Bag Machine	293,353	February 12, 1884
Purvis, William B.	Fountain Pen	419,065	January 7, 1890
Purvis, William B.	Paper Bag Machine	420,099	January 28, 1890
Purvis, William B.	Paper Bag Machine	430,684	June 24, 1890
Purvis, William B.	Paper Bag Machine	434,461	August 19, 1890
Purvis, William B.	Paper Bag Machine	435,524	September 2, 1890
Purvis, William B.	Paper Bag Machine	460,093	September 22, 1891
Purvis, William B.	Electric Railway	519,291	May 1, 1894
Purvis, William B.	Paper Bag Machine	519,348	May 8, 1894
Purvis, William B.	Paper Bag Machine	519,349	May 8, 1894
Purvis, William B.	Paper Bag Machine	530,650	December 1, 1894

PATENTEE	TITLE OF INVENTION	PATENT NUMBER	ISSUE DATE
Purvis, William B.	Magnetic Car Balancing Device	539,542	May 21, 1895
Purvis, William B.	Paper Bag Machine	578,361	March 9, 1897
Purvis, William B.	Electric Railway System	588,176	August 17, 1897
Queen, William	Guard for Companion Ways or Hatches	458,131	August 18, 1891
Quick, Nathaniel R., et al.	Carbon Transducer with Electrical Contact	4,387,276	June 7, 1983
Quick, Nathaniel R.	Apparatus and Method for Processing Wire Strand Cable	4,401,479	August 30, 1983
Quick, Nathaniel R., et al.	Electrical Contact Means with Gold Nickel Overlay	4,480,014	October 30, 1984
Quick, Nathaniel R.	Apparatus and Method for Processing Wire Strand Cable	4,529,566	July 16, 1985
Quick, Nathaniel R.	Apparatus and Method for Processing Wire Strand Cable	4,534,310	August 13, 1985
Quick, Nathaniel R., et al.	Direct Writing of Conductive Patterns	4,691,091	September 1, 1987
Quigless, Kirk	Dispensable-Head Manual Toothbrush	5,737,792	April 14, 1998
Randall, Carol C.	Ear Brace	4,971,072	November 20, 1990
Ransom, Victor L.	Traffic Data Processing	3,231,866	January 25, 1966
Ransom, Victor L.	Method and Apparatus for Gathering Peak Load Traffic Data	3,866,185	February 11, 1975
Ratchford, Debrilla M.	Suitcase with Wheels and Transporting Hook	4,094,391	June 13, 1978
Ray, Ernest P.	Chair Supporting Device	620,078	February 21, 1899
Ray, Lloyd P.	Dust Pan	587,607	August 3, 1897
Redmond, Sidney D., et al.	Torpedo Arrester or Insulator	2,348,094	May 2, 1944
Redmond, Joseph M., et al.	Resistor Sensing Bit Switch	3,736,573	May 29, 1973
Reeberg, Christiaan	Hold Steady Strap	4,155,636	May 22, 1979
Reed, Judy W.	Dough Kneader and Roller	305,474	September 23, 1884
Reid, Tahira, et al.	Jump Rope Device	5,961,425	October 5, 1999
Reynolds, Humphrey H.	Window Ventilator for Railroad Cars	275,271	April 3, 1883

Reynolds, Humphrey H.	Safety Gate for Bridges	437,937	October 7, 1890
Reynolds, Mary Jane	Hoisting and Loading Mechanism	1,337,667	April 20, 1920
Reynolds, Robert R.	Non-Refillable Bottle	624,092	May 2, 1899
Rhodes, Jerome Bonaparte	Water Closet	639,290	December 19, 1899
Richards, Donna E.	Loose Leaf Retainer for File Folders	4,932,804	June 12, 1990
Richards, Levie	Ointment for Treatment of Arthritis	4,271,154	June 2, 1981
Richardson, Albert C.	Hame Fastener	255,022	March 14, 1882
Richardson, Albert C.	Churn	446,470	February 17, 1891
Richardson, Albert C.	Casket-Lowering Device	529,311	November 13, 1894
Richardson, Albert C.	Insect Destroyer	620,362	February 28, 1899
Richardson, Albert C.	Bottle	638,811	December 12, 1899
Richardson, Alfred G., et al.	Method for Fabricating an Optical Fiber Cable	4,484,963	November 27, 1984
Richardson, William H.	Cotton Chopper	343,140	June 1, 1886
Richardson, William H.	Child's Carriage	405,599	June 18, 1889
Richardson, William H.	Child's Carriage	405,600	June 18, 1889
Richey, Charles V.	Car Coupling	587,650	June 15, 1897
Richey, Charles V.	Railroad Switch	587,657	August 3, 1897
Richey, Charles V.	Railroad Switch	592,448	October 26, 1897
Richey, Charles V.	Fire Escape Bracket	596,427	December 28, 1897
Richey, Charles V.	Combined Cot, Hammock, and Stretcher	615,907	December 13, 1898
Richey, Charles V.	Telephone Call Register	1,037,053	August 27, 1912
Richey, Charles V.	Telephone Register and Lock-out Device	1,063,599	June 3, 1913
Richey, Charles V.	Lockout for Outgoing Calls for Telephone Systems	1,812,984	July 7, 1931
Richey, Charles V.	Time Control System for Telephones	1,897,533	February 14, 1933
Rickman, Alvin Longo	Overshoe	598,816	February 8, 1898
Ricks, James	Horseshoe	338,781	March 30, 1886
Ricks, James	Overshoes for Horses	626,245	June 6, 1899
Rillieux, Norbert	Improvement in Sugar-Works	3,237	August 26, 1843
Rillieux, Norbert	Improvement in Sugar-Making	4,879	December 10, 1846

PATENTEE	TITLE OF INVENTION	PATENT NUMBER	ISSUE DATE
Rillieux, Norbert	Improvement in Sugar-Making	Reissue 439	March 17, 1857
Roberson, William A.	Portable Laundry	748,986	January 5, 1904
Roberson, William A.	Convertible Cot	780,815	January 24, 1905
Robert, Andre	Method of Reducing the Undesirable Gastrointestinal Effects of Prostaglandin Synthetase Inhibitor	4,061,742	December 6, 1977
Robert, Andre	Cytoprotective Prostaglandins	4,081,553	March 28, 1978
Robert, Andre	Treatment of Inflammatory Diseases of the Mammalian Large Intestine	4,083,998	April 11, 1978
Robert, Andre	Cytoprotective Prostaglandins	4,088,784	May 9, 1978
Robert, Andre	Gastric Cytoprotection with Non-Antisecretory Doses of Prostaglandins	4,097,603	June 27, 1978
Robert, Andre	Preventing Enteropooling Induced Diarrhea	4,208,427	June 17, 1980
Robert, Andre, et al.	Method for Preventing Renal Papillary Necrosis	4,397,865	August 9, 1983
Robert, Andre, et al.	Cytoprotective Use of Oxamate Derivatives	4,439,445	March 27, 1984
Robert, Andre, et al.	Method of Preventing Pancreatitis Utilizing 2-Amino-Cycloaliphatic Amides	4,891,382	January 2, 1990
Roberts, Louis W.	High-Frequency-Transmission Control Tube	2,678,408	May 11, 1954
Roberts, Louis W., et al.	Electrode Support for Electron Discharge Devices	2,945,983	July 19, 1960
Roberts, Louis W.	High Power Microwave Switching Device	3,017,534	January 16, 1962
Roberts, Louis W.	Gaseous Discharge Device	3,072,865	January 8, 1963
Roberts, Louis W.	Device for Gas Amplication by Stimulated Emission and Radiation	3,257,620	June 21, 1966
Roberts, Louis W., et al.	Gallium-Wetted Movable Electrode Switch	3,377,576	April 9, 1968
Robinson, Daniel E., et al.	Cord Sets with Power Factor Control	4,417,196	November 22, 1983
Robinson, Daniel E., et al.	Remotely Actuable Line Disconnect Device	4,485,271	November 27, 1984
Robinson, Daniel E., et al.	Remotely Controlled Crossconnection System	4,533,914	August 6, 1985

Robinson, Elbert R.	Electric Railway Trolley	505,370	September 19, 1893
Robinson, Elbert R.	Casting Composite or Other Car Wheels	594,286	November 23, 1897
Robinson, Elbert R.	Switch	866,306	September 17, 1907
Robinson, Elbert R.	Rail	886,541	May 5, 1908
Robinson, Elbert R.	Cast-Iron Axle	887,848	May 19, 1908
Robinson, Hassel	Traffic Signals for Automobiles	1,580,218	April 13, 1926
Robinson, James H.	Life-Saving Guard for Locomotives	621,143	March 14, 1899
Robinson, James H.	Life-Saving Guard for Street Cars	623,929	April 25, 1899
Robinson, John	Dinner Pail	356,852	February 1, 1887
Robinson, Natalie F. G.	Time to Win	5,513,852	May 7, 1996
Robinson, Neale Moore	Vehicle Wheel	1,422,479	July 11, 1922
Rolls, James P.	Delta[1] Dehydrogenation of Corticoids without Side Chain Degradation by Septomyxa	4,088,537	May 9, 1978
Romain, Arnold	Passenger Register	402,035	April 23, 1889
Rose, Raymond E.	Control Apparatus	3,618,388	November 9, 1971
Ross, Archia L.	Runner for Stoops	565,301	August 4, 1896
Ross, Archia L.	Bag Closure	605,343	June 7, 1898
Ross, Archia L.	Trousers Support or Stretcher	638,068	November 28, 1899
Ross, Joseph	Hay Press	632,539	September 5, 1899
Ross, Leonard W., Jr.	Tarp Enclosure for Flat Bed Trailer and Truck Bodies	4,342,480	August 3, 1982
Rosten, David N.	Feather Curler	556,166	March 10, 1896
Rowe, V. Lopez	Bicycle Drinking Apparatus	4,095,812	June 20, 1978
Royster, Ronald B., Sr.	Computer Controlled Stolen Vehicle Detection System	3,656,111	April 11, 1972
Russell, Edwin Roberts, et al.	Adsorption-Bismuth Phosphate Method for Separating Plutonium	2,942,937	June 28, 1960
Russell, Edwin Roberts, et al.	Removal of Cesium from Aqueous Solution by Ion Exchange	3,296,123	January 3, 1967
Russell, Edwin Roberts, et al.	Thorium Oxide or Thorium-Uranium Oxide with Mg Oxide	3,309,323	March 14, 1967
Russell, Jesse E.	Base Station for Mobil Radio Telecommunication System	5,084,869	January 28, 1992

PATENTEE	TITLE OF INVENTION	PATENT NUMBER	ISSUE DATE
Russell, Jesse E., et al.	Multi-band Wireless Radiotelephone Operative in a Plurality of Air Interface of Differing Wireless Communications Systems	5,406,615	April 11, 1995
Russell, Jesse E., et al.	Universal Wireless Radiotelephone System	5,574,775	November 12, 1996
Russell, Jesse E., et al.	Intelligent Wireless Signaling Overlay for a Telecommunication Network	5,583,914	December 10, 1996
Russell, Jesse E., et al.	Broadband Wireless System and Network Architecture Providing Broadband/Narrowband Service	5,592,470	January 7, 1997
Russell, Jesse E., et al.	Wireless Telecommunication Base Station for Integrated Wireless Services with ATM Processing	5,600,633	February 4, 1997
Russell, Jesse E., et al.	Multiple Call Waiting in a Packetized Communication System	6,633,635	October 14, 2003
Russell, Joseph L., et al.	Preparation of Tungsten Hexafluoride	3,995,011	November 30, 1976
Russell, Lewis A.	Guard Attachment for Beds	544,381	August 13, 1895
Ryder, Earl	High Silicon Cast Iron	3,129,095	April 14, 1964
Saab, Acie J.	Picture Postcard	4,079,881	March 21, 1978
Sammons, Walter H.	Comb	1,362,823	December 21, 1920
Sammons, Walter H.	Hair-Dressing Device	1,483,988	February 19, 1924
Sammons, Walter H.	Comb	Reissue 15,808	April 1, 1924
Samms, Adolphus	Rocket Engine Pump Feed System	3,000,179	September 19, 1961
Samms, Adolphus	Multiple Stage Rocket	3,199,455	August 10, 1965
Samms, Adolphus	Air-Breathing Rocket Booster	3,218,974	November 23, 1965
Samms, Adolphus	Rocket Motor Fuel Feed	3,310,938	March 28, 1967
Samms, Adolphus	Emergency Release for Extraction Chute	3,257,089	June 21, 1966
Sampson, Charles T., Sr.	Fishhook	2,591,013	April 1, 1952
Sampson, Charles T., Sr.	Fishing Device	2,736,980	March 6, 1956

Name	Invention	Patent No.	Date
Sampson, George T.	Sled Propeller	312,388	February 17, 1885
Sampson, George T.	Clothes Dryer	476,416	June 7, 1892
Sampson, Henry T.	Binder System for Propellants and Explosives	3,140,210	July 7, 1964
Sampson, Henry T.	Case Bonding System for Cast Composite Propellants	3,212,256	October 19, 1965
Sampson, Henry T.	Gamma-Electric Cell	3,591,860	July 6, 1971
Sampson, Henry T.	Process for Case Bonding Cast Composite Propellant Grains	3,734,982	May 22, 1973
Samuels, John Clifton	A Cathode-Follower Oscillator	2,874,290	February 17, 1959
Sanders, Estelle, et al.	Scalp Massaging Implement	4,308,860	January 5, 1982
Sanderson, Dewey S. C.	Urinalysis Machine	3,522,011	July 28, 1970
Sanderson, Ralph W.	Hydraulic Shock Absorber	3,362,742	January 9, 1968
Saxton, Olivia	Anchor for Furniture Including TV Sets	4,118,902	October 10, 1978
Saxton, Richard L.	Pay Telephone with Sanitized Tissue Dispenser	4,392,028	July 5, 1983
Scharschmidt, Virginia	Safety Window Cleaning Device	1,708,594	April 9, 1929
Scott, Blanton, Jr.	Photographic Film Magazine	3,719,130	March 6, 1973
Scott, Howard L.	Treating Human, Animal, and Synthetic Hair with Water-Proofing Composition	3,568,685	March 9, 1971
Scott, Robert P.	Corn Silker	524,223	August 7, 1894
Scottron, Samuel R.	Adjustable Window-Cornice	224,732	February 17, 1880
Scottron, Samuel R.	Cornice	270,851	January 16, 1883
Scottron, Samuel R.	Pole Tip	349,525	September 21, 1886
Scottron, Samuel R.	Curtain Rod	481,720	August 30, 1892
Scottron, Samuel R.	Supporting Bracket	505,008	September 12, 1893
Seale, Glenn C., et al.	Genealogy Apparatus	4,201,386	May 6, 1980
Shanks, Stephen C.	Sleeping Car Berth Register	587,165	July 21, 1897
Shaw, Earl D.	Free-Electron Amplifier Device with Electromagnetic Radiation Delay Element	4,529,942	July 16, 1985
Shivers, Clarence L.	Passive Ambience Recovery System for Reproduction of Sound	4,837,825	June 6, 1989

PATENTEE	TITLE OF INVENTION	PATENT NUMBER	ISSUE DATE
Shivers, Clarence L.	Passive Ambience Recovery System for the Reproduction of Sound	4,882,753	November 21, 1989
Shorter, Dennis W.	Feed Rack	363,089	May 17, 1887
Silvera, Esteban	Ram-Valve Level Indicator	3,718,157	February 27, 1973
Sluby, Thomas Buchanan	Milk Bottle Stopper	1,052,289	February 4, 1913
Smartt, Brinay	Reversing-Valve	799,498	September 12, 1905
Smartt, Brinay	Reversing-Valve	837,427	December 4, 1906
Smartt, Brinay	Valve Gear	935,169	September 28, 1909
Smartt, Brinay	Rotary Valve	981,019	January 10, 1911
Smartt, Brinay	Wheel	1,052,290	February 4, 1913
Smith, Bernard	Glass Laser Window Sealant Technique	3,616,523	November 2, 1971
Smith, Bernard, et al.	Method of Making a High Current Density Long Life Cathode	4,078,900	March 14, 1978
Smith, Bernard	Method of Forming an Efficient Electron Emitter Cold Cathode	4,149,308	April 17, 1979
Smith, Bernard	Method of Making Ruggedized High Current Density Cathode	4,236,287	December 2, 1980
Smith, Bernard, et al.	EBS Device with Cold-Cathode	4,410,832	October 18, 1983
Smith, Bernard, et al.	Method of Making a High Current Density Cathode	4,444,718	April 24, 1984
Smith, Bernard, et al.	Method of Preparing Nonlaminating Anisotropic Boron Nitride	4,544,535	October 1, 1985
Smith, Bernard, et al.	Method of Making Long Lived High Current Density Cathode	4,708,681	November 24, 1987
Smith, Bernard, et al.	Method of Making a Cathode from Tungsten and Iridium Powders	4,808,137	February 28, 1989
Smith, Bernard, et al.	Method of Making a Cathode from Tungsten and Iridium Powders	4,818,480	April 4, 1989

Name	Title	Patent No.	Date
Smith, Betty J., et al.	Multicharacter Doll	4,921,459	May 1, 1990
Smith, Bruce K., et al.	Soap Saving Method and Apparatus	5,030,405	July 9, 1991
Smith, Charles R., Sr.	Hoist	2,305,202	December 15, 1942
Smith, Herman W.	Omega-Aryl-13,14-Didehydro-PGF Compounds	4,276,429	June 30, 1981
Smith, Herman W.	Structural Analogues of 5,6,-Dihydro PG.sub.1	4,294,759	October 13, 1981
Smith, Herman W.	Trans-4,5,13,14-Tetrahydro-PGI.sub.1	4,301,078	November 17, 1981
Smith, Herman W., et al.	6-Aryluracils	4,495,349	January 22, 1985
Smith, Herman W.	Analogs of 5,6-Dihydro PGI.sub.2	4,496,742	January 29, 1985
Smith, Herman W., et al.	Process for the Preparation of 1,3-Oxazine-4-ones	4,521,599	June 4, 1985
Smith, Herman W.	Use of 5,6,7,8-Tetrahydroquinoline and 5,6-Dihydropyridines	4,576,949	March 18, 1986
Smith, Herman W.	Processes for Preparation of 6-Aryluracils	4,578,466	March 25, 1986
Smith, Herman W.	Use of 6-Aryluracils as Anti-inflammatory and Antiarthritic Agents	4,593,030	June 3, 1986
Smith, Herman W.	6-Aryluracils and Selected Novel Intermediates	4,625,028	November 25, 1986
Smith, Herman W.	Cyclopentapyrazole and Tetrahydroindazole Compounds and Their Use	4,851,425	July 25, 1989
Smith, Herman W.	Phosphonic Acid Derivatives	5,298,498	March 29, 1994
Smith, Herman W.	Bisphosphonic Acid Derivatives	5,360,797	November 1, 1994
Smith, Herman W.	Diaromatic Substituted Compounds as Anti-HIV-1 Agents	5,563,142	October 8, 1996
Smith, James	Aeroplane	1,047,581	December 17, 1912
Smith, John Winsor	Improvement in Games	647,887	April 17, 1900
Smith, Jonathan S., II, et al.	Yttrium, Dysprosium, and Ytterbium Alkoxides and Process	3,278,571	October 11, 1966
Smith, Jonathan S., II, et al.	Yttrium, Dysprosium, and Ytterbium Alkoxides	3,356,703	December 5, 1967
Smith, Jonathan S., II, et al.	Transparent Zirconia Composition	3,432,314	March 11, 1969
Smith, Jonathan S., II, et al.	Method for Making High Purity and High Yield Tertiary-Amyl Acetate	3,489,796	January 13, 1970
Smith, Jonathan S., II, et al.	Transparent Zirconia and Process for Making	3,525,597	August 25, 1970
Smith, Jonathan S., II, et al.	Producing High Purity Submicron Barium and Strontium Titanate	3,647,364	March 7, 1972

PATENTEE	TITLE OF INVENTION	PATENT NUMBER	ISSUE DATE
Smith, Joseph H.	Lawn Sprinkler	581,785	May 4, 1897
Smith, Joseph H.	Lawn Sprinkler	601,065	March 22, 1898
Smith, Mildred Austin	Family Relationship Card Game	4,230,321	October 28, 1980
Smith, Peter D.	Potato Digger	445,206	January 27, 1891
Smith, Peter D.	Grain Binder	469,279	February 23, 1892
Smith, Robert T.	Spraying Machine	1,970,984	August 21, 1934
Smith, Samuel C.	Hardness Tester	3,956,925	May 18, 1976
Smith-Green, E. D.	Mechanism for Cleaning Shell-Fillers	1,232,401	July 3, 1917
Smithea, Clarence O.	Auxiliary Retention Belt and Support for Seat of Open Vehicles	3,940,166	February 24, 1976
Smoot, Lanny S.	Optical Receiver Circuit with Active Equalizer	4,565,974	January 21, 1986
Smoot, Lanny S.	Teleconferencing Facility with High Resolution Video	4,890,314	December 26, 1989
Smoot, Lanny S.	Teleconferencing Terminal with Camera behind Display Screen	4,928,301	May 22, 1990
Snow, William, et al.	Liniment	437,728	October 7, 1890
Snowden, Maxine W.	Rain Hat	4,378,606	April 5, 1983
Souther, Benjamin F.	Hose Storage Reel	2,438,306	March 23, 1948
Spears, Harde	Improvement in Portable Shields for Infantry and Artillery	110,599	December 27, 1870
Spencer, Jerrald, et al.	Light Show Mechanism	5,269,719	December 14, 1993
Spight, Carl	Machine Vision System Utilizing Programmable Optical Parallel Processing	4,462,046	July 24, 1984
Spikes, Richard B.	Billiard Rack	972,277	October 11, 1910
Spikes, Richard B.	Combination Milk Bottle Opener and Bottle Cover	1,590,557	June 29, 1926
Spikes, Richard B.	Method and Apparatus for Obtaining Average Samples and Temperature of Tank Liquids	1,828,753	October 27, 1931
Spikes, Richard B.	Automatic Gear Shift	1,889,814	December 6, 1932

Name	Invention	Patent No.	Date
Spikes, Richard B.	Transmission and Shifting Means	1,936,996	November 28, 1933
Spikes, Richard B.	Horizontally Swinging Barber's Chair	2,519,936	August 8, 1950
Spikes, Richard B.	Automatic Safety Brake System	3,015,522	January 2, 1962
Stafford, Osborne C.	Microwave Phase Shift Device	3,522,558	August 4, 1970
Stallworth, Elbert	Electric Heater	1,687,521	October 16, 1928
Stallworth, Elbert	Electric Chamber	1,727,842	September 10, 1929
Stallworth, Elbert	Alarm Clock Electric Switch	1,972,634	September 4, 1934
Stanard, John	Oil Stove	413,689	October 29, 1889
Stanard, John	Refrigerator	455,891	July 14, 1891
Stanton, Horace D., et al.	In Situ Cured Booster Explosive	4,385,948	May 31, 1983
Stanton, Horace D., et al.	Polymer Modified TNT Containing Explosives	4,445,948	May 1, 1984
Stanton, Horace D., et al.	Extrudable PBX Molding Powder	4,952,255	August 28, 1990
Starks, Zeston	Protector for Plants	1,904,700	April 18, 1933
Starks, Zeston	Container	1,910,646	May 23, 1933
Starks, Zeston	Protector and Supporter for Plants	1,916,868	July 4, 1933
States, John B., Sr.	Material and Methods for Oil Spill Control and Cleanup	4,248,733	February 3, 1981
States, John B., Sr., et al.	Odor-Reducing, Nutrient-Enhancing Composition	5,574,093	November 12, 1996
Stephens, George B. D.	Cigarette Holder and Ash Tray	2,762,377	September 11, 1956
Stevens, Emeline	Pillow-like Body Supports and Protectors and System of Same	5,103,516	April 14, 1992
Stewart, Albert Clifton	Redox Couple Radiation Cell	3,255,044	June 7, 1966
Stewart, Albert Clifton	Electric Cell	3,255,045	June 7, 1966
Stewart, Earl M., et al.	Arch and Heel Support	2,031,510	February 18, 1936
Stewart, Enos W.	Punching Machine	362,190	May 3, 1887
Stewart, Enos W.	Machine for Forming Vehicle Seat Bars	373,698	November 22, 1887
Stewart, Eugene	Fare Computer	4,800,502	January 24, 1989
Stewart, Isaac, Jr.	Sno-Rak	4,547,011	October 15, 1985
Stewart, Marvin Charles	Arithmatic Unit for Digital Computers	3,395,271	July 30, 1968
Stewart, Marvin Charles	System for Interconnecting Electrical Components	3,605,063	September 14, 1971
Stewart, Thomas	Metal Bending Machine	375,512	December 27, 1887

PATENTEE	TITLE OF INVENTION	PATENT NUMBER	ISSUE DATE
Stewart, Thomas W.	Mop	499,402	June 13, 1893
Stewart, Thomas W., et al.	Station Indicator	499,895	June 20, 1893
Stilwell, Henry F.	Means for Delivery of Mail and Other from Aeroplanes while in Motion	1,841,766	January 19, 1932
Stokes, Rufus	Exhaust Purifier	3,378,241	April 16, 1968
Stokes, Rufus	Air Pollution Control Device	3,520,113	July 14, 1970
Sutton, Edward H.	Improvement in Cotton Cultivators	149,543	April 7, 1874
Sweeting, James A.	Device for Rolling Cigarettes	594,501	November 30, 1897
Sweeting, James A.	Combined Knife and Scoop	605,209	June 7, 1898
Tankins, Sacramenta G.	Comb	1,339,632	May 11, 1920
Tankins, Sacramenta G.	Method and Means for Treating Human Hair	1,845,208	February 16, 1932
Tate, Charles W.	Flexible and Transparent Lubricant Housing	3,423,959	January 28, 1969
Taylor, Aiken C.	Combined Cotton Planter and Fertilizer Distributor	827,328	July 31, 1906
Taylor, Asa J.	Machine for Assembling and/or Disassembling the Parts of Spring Tensioned Devices	2,286,695	June 16, 1942
Taylor, Asa J.	Device for Dislodging Valve-Assemblies of Internal-Combustion Engines	2,365,023	December 12, 1944
Taylor, Asa J.	Fluid Joint	2,434,629	January 13, 1948
Taylor, Benjamin H.	Improvement in Rotary Engines	202,888	April 23, 1878
Taylor, Benjamin H.	Slide Valve	585,798	July 6, 1897
Taylor, Don A.	Individually Packaged Frozen Confection	2,735,778	February 21, 1956
Taylor, Don A.	Floor Mats for Automobiles	2,810,671	October 22, 1957
Taylor, Don A.	Floor Mats for Automobiles	2,810,672	October 22, 1957
Taylor, Don A.	Baton	3,003,385	October 10, 1961
Taylor, Don A.	Air Intake Scoop for Ventilating Seat Cushion	3,039,817	June 19, 1962
Taylor, Don A.	Measuring Tape Tension Holder	3,100,941	August 20, 1963

Taylor, Don A.	Detachable Ventilating Seat Cover for Automobile Seats	3,101,037	August 20, 1963
Taylor, Don A.	Ventilating Hood for Seat Cushions	3,101,660	August 27, 1963
Taylor, Don A.	Finger Grip Pad for Bowling Balls	3,113,775	December 10, 1963
Taylor, Don A.	Molding Apparatus	3,748,075	July 24, 1973
Taylor, Don A.	Apparatus for Molding Strip Material	3,829,271	August 13, 1974
Taylor, Don A.	Method for Forming Hollow Article	3,832,437	August 27, 1974
Taylor, Don A.	Molding Apparatus	3,836,307	September 17, 1974
Taylor, Don A.	Apparatus for Transfer Molding Thermosetting Materials	3,843,289	October 22, 1974
Taylor, Don A.	Particle Filled Self-Conformable Cushion and Method	3,971,839	July 27, 1976
Taylor, Don A.	Injection Cylinder Unit Mold and Mold Handling Apparatus	3,981,661	September 21, 1976
Taylor, Don A.	Heating System	3,993,244	November 23, 1976
Taylor, Moddie D.	Preparation of Anhydrous Alkaline Earth Halides	2,801,899	August 6, 1957
Taylor, Moddie D.	Ion Exchange Adsorption Process for Plutonium Separation	2,992,249	July 11, 1961
Taylor, Moddie D.	Preparation of Anhydrous Lithium Salts	3,049,406	August 14, 1962
Thomas, Arend J.	Electric Heating Apparatus for Heat Treating Pharmaceuticals	4,273,992	June 16, 1981
Thomas, Edward H. C.	Automobile Key and License Holder	1,693,006	November 27, 1928
Thomas, Samuel E.	Waste Trap	286,746	October 16, 1883
Thomas, Samuel E.	Waste Trap for Basins, Closets, etc.	371,107	October 4, 1887
Thomas, Samuel E.	Process of Casting	386,941	July 31, 1888
Thomas, Samuel E.	Pipe Connection	390,821	October 9, 1888
Thomas, Valerie L.	Illusion Transmitter	4,229,761	October 21, 1980
Thompson, John P.	Motor Vehicle Elevating and Parking Device	2,086,142	July 6, 1937
Thompson, Joseph Ausbon, Jr.	Foot Warmer	2,442,026	May 25, 1948
Thompson, Joseph Ausbon, Jr.	Moist/Dry Lavatory and Toilet Tissue	3,921,802	November 25, 1975
Thompson, Oliver L.	Vehicle Parking Attachment	1,541,670	June 9, 1925
Thornton, Benjamin F.	Apparatus for Automatically Recording Telephonic Messages	1,831,331	November 10, 1931

PATENTEE	TITLE OF INVENTION	PATENT NUMBER	ISSUE DATE
Thornton, Benjamin F.	Apparatus for Automatically Transmitting Messages Over a Telephone Line	1,843,849	February 2, 1932
Thornton, Benjamin F., et al.	Underarm Perspiration Pad	2,911,647	November 10, 1959
Thurman, John S.	Vehicle Motion Signalling System	4,594,574	June 10, 1986
Todd, Melvin I., et al.	Hoodliner	5,164,254	November 17, 1992
Toland, Mary H.	Float-Operated Circuit Closer	1,339,239	May 4, 1920
Toliver, George	Propeller for Vessels	451,086	April 28, 1891
Tolliver, Peter M.	Corona Generating Device	3,965,400	June 22, 1976
Tolliver, Peter M.	Lateral View Extender Device	4,493,538	January 15, 1985
Tolliver, Peter M.	Lawn Rake with Debris Pile Capability	5,303,536	April 19, 1994
Toomey, Richard E. S., et al.	Airplane Appliance to Prevent Ice Formation	1,749,858	March 11, 1930
Truedell, Brenda A., et al.	2-N-Acylated and 2-N-Alkylated Derivatives and Process	4,424,344	January 3, 1984
Truedell, Brenda A., et al.	1-N-Acylated and 1-N-Alkylated Derivatives and Process	4,424,345	January 3, 1984
Truedell, Brenda A., et al.	1-N-Acylated and 1-N-Alkylated Derivatives	4,468,512	August 28, 1984
Truedell, Brenda A., et al.	2'-N-Acylated and 2'-N-Alkylated Derivatives	4,468,513	August 28, 1984
Truesdale, Carlton, et al.	Increasing the Retention of GeO.sub.2 during Production of Glass Articles	5,641,333	June 24, 1997
Tucker, Cleveland T.	Door Car Starter	4,291,653	September 29, 1981
Turner, Albert Walter	Lever Assemblies for Augmenting Prime Mover Power	4,113,047	September 12, 1978
Turner, Allen H., et al.	Electrostatic Paint System	3,017,115	January 16, 1962
Turner, Allen H., et al.	Electrostatic Painting	3,054,697	September 18, 1962
Turner, Allen H., et al.	Electrodeposition Process and Apparatus	3,399,126	August 27, 1968
Turner, Allen H., et al.	Electron Discharge Control	3,418,155	December 24, 1968
Turner, Allen H.	Electron Induced Deposition of Organic Coatings	3,462,292	August 19, 1969
Turner, Collatius, et al.	Alarm for Boilers	566,612	August 25, 1896
Turner, Collatius, et al.	Steam Cage	566,613	August 25, 1896
Turner, Collatius, et al.	Alarm for Water Containing Vessels	598,572	February 8, 1898

Name	Title	Patent No.	Date
Turner, Cyril	Sloped Gutter Assembly	5,678,359	October 21, 1997
Turner, George W.	Spring Motor for Fans	1,214,848	February 6, 1917
Turner, Madeline M.	Fruit Press	1,180,959	April 25, 1916
Turner, Posie C.	Compact Foldable Bootjack with Positive Locking Device	4,226,346	October 7, 1980
Turner, Ronald Leon	Food Container	6,269,964	August 7, 2001
Turner, Willie L.	De-ending Shears	4,428,119	January 31, 1984
Turpin, Robert A., Jr., et al.	Odor-Reducing, Nutrient-Enhancing Composition	5,574,093	November 12, 1996
Valdes, Mario A.	Pipeable Gelled Food and Ethyl Alcohol Beverages	5,019,414	May 28, 1991
Vincent, Simon	Woodworking Machine	1,361,295	December 7, 1920
Wade, William L., Jr.	Method of Making Magnetic Ferrite Films	3,096,206	July 2, 1963
Wade, William L., Jr., et al.	Method of Coating a Substrate with Magnetic Ferrite Film	3,197,334	July 27, 1965
Wade, William L., Jr., et al.	Method of Making a Porous Carbon Cathode, a Porous Carbon Cathode so made, and Electrochemical Cell	4,514,478	April 30, 1985
Wade, William L., Jr., et al.	Method of Pretreating Carbon Black Powder	4,526,881	July 2, 1985
Wade, William L., Jr., et al.	Method of Pretreating Carbon Black Powder	4,543,305	September 24, 1985
Wade, William L., Jr., et al.	High Capacity Inorganic Oxyhalide Electrochemical Cell	4,560,628	December 24, 1985
Wade, William L., Jr., et al.	Method of Washing Solids with Liquified Gases	4,816,080	March 28, 1989
Walker, M. Lucius, Jr., et al.	Laminar Fluid NOR Element	3,478,764	November 18, 1969
Walker, Moses Fleetwood	Cartridge	458,026	August 18, 1891
Walker, Moses Fleetwood	Film End Fastener for Motion Picture Film Reels	1,328,408	January 20, 1920
Walker, Moses Fleetwood	Motion Picture Film Reel	1,348,813	July 6, 1920
Walker, Moses Fleetwood	Alarm for Motion Picture Film Reel	1,348,609	August 3, 1920
Walker, Peter	Machine for Cleaning Seed Cotton	577,153	February 16, 1897
Walker, Peter	Bait Holder	600,241	March 8, 1898
Waller, Joseph W.	Shoemaker's Cabinet or Bench	224,253	February 3, 1880
Warde, Cardinal, et al.	Microchannel Spatial Light Modulator	4,481,531	November 6, 1984
Warde, Cardinal, et al.	Charge Transfer Signal Processor	4,794,296	December 27, 1988

PATENTEE	TITLE OF INVENTION	PATENT NUMBER	ISSUE DATE
Warde, Cardinal, et al.	Completely Cross-Talk Free High Speed Resolution 2-D Bistable Light Modulation	4,800,263	January 24, 1989
Warde, Cardinal, et al.	Low-Cost Substantially Cross-Talk Free High Spatial Resolution 2-D Bistable Light Modulator	4,822,993	April 18, 1989
Warde, Cardinal, et al.	High Spatial Resolution 2-D Bistable Light Modulator	4,851,659	July 25, 1989
Warde, Cardinal, et al.	Charge Transfer Signal Processor and Charge Transfer, Feedthrough Plate Fabrication Assembly and Method	4,863,759	September 5, 1989
Warner, Isiah M., et al.	Degassing Process and Apparatus for Removal of Oxygen	4,516,984	May 14, 1985
Warren, Richard	Display Rack	1,619,900	March 8, 1927
Washington, Andrew D.	Shoe Horn	728,788	May 19, 1903
Washington, Wade	Corn Husking Machine	283,173	August 14, 1883
Watkins, Isaac	Scrubbing Frame	437,849	October 7, 1890
Watts, Julius R.	Bracket for Miner's Lamp	493,137	March 7, 1893
Watts, Orlando	Stencil Cutting Machine	1,305,847	June 3, 1919
Weatherby, Dennis W.	Automatic Dishwasher Detergent Composition	4,714,562	December 22, 1987
Weaver, Rufus J.	Stairclimbing Wheelchair	3,411,598	November 19, 1968
Webb, Henry C.	Clearing Plow	1,226,425	May 15, 1917
Weir, Charles E.	High-Pressure Optical Cell	3,079,505	February 26, 1963
Weir, Charles E.	High-Pressure Optical Cell for Raman Spectrography	3,610,757	October 5, 1971
West, Edward H.	Weather Shield	632,385	September 5, 1899
West, James E., et al.	Electroacoustic Transducer	3,118,022	January 14, 1964
West, James E., et al.	Electrostatic Transducer	3,118,979	January 21, 1964
West, James E., et al.	Method of Measuring the Volume Resistivity of Thin, Solid Dielectric Material	3,496,461	February 17, 1970
West, James E., et al.	Directional Microphone	3,573,399	April 6, 1971
West, James E., et al.	Directional Microphone	3,573,400	April 6, 1971

West, James E., et al.	3,644,605	February 22, 1972	Method of Producing Permanent Electret Charges in Dielectric Materials
West, James E., et al.	3,652,932	March 28, 1972	Method and Apparatus for Measurement of Surface Charge of an Electret
West, James E., et al.	3,668,417	June 6, 1972	Touch-Sensitive Switch Employing Electret Foil
West, James E., et al.	3,705,312	December 5, 1972	Preparation of Electret Transducer Elements
West, James E., et al.	3,711,941	January 23, 1973	Fabrication of Electret Transducer Elements
West, James E., et al.	3,715,500	February 6, 1973	Unidirectional Microphones
West, James E., et al.	3,750,149	July 31, 1973	Multi-unit Electret Touch Selector
West, James E., et al.	3,930,066	December 30, 1975	Technique for Fabrication of Foil Electret
West, James E., et al.	3,945,112	March 23, 1976	Technique for Fabrication of Foil Electret
West, James E., et al.	4,008,376	February 15, 1977	Loudspeaking Teleconferencing Circuit
West, James E.	4,248,808	February 3, 1981	Technique for Removing Surface and Volume Charges
West, James E., et al.	4,429,189	January 31, 1984	Electret Transducer with a Selectively Metalized Backplate
West, James E., et al.	4,429,191	January 31, 1984	Electret Transducer with Variably Charged Electret Foil
West, James E., et al.	4,429,192	January 31, 1984	Electret Transducer with Variable Electret Foil Thickness
West, James E., et al.	4,429,193	January 31, 1984	Electret Transducer with Variable Effective Air Gap
West, James E., et al.	4,434,327	February 28, 1984	Electret Transducer with Variable Actual Air Gap
West, James E., et al.	4,524,247	June 18, 1985	Integrated Electroacoustic Transducer with Built-in Bias
West, James E., et al.	4,598,590	July 8, 1986	Electret Transducer for Blood Pressure Measurement
West, James E., et al.	4,612,145	September 16, 1986	Method for Producing Electret-Containing Devices
West, James E., et al.	4,675,906	June 23, 1987	Second Order Toroidal Microphone
West, James E., et al.	4,742,548	May 3, 1988	Unidirectional Second Order Gradient Microphone
West, James E., et al.	4,802,227	January 31, 1989	Noise Reduction Processing Arrangement for Microphone Arrays
West, James E., et al.	4,965,775	October 23, 1990	Image Derived Directional Microphones
West, James E., et al.	5,093,570	March 3, 1992	Discriminating Electret Radioactivity Detector System and Method for Measuring Radon Concentration
West, James E., et al.	5,303,307	April 12, 1994	Adjustable Filter for Differential Microphones
West, James E., et al.	5,388,163	February 3, 1995	Electret Transducer Array and Fabrication Technique

PATENTEE	TITLE OF INVENTION	PATENT NUMBER	ISSUE DATE
West, James E., et al.	Adjustable Filter for Differential Microphones	5,586,191	December 17, 1996
West, John W.	Improvement in Wagons	108,419	October 18, 1870
West, Thomas P.	Clasp for Shoes or Other Articles	320,104	June 16, 1885
West, Willis H.	Window Ventilator	1,209,366	December 19, 1916
White, Charles Fred	Timing Device	1,018,799	February 27, 1912
White, Daniel L.	Extension Steps for Cars	574,969	January 12, 1897
White, John T.	Lemon Squeezer	572,849	December 8, 1896
Wicks, Jerome L.	Patio Door and Window Guard System	4,325,203	April 20, 1982
Wicks, Jerome L., et al.	Door Security Device	4,601,503	July 22, 1986
Wiggins, Reatha L.	Plurality of Aspirators	3,430,628	March 4, 1969
Willard, John Wesley, Sr.	Method of Washing Soiled Culinary Articles	3,874,927	April 1, 1975
Willard, John Wesley, Sr.	Method of Cleaning Glass Windows and Mirrors	3,915,738	October 28, 1975
Willard, John Wesley, Sr.	Method of Washing Textile Materials	3,923,456	December 2, 1975
Willard, John Wesley, Sr.	Method of Growing Plants in Soil	4,067,712	January 10, 1978
Willard, John Wesley, Sr.	Method of Improving the Fertility of Soil and the Soil thus Prepared	4,067,713	January 10, 1978
Willard, John Wesley, Sr.	Method of Watering Plants and/or Feeding Nutrients to Plants	4,067,714	January 10, 1978
Willard, John Wesley, Sr.	Method of Transplanting Plants	4,067,715	January 10, 1978
Williams, Carter	Canopy Frame	468,280	February 2, 1892
Williams, Eugene, Sr.	Audiovisual Interview Portfolio	4,255,872	March 17, 1981
Williams, Isaac C.	Fire Place	315,367	April 7, 1885
Williams, James P.	Pillow Sham Holder	634,784	October 10, 1899
Williams, Louise H.	Collapsible Receptacle	2,405,627	August 13, 1946
Williams, Paul E.	Helicopter	3,065,933	November 27, 1962
Williams, Philip B.	Electromagnetic Electric Railway Track Switch	648,092	April 24, 1900

Name	Invention	Number	Date
Williams, Philip B.	Electrically Controlled and Operated Railway Switch	666,080	January 15, 1901
Williams, Robert	Method and Apparatus for Disinfecting Objects	5,171,523	December 15, 1992
Williamson, Michael A., et al.	Accelerator Combinations for Anaerobic Polymerization	4,631,325	December 23, 1986
Williamson, Samuel R., et al.	Acoustic Light Deflection Cells	3,614,204	October 19, 1971
Willis, Lovell J.	Portable Minature Waterfall	3,901,439	August 26, 1975
Wilson, Donald Claude	Flying Saucer Toy	4,228,616	October 21, 1980
Winn, Frank	Direct Acting Steam Engine	394,047	December 4, 1888
Winters, Joseph R.	Fire Escape Ladder	203,517	May 7, 1878
Winters, Joseph R.	Improvement in Fire Escape Ladders	214,224	April 8, 1879
Wise, John D.	Driverless Lawn Mower	3,415,335	December 10, 1968
Wise, John D.	Driverless Lawn Mower	3,566,988	March 2, 1971
Wise, John D.	Automatic House Painter	3,611,983	October 12, 1971
Wise, John D.	Automatic House Painter	3,847,112	November 12, 1974
Wise, John D.	Envelope Contents Removal	4,866,915	September 19, 1989
Wood, Francis J.	Potato Digger	537,953	April 23, 1895
Woodard, Dudley G.	Vinylidene Chloride Copolymer Latices and Products	3,235,525	February 15, 1966
Woodard, Dudley G.	Preparation of Water Soluble Acrylic Copolymers	3,574,175	April 6, 1971
Woodard, Dudley G., et al.	Polyvinylidene Chloride Latex and Process	3,317,449	May 2, 1967
Woodard, Dudley G.	Stringed Instruments with Improved Strings due to Irradiation and Process	3,842,705	October 22, 1974
Woodard, Dudley G.	Rapidly Crystallizing Vinylidene Chloride-Acrylonitrile Copolymer	3,642,735	February 15, 1972
Woods, Granville T.	Steam Boiler Furnace	299,894	June 3, 1884
Woods, Granville T.	Telephone Transmitter	308,876	December 2, 1884
Woods, Granville T.	Apparatus for Transmission of Messages by Electricity	315,368	April 7, 1885
Woods, Granville T.	Relay Instrument	364,619	June 7, 1887
Woods, Granville T.	Polarized Relay	366,193	July 5, 1887
Woods, Granville T.	Electromechanical Brake	368,265	August 16, 1887
Woods, Granville T.	Telephone System and Apparatus	371,241	October 11, 1887

PATENTEE	TITLE OF INVENTION	PATENT NUMBER	ISSUE DATE
Woods, Granville T.	Electromagnetic Brake Apparatus	371,655	October 18, 1887
Woods, Granville T.	Railway Telegraphy	373,383	November 15, 1887
Woods, Granville T.	Induction Telegraph System	373,915	November 29, 1887
Woods, Granville T.	Overhead Conducting System for Electric Railway	383,844	May 29, 1888
Woods, Granville T.	Electromotive Railway System	385,034	June 26, 1888
Woods, Granville T.	Tunnel Construction for Electric Railway	386,282	July 17, 1888
Woods, Granville T.	Galvanic Battery	387,839	August 14, 1888
Woods, Granville T.	Railway Telegraphy	388,803	August 28, 1888
Woods, Granville T.	Automatic Safety Cut-out for Electric Circuits	395,533	January 1, 1889
Woods, Granville T.	Electric Railway System	463,020	November 10, 1891
Woods, Granville T.	Electric Railway Conduit	509,065	November 21, 1893
Woods, Granville T.	System of Electrical Distribution	569,443	October 13, 1896
Woods, Granville T.	Amusement Apparatus	639,692	December 19, 1899
Woods, Granville T.	Incubator	656,760	August 28, 1900
Woods, Granville T.	Electric Railway	667,110	January 29, 1901
Woods, Granville T.	Electric Railway System	678,086	July 9, 1901
Woods, Granville T.	Regulating and Controlling Electrical Translating Device	681,768	September 3, 1901
Woods, Granville T.	Electric Railway	687,098	November 19, 1901
Woods, Granville T.	Automatic Air Brake	701,981	June 10, 1902
Woods, Granville T.	Electric Railway System	718,183	January 13, 1903
Woods, Granville T.	Electric Railway	729,481	May 26, 1903
Woods, Granville T. and Lyates	Railway Brake Apparatus	755,825	March 29, 1904
Woods, Granville T. and Lyates	Railway Brake Apparatus	795,243	July 18, 1905
Woods, Granville T. and Lyates	Safety Apparatus for Railways	833,193	October 16, 1906
Woods, Granville T. and Lyates	Safety Apparatus for Railways	837,022	November 27, 1906
Woods, Granville T. and Lyates	Vehicle Controlling Apparatus	867,180	September 24, 1907
Wormley, James	Life-Saving Apparatus	242,091	May 24, 1881

NOTES

The noncited characterization of an innovation is taken from the patent grant itself. Appendix II provides the listing of inventor, invention, patent number, and date.

PREFACE

1. Martin Luther King, "Paul's Letter to American Christians," in *Strength to Love* (New York: Harper and Row, 1963), pp. 137–138.

2. Lawrence Muhammad, "Slave Left His Mark on History and Cave," *Courier-Journal* [Louisville, Kentucky], February 22, 1996, p. 1.

3. See Martin Williams, "Scott Joplin, the Ragtime King, Rules Once More," *Smithsonian*, October 1974, pp. 108, 109, 114, 116–118.

4. See James M. Trotter, *Music and Some Highly Musical People* (Boston: 1878; reprint, Chicago: Afro-American Press, 1969), pp. 114–130; Giles B. Jackson and D. Webster Davis, *The Industrial History of the Negro Race of the United States* (Richmond, Va.: Giles B. Jackson, 1908), p. 129; and Benjamin Verdery, "Contemporary Classical, Justin Holland, Classical Pioneer," *Guitar Player*, May 1989, p. 112.

5. R. R. Wright, "The Negro as an Inventor," *A.M.E. Church Review* 2, no. 14 (April 1886): 397.

6. Rayford W. Logan and Michael R. Winston, eds., *Dictionary of American Negro Biography* (New York: W. W. Norton & Company, 1982), pp. 12–13.

7. Paul E. Sluby, Sr., *History of the Columbian Harmony Society and of Harmony Cemetery* (Washington, D.C.: privately printed, revised 2001), p. 81. By the middle of the twentieth century, nearly all black beneficial organizations faded. In 1863 at Philadelphia, Pennsylvania, Americans of African descent established the fraternal order known as the General Grand Accepted Order of Brothers and Sisters of Love and Charity. Although some branches became powerful entities for prudence, relief and community improvement in the early 1900s, the order vanished.

8. W. P. Burrell and D. E. Johnson, Sr., *Twenty-Five Years History of the Grand*

Fountain of the United Order of True Reformers, 1881–1905 (Richmond, Va.: Grand Fountain of United Order of True Reformers, 1909), passim.

9. Logan and Winston, *Dictionary of American Negro Biography*, pp. 626–627. See also Jackson and Davis, *Industrial History*, p. 135, and Patricia Carter Ives, "Richmond's Black Heritage," *Richmond Afro-American*, February 20, 1982, p. 23.

10. See Frederick E. Drinker, *Booker T. Washington* (Philadelphia: National Publishing Co., 1915), p. 223; Monroe N. Work, ed., *Negro Year Book, 1918–1919* (Tuskegee, Ala.: Negro Year Book Publishing Company, 1919), p. 250. Black women similarly established an association and named it the Colored Young Women's Christian Association. Its roots began in Philadelphia in the early 1870s, but the women did not form a national board until 1907. Appointed to the board, Mrs. William A. Hunton founded student and city alliances in Brooklyn, New York; Baltimore, Maryland; and Washington, D.C. In one entry in the *Negro Year Book, 1918–1919*, at "February 6, 1800," is the unusual mention for schooling of blacks as follows: "Robert Pleasants, of Henrico County, Virginia, left by will, a school house and 350 acres of land . . . to be used 'forever or so long as the Monthly Meeting of Friends in that county may think it necessary for the benefit of the children and descendants of those who have been emancipated by me, or other black children whom they think proper to admit.' " See Carter G. Woodson and Charles H. Wesley, *The Negro in our History* (Washington, D.C.: Associated Publishers, 1972), pp. 562–565, for a discussion of education for African Americans.

11. *The Proceedings of the National Negro Business League, Boston, 1900* (Boston: J. R. Hamm, 1901), introduction. The Southern Aid Life Insurance Company, the oldest black-owned life insurance company in the country, founded in 1893, presently has millions of dollars in assets. As an outgrowth of the National Benefit Society, the Virginia Mutual Benefit Life Insurance Company began with $12,500 in assets and is now a top African American insurance company with a huge staff that maintains district offices in Virginia and in Washington, D.C.

12. Burrell and Johnson, *Twenty-Five Years History*, p. 96; Patricia Carter Ives, "Jackson Ward . . . Citadel of Black Business," *Richmond Afro-American*, February 13, 1982, p. 33.

13. Charles M. Christian, *Black Saga: The African American Experience, a Chronology* (Washington D.C.: Civitas Counterpoint 1995), p. 349.

14. Logan and Winston, *Dictionary of American Negro Biography*, 568.

15. Carter G. Woodson, *Negro Makers of History* (Washington, D.C.: Associated Publishers, 1928), p. 73, and Work, *Negro Year Book, 1918–1919*, p. 422.

16. See Woodson, *Negro Makers of History*, pp. 167–168. The pharmacies were the first black business enterprises in the community; see Drinker, *Booker T. Washington*, p. 202.

17. *Bulletin*, Medico-Chirurgical Society of the District of Columbia, January 1949.

18. Leonard Medical School of Shaw University in Raleigh, North Carolina, began in 1882, Louisville National Medical School in Kentucky opened in 1887, and Flint Goodrich Medical School in New Orleans originated in 1889. In Tennessee, the Knoxville Medical School opened its doors in 1895. Five years later, the University of West Tennessee set up a medical facility, and around 1902 in the same state, the Chattanooga National Medical College was founded. Lincoln University in Pennsylvania opened a medical school in 1870, but closed it in 1876.

Virginia Union University at Richmond toyed with the notion of establishing a medical department before 1920, but abandoned the idea due to many problems.

INTRODUCTION

1. *The Story of the United States Patent Office* (Washington, D.C.: Pharmaceutical Manufacturers Association with the cooperation of the U.S. Department of Commerce, 1965), pp. 1–3, 6.

2. Kelly Miller, "The Negro 'Stephen Foster,' " *Etude*, July 1939, p. 432. See also Eileen Southern, *The Music of Black Americans: A History* (New York: W. W. Norton & Company, 1971), pp. 265–266, Lewis Horace Bland, "James Allen Bland, Negro Composer," master's thesis submitted to the Graduate Division, Howard University, June 1968, passim; Washington, D.C., *Boyd's Directory of the District of Columbia*, 1865–1882.

3. Miller, *Etude*, p. 432.

4. Michael Walsh, "Henry Edwin Baker, Jr., a Contextual Biography," paper, Miami University, Oxford, Ohio, March 31, 1997; Andrew F. Hilyer, *The Twentieth Century Union League Directory* (Washington, D.C., January 1901), p. 30; and Herbert Jones, Sr., former patent office employee, interview with author, October 8, 1984.

5. Walsh, "Henry Edwin Baker, Jr."

6. Ibid.

1: ONCE UPON A TIME

1. Ali A. Mazrui, *The Africans* (Boston: Little Brown & Company, 1986), p. 4.

2. See C. R. Gibbs, *Black Inventors from Africa to America* (Silver Spring, Md.: Three Dimensional Publishing Company, 1995), pp. 10–57. Also see Mazrui, *Africans*, pp. 42–49; and Anthony T. Browder, *Nile Valley Contributions to Civilization* (Washington, D.C.: Institute of Karmic Guidance, 1992), passim.

3. Ivan Van Sertima, *Blacks in Science: Ancient and Modern* (London: Transaction Books, 1983), pp. 5–6.

4. Gibbs, *Black Inventors*, pp. 39, 55; Mazrui, *Africans*, p. 38.

5. Gibbs, *Black Inventors*, p. 56.

6. See Ali A. Mazrui and Toby K. Levine, *The Africans: The Reader* (New York: Praeger, 1986), passim; and J(oel) A. Rogers, *Africa's Gift to America* (St. Petersburg, Fla.: Helga M. Rogers, 1961), pp. 6–25.

7. Mazrui, *Africans*, p. 95.

8. Woodson and Wesley, *Negro in Our History*, pp. 26–27.

9. Portia James, *The Real McCoy* (Washington, D.C.: Smithsonian Institution, 1989), p. 17.

10. Ibid.

2: EARLY CREATIVE MINDS

1. Logan and Winston, *Dictionary of American Negro Biography*, p. 22.

2. Ibid., pp. 23–24.

3. See James, *Real McCoy*, pp. 33–35.

4. Henry E. Baker, *The Colored Inventor* (New York: Crisis Publishing Co., 1913), p. 6.

5. Ibid. See also James, *Real McCoy*, pp. 33–34; Logan and Winston, *Dictionary of American Negro Biography*, pp. 234–235.

6. Personal knowledge of author; James, *Real McCoy*, pp. 35–36; Logan and Winston, *Dictionary of American Negro Biography*, pp. 582–583; and Robert C. Hayden, *Eight Black American Inventors* (Reading, Mass.: Addison-Wesley, 1972), pp. 32–43.

7. James, *Real McCoy*, pp. 39–40; Gibbs, *Black Inventors*, p. 85.

8. James, *Real McCoy*, pp. 54–55; Kenneth W. Dobyns, *The Patent Office Pony: A History of the Early Patent Office* (Fredericksburg, Va.: Sergeant Kirkland's Museum and Historical Society, 1994), p. 36.

9. Dobyns, *Patent Office Pony*, p. 36. See also John E. Ehrenhard and Mary R. Bullard, *Stafford Plantation Cumberland Island National Seashore, Georgia* (Tallahassee, Fla.: National Park Service, 1979), passim.

10. Woodson and Wesley, *Negro in Our History*, p. 230.

11. Dobyns, *Patent Office Pony*, p. 37. See also *The 1999 National Inventors Hall of Fame Black Book*, 27th ed. (Washington, D.C.: U.S. Department of Commerce, Patent and Trademark Office, 1999), p. 5. A similar discussion of the claim that a black was principally involved with Cyrus McCormick's mechanical reaper, a grain harvester built in Virginia in 1831, is centered around his slave Jo Anderson. While McCormick is given patent credit in 1834 for the invention, Anderson is said to have given him "valuable assistance" during its construction. A picture of McCormick and Anderson is in Rogers, *Africa's Gift to America*, p. 227.

12. S. N. Hawks, Jr., *Principles of Flue-Cured Tobacco Production* (Raleigh, N.C.: Author, 1970), pp. 4–5.

13. Nannie May Tilley, *The Bright Tobacco Industry, 1860–1929* (Manchester, N.H.: Ayer Company Publishers Inc., 1945), pp. 150–151.

14. *Anglo-African*, April 1859, Vol. 1, pp. 126–128. Also see Gibbs, *Black Inventors*, p. 72 and Herbert Aptheker, ed., *A Documentary History of the Negro People in the United States* (New York: Citadel, 1951), pp. 420–422.

15. Rogers, *Africa's Gift to America*, pp. 228, 230.

16. *Digest of Patents, United States, 1770–1839*, U.S. Patent and Trademark Office, index, p. 469.

17. "Horse Hay Rake," *Farmer's Cabinet* 3 (February 15, 1839): 226. See also "Horse Rake," *Scientific American* 3, no. 8 (November 13, 1847): 59.

18. "Genius of the Colored Man," *New Ideas, Philadelphia*, September 1895, p. 31.

19. Logan and Winston, *Dictionary of American Negro Biography*, pp. 525–527. See also Louis Haber, *Black Pioneers of Science and Invention* (New York: Harcourt, Brace & World, 1970) pp. 15–19.

20. Logan and Winston, *Dictionary of American Negro Biography*, pp. 525–527.

21. William H. Quick, *Negro Stars in All Ages of the World* (Henderson, N.C.: D. E. Aycock, 1890), pp. 240–241.

22. Dobyns, *Patent Office Pony*, p. 152.

23. J. Hubley Ashton, ed., *Official Opinions of the Attorneys General of the United States Advising the President and Heads of Departments in Relation to Their Official Duties*, vol. 9 (Washington, D.C.: W. H. & O. H. Morrison, 1866), pp. 171–172; John Boyle,

"Patents and Civil Rights in 1857–8," *Journal of the Patent Office Society* 42 (1960): 789.

24. Boyle, "Patents and Civil Rights," pp. 792–794.

25. *Acts and Resolutions of the Second Session of the Provisional Congress of the Confederate States, 1861* (Montgomery, Ala.: Wimbush & Co., 1862), p. 83; James M. Matthews, ed., *Statutes at Large of the Confederate States of America*, July 1861, p. 54.

26. Dorothy Cowser Yancy, "The Stuart Double Plow and Double Scraper: The Invention of a Slave," *Journal of Negro History* 69 (1984): 48–51.

27. Janet Sharp Hermann, *The Pursuit of a Dream* (New York: Oxford University Press, 1981), pp. 17–18; Henry E. Baker, "Inventions of the Negro," *Colored American*, November 14, 1903, p. 8; and "The Negro in the Field of Invention," *Journal of Negro History* 2 (1917): 21–36.

28. "Western Sanitary Fair, An Important Invention," *Cincinnati Daily Gazette*, December 25, 1863, p. 3.

29. Letter to the Honorable W. E. Simonds from patent solicitor James H. Layman, of Cincinnati, Ohio, Room H, Opera House, April 23, 1892, received at the Office of Commissioner of Patents, April 26, 1892, Box 120, Files of Commissioner.

30. See James, *Real McCoy*, p. 76.

31. Max W. Tucker, "The Patent Office of the Confederacy," *Journal of the Patent Office Society* 3 (1920–1921): 596–600.

32. Ibid. See also Henry Putney Beers, *Guide to the Archives of the Government of the Confederate States of America* (Washington, D.C.: National Archives, 1968), pp. 402–403.

3: UNDER HIS OWN PERSONAGE: DUTIFULLY LOGGED

1. Haber, *Black Pioneers*, pp. 32–33; Logan and Winston, *Dictionary of American Negro Biography*, p. 429; Woodson, *Negro Makers of History*, p. 305; and Patricia Carter Ives, *Creativity and Inventions: The Genius of Afro-Americans and Women in the United States, and Their Patents* (Arlington, Va.: Research Unlimited, 1987). Mention is made of Matzeliger's inventions in numerous publications, for example, in Baker, *Colored Inventor*, G. F. Richings, *Evidences of Progress among Colored People* (Philadelphia: George S. Ferguson Co., 1905), and Jackson and Davis, *Industrial History*. Additionally, current acknowledgments cite Matzeliger's patents.

2. Vital records, state of Massachusetts.

3. Asa J. Davis, "The Two Autobiographical Fragments of George W. Latimer," *Journal of the Afro-American Historical and Genealogical Society* 1 (summer 1930): 3–18; Winifred Latimer Norman and Lily Patterson, *Lewis Latimer* (New York: Chelsea House, 1994), pp. 19–27.

4. Haber, *Black Pioneers*, pp. 49–59. See also Glennette Tilley Turner, *Lewis Howard Latimer* (Englewood Cliffs, N.J.: Silver Burdett Press, 1991), and Janet M. Schneider and Bayla Singer, eds., *Blueprint for Change: The Life and Times of Lewis H. Latimer* (New York: Queens Borough Public Library, 1995).

5. Turner, *Lewis Howard Latimer*, p. 30.

6. Haber, *Black Pioneers*, pp. 57–59; "Lewis H. Latimer, Edison's Assistant, Dies at Age of 81," [New York] *Amsterdam News*, December 19, 1928.

7. See Harber, *Black Pioneers*, p. 59, and Turner, *Lewis Howard Latimer*, p. 106.

8. Samuel R. Scottron, "Manufacturing Household Articles," *Colored American Magazine*, December 1906, pp. 621–624.

9. Personal interview with Binga's descendant Anthony J. Binga of Richmond, Virginia, 1980.

10. Paul E. Sluby, Sr., "History of the Columbian Harmony Society," speech by Sluby as secretary of the society at memorial dedication and grave plaque unveiling for Osborne Perry Anderson, November 11, 2000, National Harmony Memorial Park, Largo, Maryland.

11. *Boyd's Directory of the District of Columbia*, 1872.

12. Ibid., 1878; interment records, Columbian Harmony Cemetery, Washington, D.C.

13. *Washington* [D.C.] *Star*, September 2, 1918.

14. Sluby, *History of the Columbian Harmony Society and of Harmony Cemetery*, p. 81.

15. *Boyd's*, 1876, and Sluby and Wormley, *History of the Columbian Harmony Society*, p. 17.

16. *Beyond the Fireworks of 76* [second work] ([Washington, D.C.]: Prepared by the Afro-American Bicentennial Corporation, circa 1972), pp. 173–183.

17. Stanton L. Wormley, Sr., Stanton L. Wormley, Jr., and Paul E. Sluby, Sr., compilers, *Wormeley-Wormley, ca. 1160–1991* (Washington, D.C.: Columbian Harmony Society, 1991), pp. 76–78.

18. Interment records, Columbian Harmony Cemetery.

19. Kelly Miller, "Obituary: Professor Hugh M. Browne," *Howard University Record*, 18, 1923–1924, p. 133.

20. Baker, *Colored Inventor*, p. 9; *Boyd's*, 1904.

21. "Negroes of Brains," *Cleveland Gazette*, November 26, 1892, p. 1. See also Paul E. Sluby, *A Lineal Perspective of John Anderson Lankford and Bishop Henry McNeal Turner*, copyright 1995 by Sara (Johnson) Bumbary, p. 13.

22. Quick, *Negro Stars*, pp. 240–242.

23. Richings, *Evidences of Progress among Colored People*, pp. 342–344.

24. Frank W. Porter III, "John Widgeon: Naturalist, Curator, and Philosopher," *Maryland Historical Magazine* 79 (winter 1994): 325–331; *Baltimore Sun*, November 15, 1908, p. 13; *Baltimore Evening Sun*, July 28, 1935, and March 8, 1937, p. 32.

25. *Baltimore Sun*, p. 13.

26. Gibbs, *Black Inventors*, p. 95; see also Richings, *Evidences of Progress among Colored People*, pp. 344–347.

27. James, *Real McCoy*, p. 87.

28. Baker, *Colored Inventor*, p. 9; personal knowledge of author; private papers in author's possession.

29. *Colored American*, November 28, 1903, p. 8.

30. Kelly Miller and Joseph R. Gay, "The Coming Men of the Race," *Progress and Achievements of the Colored People* (Washington, D.C.: Austin Jenkins Co., [1917]), p. 23.

31. Information obtained from certified genealogist Paul E. Sluby, Sr.

32. J. L. Nichols and William H. Crogman, *Progress of a Race* (1920; reprint, New York: Arno Press, 1969), p. 247.

33. "Fleet Walker Scores Big," *Cleveland Gazette*, July 2, 1921.

34. Jerry Malloy, "Moses Fleetwood Walker, Out at Home," *The National Pastime* (Cooperstown, N.Y.: Society for American Baseball Research, 1983), p. 19.

4: PROGRESSIVE ACHIEVEMENT: EXPOSING EBONY TALENT

1. Gibbs, *Black Inventors*, p. 88.

2. Logan and Winston, *Dictionary of American Negro Biography*, pp. 413–414; Also see Haber, *Black Pioneers*, pp. 35–36; Hayden, *Eight Black American Inventors*; and Ives, *Creativity and Inventions*, p. 44.

3. Logan and Winston, *Dictionary of American Negro Biography*.

4. Ives, *Creativity and Inventions*, p. 44; Haber, *Black Pioneers*, pp. 41–48; Logan and Winston, *Dictionary of American Negro Biography*, pp. 663–665. See also Michael C. Christopher, "Granville T. Woods," *Journal of Black Studies 2* (March 1981): 269–276; and Patricia Carter Sluby, "Minority Inventive Genius: A Look at Spirited American People," *Journal of the Afro-American Historical and Genealogical Society* 11 (spring and summer 1990): 54.

5. Ives, *Creativity and Inventions*, p. 57; Vital records, state of Ohio.

6. Vital records, state of Ohio.

7. Ives, *Creativity and Inventions*, p. 29.

8. A. S. "Doc" Young, "Railroad Show: Recalls Inventive Genius of Robinson, Dammond," *Chicago Defender*, June 25, 1949, p. 20.

9. Patricia Carter Ives, "Some Black Inventors Who Changed the Course of Industries," *Washington Afro-American*, February 25, 1984, p. 17 and February 2, 1985.

10. Young, *Chicago Defender*, p. 20.

11. Jackson and Davis, *Industrial History*, p. 21.

12. Young, *Chicago Defender*, 1949, p. 20.

13. Ibid.

14. Quick, *Negro Stars*, p. 240.

15. Letter from the Honorable B. K. Bruce to the Honorable Marcellus Gardner, March 20, 1885, Department of the Interior, National Archives, New Orleans, Black Inventors, Box 119.

16. Gardner to the Honorable R. G. Dyrenforth, ibid.

17. See brochure, Woodlawn Cemetery Association, Washington, D.C.; interment records, Woodlawn Cemetery, Washington, D.C.

18. Congressman G. W. Murray, *Congressional Record, House*, 53rd Congress, Second Session, August 10, 1894, pp. 8382–8383. Congressman Floyd Flake of New York introduced House Joint Resolution 377 in the House of Representatives, October 15, 1987, designating March 27, 1988, as "National Black American Inventors Day."

19. See D. W. Culp, ed., *Twentieth Century Negro Literature* (1902; reprint, New York: Arno Press, 1969); James, *The Real McCoy*, p. 77.

20. Baker, *Colored Inventor*, p. 9.

21. Ibid., p. 6. See also W. E. Burghardt Du Bois, "The American Negro at Paris," *American Monthly Review of Reviews* 22 (November 1900): 575–577.

22. Baker, *Colored Inventor*, p. 3.

23. Ibid., p. 6.

24. Ibid.

25. Jackson and Davis, *Industrial History*, p. 147.

26. Ibid., p. 196.

5: ONWARD, SOLDIERS OF FORTUNE

1. Haber, *Black Pioneers*, p. 69.

2. Ives, *Creativity and Inventions*, pp. 48, 50.

3. John Hope Franklin, "The Gift of Service," speech delivered at the induction of George Washington Carver into the Hall of Fame for Great Americans at Tuskegee Institute on April 23, 1977.

4. Haber, *Black Pioneers*, pp. 73–85; Ives, *Creativity and Inventions*, pp. 32–35; and Logan and Winston, *Dictionary of American Negro Biography*, pp. 92–95. See also Barry MacKintosh, "George Washington Carver and the Peanut," *American Heritage*, November 1977, pp. 67–72; *George Washington Carver, 1864–1943* (New York: Hall of Fame for Great Americans, 1977).

5. Haber, *Black Pioneers*, pp. 73–85; Ives, *Creativity and Inventions*, 32–35; and Logan and Winston, *Dictionary of American Negro Biography*, pp. 92–95.

6. James W. Butcher Papers, 1910–1949, MS 507, Special Collections, Historical Society of Washington, D.C.

7. Work, *Negro Year Book, 1918–1919*, pp. 7–8.

8. "Bringing Our Unsung Technical Achievers to Light," *National Technical News*, December 1992, pp. 1, 3.

9. Patrica Carter Ives, "Creativity and Inventions," *NSBE News*, September/October 1985, p. 39.

10. Agreement (attested to by John Scudder and Charles R. Drew), Liber Y192, p. 332, Digest of Assignments, U.S. Patent and Trademark Office, p. 201.

11. From letter of Dr. Walter R. Johnson titled "April 1, 1950," dated November 15, 1982. See also "Dr. Drew Killed in Crash," *Washington Afro-American*, April 4, 1950, and Richard Hardwick, *Charles Richard Drew* (New York: Charles Scribner's Sons, 1967).

12. Johnson letter.

13. From telephone conversation with Omohundro's widow, May 10, 2000.

14. From personal interview with author, 1977.

15. "Percy Julian, Chemist, Developer of Cortisone," *Washington Star*, April 21, 1975. See also Ives, *Creativity and Inventions*, pp. 36–39; Haber, *Black Pioneers*, pp. 87–101; Gibbs, *Black Inventors*, p. 161.

16. *Washington Star*.

17. Logan and Winston, *Dictionary of American Negro Biography*, p. 366.

18. Ives, *Creativity and Inventions*, pp. 13–14; Wil Haygood, *King of the Cats: The Life and Times of Adam Clayton Powell, Jr.* (Boston: Houghton Mifflin, 1993), p. 90.

19. From personal papers of inventor.

20. "Johnson to Be Freed," *Cleveland Gazette*, July 2, 1921; Dick Schaap and the Lampman, introductory essays in *Jack Johnson Is a Dandy: Autobiography* (New York: Chelsea House, 1969), passim.

21. Schaap and the Lampman, *Jack Johnson Is a Dandy*, p. 11.

22. "Supreme Court Denies Turner Appeal," *Washington Afro-American*, May 21, 1988.

23. Peter Baker, "At Virginia's Death House, an Eye for an Eye, Face to Face," *Washington Post*, June 3, 1995.

24. Kitta MacPherson, "Turn-Signal 'Inventor' Boosted Posthumously," *Sunday Star-Ledger* [Newark, N.J.], February 22, 1987, p. 40.

25. Jon Hiratsuka, "Woman Claims Suspenders Invented by Lynchburg Man," *News and Daily Advance* [Lynchburg, Va.], July 31, 1983; communication from daughter, Alice Green, August 18, 1998.

26. Marvin Grosswirth, "People in Science: Meredith C. Gourdine," *SciQuest*, April 1982, pp. 22–24; Frank Litsky, "Meredith Gourdine, 69, Athlete and Physicist," *New York Times*, November 24, 1998, p. A29.

27. Nancy Stevens, "C.R. Inventor Predicts Security System Revolution," *Cedar Rapids* [Illinois] *Gazette*, February 20, 1979; Michael Paul Williams, "Was Black Inventor Ripped Off?" *Richmond* [Virginia] *Times-Dispatch*, June 15, 1998, p. B1.

28. J. Richard Everett, "Patents: Potential Economic Benefits for Minority-Run Universities," in *Patent Policy: Government, Academic, and Industry Concepts*, ed. Willard Marcy (Washington, D.C.: American Chemical Society, 1978), pp. 69–77.

6: AMONG WOMEN AND FAMILY

1. Unpublished speech by Maggie Lena Walker, before an assembly, 1909.

2. Charlotte Smith, "Colored Woman Inventor," *Woman Inventor*, April 1890, p. 3, column 2. See also Ives, *Creativity and Inventions*, p. 17.

3. Charlotte Smith, "Ancient and Modern," *Woman Inventor*, April 1890, p. 3, column 3.

4. Mrs. N. F. Mossell, *The Work of the Afro-American Woman* (New York: Oxford University Press, 1894), p. 25.

5. Ibid.

6. Smith, "Colored Woman Inventor," p. 1.

7. Federal Population Enumeration, Twelfth Census of States, New York, 1900.

8. Jeanne Madeline Weimann, *The Fair Women* (Chicago: Academy Chicago, 1981), p. 269.

9. Ann Massa, "Black Women in the 'White City,' " *American Studies* 8 (1974): 336.

10. "A Woman Inventor," *Colored American Magazine*, April 1907, p. 292. See also James, *The Real McCoy*, p. 80.

11. A'Lelia Perry Bundles, *Madame C. J. Walker: Entrepeneur* (New York: Chelsea House, 1991), pp. 19–27. See also Logan and Winston, *Dictionary of American Negro Biography*, pp. 621–622.

12. Bundles, *Madame C. J. Walker: Entrepreneur*, pp. 102–103.

13. Christi Parsons, "63 Years Inventor Glad She Made Waves," *Chicago Tribune*, November 3, 1989.

14. "Banking by the Bible: Business Beat," *Chicago Tribune*, October 27, 1989; Program for Annual Dinner in Honor of the Federal Judiciary, Patent Law Association of Chicago, November 3, 1989; "Inventors," *Women in World History* (New York: Columbia University Press, 2000), vol. 7, pp. 678–680.

15. Interview with relative John Newsome, a former U.S. patent examiner, May 19, 2000.

16. "Woman Inventor Gives France Invalid Feeder," *Norfolk* [Virginia] *Journal and Guide*, 1952; "Woman Invents Invalid Feeder," *Newark* [New Jersey] *Sunday News*, September, ?.

17. Interviews with Patricia Bath 1997–2002; "Cataract Surgery Inventor to Be Feted," *Wave Community Newspapers*, February 14, 1995 pp. A–B; Charles H. Epps, Jr., Davis G. Johnson, and Audrey Vaugn, *African-American Medical Pioneers* (Rockville, Md.: Betz Publishing, 1994), p. 6.

18. "Inventor Makes Good on a Third-Grade Notion," *New York Times*, February 14, 2000, section C, p. 8.

19. Ives, *Creativity and Inventions*, p. 22; Jean F. Blashfield, *Women Inventors* (Minneapolis: Capstone Press, 1996), p. 14. See also Joan O'Sullivan, "The Unsinkable Mildred Smith," *Living Today*, King Features Syndicate, October 20, 1982.

20. Blashfield, *Women Inventors*, p. 15; Obituary, Mildred Austin Smith, distributed at her funeral in August 1993.

21. Telephone interview with John P. Beckley, May 17, 2000.

22. Ibid.

23. "Inventions of the Negro," *Colored American*, November 14, 1903, p. 8; and "Inventions: Devices Designed by Afro-Americans on File at the Nation's Capital," *Cleveland Gazette*, November 28, 1903, p. 1.

24. Federal Population Enumeration 1880; Daniel Smith Lamb, compiler and editor, *Howard University Medical Department, Washington, D.C.* (City of Washington, 1900), p. 235.

25. Letter (autobiography) from Albert W. Turner to author, June 1992.

26. Bruce Watson, "If a = Math and b = Magic, Then a + b = the Algebra Project," *Smithsonian* 26 (February 1996): 114–124; Peter Michelmore, "Bob Moses's Crusade," *Reader's Digest*, March 1995, pp. 107–111. See also Bell Gale Chevigny, "Mississippi Learning: Algebra as Political Curriculum," *Nation*, March 4, 1996, pp. 16–21; and Robert P. Moses, "Remarks on the Struggle for Citizenship and Math/Science Literacy," *Journal of Mathematical Behavior* 13 (1994): 107–111.

7: THE NEW AGE: THE LEADING EDGE OF TECHNOLOGY

1. Christian, *Black Saga*, p. 480.

2. Haber, *Black Pioneers*, pp. 103–111.

3. Vivian Ovelton Sammons, *Blacks in Science and Medicine* (New York: Hampshire Publishing Corp., 1990), p. 109.

4. Carl Spight, "High Technology," *NSBE Journal* 2 (October 1986): 42.

5. See "Mark Dean and Denis Moeller to Be Inducted into the National Inventors Hall of Fame," News Release, Inventure Place, Akron, Ohio, June 16, 1997.

6. Ibid.

7. Van Sertima, *Blacks in Science*, p. 289; interviews of James E. West with author. See *The 1999 National Inventors Hall of Fame Black Book*, 27th ed., p. 149.

8. Interviews of James E. West with author.

9. Van Sertima, *Blacks in Science*, pp. 288–289; "Profile," *NTA Journal*, October 1987, p. 59.

10. "Profile," *NTA Journal*, July 1988, p. 68.

11. Ibid., p. 56.

12. Van Sertima, *Blacks in Science*, p. 228.

13. "Profile," *NTA Journal*, October 1987, p. 66.

14. Ibid., p. 68.

15. Ibid., p. 29.

16. "James C. Letton," *NTA Journal*, spring 1991, p. 29.

17. Ibid.

18. Jay Mathes, "Escaping the Office to Unlock Ideas," *Washington Post*, December 27, 1991; "The Man behind the Curtain (of Water)," *Washington Post*, July 9, 2002, p. C14; and personal interviews of Lonnie Johnson with author, 1992. See also Fred M. B. Amram, *African-American Inventors* (Mankato, Minn.: Capstone Press, 1996), pp. 9–13.

19. "David Gittens: 'Future Link' Aircraft Designer," *Innovator Lives* (circular), Lemelson Center for the Study of Invention and Innovation, National Museum of American History, Smithsonian Institution, 1997.

20. See "Making a Powerful Workstation," *Black Enterprise*, February 1990, p. 112; "Special Effects Wiz," *Ebony*, February 1993, pp. 55–58.

21. "Making a Powerful Workstation," *Black Enterprise*.

22. Personal interviews with inventor Francis S. Bernard.

23. J. Clay Smith, Jr., Introduction in *The Genetic Engineering Revolution: A New Century Reality. Bibliographic Index (1981–1986)* (Washington, D.C.: Howard University School of Law, 1986).

24. "Biochemical Genomics," *Chemical and Engineering News*, November 8, 1999, p. 5.

25. Mark Walters, Melinda Patience, Wendy Leisenring, James Eckman, Paul Scott, William C. Mentzer, Sally C. Davies, Kwaku Oheme-Fremong, Francoise Bernaudin, Dana C. Matthews, Rainer Storb, and Keith N. Sullivan, "Bone Marrow Transplantation for Sickle Cell Disease," *New England Journal of Medicine* 335, no. 6 (August 6, 1996): 369–376.

26. John L. Petersen, *The Road to 2015: Profiles of the Future* (Corte Madera, Calif.: Waite Group Press, 1994), p. 28.

27. Ibid.

28. For general references for this chapter, see *Black Enterprise*, February 1990, December 1995, March 1998, June 1999, and August 2001; *NSBE Journal*, February 1988; *Black Collegian*, January/February 1985; *NTA Journal*, July 1987, October 1987, January 1988, July 1988, summer 1990, summer 1991, and spring 1992; *Ebony*, February 1990, February 1993, and December 1999; and *Emerge*, July/August 1999.

CONCLUSION

1. Letter of Conrad Groves to author, October 15, 1991.

2. Susan Gervasi, "For Teen, It's All a Matter of Time," *Prince George's Journal*, July 12, 2002, pp. A1, A5.

BIBLIOGRAPHY

ABBREVIATIONS

AAM	*Anglo-African Magazine*
AMRR	*American Monthly Review of Reviews*
BE	*Black Enterprise*
JAAHGS	*Journal of the Afro-American Historical and Genealogical Society*
JNH	*Journal of Negro History*
JPOS	*Journal of the Patent Office Society*
MHM	*Maryland Historical Magazine*
NAAHK	*National Afro-American History Kit*
NCQ	*Negro College Quarterly*
NHB	*Negro History Bulletin*
NSBEJ	*National Society of Black Engineers Journal*
TT	*Technology Transfer*

BOOKS AND GENERAL REFERENCES

Adams, Russell L. *Great Negroes, Past and Present.* Chicago: Afro-American Publishing Co., 1969.

Alexander, Fred M. *Education for the Needs of the Negro in Virginia.* Washington, D.C.: Southern Education Foundation, 1943.

Amram, Fred M. B. *African-American Inventors.* Mankato, Minn.: Capstone Press, 1996.

Baker, Henry Edwin. *The Colored Inventor: A Record of Fifty Years.* New York: Crisis Publishing Company, 1913.

Balsam, M. S., and Edward Sagarin. *Cosmetics, Science, and Technology.* New York: Wiley-Interscience, 1957.

Becoat, Bill. *Dream Peddler: The Story of an Entrepreneur.* St. Louis, Mo.: Fokl Power/ Publishers, 1995.

Bennett, Lerone, Jr. *Before the Mayflower.* Chicago: Johnson Publishing Company, 1962.

Blashfield, Jean F. *Women Inventors*. Minneapolis: Capstone Press, 1996.

Bundles, A'Lelia Perry. *Madam C. J. Walker, Entrepreneur*. New York: Chelsea House, 1991.

Burt, McKinley, Jr. *Black Inventors of America*. Portland, Oreg.: National Book Company, 1989.

Carwell, Hattie. *Blacks in Science*. Hicksville, N.Y.: Exposition Press, 1977.

Christian, Charles M. *Black Saga: The African American Experience, a Chronology*. Washington, D.C.: Civitas Counterpoint, 1995.

Cobb, William Montague. *The First Negro Medical Society: A History of the Medico–Chirurgical Society of the District of Columbia, 1884–1939*. Washington, D.C.: Associated Publishers, 1939.

Cromwell, John W. *The Negro in American History*. Washington, D.C.: American Negro Academy, 1914.

Culp, Daniel Wallace, ed. *Twentieth Century Negro Literature: or, A Cyclopedia of Thought on the Vital Topics Relating to the American Negro by 100 of America's Greatest Negroes*. 1902. Reprint, New York: Arno Press, 1969.

Curtis, James L. *Blacks, Medical Schools, and Society*. Ann Arbor: University of Michigan Press, 1971.

Davis, John P., ed. *The American Negro Reference Book*. Englewood Cliffs, N.J.: Prentice-Hall, 1966.

Davis, John W., and Garrett H. Watkins. *Black Honorary Shipmasters*. NAAHK. J. Rupert Picott, series ed. Washington D.C.: The Association for the Study of Afro-American Life and History, Inc., n.d.

Diggs, Irene. *Black Innovators*. Chicago: Institute of Positive Education, 1975.

Dobyns, Kenneth W. *The Patent Office Pony: A History of the Early Patent Office*. Fredericksburg, Va.: Sergeant Kirkland's Museum and Historical Society, 1994.

Du Bois, William E. B. *The Health and Physique of the Negro American*. Atlanta University Publications, no. 11. Reprint of the 1906 edition, New York: Arno Press and the New York Times, 1968.

Engs, Robert. *Freedom's First Generation*. Philadelphia: University of Pennsylvania Press, 1979.

Fletcher, Tom. *100 Years of the Negro in Show Business*. Reprint, New York: Da Capo Press, 1984.

Frazier, E. Franklin. *The Negro Family in the United States*. Chicago: University of Chicago Press, 1966.

Gay, Joseph R. *Self-Education for a Rising Race: Showing Progress of the Colored Americans*. Nashville, Tenn.: Southwestern Co., 1913.

Gibbs, Carroll R. *The Afro-American Inventor*. Washington, D.C.: Author, 1975.

———. *Black Inventors from Africa to America: Two Million Years of Invention and Innovation*. Silver Spring, Md.: Three Dimensional Publishing Company, 1995.

Gilmore, Al-Tony. *Bad Nigger! The National Impact of Jack Johnson*. Port Washington, N.Y.: Kennikat Press, 1975.

Graham, Shirley. *Your Most Humble Servant*. New York: Julian Messner, 1949.

Guzman, Jessie Parkhurst, ed. *Negro Year Book, 1952*. New York: William H. Wise & Company, 1952.

Haber, Louis. *Black Pioneers of Science and Invention*. New York: Harcourt, Brace & World, 1970.

Harris, Middleton A., Ernest Smith, Morris Levitt, and Roger Furman. *The Black Book*. New York: Random House, 1974.

Hawks, S. N., Jr. *Principles of Flue-Cured Tobacco Production*. Raleigh, N.C.: S. N. Hawks, Jr. 1970.

Hayden, Robert C. *Eight Black American Inventors*. Reading, Mass.: Addison-Wesley, 1972.

Haygood, Wil. *King of the Cats: The Life and Times of Adam Clayton Powell, Jr.* Boston: Houghton Mifflin, 1993.

Hermann, Janet Sharp. *The Pursuit of a Dream*. New York: Oxford University Press, 1981.

Hine, Darlene Clark, ed. *Black Women in America*. Brooklyn, N.Y.: Carlson Publishing, 1993.

————. *Black Women in the Nursing Profession: A Documentary History*. New York: Garland, 1985.

Ho, James K. K., ed. *Black Engineers in the United States: A Directory*. Washington, D.C.: Howard University Press, 1974.

Holt, Rackham, *George Washington Carver: An American Biography*. Garden City, N.Y.: Doubleday, Doran & Company, 1943.

Ives, Patricia Carter. *Creativity and Inventions: The Genius of Afro-Americans and Women in the United States and Their Patents*. Arlington, Va.: Research Unlimited, 1987.

————. "Minority Inventive Genius: A Look at Spirited American People." In *Bicentennial Celebration, United States Patent and Copyright Laws: Proceedings, Events, Addresses, May 7 through 11, 1990, Washington, D.C.* Washington, D.C.: Foundation for a Creative America, 1991; Washington, D.C.: Port City Press, Crabtree & Jamison, Clark Boardman Co., 1991.

Jackson, Giles, B., and Daniel Webster Davis. *The Industrial History of the Negro Race of the United States*. Richmond, Va.: Presses of The Virginia Press, 1908.

James, Portia. *The Real McCoy: African-American Invention and Innovation, 1619–1930*. Washington, D.C.: Smithsonian Institution, 1989.

Klein, Aaron E. *The Hidden Contributors: Black Scientists and Inventors in America*. Garden City, N.Y.: Doubleday, 1971.

Lerner, Max. *America as a Civilization*. New York: Simon & Schuster, 1957.

Lewis, David Levering. *When Harlem Was in Vogue*. New York: Vintage Books, 1982.

Link, Jim. *Portrait of a Professional: The Nat the Bush Doctor Story*. Tuxedo, Md.: H&H Printing Company, 1986.

Logan, Rayford W. *The Negro in the United States: A Brief History*. Princeton, N.J.: Van Nostrand, 1957.

Logan, Rayford W., and Michael R. Winston, eds. *Dictionary of American Negro Biography*. New York: W. W. Norton & Company, 1982.

Macdonald, Anne L. *Feminine Ingenuity: Women and Invention in America*. New York: Ballantine Books, 1992.

Mackintosh, Barry. *Booker T. Washington: An Appreciation of the Man and His Times*. Washington, D.C.: National Park Service, U.S. Department of the Interior, 1972.

Mazrui, Ali A. *The Africans*. Boston: Little, Brown & Company, 1986.

Miller, Kelly, and Joseph R. Gay. *Progress and Achievements of the Colored People*. Washington, D.C.: Austin Jenkins Co. [1917].

Mitchell, Barbara. *Shoes for Everyone: A Story about Jan Matzeliger*. Minneapolis: Carolrhoda Books, 1986.

Morsbach, Mabel. *The Negro in American Life*. New York: Harcourt, Brace, & World, 1967.

Moses, Robert P., and Charles E. Cobb, Jr. *Radical Equations: Math Literacy and Civil Rights*. Boston: Beacon Press, 2001.

Norman, Winifred Latimer, and Lily Patterson. *Lewis Latimer, Scientist*. New York: Chelsea House, 1994.

Pathfinders: African American Scientists and Inventors. Boston: Edison, n.d.

Penn, I. Garland. *The Afro-American Press and Its Editors*. Springfield, Mass.: Willey & Co., 1891.

Petersen, John L. *The Road to 2015: Profiles of the Future*. Corte Madera, Calif.: Waite Group Press, 1994.

Ploski, H. A., and R. C. Brown, eds. *The Negro Almanac*. New York: 1967.

Porter, Gladys L. *Three Negro Pioneers in Beauty Culture*. New York: Vantage Press, 1966.

The Proceedings of the National Negro Business League, Boston, 1900. Boston: J. R. Hamm, 1901.

Quarles, Benjamin. *The Negro in the Making of America*. New York: Collier, 1964.

Quick, William H. *Negro Stars in All Ages of the World*. Henderson, N.C.: D. E. Aycock, 1890.

Reasons, George, and Sam Patrick. *They Had a Dream*. Vols. 1 and 2. Los Angeles: Los Angeles Times Syndicate, 1969, 1970.

Redding, J. Saunders. *On Being Negro in America*. Indianapolis: Bobbs-Merrill, 1951.

Richings, G. F. *Evidences of Progress among Colored People*. Philadelphia: George S. Ferguson Co., 1905.

Rogers, Joel A. *World's Great Men of Color*. Vol. 2. New York: Collier Books, 1972.

Sammons, Vivian Ovelton, comp. *Blacks in Science and Medicine*. New York: Hemisphere Publishing Corporation, 1990.

Schaap, Dick, and the Lampman. Introductory essays in *Jack Johnson Is a Dandy; Autobiography*. New York: Chelsea House, 1969.

Schneider, Janet M., and Bayla Singer, eds. *Blueprint for Change: The Life and Times of Lewis H. Latimer*. New York: Queens Borough Public Library, 1995.

Showell, Ellen H., and Fred M. B. Amram. *From Indian Corn to Outer Space*. Peterborough, N.H.: Cobblestone Publishing, 1995.

Sluby, Paul E., Sr., and Stanton L. Wormley, Jr. *History of the Columbian Harmony Society and of Harmony Cemetery*. [Washington, D.C.]: privately printed, revised 2001.

Spradling, Mary Mace, ed. *In Black and White*. 3rd ed., supplement. Detroit: Gale Research Co., 1985.

Stanley, Autumn. "From Africa to America: Black Women Inventors." In *The Technological Woman: Interfacing with Tomorrow*, ed. Jan Zimmerman. New York: Praeger, 1983.

———. *Mothers and Daughters of Invention: Notes for a Revised History of Technology*. Metuchen, N.J.: Scarecrow Press, 1993.

Trotter, James M. "Justin Holland, The, Eminent Author and Arranger." In *Music and Some Highly Musical People*. Boston, 1878. Reprint, Chicago: Afro-American Press, 1969.

Turner, Glennette Tilley. *Lewis Howard Latimer.* Englewood Cliffs, N.J.: Silver Burdett Press, 1991.

Van Sertima, Ivan. *Blacks in Science: Ancient and Modern.* London: Transaction Books, 1983.

Vare, Ethlie Ann, and Greg Ptacek. *Mothers of Invention from the Bra to the Bomb: Forgotten Women and Their Unforgettable Ideas.* New York: William Morrow and Company, 1988.

Williams, James C., comp. *At Last Recognition in America: A Reference Handbook of Unknown Black Inventors and Their Contributions to America.* Chicago: B.C.A. Publishing Corp., 1978.

Winslow, Eugene, ed. *Black Americans in Science and Engineering: Contributors of Past and Present.* Chicago: Afro-Am Publishing Co., 1984.

Woodson, Carter Goodwin. *Negro Makers of History.* Washington, D.C.: Associated Publishers, 1928.

Woodson, Carter G., and Charles H. Wesley. *The Negro in Our History.* Washington, D.C.: Associated Publishers, 1972.

Work, Monroe, ed. *Negro Year Book, 1918–1919.* Tuskegee, Ala.: Negro Year Book Publishing Company, 1919.

Wormley, Stanton L., and Lewis H. Fenderson, eds. *Many Shades of Black.* New York: William Morrow & Company, 1969.

Yancet, Dorothy Cowser. *Twentieth Century Black Patentees—A Survey.* NAAHK. J. Rupert Picott, series ed. Washington, D.C.: Association for the Study of Afro-American Life and History, 1979.

PERIODICALS

"A Look Ahead to the Dawn of the Next Millennium." *Newsweek,* January 27, 1997, p. 49.

Adams, Howard G. "Insights on Engineering: Conversation with Howard University Dean M. Lucius Walker, Jr." *Black Collegian,* January/February 1985, p. 99–102.

"Africa in Discovery and Invention" and "The American Negro as an Inventor." *NHB* 3, no. 6 (March 1940): 81–84, 94–95.

"America's Top HMOs." *U.S. News and World Report,* October 5, 1998, pp. 64–72.

Amram, Fred M., and Jane A. Morgan. " 'Inventor' Is a Masculine Word." *US Woman Engineer,* December 1980, pp. 1–5, 314.

"Architects of the Future." *BE,* February 1990, pp. 79–116.

Baker, Henry E. "The Negro in the Field of Invention." *JNH* 2 (1917): 21–36.

"Biochemical Genomics." *Chemical and Engineering News,* November 8, 1999, p. 5.

"Black Inventors." *Ebony,* February 1990, pp. 128–134.

Borman, Stu. "Black Chemist Percy Julian Commemorated on Postage Stamp." *Chemical and Engineering News* 71, no. 5 (February 1, 1993): 9–12.

Boyle, John. "Patents and Civil Rights in 1857–8." *JPOS* 42 (1960): 789, 792–794.

Chappell, Kevin. "How Black Inventors Changed America." *Ebony,* February 1997, pp. 40, 46, 48, 50.

Chevigny, Bell Gale. "Mississippi Learning: Algebra as Political Curriculum." *Nation,* March 4, 1996, pp. 16–21.

"Chronology of American Technology." *Industrial Research*, November 15, 1976.

"The Cover: Charles Richard Drew, MD." *JAMA: The Journal of the American Medical Association* 269, no. 5 (February 3, 1993).

Davis, Asa J. "The Two Autobiographical Fragments of George W. Latimer." *JAAHGS* 1 (summer 1930): 3–18.

"The Doctors Are In." *BE*, August 2001, pp. 72–93.

Douglass, Frederick. "Thomas L. Jinnings." *AAM* 1 (April 1859): 126–128.

Du Bois, William E. B. "The American Negro at Paris." *AMRR* 22 (November 1900): 575–577.

Fairbanks, Charles H., and Sue A. Mullins-Moore. "How Did Slaves Live?" *Early Man: Magazine of Modern Archeology* 2, no. 2 (summer 1980): 2–6.

Frederico, P. J. "Colonial Monopolies and Patents." *JPOS* 11 (August 1929): 358–365.

———. "Origin and Early History of Patents." *JPOS* 11 (July 1929): 292–305.

———. "The Patent Office Fire of 1836." *JPOS* 19, no. 11 (1937): 804–833.

———. "State Patents." *JPOS* 13 (April 1931): 166–176.

Gaboury, William J. "George Washington Murray and the Fight for Political Democracy in South Carolina." *JNH* 62, no. 3 (July 1977): 258–269.

Gibbs, C. R. "A New First." *American Visions*, August 1987, p. 8, 11–12.

Gray, Garry. "H. C. Haynes, Barber and Inventor." *NHB* 40, no. 5 (September–October 1977): 750–752.

Grosswirth, Marvin. "People in Science: Meredith C. Gourdine." *SciQuest*, April 1982, pp. 22–24.

Gullette, Robert L. "State Legislation Governing Ownership Rights in Inventions under Employee Invention Agreements." *JPOS* 62, no. 12 (December 1980): 732–760.

Haywood, Charles. "Famous Men of Flushing: James A. Bland, Prince of Colored Songwriters." Discourse, Flushing Historical Society, New York, 1944.

Herbert, Solomon J. "Bioengineering." *NSBEJ* 3, no. 3 (February 1988): 54–57.

"Horse Hay Rake." *Farmer's Cabinet* 3 (February 15, 1839): 226.

Howard, Sharon M. "First Black Female Millionairess, Madam C. J. Walker." *Blac Tress*, November 1980.

Ives, Patricia Carter. "Giles Beecher Jackson." *NHB* 38, no. 8 (December 1975): 480–483.

———. "Patent and Trademark Innovations of Black Americans and Women." *JPOS* 62, no. 2 (February 1980): 108–126.

Ives, Patricia C., and Vertie F. Ives, Jr. "The Dark Side of Washington." *Annual of the Freedom Fund Committee, NAACP, D.C. Branch*, 1971 and 1973.

Jenkins, Edward S. "Bridging the Two Cultures, African Black Scientists and Inventors." *Journal of Black Studies* 21, no. 3 (March 1991): 313–324.

King, Anita. "Family Tree." *Essence*, February 1976, p. 17.

MacKintosh, Barry. "George Washington Carver and the Peanut." *American Heritage*, November 1977, pp. 67–72.

"Masters of Discovery." *U.S. News and World Report*, August 17–24, 1998, pp. 28–36.

Mastin, Oscar. "Patent System Originated with U.S. Constitution." *Commerce People, U.S. Department of Commerce*, June 1987: 1.

Mattis, Richard L. "The First 1,000 Inventions." *Cobblestone* 13, no. 2 (February 1992): 4–8.

Mehagian, J. Douglas. "GE Innovators." *American Legacy*, winter 2002, p. 20.

Michelmore, Peter. "Bob Moses's Crusade." *Reader's Digest*, March 1995, pp. 107–111.

Miller, Kelly. "Obituary: Professor Hugh M. Browne." *Howard University Record* 18 (1923–1924): 133.

Morse, Excellenza L. "Women in Patent Work." *JPOS* 17, no. 4 (April 1935): 328–334.

Murray, Daniel. "Who Invented the Cotton Gin?" *Voice of the Negro* 2, no. 2 (February 1905): 96–102.

Oman, Ann. "Mothers of Invention." *Washington Woman*, May 1984, 18–24.

"Past, Present, Future." *TT* 3, no. 9 (September 1981): 5–6; *TT* 4, no. 1 (January 1982), pp. 5–6.

Patterson, Pat. "200 Years of Economic Development." *BE*, July 1975.

Porter, Frank W., III. "John Widgeon: Naturalist, Curator, and Philosopher." *MHM* 79, no. 4 (winter 1984): 325–331.

Rossman, Joseph. "The Negro Inventor." *JPOS* 12 (1930): 549–553.

———. "Women Inventors." *JPOS* 10 (1927): 18–30.

Scott, Matthew S. "Wonderful World at Disney" and "Entertainment in Cyberspace." *BE*, December 1995, pp. 58–64, 66–72.

Scottron, Samuel R. "Manufacturing Household Articles." *Colored American Magazine*, December 1906, pp. 621–624.

Sluby, Patricia Carter. "Black Women and Inventions." *Sage: A Scholarly Journal on Black Women* 6, no. 2 (Fall 1989): 33–35.

———. "Black Women and Inventions." *Women's History Network News*, January 1993, pp. 4–5.

———. "Congratulations to PTOS Members, Winners of the Law Library Contest!!!" *PTOS Unofficial Gazette* 24, no. 5 (July–August 1995): 1.

———. "Paths to the Past for Youth: It's in the Blood." *Bookmark: Family History Resources*, New York State Library, Albany, spring 1991, pp. 183–188.

Spight, Carl. "High Technology." *NSBEJ* 2, no. 1 (October 1986): 42–48.

Verdery, Benjamin. "Contemporary Classical: Justin Holland, Classical Pioneer." *Guitar Player*, May 1989, p. 112.

Walston, Mark. "Maryland Inventors and Inventions, 1830–1860." *MHM* 80, no. 1 (1985): 66–70.

Watson, Bruce. "If a = Math and b = Magic, Then a + b = the Algebra Project." *Smithsonian* 26, no. 11 (February 1996): 114–124.

Williams-Harold, Bevolyn. "You've Got It Made." *BE*, June 1999, pp. 262–266.

Wright, Clarence W. "Some Recent Negro Men of Science." *NCQ* 1, no. 4 (December 1943): 108–109.

Wright, R. R. "The Negro as an Inventor." *A.M.E. Church Review* 2, no. 14 (April 1886): 397–411.

Yancy, Dorothy Cowser. "Four Black Inventors with Patents." *NHB* 39, no. 4 (April 1976): 574–576.

NEWSPAPERS

Baker, Peter. "At Virginia's Death House, an Eye for an Eye, Face to Face [Willie Lloyd Turner]." *Washington Post*, June 3, 1995.

"Black History for the Month of February." *Washington* [D.C.] *Afro-American*, February 1, 1983.

Brinkley, Ora. "Ora." *Philadelphia Tribune*, February 1977.

"Chemist W. Lincoln Hawkins, National Medal Recipient, Dies." *Washington Post*, August 23, 1992.

"Early Black Inventors (History Series)." *Richmond* [Virginia] *Afro-American*, October 16–20, 1973.

"Fleet Walker Scores Big" and "Johnson to Be Freed!" *Cleveland* [Ohio] *Gazette*, July 2, 1921.

Gardner, Greg. "Woman Finds Roots in Patent Search." *New York Amsterdam News*, August 31, 1985.

"Genius of the Colored Man." *New Ideas, Philadelphia*, September 1895.

Gervasai, Susan. "Ideas: Birth of a Notion." *Washington Post*, Style Plus, April 24, 1990.

Greene, Robert Ewell. "Tinkering Led to Discoveries." *Washington* [D.C.] *Afro-American*, February 2, 1985.

"Gung H2O: Water Saver Invented by Local Man." *Washington* [D.C.] *Afro-American*, August 21, 1999.

"Hawkins to Receive National Technology Medal." *Bell Labs News*, June 22, 1992.

"He Tells His Own Life Story." *New York World*, September 27, 1890.

"Health." *Washington Post*, August 25, 1998.

Hiratsuka, Jon. "Woman Claims Suspenders Invented by Lynchburg Man." *News and Daily Advance* [Lynchburg, Va.], July 31, 1983.

Ives, Patricia Carter. "Inventors through the Years." *PatentTalk*, Employee Bulletin, no. 291, U.S. Department of Commerce, Patent and Trademark Office, August 9, 1978.

———. "Some Black Inventors Who Changed the Course of Industries." *Washington* [D.C.] *Afro-American*, February 2, 1985.

Kelly, Chris. "Woman Never Suspended Fight for Recognition of Inventor Dad." *Post* [Martin County, Florida], June 25, 1985.

"Lewis H. Latimer, Edison's Assistant, Dies at Age of 81." *New York Amsterdam News*, December 19, 1928.

Litsky, Frank. "Meredith Gourdine, 69, Athlete and Physicist." *New York Times*, November 24, 1998.

MacPherson, Kitta. "Turn-Signal 'Inventor' Boosted Posthumously." *Sunday Star-Ledger* [Newark, N.J.], February 22, 1987.

"Outlook." *Washington Post*, July 15, 2001.

Shaw, Donna. "How an Idea for a Better Diaper Became a Legal Morass." *Philadelphia Inquirer*, January 23, 1990.

Stevens, Nancy, "C.R. Inventor Predicts Security System Revolution." *Cedar Rapids* [Illinois] *Gazette*, February 20, 1979.

"Supreme Court Denies Turner Appeal." *Washington Afro-American*, May 21, 1988.

"Three of America's Top Physical Scientists" *Philadelphia Tribune*, June 18, 1977.

"24 Black Inventors Cited Here." *Philadelphia Tribune*, February 3, 1977.

Weiss, Rick. "First Human Embryos Are Cloned in U.S." *Washington Post*, November 26, 2001.

Williams, Michael Paul. "Was Black Inventor Ripped Off?" *Richmond* [Virginia] *Times-Dispatch*, June 15, 1998.

The Woman Inventor. Ed. and pub. by Charlotte Smith, Washington, D.C., April 1890 and June 1891.

"Worker Honored [Joseph Turner]" [Charleston, W.V.] [unknown] October 11, 1942.

Young, A. S. "Doc." "Railroad Show: Recalls Inventive Genius of Robinson, Dammond." *Chicago Defender*, June 25, 1949.

PAMPHLETS, CATALOGS, AND DIRECTORIES

Amram, Fred, Guest Curator, and Timothy Trent Blade, Exhibition Designer. "Her Works Praise Her: An Exhibition of Inventions by Women. Goldstein Gallery, University of Minnesota, Minneapolis, June 12–December 16, 1988.

Malloy, Jerry. "Moses Fleetwood Walker, Out of Home," *The National Pastime* (Cooperstown, N.Y.: Society for American Baseball Research, 1983), p. 14.

"Mark Dean and Dennis Moeller to Be Inducted into the National Inventors Hall of Fame." *News release*, Inventure Place [Akron, Ohio], June 16, 1977.

"National Black American Inventors Day." *News release*, Congressman Floyd H. Flake, 6th District, New York, Washington, D.C., March 27, 1988.

Smith, J. Clay, Jr. Introduction. *The Genetic Engineering Revolution: A New Century Reality, Bibliographic Index (1981–1986)*. Howard University School of Law. New Century Research, October 7, 1986.

Tenth Annual Program, African American History Month. "Shaping the Future: Historically Black Colleges and Universities." National Academy of Sciences, National Academy of Engineering, Institute of Medicine, National Research Council, February 27, 1996.

MANUSCRIPT SOURCES

Bird, Betty, Robie Lange, Bill Lebovich, Glen Leiner, Susan Pearl, Thomas Tyler Pottersfield, Jr., Nancy, Schwartz, and Dreck Spurlack Wilson. " . . . and the Walls Came Tumbling Down: The Early African-American Architects of the District of Columbia and Tidewater Virginia." January 1995.

Butcher, James W. Papers, 1910–1949. Historical Society of Washington, D.C.

Hunter, Bertina (chairperson, Black Heritage Committee) and Mabel B. Perry (Basileus). "Achievements of Black Women, 1600–1900's." Alpha Kappa Alpha Sorority, Beta Alpha Omega Chapter, Newark, N.J., February 1988. Typed.

Ives, Patricia C. "Historical Data." Presentation in exhibition on women in the patent system at the National Inventors' Day Exposition, U.S. Patent and Trademark Office, Arlington, Va., 1971, 1973. Typed.

Letter from Patricia Braxton (wife of inventor) to author, February 4, 1997.

Letter from Patricia Crawford Dunn to author, December 1971.

Letter from Lawrence Fleming (registered patent agent) to author, May 27, 1980.

Letter from Alice Hall Green (daughter of inventor) to author, August 18, 1998.

Letter from Conrad Groves (inventor) to author, October 15, 1991.

Letters from Jerry Malloy (journalist) to author, July 15, 1991; October 23, 1993; December 10, 1993.

Letter from Lloyd McAulay (patent attorney) to author, February 24, 1982.

Letter from Nathaniel R. Quick, Ph.D. (inventor) to author, January 28, 1990.

Letter from Tim Rives (National Archives, Central Plains Region) to author, December 14, 2000.

Letter from Richard L. Saxton and Olivia Saxton (inventors) to Simeon Booker of Johnson Publishing Company, April 17, 1986 [given to author].

Letter from Bruce K. Smith (inventor) to author, March 18, 1993.

Letter from James G. Spady (lecturer and author) to author, December 30, 1980.

Letter (autobiography) from Albert W. Turner, Sr. (inventor), to author, June 1992.

Letters from Glennette Tilley Turner (wife, granddaughter, and mother of inventors) to author, July 1, 1992; December 23, 1997.

Letter from Benjamin Verdery (classical guitarist and professor) to author, June 26, 1990.

Letter from Barbara Wyche (researcher) to author, January 14, 1992.

Rogers, Ira. "And They Were Giants: A Proposal to the National Endowment for the Humanities." [Chicago], 1978. Photocopied.

Sluby, Patricia Carter. "African Americans in the Health Sciences: The Art of Healing, a Spiritual Celebration." Program given at Christ United Methodist Church. Washington, D.C., February 23, 1997.

———. "Patent Records Have . . . a Sister Act—It's in the Blood." Speech given at 17th Annual Conference of the Afro-American Historical and Genealogical Society, Washington, D.C., April 1995. Typed.

———. "Recognizing African American Inventive Genius, 1821–1995: A Spiritual Celebration." Program given at Christ United Methodist Church. Washington, D.C., February 26, 1995.

Strasser, Terry. "African-American Invention in New York State." [New York State Library], [paper], 1991.

Williams, Jr., Sidney B., and Pat Sluby. "History of African American Intellectual Property Law Practitioners." Temple Hills, Maryland, September 1, 1998. Typed.

OFFICIAL DOCUMENTS, REPORTS, AND PUBLICATIONS

Boyd's Directory of the District of Columbia. Washington, D.C.: William Ballantyne & Sons, 1865–1869, 1870–1884, 1889, 1890, 1897.

Smithsonian Institution. National Museum of American History. Lemelson Center for the Study of Invention and Innovation. "David Gittens: 'Future Link' Aircraft Designer." [flyer] *Innovative Lives*, May 7, 1997.

U.S. Congress. House. Representative Floyd H. Flake of New York speaking for a joint resolution designating March 27, 1988, as "National Black American Inventors Day." H. 8672. October 14, 1987.

———. Representative Garcia of New York speaking for a joint resolution (H.J.

Res. 377) designating March 27, 1988, as "National Black American Inventors Day." H965. March 17, 1988.

———. Representative George W. Murray of South Carolina speaking for the amendment offered by the Representative Durborow of Illinois on the Cotton States Exposition. 53rd Cong., 2nd sess. *Congressional Record*, August 10, 1894.

U.S. Department of Commerce. Commerce News. "More Women than Men Were Attending College in 1979, Census Report Shows." August 24, 1980.

U.S. Department of Commerce. Patent and Trademark Office. *Buttons to Biotech: U.S. Patenting by Women, 1977 to 1988.* Office of Documentation Information, Technology Assessment and Forecast Program, January 1990.

———. *Profile of Female Inventors.* Gerald Mossinghoff and Barbara Luxenburg, compilers. Office of Technology Assessment and Forecast, 1984.

———. *A Women's Place Is in the Patent Office.* [Washington, D.C.], [1990].

U.S. Department of Labor. *Women's Contribution in the Field of Invention: A Study of the Records of the United States Patent Office.* Women's Bureau Bulletin 28: Ed. Mary Anderson. Washington, D.C.: Government Printing Office, 1923.

U.S. Patent Office. *Women Inventors to Whom Patents Have Been Granted by the United States Government, 1790 to July 1, 1888.* Compiled under the direction of the Commissioner of Patents. Washington, D.C.: Government Printing Office, 1888.

———. *Women Inventors to Whom Patents Have Been Granted by the United States Government, July 1, 1888 to October 1, 1892.* Appendix No. 1. Compiled under the direction of the Commissioner of Patents. Washington, D.C.: Government Printing Office, 1892.

———. *Women Inventors to Whom Patents Have Been Granted by the United States Government, October 1, 1892 to March 1, 1895.* Arranged chronologically and by classes. Appendix No. 2. Compiled under the direction of the Commissioner of Patents. Washington, D.C.: Government Printing Office, 1895.

Vital records: Alabama, Illinois, Michigan, New York, Ohio.

INDEX

About the Author

PATRICIA CARTER SLUBY is a Registered Patent Agent and a former United States primary patent examiner. She is also a lecturer and free-lance writer who has appeared on television and radio shows to discuss minority inventors. She is the past president of the National Intellectual Property Law Association. Her book *Creativity and Inventions: The Genius of Afro-Americans and Women in the United States and Their Patents* (1987) details the inventive nature of minorities in America.